Mary Somerville was born on 26 December 1780 in a manse at Jedburgh, the home of her mother's sister. She was fifth child of William George Fairfax a Lieutenant in Nelson's navy (later a Vice-Admiral) and his second wife, Margaret Charters. Four of the couple's seven children survived. They were brought up in Burntisland where Mary Somerville spent her childhood and adolescence. She attended a school in Musselburgh whose chief aim was to teach girls how to be gracious. Despite the obstacles that were put in her way she pursued her own interests in mathematics and the classics.

In 1804 she married her cousin Samuel Greig and they went to stay in London, but she was left with two young children when her husband died only three years later at the age of twenty-nine. Mary returned to her parents' home where she continued her studies in algebra and geometry.

In 1812 she married another of her cousins, William Somerville, an army doctor. The couple soon moved to London again where William took up a post as physician at the Chelsea Hospital. Mary Somerville continued her studies and was in her early forties when her scientific interests began to make their mark. In 1831 she published a translation of Laplace's *Mécanique Céleste* originally intended as one of the publications of the Society for the Diffusion of Useful Knowledge but in the end published by John Murray. This work was soon adopted for courses in Cambridge and made her reputation. It was followed by *The Connexion of the Physical Sciences* in 1834 and the award of a government pension the following year. Scientists throughout Europe honoured Mary Somerville and her work was widely translated.

William's poor health took the family to Italy and when he retired in 1840 the Somervilles moved there permanently, living mainly in Florence and Rome. When William died in 1860 Mary moved to Naples where she spent the rest of her life. During this time she produced a study of physical geography (1848) and a book on molecular and microscopic science.

Mary Somerville died in 1872 and her *Recollections*, edited and selected with a commentary by her daughter were published in 1873. These memoirs give a fascinating picture of her life and times and her meetings with many famous writers and scientists of the day. Somerville College at Oxford is named after her, and the present edition has been re-edited by Dorothy McMillan, drawing on manuscripts held at that college.

Dorothy McMillan is a Senior Lecturer in English Literature and currently Head of the School of English and Scottish Language and Literature at the University of Glasgow. With Douglas Gifford she has edited *A History of Scottish Women's Writing* (EUP, 1997) which includes chapters by her on travel and memoir writing of the eighteenth and nineteenth centuries and on twentieth-century poetry. Other publications on women's writing include her anthology of non-fiction writing, 1700–1900: *The Scotswoman at Home and Abroad* (ASLS, 1999) and various chapters and articles on Joanna Baillie, Ann Radcliffe, Jane Austen, Elizabeth Barrett Browning, Liz Lochhead and Kathleen Jamie. She is preparing an anthology of twentieth-century Scottish women's poetry for Canongate.

She is currently President of the Association for Scottish Literary studies.

Queen of Science

Personal Recollections of
MARY SOMERVILLE

Edited and Introduced by
Dorothy McMillan

★

CANONGATE
CLASSICS
102

First published in 1873 as *Personal Recollections, from Early Life to Old Age, of Mary Somerville* by John Murray, London. First published as a Canongate Classic in 2001 by Canongate Books Ltd, 14 High Street, Edinburgh EH1 1TE. Introduction and Notes copyright © Dorothy McMillan 2001.

The publishers gratefully acknowledge general subsidy from the Scottish Arts Council towards the Canongate Classics series and a specific grant towards the publication of this volume.

Set in 10pt Plantin by Hewertext Ltd, Edinburgh. Printed and bound in Great Britain by Omnia Books Ltd, Glasgow.

10 9 8 7 6 5 4 3 2 1

CANONGATE CLASSICS
Series Editor: Roderick Watson
Editorial Board: J.B. Pick, Cairns Craig, Dorothy McMillan

British Library Cataloguing-in-Publication Data
A catalogue record for this book is available on request from the British Library

ISBN 1 84195 136 6

www.canongate.net

Contents

Acknowledgments   ix
Introduction   xi
Editorial Practice   xliii

ONE
Introduction – Parentage – Life in Scotland in
the Last Century – Early Education – School   1

TWO
Freedom – Religious Education – Jedburgh   20

THREE
Edinburgh – Youthful Studies and Amusements –
Politics – the Theatres of the Time   33

FOUR
Edinburgh Supper Parties – Tour in the Highlands –
Mutiny in the Fleet – Battle of Camperdown   48

FIVE
First Marriage (1804) – Widowhood – Studies –
Second Marriage   61

SIX
Somerville Family – Dr Somerville's Character –
Letters – Journey to the Lakes – Death of Sir William
Fairfax – Reminiscences of Sir Walter Scott   70

SEVEN
Life in Hanover Square – Visit to France – Arago –
Cuvier – Rome   85

EIGHT
Education of Daughters – Dr Wollaston – Dr Young –
The Herschels   104

NINE

Society in London – Coronation of George IV – Letter
to Dr Somerville   115

TEN

Death of Margaret Somerville – Letter from Mrs
Somerville to the Rev. Dr Somerville – Life at Chelsea –
The Napiers – Maria Edgeworth – Tour in
Germany   124

ELEVEN

Letter from Lord Brougham – Writes 'Mechanism of
the Heavens' – Anecdote of the Roman Improvisatrice
– Letters from Sir John Herschel and Professor
Whewell – Elected Hon. Member of the Royal
Astronomical Society – Notice in the Académie des
Sciences, and Letter from M. Biot – Pension – Letter
from Sir Robert Peel – Begins to Write on the Connexion
of the Physical Sciences – Visit to Cambridge –
Letters from Professor Sedgwick and Laplace   131

TWELVE

Paris – Arago, Lafayette, MM. Bouvard, Poisson,
Lacroix, &c., Marquise de Laplace, Dupin,
F. Cooper – Legitimiste Society – Majendie –
Visit Baron Louis – Letter from Lafayette   149

THIRTEEN

Return to England – Letter from Hallam – Treatise on
the form and Rotation of the Earth and Planets –
Second Edition of The 'Connexion of the Physical
Sciences' – Letters from Maria Edgeworth, Miss
Berry, Lord Brougham, Mrs Marcet, Admiral
Smyth – Double Stars – Eclipse of Double Stars –
Letter from Admiral Smyth – Sir William Herschel –
Nebulæ – Letter from Lord Rosse – Letter from
Sir John Herschel – Sir James South's Observatory –
Mr John Murray – Miss Berry – Lord Dudley – Mr
Bowditch and Other Distinguished Americans – Mrs
Browning Washington – Letter from the Rev. Dr

Tuckerman – Sir William Fairfax Attacked by
Highwaymen   159

FOURTEEN

Rome, Naples, and Como – Baden – Winter at
Florence – Siena – Letter from Lord Brougham –
Mr Mountstuart Elphinstone – Life at Rome –
Campagna Cattle   185

FIFTEEN

Albano – Popular Singing – Letters from Mrs
Somerville – Gibson – Perugia   Comet of 1843 –
Summer at Venice – Letters from Mrs Somerville
and Miss Joanna Baillie – Elected Associate of the
College of Resurgenti and R. I. Academy of Science
at Arezzo   196

SIXTEEN

Publishes 'Physical Geography' – Letter from
Humboldt – Christmas at Collingwood – Letter from
Mrs Somerville – Faraday – Letter from Faraday –
Keith Johnston's Maps – Winter at Munich –
Salzburg – Lake of Garda – Miniscalchi – Poem by
Caterina Brenzoni – Letter from Brenzoni – Letter from
Mrs Somerville – Éloge by Miniscalchi – Winter at
Turin – Baron Plana – Camillo Cavour – Colline
near Turin – Genoa – Teresa Doria – Florence –
Miss F. P. Cobbe – Vivisection – Excursions in the
Neighbourhood – Cholera – Misericordia – Pio Nono
in Tuscany – Comet – Tuscan Revolution – War in
Lombardy – Entry of Victor Emmanuel into
Florence – Letters from Mrs Somerville – My
Father's Death – Letter from Miss Cobbe   232

SEVENTEEN

Spezia – Genoa – Begins Molecular and Microscopic
Science – Turin – Spezia – British Fleet – Letters from
Mrs Somerville – Garibaldi – Severe Illness – Florence –

My Brother's Death – Naples – Eruption of Vesuvius
– J. S. Mill – Change in Public Opinion on Women's
Education – Eighty-Ninth Year – Describes her Own
Character – Thoughts on a Future Life – Progress
in Knowledge of Geography – Victoria Medal –
Medal from Royal Italian Geographical Society –
Letter from Menebrea – Rome, Capital of Italy –
Aurora Borealis   266

EIGHTEEN

Eclipse – Visits of Scientific Men – Life at Naples –
Darwin's Books – Remarks on Civilisation – Fine
Aurora Borealis – Death of Herschel – Summer at
Sorrento – Bill for Protection of Animals – Ninety-
Second Year – Letter from Professor Sedgwick –
Grand Eruption of Vesuvius – Last Summer at
Sorrento, Plants Found There – Conclusion   285

Brief Biographies   303
Translations of Letters   387
Notes   397
Bibliography   415
Index   419

Acknowledgments

Passages from the drafts of the *Recollections* and quotations from letters in the Somerville Collection deposited in the Bodleian Library, Oxford, are quoted by kind permission of Somerville College, Oxford. Quotation from the Herschel Papers in the Library of the Royal Society is by kind permission of the President and Council of the Royal Society. I should like to thank the staff in the Modern Papers section of the Bodleian Library and the librarians of the Royal Society for all their assistance. As usual, the staff of Special Collections of Glasgow University Library have been most helpful. I particularly thank my colleagues Robert Cummings and Nicola Trott for their assistance: any remaining errors and infelicities are, of course, my responsibility.

I am grateful to Canongate and to my colleagues on the Canongate Classics committee for recognising the value of this project. Rory Watson has been a constant support.

Introduction

Cheerful though wise, though learned, popular,
Liked by the many, valued by the few,
Instructs the world, yet dubbed by none a Blue.

Mary Somerville was one of the most remarkable women of her time, or indeed of any time. During her long life she moved from obscure private life in the little town of Burntisland in Fife, to the celebrity of being an internationally acclaimed mathematician, astronomer, physical scientist and geographer. When she died in her 92nd year, obituaries appeared in newspapers and journals all over Europe and in America: the *Morning Post* obituary called her, with complete confidence, 'the Queen of science' (Mon. 2 Dec. 1872). Throughout her long life she was a respected presence in body or in correspondence on various British, European and American scientific scenes. The work for which she is probably still best remembered is her translation of Laplace's *Mécanique céleste* as *The Mechanism of the Heavens* in 1831; her most ambitious work was probably *On the Connexion of the Physical Sciences* (1834), which ran to nine British editions in her lifetime; but there is also *Physical Geography*, two vols. (1848), which, as she points out in her *Recollections*, 'went through nine editions, has been translated into German and Italian [. . .] and went through various editions in the United States' (p. 162); and *On Molecular and Microscopic Science*, which she published when she was in her 89th year, and which *The Morning Post* suggests was her *magnum opus*.

Mary Somerville was born on 26 December 1780 in the

manse at Jedburgh, the home of her mother's sister, who was married to the local minister, the Rev. Dr Thomas Somerville. She was the fifth child of Lieutenant (later Vice-Admiral) William George Fairfax and his second wife, Margaret Charters. Fairfax had just embarked on a long period of sea duty and his pregnant wife was living at her sister's home when the child was born. Mrs Fairfax was ill after the confinement and the baby, Mary, was suckled by her aunt. Mary Somerville points out that since her second husband was her aunt's elder son, she was nursed by her mother-in-law (p. 9). The Fairfax family was from Yorkshire and was connected to Sir Thomas Fairfax, commander of the New Model Army, which defeated Charles I; the family also had American connections (p. 150). The Charters family was also an old family, related to several other notable Scottish families.

Four of Margaret Charters's seven children survived: Samuel, Mary, Margaret and Henry. They were brought up in Burntisland in a house that is still standing. In her *Personal Recollections* Mary Somerville describes her childhood and adolescence in Burntisland and at school in Musselburgh, as well as her social life as a fairly well-connected young lady in Edinburgh. The explanation of the difficulties she surmounted to acquire the education she craved is best experienced through her own words.

By 1804, when she married her cousin, Samuel Greig, her unconventional desire to learn geometry, algebra and the classics was already well established, in spite of the obstacles placed in her way, even by those who loved her. Greig was the son of Admiral Sir Samuel Greig, who had gone to Russia in 1763 to organise Catherine II's navy. To allow the young couple to marry, Greig was appointed Russian consul in London and Mary moved into his house there. Neither the house nor the marriage seems to have been very comfortable. Samuel Greig died in 1807, aged only 29, leaving Mary Somerville with two young children, Woronzow, called after the Russian Ambassador in London, and William George. As a widow back in her parents' home, Mary Somerville had the means and the independence to pursue her studies. And this she did until in 1812 she married again, again to a cousin, William Somerville, an army doctor. The story of this happy union is embedded in the *Recollections*. There was at first a brief period in Edinburgh, then the family settled in London, where in 1819 William Somerville, after some vicissitudes, became Physician at Chelsea Hospital. During the next two decades the Somervilles played a significant part in the intellectual life of London: their acquaintance embraced the worlds of science, arts and politics.

Mary Somerville was in her late 40s when she embarked on her life as a writer on science. Her first work, the translation of the *Mécanique céleste* of the French astronomer and mathematician, Laplace, was undertaken, as she explains, at the suggestion of Henry Brougham (p. 131). It was published in 1831 to general acclamation: the trajectory of Mary Somerville's professional life was set. William Somerville's health sent the family travelling to Italy in 1838; in 1840 he retired and the Somervilles lived in various locations in Italy. William Somerville died in 1860 and Mary herself in Naples in 1872.

Mary Somerville's successful life, nevertheless, included private tragedy. William George Greig died at only nine; the first child, a boy, of her second marriage died in infancy; and, worst of all, the Somervilles' eldest girl, Margaret, from whom they had expected much, died in 1823, aged ten. Woronzow Greig married Agnes Graham in 1837 and became a successful barrister but died without legitimate issue in 1865, seven years before his mother. The remaining daughters, Martha Charters and Mary Charlotte Somerville, died unmarried only a few years after their mother. Her heirs were the children of her younger brother, Henry Fairfax.

The *Personal Recollections* were published the year after Mary Somerville's death. According to her daughter and editor, Martha Somerville, they were mostly 'noted down' during the last years of her life (p. 2) and they have, even after editing, all the immediacy of a diary – the seeming freshness of youth informs them throughout. It turns out, however, that 'noted down' does less than justice to the care with which Mary Somerville prepared her *Recollections*. They exist in three versions in the Somerville Collection, deposited in the Bodleian Library – a rough outline in an 1859 notebook;[1] a first draft, wholly in Mary Somerville's hand, probably completed about 1869[2] and a second draft in Martha Somerville's hand with interpolations in Mary Somerville's hand.[3]

Mary Somerville undoubtedly intended the memoirs for publication before or after her death. In the original rough notes, she gives as her reason for writing 'to prevent others misrepresenting me after my death, and to encourage other women'. There would be little point in such an aim if the autobiography was to remain private. But since she could have changed her mind, it is worth citing a letter from Sir John Herschel, Mary Somerville's lifelong friend, and adviser on her scientific manuscripts. In March 1869 Sir John writes to Mary Somerville apologising for having taken more than a month to respond to the manuscript of her autobiography, which she had sent to him.[4] Herschel is, he says, in almost every respect impressed by the narrative, but he is equivocal about immediate publication, believing that the exemplary life that it unfolds might have more effect on the public, 'the many-headed monster', after its subject's death. He also recommends the excision of some fairly lengthy passages which involve a 'recital of specific features in the history of scientific progress and modern discovery': he believes that the lay reader will find them dull and the expert reader inadequate. Both suggestions seem to have been accepted.

Herschel is impressed with the unaffectedness of the autobiography – 'Nothing can be more pleasing and simple than the *personal narration,* the account of your strong early interest in those studies which you ultimately pursued with such extraordinary success and your self-taught progress in them under the most discouraging circumstances.' The case for offering this edition of the *Recollections* to a new public more than 100 years after original publication depends in part on my belief that Herschel's comment still holds, that Mary Somerville's life remains an exemplary one, from which we have much to learn. I presume that the memoirs of a once-celebrated individual will have a special force and interest and additionally Mary Somerville's representation of the age – and here the age means nearly a century, during which both Europe and the world beyond changed radically – is presented in a clear and penetrating manner in her *Recollections*.

The *Recollections* were very well received on their initial publication, reviewed in a number of national and local newspapers and journals. There had been a number of obituaries the year before, Mary Somerville's achievements were still before the public. Those who were against the further advancement of women could use her example to point out how few women were like her and those who supported women's causes could argue for how much women could achieve, even under adverse circumstances, if they would but persevere. But, as far as women's rights were concerned, Mary Somerville was of a previous generation, a previous era indeed, and shortly after her death advocates of the cause closer to the moment were needed. And so it was that her personal life-writing, like her scientific works, fell out of print until AMS Press in 1975 reprinted the American edition of 1876.[5] This has not, however, really made the *Recollections* accessible to a general readership and it is to this readership that the present edition is addressed.

Had Mary Somerville been a literary woman of comparable stature in her field, like George Eliot, or even her own close acquaintance, Harriet Martineau°, or had she led a more adventurous life, like Fanny Kemble, Mary Somerville's *Recollections* would almost certainly by now have been republished, or her voluminous correspondence edited. But Mary Somerville was not literary, nor did she lead a dangerous or rackety life. Yet no other memoirist writes quite like Mary Somerville and this is in part because she is not self-consciously literary. Her voice is peculiarly transparent. Her rationale for the memoirs is actually quite aggressive, since to see oneself as an example is not really modest but Martha's editing tries to turn assertiveness into self-deprecation. Mary Somerville begins, 'My life has been domestic and quiet. I have no events to record that could interest the public, my only motive in writing it is to show my country women that self education is possible under the most unfavourable and even discouraging circumstances.'[6] Martha begins with *her* voice rather than her mother's, paraphrasing her mother's words: 'The life of a woman entirely devoted to her family duties and to scientific pursuits affords little scope for a biography.' Thus, what in Mary Somerville's voice is a challenge to the reader to find her struggle less than interesting becomes in Martha's voice apologetic. Martha turns what is a contrast between the privacies of a life and the fame and achievements of the woman who lived it into a rather weak insistence that Mary Somerville was first and foremost a wife and mother. How can a new edition cope with this kind of problem?

The autobiography exists in three drafts. First there is the notebook of 1859 which sketches out shape and motivation; then there is an extensive draft entirely in Mary Somerville's hand; most but not all of this draft reaches the printed version with some changes in arrangement as well as changes in spelling and punctuation. The punctuation of this first version is very light and some additional punctuation is certainly needed for print and, since Mary Somerville is avowedly a bad speller (see p. 97), the corrections of her spelling (probably not as insecure as Joanna Baillie's) are uncontentious. This first draft peters out towards the end so that there is no firm conclusion to what was still a continuing life. The second draft is largely a copy of the first in Martha Somerville's hand, with marginal comments and additions in Mary Somerville's hand, and a few additional sheets wholly in Mary Somerville's hand. There are also editorial comments in the margin in a third hand, probably Mary Charlotte's, mostly injunctions to omit or confirmations that something has been omitted, which suggests that the final version was known at this stage. There are some additions in this version, most but not all of which appear in the printed text.

This edition does not pretend to be a complete re-editing of the recollections – indeed this would be impossible at this distance. Mary Somerville's own final intentions are not completely clear and minor changes are usually not worth commenting upon. The text, as we have it, loses some of the colloquial flow of the first draft, simply by introducing punctuation, but I am persuaded that Mary Somerville would have expected her text to be corrected by the printers (see again her comments on p. 97). There is no doubt, however, that there are some editorial decisions taken by Martha, probably in conjunction with the younger daughter, Mary, but some, more worryingly, on the advice of Frances Power Cobbe, who worshipped Mary Somerville and probably wished to smooth out some of her imperfections. Letters from Frances Cobbe to Martha suggest a fair amount of input into the printed text:

> I think your Introduction is most touching and so genuine and honest, it is sure to go straight to the reader's heart [. . .]. I have only made a few verbal

alterations twisting some of the sentences a little (so
as to avoid the little colloquialisms you fall into of
ending your sentences with a preposition and dividing some of them a little differently). But I would not
touch the substance of what you say for anything.
[. . .] Dear Martha I feel *quite* happy now about the
work. The book will make the world love your Mother
more and not admire her an atom the less.[7]

The intention of making Mary Somerville loveable has
moved well away from Mary Somerville's own aim.

The most extensive biographical work on Mary Somerville is by Elizabeth Chambers Patterson who has published
both a brief account of Mary Somerville's whole life, *Mary
Somerville, 1780–1872,* 1979[8] and a scholarly study of the
most significant period of Mary Somerville's professional
life, *Mary Somerville and the Cultivation of Science, 1815–
1840,* 1983.[9] The latter is an indispensable *vademecum* for
anyone who wants to look deeper into Mary Somerville's
professional life. Elizabeth Patterson uses the *Personal
Recollections,* as well as the extensive Somerville archive
deposited in the Bodleian Library to establish both biographical facts and feelings at any given point. She deals
only briefly with the genealogy of the printed text of the
Recollections. Here is what she says:

Her last work was an autobiography, begun in her
eighty-ninth year and completed before her death in
1872. A heavily edited version of this work was published in 1873 [. . .]. Her daughter, Martha, advised by
their friend Frances Power Cobbe (1822–1904),
omitted from the printed life markedly scientific sections of the manuscript, as well as many references to
persons and events they judged uninteresting or un-
suitable as contents. A selection of letters to Mary
Somerville from eminent persons was woven into the

text. [. . .] *Personal Recollections* emerges with many Victorian touches that would have been foreign to Mary Somerville herself (EP, 194).

This is true but, nevertheless, the effect of the Victorian touches is most interesting. The processes of the production of the final text, and hence of the version of Mary Somerville that her remaining family and friends wished to present to the world, are in themselves valuable and worth preserving but, at the same time, I think it worth restoring some of the rougher edges of the earlier drafts.

I have not restored the scientific sections that Herschel advised cutting.[10] Other omitted passages are, however, too good to lose: I have, therefore, interpolated in the 1873 printed text some passages from first and second drafts. I have added nothing which is not in Mary Somerville's hand, nor have I added without comment any passages, even though in her hand, if she herself has scored them out. It will be clear that the additional passages are mostly anecdotes which Martha, possibly Mary, and Frances Power Cobbe presumably deemed too trivial to be included but a modern audience may have a different notion of what is trivial. Some of the anecdotes were clearly offensive to a Victorian sensibility, although they did not upset Mary Somerville's own more robust taste: the story of her being taught to swear as a child seems to have been copied in Martha's hand into the second draft, but a marginal note says that it 'must go' and the offending passage has been snipped out of the manuscript. While the story is not in itself exceptional – what family cannot produce some similar embarrassing account? – the determined excision of it is significant. Other omissions seem minor, yet cumulatively, when added to the printed text, they work to produce a Mary Somerville far more concerned with her outer self, with her appearance. In the drafts Mary Somerville comments fairly regularly on her appearance and, by taking the comments out of her mother's mouth and putting them into her own, Martha turns legitimate self-concern, even occasionally self-absorption and vanity, into daughterly eulogy. Similarly, Mary Somerville's youthful and not so youthful resentments are smoothed away, producing a more emollient personality than appears in the drafts. Occasionally, as with the story of the mean friend (p. 222), there may have been relatives still alive to offend but, more generally, the omissions paper over cracks in Mary Somerville's serenity that, revealed, make her a little less noble but more congenial. To remember an insult for 50 years, as Mary Somerville does with Mrs Oswald's outrageous rudeness (p. 44) may not be saintly but it is, to imperfect mortal readers, understandable.

At the same time, it would be another kind of falsification to try to remove the effects of Martha's editing since the presentation of the mother by the daughter has a special quality in itself: Martha adds as well as taking away. She adds, of course, her own comments on both her parents; insists; just as tartly as her mother, that the obituaries were quite wrong in suggesting that Mary Somerville's first husband assisted her studies, and she adds letters from contemporaries which act as personal and professional validations of Mary Somerville. I have, therefore, tried to provide a text that can be read simultaneously as the version of a Victorian daughter, Martha, and the production of her mother. The intended result is to offer a plurality of Mary Somervilles, all with their special kind of truth. I should like to look now a little more closely at some of these Mary Somervilles, trying to show that, although plural, they are not separate.

FEMINIST, MATHEMATICIAN, ASTRONOMER, BOTANIST, GEOGRAPHER – SCIENTIST:

In this section I am particularly indebted to Elizabeth Patterson's searching study. Its introduction (i–xiii) offers an admirable summation of the changing state of British science in the years 1815 to 1840, roughly the period of Mary Somerville's London residence (allowing, of course, for her continental tours). Elizabeth Patterson sets out to answer the question: 'How did Mary Somerville move from self-taught provincial to celebrated scientific lady?' (EP, xiii), and does so against a wide understanding of the nature and status of science in the period.

How far, then, were the dice loaded against Mary Somerville because of her sex? The declared aim of the autobiography is to show how it is possible for a woman to overcome obstacles and achieve a high place in a male world. The narrative tries to encourage those who might often feel discouraged, for, although female education was easier to obtain when Mary Somerville wrote her *Recollections* than it was when she began her courses of private study, it remained difficult and many prejudices persisted which showed themselves still in her obituaries and even in the reviews of her *Recollections*. It was her achievement to be exemplary as a woman and as a scientist, to reach her goals without sacrificing relatively conventional femininity. Indeed, one of the prejudices that she never attacks, in fact probably shares, is the deeply embedded fear that commitment to the life of the mind might produce aggression or frumpishness in a woman.

Most of Mary Somerville's explicit resentments in the *Recollections* are reserved for the problems of the early stages of her life. She explains how more or less anything was thought good enough for female education. Her father does not want her to become a 'savage' but a little learning is obviously deemed enough to prevent this. She is particularly good on the way in which the production of female deportment at Miss Primrose's school is a form of torture and of intellectual imprisonment too:

Then a steel rod, with a semi-circle which went under the chin, was clasped to the steel busk in my stays. In

> this constrained state I, and most of the younger girls,
> had to prepare our lessons. (p. 18)

When she is released, becoming like a 'wild animal escaped
out of a cage' (p. 20), she moves closer to a holistic
response to the natural world, which is the kind of response
that ultimately underpins her scientific thinking. All forms
of life-writing are potentially suspect, insofar as they attempt to identify the future in the past but Mary Somerville's depiction of her response to her natural environment
at Burntisland carries the stamp of authenticity:

> There was a small pier on the sands for shipping
> limestone brought from the coal mines inland. I was
> astonished to see the surface of these blocks of stone
> covered with beautiful impressions of what seemed to
> be leaves; how they got there I could not imagine, but
> I picked up the broken bits, and even large pieces, and
> brought them to my repository. (p. 21)

The human environment was less kind and Mary Somerville's struggle against prejudice and indifference to acquire
a classical and scientific education is equally authentically
presented.

While it was truly hard for Mary Somerville to become
proficient in mathematics through private study, there is
little doubt nevertheless that once she had done a certain
amount herself there were plenty of male practitioners who
were anxious to assist her in an unpatronising manner. Her
early loneliness and despondency (p. 37 and p. 60) were
consequences of the limitations of her family circle but
once she had won independence as a widow and, even
better, married a second, supportive husband, the scientific
world did not try to keep her out. And so, in the end, Mary
Somerville got her scientific education in much the same
way as any man from an unprivileged background at the

time – through the generosity of a developing group of scientific men, amateur and professional, who were anxious not to fence off their patch but rather to invite in those who loved to learn.[11] William Wallace, who supported Mary Somerville's activities in mathematics during her first widowhood (p. 66), and Michael Faraday were both bookbinders' apprentices before their talents and the assistance of richer men placed them in significant positions in the scientific establishment. It is a proper tribute to this network, which shows itself throughout the *Recollections*, that Mary Somerville's most ambitious book was *On the Connexion of the Physical Sciences*, an attempt to do for science itself what all these lovers of truth were doing for each other – establishing a network of connections.

The scientific establishments of Britain and Europe were not, of course, free from competitiveness, aggression and snobbishness. Elizabeth Patterson's account of the internal struggles between various factions of the Royal Society shows that the struggles at the Royal Society often had a gentlemen-versus-players aspect. But there is very little suggestion in or out of the *Recollections* of any aggression towards Mary Somerville, any feeling that she was an interloper.

Mary Somerville, then, may have been hindered at home, nagged by her prospective sister-in-law, denounced from the pulpit and spoken against in the House, but the scientific world in London, in Paris, in Geneva and, finally in the relative scientific backwater of Italy,[12] opened its arms to her. To her these men were exceptionally civil, an effect perhaps of her own feminine civility.

It was no doubt Mary Somerville's fortune, in the end, to be little and shy (pp. 48–9). If we look at the letters from scientists and mathematicians included in the volume, they are remarkable for a composite idiom, which I think we owe to a very large extent to the very nature of Mary Somerville. Of course, it is not that before her career scientists obsec sively focused on their work in their letters and refused the pleasantries of social intercourse, but, nevertheless, a special tone of civility enters professional letters from Mary Somerville's correspondents. Also illuminating in terms of epistolary discourse and gender are letters written by scientists to Mary Somerville's husband. Sir John Herschel's letter of 17 July 1830 to William Somerville (p. 174) is principally about the recognition of his wife, yet at the same time it is clearly an exchange between 'chaps', as it were. It is obvious that William Somerville found himself in no way emasculated by the abilities of his wife and no more did his acquaintance worry about his status, even after he retired because of ill-health.

But perhaps there is a problem with the civility of the letters to Mary Somerville from scientists, perhaps they are altogether too civil. There may well be a line, too fine to discern with security, between the civil and the patronising. Yet the amount of time spent on talking to and writing to Mary Somerville by these men can only be justified by something more than gallantry, and there is also, outside the *Recollections*, the evidence of the kind of letter that Martha Somerville did not include in her edition because it would be beyond the comprehension of ordinary readers. These letters, full of detailed equations and abstruse speculations, are exchanged with Herschel, Babbage and Lubbock, among many others. Again, with mostly trivial or petulant exceptions, contemporary reviews treat Mary Somerville's work in a wholly unpatronising manner.[13]

Mary Somerville, then, both suffers from and profits from her femininity and it can be argued that this has been the constant problem for female achievers. It is a problem that Mary Somerville negotiated with more success than, for example, Mary Wollstonecraft, who continues to be castigated for being too womanly and not womanly enough, or, to choose the same field as Somerville, the unfortunate Ada Lovelace whose 'womanly' behaviour brought her close to disgrace and who died in great pain from her woman's body (see 'Brief Biographies' pp. 349–50). But Mary Somerville is herself insecure about this female body which she cannot quite reconcile with the notion of a sexless mind; she fears, in truth, that the mind, like the body, is gendered, and gendered by the body. The passage that reveals these fears most clearly was cut out of the published text and I have restored it:

> In the climax of my great success, the approbation of some of the first scientific men of the age and of the public in general I was highly gratified, but much less elated than might have been expected, for although I had recorded in a clear point of view some of the most refined and difficult analytical processes and astro-nomical discoveries, I was conscious that I had never made a discovery myself, that I had no originality. I have perseverance and intelligence but no genius, that spark from heaven is not granted to the sex, we are of the earth, earthy, whether higher powers may be alotted to us in another state of existence God knows, original genius, in science at least, is hopeless in this.
> (p. 145)

Martha and Mary Somerville and Frances Power Cobbe must have felt at the time that this was an unnecessary hostage to fortune. In the obituaries in 1872 there were already signs of a willingness to downgrade her achieve-ment. The *Saturday Review*, which also credits the erro-neous story that her first husband was supportive, insists that she was an interpreter and expounder, not a disco-verer:

> It is not invidious, still less discourteous, in us to say that the one is to the other as moonlight is to sunlight. Receptive, bright and keen, the mind of woman may

give back or diffuse the rays of knowledge for the source or emanation of which a stronger and more original power is necessary.[14]

In the light of Mary Somerville's resigned, even depressed, acquiescence in the secondary position of women as innovative scientists, it is obviously important that John Couch Adams told her husband that it was a suggestion from *On the Connexion of the Physical Sciences* that put it into his head to calculate the orbit of Neptune. Furthermore it was the impact of Mary Somerville's *Connexion of the Physical Sciences* that produced the word 'scientist' in the first place. Reviewing the book in the *Quarterly*, William Whewell speaks of Mary Somerville's laudable insistence on connection at a time when there was an 'increasing proclivity to separation and dismemberment' in the sciences and he proposes the use of a new term, one possibility being 'scientist', on the model of 'artist, sciolist, economist and atheist'.[15] It is also in this review that Whewell rehearses arguments about female and male intellect that are with us still. He does believe that 'there is a sex in minds' and while he does not simply privilege male over female, the sex of his own mind is never far away:

> One of the characteristics of the female intellect is a clearness of perception as far as it goes; with them action is the result of feeling; thought of seeing; their practical emotions do not wait for instruction from speculation; their reasoning is undisturbed by the prospect of its practical consequences. (*QR*, 65)

Diminishing though this seems, Whewell plucks out of it a kind of victory for female intellect:

> But, from the peculiar mental character to which we have referred, it follows, that when women are phi-

losophers, they are likely to be lucid ones; that when
they extend the range of their speculative views, there
will be a peculiar illumination thrown over the prospect. If they attain to the merit of being profound,
they will add to this the great excellence of being also
clear. (*QR*, 66)

Yet, as soon as difference is admitted, and both men and
women at the time did admit it, it becomes impossible
within the historical context to do other than privilege the
male in the very act of elevating the female. It cannot really
be denied that in spite of all the attention and assistance
that Mary Somerville received and the accolades she won,
this was still a man's world. With the exceptions of Mary
Somerville herself and Ada Lovelace, most of the other
women involved in the scientific world were involved
because of the assistance they gave their husbands or
because, like Jane Marcet, they were popularisers in a
way that Mary Somerville never was. Yet it was Jane
Marcet who first inspired Faraday (p. 92), and that is
surely something. But Mrs Kater, Mrs Sabine, Mrs Lyell
gave their devoted services to their husbands and are
remembered as helpmeets, although Elizabeth Sabine
translated Humboldt's *Kosmos*. Sometimes, indeed, it
has been necessary, as with Mrs Lowry, to go to a biography
of a husband to get any information about a wife. In this
sense, Mary Somerville is assisted by not having had a
scientific partner.

The public honours she received, although numerous
and welcome, were also usually secondary: she was generally an honorary, not a full, member of learned societies.
When Herschel writes to William Somerville (p. 175) that
he hears that a recent vote of the Astronomical Society
makes Mary Somerville his *colleague* he is exaggerating,
since her membership of the Society, like that of his aunt,
Caroline Herschel, was an honorary one. Nevertheless,

Mary Somerville's pension from the Civil List was in line with the awards made to her male contemporaries: she received, as she explains (p. 144), £200 from Robert Peel's administration and when the succeeding Whig administration added £100 to this, Mary Somerville was in receipt of an amount equivalent to the pensions of Airy, Faraday and Brewster among others (EP, 161).

THE SCOTSWOMAN:

Whewell concludes his review by quoting the verses that I have chosen as my epigraph, which compare Mary Somerville to Hypatia and Madame Agnesi, the only two earlier women believed to be distinguished in mathematics: 'Three women in three different ages born, /Greece, Italy, and England did adorn.' Accepting the justice of the claim, Whewell, nevertheless, points out that Madame Agnesi and Mary Somerville were born in the same century and that, 'though Hypatia talked Greek as Mrs Somerville does English, the former was an Egyptian, and the latter, we are obliged to confess, is Scotch by her birth, though we are very happy to claim her as one of the brightest ornaments of England' (*QR*, 68). Mary Somerville was a Scot living outside Scotland at a time when nationality was a peculiarly pressing issue and the positioning of an intellectual north or south of the border was a contentious business. For example, if Mary Somerville could not have been great without leaving Scotland, we might well feel that Scott could not have been great if he had done. But Scott died the year after the *Mechanism of the Heavens* was published. Scotland's intellectual heyday was fading despite the continued ascendancy of 'Scotch Reviewers'.

Mary Somerville's relationship with her native country was complex. Her closeness to Joanna Baillie may well have derived from the shared sense of both being and not being Scottish. They both retained their Scottish accents: Joanna

Baillie's was apparently even more marked,[16] but Mary Somerville was always self-conscious about her accent (p. 97). However far she travelled physically and intellectually from her native land, she carried its continued impress in her speech.

Her religious sense too was shaped by Scotland, both in what underpinned it and in what she rejected. Her love for the natural world, which affected every aspect of her personal and professional life, came out of her early years in Burntisland and Jedburgh. As is, of course, very often the case with memoirs, the sections which deal with childhood experiences are among the most vivid and most moving. It is from these early experiences that she derived a feeling for the history inherent in things and places that anchors her to the beauties of the living world:

> Some of the plum and pear trees were very old, and were said to have been planted by the monks. Both were excellent in quality, and very productive. [. . .] The precipitous banks of red sandstone are richly clothed with vegetation, some of the trees ancient and very fine, especially the magnificent one called the capon tree, and the lofty king of the wood, remnants of the fine forests which at one time had covered the country. (p. 30)

And it was in these early days too that she developed the love for birds that she carried with her to the end.

But if Scotland taught her how to love God's creation, it also gave her much to reject in the narrowness of the Calvinism of some of her religious teaching. On the whole, Mary Somerville makes light of the gloomier and harsher aspects of Scottish Calvinism but clearly it was one of the factors that made her less than wholly sorry to leave her native land. Nevertheless, she carries with her on her first departure from Scotland a sense of democratic community in the 'Scotch Kirk' that she misses in the 'coldness and formality of the Church of England' (p. 63). That sense of closeness of the individual to the creation and the Creator never left Mary Somerville. She did not need to commit herself to the narrowness of the Evangelical movement to be close to God. And her tolerance of the views of others, even of atheism, derives from an early security in the goodness of Christians like her mother and her uncle and father-in-law, the Rev. Thomas Somerville.

At the same time, she was aware that continued residence in Scotland would have stifled her intellectual life and it was important to her that her second husband, William Somerville, had travelled widely and was 'emancipated from Scotch prejudices' (p. 73). A letter written from Scotland in 1837 to her daughters in London recommends them to think hard before marrying Scotsmen and make it quite clear that she regards her departure from her native country as a fortunate escape (EP, 185–86). The letter is crossed ferociously, partly to conceal its contents from a casual glance: it is very difficult to decipher:

> I never should have written a word and you two
> would have been worried to death and stupid [?] like
> the rest, so all is for the best. Jedburgh my birthplace I
> saw without pleasure and left without regret, yet the
> vale is most beautiful but a place however lovely is
> only agreeable in solitude or good society neither of
> which charm does it possess. If you marry Scotch-
> men, take care they are good ones. The Scotch are
> like foreigners in one respect, the very high *alone* are
> tolerable and they not always.[17]

This is, however, a letter written in surprising bitterness of spirit, full of irritation with some of her Scottish acquaintance and also, alas, with the family of her son's bride. She quotes her brother Henry as saying that the gentlemen of the new generation are not fit society for Martha and Mary, as feeling that Woronzow's imminent marriage to Agnes Graham will not bring a good 'connexion' and that Woronzow might have done much better. Mary Somerville agrees that her brother is the only *gentleman* and his wife and her sister the only *ladies* she has seen since she came, but she believes that Woronzow's happiness is most important and everyone speaks well of Agnes. There is an uncharacteristic coarseness about this which can perhaps only come out of encounters with our nearest and dearest. The oppressiveness of provincial society is hardly a peculiarly Scottish problem.

Her local places were certainly proud of *her*. The *Kelso Chronicle* reviewed her *Personal Recollections*, entirely unresentful of the occasional slight to Scotland, justly recognising that 'Mary Somerville lived so as to get the greatest possible amount of happiness out of her long life' (n.d. after 18 Dec. 1873) and the *Kelso Mail* (25 March 1874), in its laudatory review, tells a doubtless apocryphal but charming story about Mary Somerville after the planting of a cedar at the residence of the Misses Ramsay, friends of her mother:

> One of the Miss Ramsays said, 'May we again all meet around it.' 'May we all meet under it' was the wish of her sister; and 'May we all meet above it' was the characteristic wish of Mrs Somerville.

DAUGHTER, WIFE AND MOTHER:
Although Mary Somerville had to contend with her parents' disapproval of her studies, and although her father worried, probably half in jest, about her ending up in a straitjacket, she obviously enjoyed close relationships with both of them in her later life and much regretted their deaths. She enjoyed a quiet domestic life with her parents after the death of her first husband and there is no doubt

that her mother was later extremely proud of her daughter's scholarly achievements and delighted by the publication of her books. She writes twice in 1831 expressing her anxiety to hear about the reception of her daughter's book – 'I am [. . .] anxious to know how your book is received by the public – write me soon, my dearest Mary.' Early in the next year she is expressing her pleasure at the book's success and her daughter's good health.[18] As for her father, Vice-Admiral of the Red, Mary Somerville was extremely proud of him and nothing in his illiberal Tory opinions could obliterate this; she always admired those who, like him, faced the hardships of the sea.

With her siblings and with her children, Mary Somerville suffered, as did most people at the time, from the frequency of infantile and premature deaths. The death of her elder brother, Sam, in India at 21, greatly affected her and the first draft of the autobiography has a double row of dots across the page after the description of his death, as if to signal an irreversible difference in her life. Like so many women of the time, she also had to suffer the pain of the deaths of her children. The most affecting childhood death certainly was that of her eldest daughter, Margaret, who died in 1823 before her eleventh birthday. The Somervilles had obviously invested a great deal in this young girl: 'She was,' Mary Somerville says, 'a child of intelligence and acquirements far beyond her tender age' (p. 124); indeed, made unscientific perhaps by grief, she feared that she may have overtaxed Margaret's young mind:

> I felt her loss the more acutely because I feared I had strained her young mind too much. My only reason for mentioning this family affliction is to warn mothers against the fatal error I have made.[19]

Mary Somerville also suffered the sorrow of having her son, Woronzow, predecease her. Of course, her longevity made this the less remarkable: Woronzow was, after all, 60 when he died. Neither of her daughters married and both lived only a few years after their mother's death. Woronzow Greig had a public life and so it is possible to know more about him than the *Recollections* reveal,[20] but Martha and Mary remain rather shadowy figures in spite of their firmer presence in the *Recollections*. Going to the letters does give the two girls clearer individual presences. Their own letters reveal quite spirited responses to the wise and the great of their mother's acquaintance; and they were educated and active women – they sailed their own boat, rode in the Roman Campagna, played instruments, sang and painted. Yet, in the letters of their parents and their friends, they are almost always 'the girls' or 'Martha and Mary', as if a kind of unit, and it is hard not to feel that they lived their lives mainly for their mother. Martha has her strongest presence as an editor of her mother's autobiography. Frances Power Cobbe confirms this in her obituary in the *Echo*: 'her husband "rose up and called her blessed", her children devoted their lives to her comfort' (3 Dec. 1872). It is a commonplace that it is difficult to be the children of famous parents and Mary Somerville's girls seem to have suffered in this way. There is no shade of resentment about this, either in or out of the published work, and it is quite clear that Mary Somerville wanted her children to be happy and independent. But could she perhaps have tried harder to detach them from her, was she too glad in the end to have them 'support her tottering steps' (p. 299)? I do not know; she herself would need to have said more, and more openly, for judgment to be passed and she does refuse openness about intimate family affairs.

In revealing the contents of Mary Somerville's rather sour letter to her daughters about Scotland and some Scots, I have already violated her insistence on the privacy of correspondence but, since the violation helps us to come closer to her feelings about her country and its people, I cannot summon a great deal of guilt. And we may slightly regret Mary Somerville's faithfulness to her decision to avoid the intimate details of her family life. Or, at least, we may feel that she regards as intimate much that we might now feel is merely everyday and that we should like to have been told. The early section of the *Recollections* remains the most delightful because the details of daily life are so sharp and because Mary Somerville's love for her father and mother and her future father-in-law emerges so clearly at this point. But some silences are verging on the obsessive in their insistence on privacy, and the silences seem to be Mary Somerville's, not Martha's. She never mentions, for example, that her mother was William Fairfax's second wife, his first wife also being from Burntisland (EP, 1). More understandably, perhaps, she fails to mention that William Somerville had been married before, and that he also had a natural child (EP, 7). Yet the existence of James Craig Somerville was never repudiated. William Somerville acknowledged his son and brought him back with him from South Africa, naming him after Sir James Craig and educating him until he graduated as a doctor of medicine from Edinburgh University. Nor did he exclude this son from his life with Mary Somerville: indeed, James Craig Somerville was fairly close to Woronzow Greig, Mary Somerville's surviving son from her first marriage. Mary Somerville's mother, writing in July 1831, asks that her 'kindest love be given to Dr James and his pretty wife'.[21]

Dr James Craig had certainly been privy to the skeleton in Woronzow's cupboard that his mother also hides from public view: it came to light at Woronzow's death that he too had had an illegitimate child, fathered when he was 19 or 20, a daughter to whom he had given financial support but whose existence he kept secret from his wife, Agnes. This obviously caused a fair amount of family commotion. Mary Somerville seems to have been a little tactless, but there was no breach of relations between mother and daughter-in-law. Nor was Mary Somerville particularly shocked, consistent with her principle that charity was to be preferred to chastity; Woronzow had lived a decent Christian life and had helped his natural daughter and her family.[22]

It does not take a very percipient reader to guess that all was not well with Mary Somerville's first marriage, although inattention and selfishness seem to have been the problems rather than anything more sinister. The short passages that I have restored from the first draft underline Samuel Greig's selfishness (p. 62). Frances Power Cobbe, reviewing the *Recollections* for the *Academy* claims that Greig was 'to the last degree harsh, stern, and unsympathising . . . Mr Greig, we believe, expressing at the last his consciousness that his widow would have had but little reason to regret his memory' (Sat., 3 Jan. 1874, 2). It is likely, however, that Cobbe was reacting with irritation to obituaries that credited Samuel Greig with assisting his wife in her studies, presumably on the assumption that no woman could master mathematics without male support. Like Martha Somerville and, indeed, Mary Somerville herself (p. 63), Frances Cobbe wants to stress his lack of sympathy and perhaps paints him blacker than he was. At any rate, he had the decency to die quickly and give Mary Somerville the independence she needed.

About the second, happy and supportive, marriage, little more need be done than to point to the testimony of the *Recollections*. But it is something of an irony that William Somerville's supportive behaviour towards his talented wife goes along with what we might now feel was an inadequately professional attitude towards his own work. His post at the Chelsea Hospital seems to have been close to a sinecure and certainly permitted a great deal of time off before his final decision to give up the position for health reasons. But, after all, this went largely unremarked at the time. And William Somerville seems to have been a re-

markable man in his way. To have moved with ease and
without apology through some of the highest intellectual
society of Europe, always allowing the superior abilities of
his wife without losing anything of his own dignity, must
have required a firm sense of self which, nevertheless,
seems to have been in no danger of becoming complacent.
The story of his good-humoured negotiation of the problems of an over-holy Sunday (p. 178) are characteristic of a
personality strong enough to be quietly assertive without
giving the outward appearance of being so.

FRIEND

One of the most attractive aspects of the *Personal Recollections* is its revelation of important friendships. The friendship with Sir John Herschel is, of course, the one that most
links the various Mary Somervilles that we have encountered: he is her scientific adviser, but he also writes to her as
a father and husband, because she is so clearly herself
mother and wife as well as intellectual woman. Female
friendships too were of great importance to Mary Somerville, notably those with Maria Edgeworth, Joanna Baillie
and, latterly, Frances Power Cobbe. We are grateful that
Martha decided to include letters from Maria Edgeworth
and Joanna Baillie; the latter, in particular, greatly assist the
formation of a whole picture of Mary Somerville. Like
Mary Somerville herself, Joanna Baillie was capable of
sharp remarks despite also being little and shy.

Among lesser acquaintance, occasionally one feels rather
bombarded by noble names. Yet one feels this as an effect
of innocence, of a kind of naivety perhaps, and in a moment
I want to suggest that this naivety is a positive quality. Nor
again is any real distinction made between the high and the
low – both are usually part of the everyday. One of the
problems for an editor is that it is tempting to spend a
disproportionate amount of time trying to find out who

everyone mentioned is. Do we need to know that the Somervilles' medical adviser was Professor Zanetti? And do we need to know if he was 'someone'? Well, Mary Somerville seems to feel that to mention her medical adviser without mentioning his name would be discourteous. She tries to show proper courtesy to everyone who crosses her path, servant or prince.

It was, as I have already indicated, the wish of Mary Somerville's daughters to provide a much more seamless version of her than I have permitted. But what does link all the Marys, that no amount of selection or editing seems to be able to fudge, is the special voice of the woman. It is, indeed, remarkable that, through all the daughterly fiddling with her text, this voice refuses to be blurred. Here we may go again to Sir John Herschel to find out what its characteristics were for her coevals. 'Nothing,' he wrote, 'can be more pleasing and simple than the *personal narration* . . . nor anything more naive, more natural and unaffected then your account of your own success – no assumption, no vanity – but only an admission (and that rather by implication) of such an amount of private satisfaction, which one must be more or less than human not to feel.'[23]

We have come to feel that naivety is not a virtue, because it is so often affected, yet to recover its special value brings us closer to Mary Somerville's unique qualities. If we think of a voice informed by naive wisdom, we go some way to defining what makes it special. This naive wisdom can be discerned in all the Mary Somervilles that I have discussed: the same unpretending clarity informs her dealings with both people and ideas.

Hers is a wholly distinctive voice, which has neither antecedent nor follower. A couple of examples may clarify its special quality: when Somerville is reporting her father's illiberality, she dramatises with the direct perception of a novelist: 'By G—, when a man cuts off his queue, the head should go with it' (p. 36). Here, the very excess of the sentiment makes the speaker more loveable than sinister. And, again, when the cruel practices of the navy are discussed, Somerville writes dispassionately and hence devastatingly. Yet, immediately afterwards, she proceeds to discuss her father's place in the very institution that she is condemning (pp. 56–58). This sophisticated perception that institutions may contain parts infinitely superior to the whole is made with a clear-mindedness so unaffected, so naive, that it is devastating. Much later, she cites the lady who believed that all those who worshipped in the Temple of Neptune must be 'in eternal misery'. Somerville asked, 'How could they believe in Christ when He was not born till many centuries after? I am sure she thought it was all the same' (p. 101). The absence of fuss in the syntax makes the implicit judgment more telling.

On larger political issues, the same naive wisdom is evident. Garibaldi is a man of genius but potentially injurious to his country (p. 245). On the slave trade and slavery she refuses to compromise (p. 299), but tolerance in religious matters is always for her a virtue (p. 277). On the right of women to education, on the other hand, she is both tart and uncompromising. Science and religion she manages to reconcile by always avoiding, as some of her contemporaries could not, the trick of alternately blaming and denying God.

These balanced judgments are a function of the varied experience of Mary Somerville. Her scientific training had made her the kind of thinker who never rejects but who never quickly becomes a proselyte: her reaction to Darwinism is telling here. Because of his devout beliefs, it took the American geologist and zoologist, James Dana, 15 years to accept a version of Darwinism. Mary Somerville describes Dana as 'an honour to his country' (p. 180) but it did not take her as long; it was perhaps easier since she had never been either a fundamentalist or an evangelical but it might still have been possible for a woman of her advanced years to react strongly against Darwin. Instead she approached his discoveries and theories as yet more evidence of what we do not know, of the mystery underlying all phenomena (p. 288). And it is the sense of that mystery that informs her opinions on secular affairs. Those who look for more fire from their pioneering women may be disappointed in her but to embrace and accommodate change may be a wiser mode than to try to force change or its acceptance on the unwilling.

The judgments come out of what, in spite of reticence and shyness, turns out to be a secure sense of identity and place. She negotiated the problems that inevitably arise within families and, although she may have been unsuccessful, she tried to give her children possibilities that she never had or did not easily secure. Mary Somerville never doubted who she was: even at her moments of greatest depression, her sense of an inner strength scarcely wavers. But place? How is it possible to speak of the security of place when she spent the last 30-odd years of her life in a more-or-less nomadic existence in Italy and elsewhere in Europe? But there are two kinds of nomad – those who are at home nowhere and those who are at home everywhere. Mary Somerville belongs to the latter group. She clearly managed with very little fuss to establish homes in the houses of others. Her intellectual baggage she always had with her and the comfort that she derived from this immaterial home seems to have assisted her in maintaining the physical comfort of others. To be sure, latterly Martha directed the household and it is hard to imagine what Mary Somerville would have done without her girls. But they presumably would not themselves have believed they had a home if she was not in it and, indeed, seem sadly not to have wished to linger on after her death.

Finally, it is Mary Somerville's insistence on the need for connection that makes her an icon for her time and its concerns. *The Connexion of the Physical Sciences* explicitly pronounces connection as an aim but all her work drives towards connection rather than separatist categorisation, and this emphasis seems characteristic of Somerville as memoirist too. For her, the desirable life is also the connected life and it is a life that does not categorise lest it stigmatise life's more homely areas. The small number of her contemporaries who tried to diminish Mary Somerville were usually those who did not understand that making marmalade and studying the calculus are not incompatible; that 'spotting muslin' is not, in spite of Veitch's remarks (p. 81), too lowly an activity for an intellectual woman, provided that her aspirations are not inhibited by it. In all areas of her activity Mary Somerville's appropriate motto was the one she herself assumed for *Molecular and Microscopic Science*: 'Deus magnus in magnis, maximus in minimis': 'God great in great things, greatest in the least'.[24]

Dorothy McMillan

I cite pagination in the manner requested by Elizabeth Patterson, whose catalogue I have also gratefully used.

1   Somerville Collection/SC: Dep. c.356, box 2, MSAU-4.
2   SC: Dep. c.355, box 5, MSAU-2.
3   SC: Dep. c.355, box 5, MSAU-3.
4   Royal Society of London Library/RSL: Herschel Papers, 2.378; J. F. W. Herschel to Mary Somerville, 14 March 1869.
5   In *Women of Letters, an AMS Reprint Series* (New York: AMS Press, 1975).
6   SC: Dep. c.355, box 5, MSAU-2, 1.
7   Somerville Collection, Dep. c.358, box 8, MSFP-19: Frances Power Cobbe to Martha Somerville, Jul. 11 [1873].
8   Elizabeth Chambers Patterson, *Mary Somerville, 1780–1872* (Oxford: Somerville College, 1979).
9   Patterson, *Mary Somerville and the Cultivation of Science, 1815–1840* (The Hague: Martinus Nijhoff, 1983). All further references will be to 'EP' with page number/s.
10 Indeed, in her reply to his letter Mary Somerville indicates that she has already taken his advice, having struck out

passages and added 'a number of anecdotes of people and things illustrative of the times which will make it more amusing, and others may occur to me as the MS will not be printed till after my death' (RSL: Herschel Papers, 2.379: Mary Somerville to Herschel, 23 March 1869).

11   It is clear, of course, that a poor *lower-class woman* could never have done what Mary Somerville did. Success in any intellectual field for working-class women was almost impossible, but in scientific fields it was unthinkable.

12   It must be noted, however, that Italian civility did not extend to allowing a woman into the observatory of the Collegio Romano without an order from the Pope (see p. 193).

13   Perhaps the most egregious example of a disparaging and ignorant review is of *The Mechanism of the Heavens* in the *Athenaeum*. Its fire is so scattered as to be ineffective but it displays an unexplained animus against learned women or, as the reviewer would have it, would-be learned women: *Athenaeum*, 221 (1832), 43–44.

14   *Saturday Review*, 7 Dec. 1872, 721–2, p.722.

15   William Whewell, review of Mary Somerville's *On the Connexion of the Physical Sciences*, 1834: *Quarterly Review*, li (1834), 154–171.

16   Maria Edgeworth reports in a letter to her mother in 1822 that Mary Somerville had a 'remarkably soft voice though speaking with a strong Scottish pronunciation – yet it is a well-bred Scotch not like the Baillies': Maria Edgeworth, *Letters from England, 1813–1844*, ed. Christina Colvin (Oxford: Clarendon Press, 1971).

17   SC. Dep. c.362, box 12, MSIF-10; Mary Somerville to Mary C. Somerville, 19 Sept. 1837 (postmarked: Kelso, 20 Sept. 1837). It seems clear that at this point Mary Somerville was staying with her husband's family and her own acquired virtue in comparison.

18   SC: Dep. c.357, box 7, MSFP-2; Margaret Charters Fairfax to Mary Somerville.

19   SC: Dep. c.355, box 5, MSAU-2, 150.

20   See John Appleby, 'Woronzow Greig (1805–1865), F.R.S., and his Scientific Interests', Notes and Records of the Royal Society of London, 53:1 (1999), 95–107.

21   SC, Dep. c.357, box 7 MSFP-2; Margaret Charters Fairfax to Mary Somerville, 15 July 1831.

22   The story may be pieced together from letters in the Somerville Collection, Dep. c.357, box 7, MSFP-11, 13 letters from

Mary Somerville to James Graham [Agnes Greig's brother] and 18 letters from James Graham to Mary Somerville. It should be stressed that no one acted in any way dishonourably in the affair; Woronzow probably simply put off the moment of revelation and then everyone suffered the tragic nuisance of his sudden death.

23 Herschel Papers, 2.378, 14 March 1869.
24 St Augustine.

Editorial Practice

Elizabeth Patterson points out that the published *Personal Recollections* include errors of date etc. Some of these are, I think, interesting in themselves, as an old woman looks back over what has constituted her life and times and some, indeed, turn out not to be errors after all (see note 44). In some cases, Mary Somerville cannot herself remember exactly when things happened but what she does know, in a way that the accurate dates cannot in themselves provide for us, is how it felt to those living at the time when extraordinary things happened. There are a number of places in the *Recollections* where Mary Somerville tells her readers that she cannot remember exactly when things occurred. This is, of course, a favourite trope of writers of autobiography to get them off the hook of falsification, which they know is always lurking for the memoirist, but it seems to me legitimate in that it retains the sense of immediate excitement by refusing to go to the books of statistics to verify memory. Elsewhere, as in the question of the earthquake at Assisi (see p. 98), I have tried to indicate how errors in dating may have occurred. Altogether, I hope the text gives the impression of a life assimilated, rather than set out according to the rule book.

I have conflated my notes and those from the original edition. When the notes are not mine, this is clearly signalled. Instead of dealing with the many people that Mary Somerville encountered in her long life in notes, I have chosen to offer brief biographies. These are signalled in the text by a degree sign. In preparing the biographies, I have been indebted to all the usual reference sources (national dictionaries of biography, subject dictionaries of biography, and the major encyclopaedias), but also particularly to Elizabeth Patterson's *Mary Somerville and the Cultivation of Science*. These debts are signalled by 'EP' with a page number where appropriate. I have followed Elizabeth Patterson's practice in giving the dates of assumption as Fellows of the Royal Society, thus showing how even the apparently non-scientific, like Woronzow Greig indeed, had amateur commitments to science.

Reading these brief biographies gives a conspectus of the life of Europe over more than a century. These are many of the people who made the modern world and a number of them were acquaintances or friends or at least in some way crossed the path of this remarkable woman.

The brief biographies do not cover everyone named in the *Recollections*. Some who are little more than names are not noted, although, if they are very interesting in themselves, I have tried to give some indication of what made them significant in their day. A number of private individuals are not included, since it is what Mary Somerville remembers of them that is significant; their achievement, in other words, is to have been remembered by her. Others, like Scott, are too famous to require to be noted. Some of the very famous, like Byron, are mentioned simply to indicate at which points their lives crossed with Mary Somerville's. Occasionally, as with Joanna Baillie, I have indulged myself with slightly longer entries, which either signal their importance for Mary Somerville or, following her own gentle but persistent feminism, privilege women who have been obscure until relatively recently.

The text is that of the first edition (London: John Murray, 1873), with interpolated passages from the first and second drafts of the autobiography in the Somerville Collection of papers in the Bodleian Library, Oxford.

The original printed text has been edited so that it is generally brought into line with modern spelling and punctuation, as in the use of italics for titles, rather than the quotation marks of the original. The exception is the letters, which are left with the idiosyncrasies that distinguish them as letters, although I have removed obvious errors such as 'Finders' for 'Flinders' on p. 94.

I have edited the passages from the drafts, silently removing spelling mistakes, of which there are fewer than might be imagined from Mary Somerville's insistence that she was a bad speller, adding light punctuation for intelligibility, and expanding ampersands; where I have added words to complete the sense, I indicate this by square brackets. Since Mary Somerville was obviously quite happy to accept the corrections of her compositors (p 97), I do not think any useful purpose is served by trying to reproduce the manuscripts exactly, especially since I use only selected passages from them. My aim throughout has been to produce a readable text while still allowing readers to see something of the original process of editing out 'unacceptable' passages.

I have brought the spelling of foreign names in both the printed text and the drafts into line with generally accepted spellings so that readers may go directly to the name in the list of brief biographies without being distracted by an uncommon or erroneous spelling.

The Bodleian shelf marks of the drafts are as follows:
First draft: Somerville Collection, Dep. c.355, box 5, MSAU-2 (signalled in the text by *1D* and page number/s).
Second draft: Somerville Collection, Dep. c.355, box 5, MSAU-3 (signalled in the text by *2D* and page number/s).

DM

PERSONAL RECOLLECTIONS

OF

MARY SOMERVILLE

ONE

Introduction – Parentage – Life in Scotland in the Last Century – Early Education – School

[1D, 1–2: this is how Mary Somerville begins her Recollections. In her daughter's editing it will be seen that much of this is taken into the initial explanatory text:

This memoir is dedicated to Martha and Mary Somerville by their affectionate mother

The Author

MY life has been domestic and quiet. I have no events to record that could interest the public. My only motive in writing it, is to show my country women that self education is possible under the most unfavourable and even discouraging circumstances. I avoid gossip, and think it dishonourable to publish letters written in confidence between friends; the only instance in which I have transgressed this law, is when they are intimately connected with the circumstances of my scientific life. In my youth the prejudice was strong against learned women, it was still more so in the preceding generation. My mother whose maiden name was Margaret Charters learnt to read she scarce knew how, and had only three months'

instruction in writing and accounts, yet she was the
daughter of Samuel Charters a gentlemanly fine-looking
man as I remember him, of good family and Solicitor
General of the Customs for Scotland. My grandfather
married Christian Murray of Kynynmont who died before
I was born. Her elder sister who was an heiress was
married to the great grandfather of the present Earl of
Minto° who took the name of Kynynmont in addition to
his own. My grandmother had a large family, four sons
and five daughters. All the sons had an excellent education
and went to India; the eldest Samuel Charters who died
chief judge of Patna was sent to travel after leaving college
while it was thought self sufficient for the daughters to be
able to read the Bible, write, and manage the house;
however, Martha Charters the eldest, who married the
Reverend Thomas Somerville° and was afterwards my
mother in law, had a little more instruction than the rest.
Besides she was clever, witty and fond of reading: she
knew Shakespeare almost by heart.]

[The life of a woman entirely devoted to her family
duties and to scientific pursuits affords little scope for a
biography. There are in it neither stirring events nor
brilliant deeds to record; and as my Mother was strongly
averse to gossip, and to revelations of private life or of
intimate correspondence, nothing of the kind will be
found in the following pages. It has been only after
very great hesitation, and on the recommendation of
valued friends, who think that some account of so
remarkable and beautiful a character cannot fail to
interest the public, that I have resolved to publish some
detached Recollections of past times, noted down by my
mother during the last years of her life, together with a
few letters from eminent men and women, referring
almost exclusively to her scientific works. A still smaller
number of her own letters have been added, either as

illustrating her opinions on events she witnessed, or else as affording some slight idea of her simple and loving disposition.

Few thoughtful minds will read without emotion my mother's own account of the wonderful energy and indomitable perseverance by which, in her ardent thirst for knowledge, she overcame obstacles apparently insurmountable, at a time when women were well-nigh totally debarred from education; and the almost intuitive way in which she entered upon studies of which she had scarcely heard the names, living, as she did, among persons to whom they were utterly unknown, and who disapproved of her devotion to pursuits so different from those of ordinary young girls at the end of the last century, especially in Scotland, which was far more old-fashioned and primitive than England.

Nor is her simple account of her early days without interest, when, as a lonely child, she wandered by the seashore, and on the links of Burntisland, collecting shells and flowers; or spent the clear, cold nights at her window, watching the starlit heavens, whose mysteries she was destined one day to penetrate in all their profound and sublime laws, making clear to others that knowledge which she herself had acquired, at the cost of so hard a struggle.

It was not only in her childhood and youth that my mother's studies encountered disapproval. Not till she became a widow, had she perfect freedom to pursue them. The first person – indeed the only one in her early days – who encouraged her passion for learning was her uncle by marriage, afterwards her father-in-law, the Rev. Dr Somerville, minister of Jedburgh, a man very much in advance of his century in liberality of thought on all subjects. He was one of the first to discern her rare qualities, and valued her as she deserved; while through life she retained the most grateful affection for him, and confided to him many doubts and difficulties on subjects of the highest importance. Nothing can be more erroneous than the statement, repeated in several obituary notices of my mother, that Mr Greig (her first husband) aided her in her mathematical and other pursuits. Nearly the contrary was the case. Mr Greig took no interest in science or literature, and possessed in full the prejudice against learned women which was common at that time. Only on her marriage with my father, my mother at last met with one who entirely sympathised with her, and warmly entered into all her ideas, encouraging her zeal for study to the utmost, and affording her every facility for it in his power. His love and admiration for her were unbounded; he frankly and willingly acknowledged her superiority to himself, and many of our friends can bear witness to the honest pride and gratification which he always testified in the fame and honours she attained.

No one can escape sorrow, and my mother, in the course of her long life, had her full share, but she bore it with that deep feeling of trust in the great goodness of God which formed so marked a feature in her character. She had a buoyant and hopeful spirit, and though her affections were very strong, and she felt keenly, it was ever her nature to turn from the shadows to all that is bright and beautiful in mortal life. She had much to make life pleasant in the great honours universally bestowed upon her; but she found far more in the devoted affection of friends, to say nothing of those whose happy lot it has been to live in close and loving intercourse with so noble and gentle a spirit.

She met with unbounded kindness from men of science of all countries, and most profound was her gratitude to them. Modest and unpretending to excess, nothing could be more generous than the unfeigned delight she shewed in recognising the genius and discoveries of others; ever jealous of their fame, and never of her own.

It is not uncommon to see persons who hold in youth opinions in advance of the age in which they live, but who at a certain period seem to crystallise, and lose the faculty of comprehending and accepting new ideas and theories; thus remaining at last as far behind, as they were once in advance of public opinion. Not so my mother, who was ever ready to hail joyfully any new idea or theory, and to give it honest attention, even if it were at variance with her former convictions. This quality she never lost, and it enabled her to sympathise with the younger generation of philosophers, as she had done with their predecessors, her own contemporaries.

Although her favourite pursuit, and the one for which she had decidedly most aptitude, was mathematics; yet there were few subjects in which she did not take interest, whether in science or literature, philosophy or politics. She was passionately fond of poetry, her especial favourites being Shakespeare and Dante, and also the great Greek dramatists, whose tragedies she read fluently in the original, being a good classical scholar. She was very fond of music, and devoted much time to it in her youth, and she painted from nature with considerable taste. The latter was, perhaps, the recreation in which she most delighted, from the opportunity it afforded her of contemplating the wonderful beauty of the world, which was a never-failing source of intense enjoyment to her, whether she watched the changing effects of light and shade on her favourite Roman Campagna, or gazed, enchanted, on the gorgeous sunsets on the bay of Naples, as she witnessed them from her much-loved Sorrento, where she passed the last summers of her life. All things fair were a joy to her – the flowers we brought her from our rambles, the seaweeds, the wild birds she saw, all interested and pleased her. Everything in nature spoke to her of that great God who created all things, the grand and sublimely beautiful as well as the exquisite loveliness of minute objects. Above all, in the laws which science unveils step by step, she found ever renewed motives for the love and adoration of their Author and Sustainer. This fervour of religious feeling accompanied her through life, and very early she shook off all that was dark and narrow in the creed of her first instructors for a purer and a happier faith.

It would be almost incredible were I to describe how much

my mother contrived to do in the course of the day. When my sister and I were small children, although busily engaged in writing for the press, she used to teach us for three hours every morning, besides managing her house carefully, reading the newspapers (for she always was a keen, and, I must add, a liberal politician), and the most important new books on all subjects, grave and gay. In addition to all this, she freely visited and received her friends. She was, indeed, very fond of society, and did not look for transcendent talent in those with whom she associated, although no one appreciated it more when she found it. Gay and cheerful company was a pleasant relaxation after a hard day's work. My mother never introduced scientific or learned subjects into general conversation. When they were brought forward by others, she talked simply and naturally about them, without the slightest pretension to superior knowledge. Finally, to complete the list of her accomplishments, I must add that she was a remarkably neat and skilful needlewoman. We still possess some elaborate specimens of her embroidery and lace-work.

Devoted and loving in all the relations of life, my mother was ever forgetful of self. Indulgent and sympathising, she never judged others with harshness or severity; yet she could be very angry when her indignation was aroused by hearing of injustice or oppression, of cruelty to man or beast, or of any attack on those she loved. Rather timid and retiring in general society, she was otherwise fearless in her quiet way. I well remember her cool composure on some occasions when we were in great danger. This she inherited from her father, Admiral Sir William Fairfax°, a gallant gentleman who distinguished himself greatly at the battle of Camperdown.

My mother speaks of him as follows among her 'Recollections,' of which I now proceed to place some portions before the reader.]

[*1D, 3:* My grandfather lived in Edinburgh but he had a house and gardens at Burntisland where the younger branches of the family resided. It was there that my mother met with my father William George Fairfax a lieutenant in the navy. The small vessel he commanded was disabled in a gale in the North Sea and he brought her to Burntisland for repair.]

My father was very good looking, of a brave and noble nature, and a perfect gentleman both in appearance and character. He was sent to sea as midshipman at ten years of age, so he had very little education; but he read a great deal, chiefly history and voyages. He was very cool, and of instant resource in moments of danger.

[*1D, 3–4:* While bottling spirits in his ship by some accident they were set on fire and the flaming liquid was running into the seams of the hold, when my father ordered the hammocks to be thrown over it, which immediately smothered the flames.]

One night, when his little vessel had taken refuge with many others from an intensely violent gale and drifting snow in Yarmouth Roads, they saw lights disappear, as vessel after vessel foundered. My father, after having done all that was possible for the safety of the ship, went to bed. His cabin door did not shut closely, from the rolling of the ship, and the man who was sentry that night told my mother years afterwards, that when he saw my father on his knees praying, he thought it would soon be all over with them; then seeing him go to bed and fall asleep, he felt no more fear. In the morning the coast was strewed with wrecks. There were no life-boats in those days; now the lives of hundreds are annually saved by the noble self-devotion of British sailors.

My mother was the daughter of Samuel Charters, Solicitor of the Customs for Scotland, and his wife Christian Murray, of Kynynmont, whose eldest sister married the great grandfather of the present Earl of Minto. [*1D, 4–5:* My grandfather was on very intimate terms with Mr Oswald of Dunnikier then holding some situation in the ministry, I forget whether Lord of the Treasury or Commissioner of the Navy, but Mrs Oswald invited his eldest daughter Martha to spend the winter with her in London where she was much in the best society. At that time sedan chairs were in fashion and one evening soon after their arrival in London on coming from the theatre Mrs Oswald's chair had gone on before, and my aunt, being a young girl, on finding herself for a moment alone, became bewildered and could not tell the chairmen where to take her. They were from Edinburgh and as soon as she told her name they declared that they would carry her all over London till they saw her in safety; being no longer afraid, she remembered her address. It was during this visit that she met with her future husband Dr Thomas Somerville, minister at Jedburgh, who was in London about the repeal of the Test and Corporation Act.[1]] My grandmother was exceedingly proud and stately. She made her children stand in her presence. My mother, on the contrary, was indulgent and kind, so that her children were perfectly at ease with her. She seldom read anything but the Bible, sermons, and the newspaper. She was very sincere and devout in her religion, and was remarkable for good sense and great strength of expression in writing and conversation. Though by no means pretty, she was exceedingly distinguished and ladylike both in appearance and manners.

My father was constantly employed, and twice distinguished himself by attacking vessels of superior force. He captured the first, but was overpowered by the second, and being taken to France, remained two years a prisoner on parole, when he met with much kindness from the Choiseul° family. At last he was exchanged, and afterwards was

appointed lieutenant on board a frigate destined for foreign
service. I think it was the North American station, for the
war of Independence was not over till the beginning of
1783. As my mother knew that my father would be absent
for some years, she accompanied him to London, though
so near her confinement that in returning home she had
just time to arrive at the manse of Jedburgh, her sister
Martha Somerville's house, when I was born, on the 26th
December, 1780. My mother was dangerously ill, and my
aunt, who was about to wean her second daughter Janet,
who married General Henry Elliot, nursed me till a wet-
nurse could be found. So I was born in the house of my
future husband, and nursed by his mother – a rather
singular coincidence.

During my father's absence, my mother lived with great
economy in a house not far from Burntisland which belonged to my grandfather, solely occupied with the care of
her family, which consisted of her eldest son Samuel, four
or five years old, and myself. One evening while my brother
was lying at play on the floor, he called out, 'O, mamma,
there's the moon rinnin' awa.' It was the celebrated meteor
of 1783.

Some time afterwards, for what reason I do not know, my
father and mother went to live for a short time at Inveresk.
[*1D, 7:* my only recollection of that period is being caught in
the act of plucking a guinea fowl for its spotted feathers.
About this time I was with my mother on a visit to her father
in Edinburgh when my uncle Thomas Charters an officer
in the Indian army then on leave, amused himself by
teaching me to swear. One day walking with my maid in
the High Street a lady asked my name and I answered,
'What's your business you damned B—.' The lady said,
'You're a bonny bairn but weel awat ye hae an ill tongue.'
My maid was so much ashamed that she caught me up in
her arms and ran home.

As all my mother's sisters were now married except the

youngest who lived in Edinburgh with my grandfather, the house at Burntisland became our permanent home.]

[This place, in which my mother's early life was spent, exercised so much influence on her life and pursuits, that I am happy to be able to give the description of it in her own words.]

———————

Burntisland was then a small quiet seaport town with little or no commerce, situated on the coast of Fife, immediately opposite to Edinburgh. It is sheltered at some distance on the north by a high and steep hill called the Bin. The harbour lies on the west, and the town ended on the east in a plain of short grass called the Links, on which the townspeople had the right of pasturing their cows and geese. The Links were bounded on each side by low hills covered with gorse and heather, and on the east by a beautiful bay with a sandy beach, which, beginning at a low rocky point, formed a bow and then stretched for several miles to the town of Kinghorn, the distant part skirting a range of high precipitous crags.

Our house, which lay to the south of the town, was very long, with a southern exposure, and its length was increased by a wall covered with fruit-trees, which concealed a courtyard, cow-house, and other offices. From this the garden extended southwards, and ended in a plot of short grass covering a ledge of low black rocks washed by the sea. It was divided into three parts by narrow, almost unfrequented, lanes. These gardens yielded abundance of common fruit and vegetables, but the warmest and best exposures were always devoted to flowers. The garden next to the house was bounded on the south by an ivy-covered wall hid by a row of old elm trees, from whence a steep mossy bank descended to a flat plot of grass with a gravel walk and flower borders on each side, and a broad gravel walk ran along the front of the house. My mother was fond of flowers, and prided herself on her moss-roses, which flourished luxuriantly on the front of the house; but my father, though a sailor, was an excellent florist. He procured the finest bulbs and flower seeds from Holland, and kept each kind in a separate bed.

The manners and customs of the people who inhabited this pretty spot at that time were exceedingly primitive.

Upon the death of any of the townspeople, a man went about ringing a bell at the doors of the friends and acquaintances of the person just dead, and, after calling out 'Oyez!' three times, he announced the death which had occurred. This was still called by the name of the Passing-bell, which in Catholic times invited the prayers of the living for the spirit just passed away.

There was much sympathy and kindness shown on these occasions; friends always paid a visit of condolence to the afflicted, dressed in black. The gude wives in Burntisland thought it respectable to provide dead-clothes for themselves and the 'gude man', that they might have a decent funeral. I once saw a set of grave-clothes nicely folded up, which consisted of a long shirt and cap of white flannel, and a shroud of fine linen made of yarn, spun by the gude wife herself. I did not like that gude wife; she was purse-proud, and took every opportunity of treating with scorn a poor neighbour who had had a *misfortune*, that is, a child by her husband before marriage, but who made a very good wife. Her husband worked in our garden, and took our cow to the Links to graze. The wife kept a little shop, where we bought things, and she told us her neighbour had given her 'mony a sair greet' – that is, a bitter fit of weeping.

The howdie, or midwife, was a person of much consequence. She had often to go far into the country, by day and by night, riding a cart-horse. The neighbours used to go and congratulate the mother, and, of course, to admire the baby. Cake and caudle were handed round, caudle being oatmeal gruel, with sugar, nutmeg, and white wine. In the poorest class, hot ale and 'scons'[2] were offered.

Penny-weddings were by no means uncommon in my young days. When a very poor couple were going to be married, the best man, and even the bridegroom himself, went from house to house, asking for small sums to enable them to have a wedding supper, and pay the town fiddler for a dance; any one was admitted who paid a penny.[3] I recollect the prisoners in the Tolbooth letting down bags from the prison windows, begging for charity.[4] I do not remember any execution taking place.

Men and old women of the lower classes smoked tobacco in short pipes, and many took snuff – even young ladies must have done so; for I have a very pretty and quaint gold snuff-box which was given to my grandmother as a marriage present. Licensed beggars, called 'gaberlunzie men', were still common. They wore a blue coat, with a tin badge, and wandered about the country, knew all that was going on, and were always welcome at the farm-houses, where the gude wife liked to have a crack (gossip) with the blue coat, and, in return for his news, gave him dinner or supper, as might be. Edie Ochiltree is a perfect specimen of this extinct race.[5] There was another species of beggar, of yet higher antiquity. If a man were a cripple, and poor, his relations put him in a hand-barrow, and wheeled him to their next neighbour's door, and left him there. Some one came out, gave him oat-cake or peasemeal bannock, and then wheeled him to the next door; and in this way, going from house to house, he obtained a fair livelihood.

My brother Sam lived with our grandfather in Edinburgh, and attended the High School, which was in the old town, and, like other boys, he was given pennies to buy bread; but the boys preferred oysters, which they bought from the fishwives, the bargain being, a dozen oysters for a halfpenny, and a kiss for the thirteenth.

These fishwives and their husbands were industrious, hard-working people, forming a community of their own in the village of Newhaven, close to the sea, and about two miles from Edinburgh. The men were exposed to cold, and often to danger, in their small boats, not always well-built nor fitted for our stormy Firth. The women helped to land and prepare the fish when the boats came in, carried it to town for sale in the early morning, kept the purse, managed the house, brought up the children, and provided food and clothing for all. Many were rich, lived well, and sometimes had dances. Many of the young women were pretty, and all wore – and, I am told, still wear – a bright-coloured, picturesque costume. Some young men, amongst others a cousin of my own, who attempted to intrude into one of these balls, got pelted with fish offal by the women. The village smelt strongly[6] of fish, certainly; yet the people were very clean personally. I recollect their keeping tame gulls, which they fed with fish offal.

Although there was no individual enmity between the boys of the old and of the new or aristocratic part of Edinburgh, there were frequent battles, called 'bickers', between them, in which they pelted each other with stones. Sometimes they were joined by bigger lads, and then the fight became so serious that the magistrates sent the city guard – a set of old men with halberds and a quaint uniform – to separate them; but no sooner did the guard appear, than both parties joined against them.

Strings of wild geese were common in autumn, and I was amused on one occasion to see the clumsy tame fat geese which were feeding on the Links rise in a body and try to follow the wild ones.

As the grass on the plot before our house did not form a fine even turf, the ground was trenched and sown with good seed, but along with the grass a vast crop of thistles and groundsel appeared, which attracted quantities of goldfinches, and in the early mornings I have seen as many as sixty to eighty of these beautiful birds feeding on it.

My love of birds has continued through life, for only two years ago, in my extreme old age, I lost a pet mountain sparrow, which for eight years was my constant companion: sitting on my shoulder, pecking at my papers, and eating out of my mouth; and I am not ashamed to say I felt its accidental death very much.

Before the grass came up on this plot of ground, its surface in the evening swarmed with earthworms, which instantly shrank into their holes on the approach of a foot. My aunt Janet, who was then with us, and afraid even to speak of death, was horrified on seeing them, firmly believing that she would one day be eaten by them – a very general opinion at that time; few people being then aware that the finest mould in our gardens and fields has passed through the entrails of the earthworm, the vegetable juices it contains being sufficient to maintain these harmless creatures. [*1D, 13:* They are admirably constructed for their manner of life; for as the underside of each ring the worm has four pairs of glassy crooked rods or feet on which it can crawl rapidly by pushing them out and in; and when it makes its burrow it forces its snout and adjacent rings into the ground and having fixed them with its hooked feet, it draws up the rest of its body and having secured it to the mouth of its hole it pushes its snout further into the earth and continues the process till the burrow is deep enough. Its walls are lubricated with mucus from the skin of the worm to prevent the earth from falling in.]

My mother was very much afraid of thunder and lightning. She knew when a storm was near from the appearance of the clouds, and prepared for it by taking out the steel pins which fastened her cap on. She then sat on a sofa at a distance from the fireplace, which had a very high chimney, and read different parts of the Bible, especially the sublime descriptions of storms in the Psalms, which made me, who sat close by her, still more afraid. We had an excellent and beautiful pointer, called Hero, a great favourite, who generally lived in the garden, but at the first clap of thunder he used to rush howling in-doors, and place his face on my knee. Then my father, who laughed not a little at our fear, would bring a glass of wine to my mother, and say, 'Drink that, Peg; it will give you courage, for we are going to have a rat-tat-too.' My mother would beg him to shut the window-shutters, and though she could no longer see to read, she kept the Bible on her knee for protection.

My mother taught me to read the Bible, and to say my prayers morning and evening; otherwise she allowed me to grow up a wild creature. When I was seven or eight years old I began to be useful, for I pulled the fruit for preserving; shelled the peas and beans, fed the poultry, and looked after the dairy, for we kept a cow.

On one occasion I had put green gooseberries into bottles and sent them to the kitchen with orders to the cook to boil the bottles uncorked, and, when the fruit was sufficiently cooked, to cork and tie up the bottles. After a time all the house was alarmed by loud explosions and violent screaming in the kitchen; the cook had corked the bottles before she boiled them, and of course they exploded. For greater preservation, the bottles were always buried in the ground; a number were once found in our garden with the fruit in high preservation which had been buried no one knew when. Thus experience is sometimes the antecedent of science, for it was little suspected at that time that by shutting out the air the invisible organic world was excluded – the cause of all fermentation and decay.

I never cared for dolls, and had no one to play with me. I amused myself in the garden, which was much frequented by birds. I knew most of them, their flight and their habits. The swallows were never prevented from building above our windows, and, when about to migrate, they used to assemble in hundreds on the roof of our house, and prepared for their journey by short flights. We fed the birds when the ground was covered with snow, and opened our windows at breakfast-time to let in the robins, who would hop on the table to pick up crumbs. The quantity of singing birds was very great, for the farmers and gardeners were less cruel and avaricious than they are now – though poorer. They allowed our pretty songsters to share in the bounties of providence. The shortsighted cruelty, which is too pre-valent now, brings its own punishment, for, owing to the reckless destruction of birds, the equilibrium of nature is disturbed, insects increase to such an extent as materially to affect every description of crop. This summer (1872), when I was at Sorrento, even the olives, grapes, and oranges were seriously injured by the caterpillars – a disaster which I entirely attribute to the ruthless havoc made among every kind of bird.

My mother set me in due time to learn the catechism of the Kirk of Scotland, and to attend the public examinations in the kirk. This was a severe trial for me; for, besides being timid and shy, I had a bad memory, and did not understand one word of the catechism. These meetings, which began with prayer, were attended by all the children of the town and neighbourhood, with their mothers, and a great many old women, who came to be edified. They were an acute race, and could quote chapter and verse of Scripture as accurately as the minister himself. I remember he said to one of them – 'Peggie, what lightened the world before the sun was made?' After thinking for a minute, she said – ' 'Deed, sir, the question is mair curious than edifying.'

Besides these public examinations, the minister made an annual visit to each household in his parish. When he came to us, the servants were called in, and we all knelt while he said a prayer; and then he examined each individual as to the state of his soul and conduct. He asked me if I could say my 'Questions' – that is, the catechism of the Kirk of

Scotland – and asked a question at random to ascertain the fact. He did the same to the servants.

[*1D, 11:* One Sunday I was surprised to see the Sexton bring a low stool and place it before the pulpit after the sermon. There was a great stir and excitement in the church, everyone rising from curiosity when a man stood upon it, and after being severely reprimanded was restored again to the privileges of the Kirk. This was probably the last instance of the cutty stool.[7] My mother had no small difficulty in evading my questions.]

When I was between eight and nine years old, my father came home from sea, and was shocked to find me such a savage. I had not yet been taught to write, and although I amused myself reading the *Arabian Nights*, *Robinson Crusoe*, and *The Pilgrim's Progress*, I read very badly, and with a strong Scotch accent; so, besides a chapter of the Bible, he made me read a paper of the *Spectator* aloud every morning, after breakfast; the consequence of which discipline is that I have never since opened that book. Hume's° *History of England* was also a real penance to me. I gladly accompanied my father when he cultivated his flowers, which even now I can say were of the best quality. The tulips and other bulbous plants, ranunculi, anemones, carnations, as well as the annuals then known, were all beautiful. He used to root up and throw away many plants I thought very beautiful; he said he did so because the colours of their petals were not sharply defined, and that they would spoil the seed of the others. Thus I learnt to know the good and the bad – how to lay carnations, and how to distinguish between the leaf and fruit buds in pruning fruit trees; this kind of knowledge was of no practical use, for, as my after-life was spent in towns, I never had a garden, to my great regret.

George the Third° was so popular, that even in Burntisland nosegays were placed in every window on the 4th of June, his birthday; and it occasionally happened that our garden was robbed the preceding night of its gayest flowers.

My father at last said to my mother, – 'This kind of life will never do, Mary must at least know how to write and keep accounts.' So at ten years old I was sent to a boarding-school, kept by a Miss Primrose, at Musselburgh, where I was utterly wretched. The change from perfect liberty to perpetual restraint was in itself a great trial; besides, being naturally shy and timid, I was afraid of strangers, and although Miss Primrose was not unkind she had an habitual frown, which even the elder girls dreaded. My future companions, who were all older than I, came round me like a swarm of bees, and asked if my father had a title, what was the name of our estate, if we kept a carriage, and other such questions, which made me first feel the difference of station. However, the girls were very kind, and often bathed my eyes to prevent our stern mistress from seeing that I was perpetually in tears. A few days after my arrival, although perfectly straight and well-made, I was enclosed in stiff stays with a steel busk in front, while, above my frock, bands drew my shoulders back till the shoulder-blades met. Then a steel rod, with a semi-circle which went under the chin, was clasped to the steel busk in my stays. In this constrained state I, and most of the younger girls, had to prepare our lessons. The chief thing I had to do was to learn by heart a page of Johnson's dictionary, not only to spell the words, give their parts of speech and meaning, but as an exercise of memory to remember their order of succession. Besides I had to learn the first principles of writing, and the rudiments of French and English grammar. The method of teaching was extremely tedious and inefficient. Our religious duties were attended to in a remarkable way. Some of the girls were Presbyterians, others belonged to the Church of England, so Miss Primrose cut the matter short by taking us all to the kirk in the morning and to church in the afternoon.

In our play-hours we amused ourselves with playing at ball, marbles, and especially at 'Scotch and English,'[8] a game which represented a raid on the debatable land, or Border between Scotland and England, in which each party tried to rob the other of their playthings. The little ones were always compelled to be English, for the bigger girls thought it too degrading.

Lady Hope, a relative of my mother, frequently invited me to spend Saturday at Pinkie. She was a very ladylike person, in delicate health, and with cold manners. Sir Archibald was stout, loud, passionate, and devoted to hunting. I amused myself in the grounds, a good deal afraid of a turkeycock, who was pugnacious and defiant.

TWO

Freedom – Religious Education – Jedburgh

[My mother remained at school at Musselburgh for a twelve-month, till she was eleven years old. After this prolonged and elaborate education, she was recalled to Burntisland, and the results of the process she had undergone are detailed in her *Recollections* with much drollery.]

SOON after my return home I received a note from a lady in the neighbourhood, inquiring for my mother, who had been ill. This note greatly distressed me, for my half-text writing was as bad as possible, and I could neither compose an answer nor spell the words. My eldest cousin, Miss Somerville, a grown-up young lady, then with us, got me out of this scrape, but I soon got myself into another, by writing to my brother in Edinburgh that I had sent him a bank-*knot* (note) to buy something for me. The school at Musselburgh was expensive, and I was reproached with having cost so much money in vain. My mother said she would have been contented if I had only learnt to write well and keep accounts, which was all that a woman was expected to know.

This passed over, and I was like a wild animal escaped out of a cage. I was no longer amused in the gardens, but wandered about the country. When the tide was out I spent hours on the sands, looking at the star-fish and sea-urchins, or watching the children digging for sand-eels, cockles, and the spouting razor-fish. I made a collection of shells, such as were cast ashore, some so small that they appeared like white specks in patches of black sand. There was a small pier on the sands for shipping limestone brought from the coal mines inland. I was astonished to see the surface of these blocks of stone covered with beautiful impressions of what seemed to be leaves; how they got there I could not imagine, but I picked up the broken bits, and even large pieces, and brought them to my repository. I knew the eggs of many birds, and made a collection of them. I never robbed a nest, but bought strings of eggs, which were sold by boys, besides getting sea-fowl eggs from sailors who had been in whalers or on other northern voyages. It was believed by these sailors that there was a gigantic flat fish in the North Sea, called a kraken.[9] It was so enormous that when it came to the surface, covered with tangles and sand, it was supposed to be an island, till, on one occasion, part of a ship's crew landed on it and found out their mistake. However, much as they believed in it, none of the sailors at Burntisland had ever seen it. The sea serpent was also an article of our faith.

In the rocks at the end of our garden there was a shingly opening, in which we used to bathe, and where at low tide I frequently waded among masses of rock covered with sea-weeds. With the exception of dulse and tangle I knew the names of none, though I was well acquainted with and admired many of these beautiful plants. I also watched the crabs, live shells, jelly-fish, and various marine animals, all of which were objects of curiosity and amusement to me in my lonely life.

The flora on the links and hills around was very beautiful, and I soon learnt the trivial names of all the plants. There was not a tree nor bush higher than furze in this part of the country, but the coast to the north-west of Burntisland was bordered by a tree- and brushwood-covered bank belonging to the Earl of Morton, which extended to Aberdour. I could not go so far alone, but had frequent opportunities of walking there and gathering ferns, foxgloves, and primroses, which grew on the mossy banks of a little stream that ran into the sea. The bed of this stream or burn was thickly covered with the freshwater mussel, which I knew often contained pearls, but I did not like to kill the creatures to get the pearls.

One day my father, who was a keen sportsman, having gone to fish for red trout at the mouth of this stream, found a young whale, or grampus, stranded in the shallow water. He immediately ran back to the town, got boats, captured the whale, and landed it in the harbour, where I went with the rest of the crowd to see the *muckle* fish.[10]

There was always a good deal of shipbuilding carried on in the harbour, generally coasting vessels or colliers. We, of course, went to see them launched, which was a pretty sight. [*2D, 15:* The name was always given by a woman standing on a platform at the stern. When the last shores were knocked away and the vessel began to move, she dashed a bottle of wine against her and gave the name which was generally that of the wife or daughter of the shipbuilder but sometimes it was fanciful as the *Morning Star*, the *Happy-Go-Lucky,* etc. As soon as the ship slipped into the water a number of the carpenters and boys who were on board rushing backwards and forwards made her roll and pitch till she was towed to a part of the pier where she lay till she was fitted with her mast and rigging.]

When the bad weather began I did not know what to do with myself. Fortunately we had a small collection of books, among which I found Shakespeare, and read it at every moment I could spare from my domestic duties. These occupied a great part of my time; besides, I had to *shew* (sew) my sampler, working the alphabet from A to Z, as well as the ten numbers, on canvas.

My mother did not prevent me from reading, but my

aunt Janet, who came to live in Burntisland after her father's death, greatly disapproved of my conduct. She was an old maid who could be very agreeable and witty, but she had all the prejudices of the time with regard to women's duties, and said to my mother, 'I wonder you let Mary waste her time in reading, she never *shews* (sews) more than if she were a man.' Whereupon I was sent to the village school to learn plain needlework. I do not remember how long it was after this that an old lady sent some very fine linen to be made into shirts for her brother, and desired that one should be made entirely by me. This shirt was so well worked that I was relieved from attending the school, but the house linen was given into my charge to make and to mend. We had a large stock, much of it very beautiful, for the Scotch ladies at that time were very proud of their napery, but they no longer sent it to Holland to be bleached, as had once been the custom. We grew flax, and our maids spun it. The coarser yarn was woven in Burntisland, and bleached upon the links; the finer was sent to Dunfermline, where there was a manufactory of table-linen.

I was annoyed that my turn for reading was so much disapproved of, and thought it unjust that women should have been given a desire for knowledge if it were wrong to acquire it. Among our books I found Chapone's° *Letters to Young Women*, and resolved to follow the course of history there recommended, the more so as we had most of the works she mentions. One, however, which my cousin lent me was in French, and here the little I had learnt at school was useful, for with the help of a dictionary I made out the sense. What annoyed me was my memory not being good – I could remember neither names nor dates. Years afterwards I studied a 'Memoria Technica,'[11] then in fashion, without success; yet in my youth I could play long pieces of music on the piano without the book, and I never forget mathematical formulæ. In looking over one of my MSS, which I had not seen for forty years, I at once recognised the formulæ for computing the secular inequalities of the moon.

We had two small globes, and my mother allowed me to learn the use of them from Mr Reed, the village schoolmaster, who came to teach me for a few weeks in the winter evenings. Besides the ordinary branches, Mr Reed taught Latin and navigation, but these were out of the question for me. At the village school the boys often learnt Latin, but it was thought sufficient for the girls to be able to read the Bible; very few even learnt writing. I recollect, however, that some men were ignorant of book-keeping; our baker, for instance, had a wooden tally, in which he made a notch for every loaf of bread, and of course we had the corresponding tally. They were called nick-sticks.

My bedroom had a window to the south, and a small closet near had one to the north. At these I spent many hours, studying the stars by the aid of the celestial globe. Although I watched and admired the magnificent displays of the Aurora,[12] which frequently occurred, they seemed to be so nearly allied to lightning that I was somewhat afraid of them. At an earlier period of my life there was a comet, which I dreaded exceedingly.

My father was Captain of the _Repulse_,[13] a fifty-gun ship, attached to the Northern fleet commanded by the Earl of Northesk°. The winter was extremely stormy, the fleet was driven far north, and kept there by adverse gales, till both officers and crew were on short rations. They ran out of candles, and had to tear up their stockings for wicks, and dip them into the fat of the salt meat which was left. We were in great anxiety, for it was reported that some of the ships had foundered; we were, however, relieved by the arrival of the _Repulse_ in Leith roads for repair.

[1D, 23: We were very gay for our house at Burntisland

was always full of the officers, and then for the first time I was on board a man-of-war.]

Our house on one occasion being full, I was sent to sleep in a room quite detached from the rest and with a different staircase. There was a closet in this room in which my father kept his fowling pieces, fishing tackle, and golf clubs, and a long garret overhead was filled with presses and stores of all kinds, among other things a number of large cheeses were on a board slung by ropes to the rafters. One night I had put out my candle and was fast asleep, when I was awakened by a violent crash, and then a rolling noise over my head. Now the room was said to be haunted, so that the servants would not sleep in it. I was desperate, for there was no bell. I groped my way to the closet – lucifer matches were unknown in those days – I seized one of the golf clubs, which are shod with iron, and thundered on the bedroom door till I brought my father, followed by the whole household, to my aid. It was found that the rats had gnawed through the ropes by which the cheeses were suspended, so that the crash and rolling were accounted for, and I was scolded for making such an uproar.

Children suffer much misery by being left alone in the dark. When I was very young I was sent to bed at eight or nine o'clock, and the maid who slept in the room went away as soon as I was in bed, leaving me alone in the dark till she came to bed herself. All that time I was in an agony of fear of something indefinite, I could not tell what. The joy, the relief, when the maid came back, were such that I instantly fell asleep. Now that I am a widow and old, although I always have a night-lamp, such is the power of early impressions that I rejoice when daylight comes.

At Burntisland the sacrament was administered in summer because people came in crowds from the neighbouring parishes to attend the preachings. The service was long and fatiguing. A number of clergymen came to assist, and as the minister's manse could not accommodate them all, we entertained three of them, one of whom was always the Rev. Dr Campbell, father of Lord Campbell.

Thursday was a day of preparation. The morning service began by a psalm sung by the congregation, then a prayer was said by the minister, followed by a lecture on some chapter of the Bible, generally lasting an hour, after that another psalm was sung, followed by a prayer, a sermon which lasted seldom less than an hour, and the whole ended with a psalm, a short prayer and a benediction. Every one then went home to dinner and returned afterwards for afternoon service, which lasted more than an hour and a half. Friday was a day of rest, but I together with many young people went at this time to the minister to receive a stamped piece of lead as a token that we were sufficiently instructed to be admitted to Christ's table. This ticket was given to the Elder on the following Sunday. On Saturday there was a morning service, and on Sunday such multitudes came to receive the sacrament that the devotions continued till late in the evening. The ceremony was very strikingly and solemnly conducted. The communicants sat on each side of long narrow tables covered with white linen, in imitation of the last supper of Christ, and the Elders handed the bread and wine. After a short exhortation from one of the ministers the first set retired, and were succeeded by others. When the weather was fine a sermon, prayers, and psalm-singing took place either in the churchyard or on a grassy bank at the Links for such as were waiting to communicate. On the Monday morning there was the same long service as on the Thursday. It was too much for me; I always came home with a headache, and took a dislike to sermons [*1D, 25:* which continues to this day and in after life I could no longer believe in the gloomy doctrines of Calvinism, but I have always kept up my early habit of reading the Bible. In youth I liked it for its sublime poetry, later in life it has been my only consolation in severe affliction.]

Our minister was a rigid Calvinist. His sermons were gloomy, and so long that he occasionally would startle the congregation by calling out to some culprit, 'Sit up there, how daur ye sleep i' the kirk.' Some saw-mills in the neighbourhood were burnt down, so the following Sunday we had a sermon on hell-fire. The kirk was very large and quaint; a stair led to a gallery on each side of the pulpit, which was intended for the tradespeople, and each division was marked with a suitable device, and text from Scripture. On the bakers' portion a sheaf of wheat was painted; a balance and weights on the grocers', and on the weavers', which was opposite to our pew, there was a shuttle, and below it the motto, 'My days are swifter than a weaver's shuttle, and are spent without *hop job*.'[14] The artist was evidently no clerk.

My brother Sam, while attending the university in Edinburgh, came to us on the Saturdays and returned to town on Monday. He of course went with us to the kirk on Sunday morning, but we let our mother attend afternoon service alone, as he and I were happy to be together, and we spent the time sitting on the grassy rocks at the foot of our garden, from whence we could see a vast extent of the Firth of Forth with Edinburgh and its picturesque hills. It was very amusing, for we occasionally saw three or four whales spouting, and shoals of porpoises at play. However, we did not escape reproof, for I recollect the servant coming to tell us that the minister had sent to inquire whether Mr and Miss Fairfax had been taken ill, as he had not seen them at the kirk in the afternoon. The minister in question was Mr Wemyss, who had married a younger sister of my mother's. [*1D, 25 verso:* He was a rigid Calvinist and by no means refined yet he was heir to a very ancient baronetcy though he never assumed the title; his son, my cousin, did but as he died unmarried the title is extinct. The Scotch clergy were of higher descent at that time than they are now.]

[*1D, 26: verso*: My uncle William had given my brother Sam a gold watch and chain of which he was very proud and used to beat his watch against my piano, but the watch was often in the hands of the watchmaker: now he broke the minute hand; then he let it fall – the string snapped and uncoiled with a whirr; at last he let it fall into the sea while catching small fish called bodles [?]¹⁵ in the harbour at Burntisland. I laughed at him and when he got it back again my mother said she hoped he would get no more presents for she had paid nearly as much as it was worth to the watchmaker.]

When I was about thirteen my mother took a small apartment in Edinburgh for the winter, and I was sent to a writing school, where I soon learnt to write a good hand, and studied the common rules of arithmetic. My uncle William Henry Charters, lately returned from India, gave me a pianoforte, and I had music lessons from an old lady who lived in the top storey of one of the highest houses in the old town. I slept in the same room with my mother. One morning I called out, much alarmed, 'There is lightning!' but my mother said, after a moment, 'No; it is fire!' and on opening the window shutters I found that the flakes of fire flying past had made the glass quite hot. The next house but one was on fire and burning fiercely, and the people next door were throwing everything they possessed, even china and glass, out of the windows into the street. We dressed quickly, and my mother sent immediately to Trotter the upholsterer for four men. We then put our family papers, our silver, &c., &c., into trunks; then my mother said, 'Now let us breakfast, it is time enough for us to move our things when the next house takes fire.' Of its doing so there was every probability because casks of turpentine and oil were exploding from time to time in a carriage manufactory at the back of it. Several gentlemen of our acquaintance who came to assist us were surprised to find us breakfasting quietly as if there were nothing unusual going on. In fact my mother, though a coward in many things, had, like most women, the presence of mind and the courage of necessity. The fire was extinguished, and we had only the four men to pay for doing nothing, nor did we sacrifice any of our property like our neighbours who had completely lost their heads from terror. I may mention here that on one occasion when my father was at home he had been ill with a severe cold, and wore his nightcap. While reading in the draw-ing-room one evening he called out, 'I smell fire, there is no time to be lost,' so, snatching up a candle, he wandered from room to room followed by us all still smelling fire, when one of the servants said, 'O, sir, it is the tassel of your nightcap that is on fire.'

On returning to Burntisland, I spent four or five hours daily at the piano; and for the sake of having something to do, I taught myself Latin enough, from such books as we had, to read Cæsar's *Commentaries*. I went that summer on a visit to my aunt at Jedburgh, and, for the first time in my life, I met in my uncle, Dr Somerville, with a friend who approved of my thirst for knowledge. During long walks with him in the early mornings, he was so kind, that I had the courage to tell him that I had been trying to learn Latin, but I feared it was in vain; for my brother and other boys, superior to me in talent, and with every assistance, spent years in learning it. He assured me, on the contrary, that in ancient times many women – some of them of the highest rank in England – had been very elegant scholars, and that he would read Virgil with me if I would come to his study for an hour or two every morning before breakfast, which I gladly did.

I never was happier in my life than during the months I

spent at Jedburgh. My aunt was a charming companion – witty, full of anecdote, and had read more than most women of her day, especially Shakespeare, who was her favourite author. My cousins had little turn for reading, but they were better educated than most girls. They were taught to write by David Brewster°, son of the village schoolmaster, afterwards Sir David, who became one of the most distinguished philosophers and discoverers of the age, member of all the scientific societies at home and abroad, and at last President of the University of Edinburgh. He was studying in Edinburgh when I was at Jedburgh; so I did not make his acquaintance then; but later in life he became my valued friend. I did not know till after his death, that, while teaching my cousins, he fell in love with my cousin Margaret. I do not believe she was aware of it. She was afterwards attached to an officer in the army; but my aunt would not allow her to go to that *outlandish* place, Malta, where he was quartered; so she lived and died unmarried. Steam has changed our ideas of distance since that time.

My uncle's house – the manse – in which I was born, stands in a pretty garden, bounded by the fine ancient abbey, which, though partially ruined, still serves as the parish kirk. The garden produced abundance of common flowers, vegetables, and fruit. Some of the plum and pear trees were very old, and were said to have been planted by the monks. Both were excellent in quality, and very productive. The view from both garden and manse was over the beautiful narrow valley through which the Jed flows. The precipitous banks of red sandstone are richly clothed with vegetation, some of the trees ancient and very fine, especially the magnificent one called the capon tree, and the lofty king of the wood, remnants of the fine forests which at one time had covered the country. An inland scene was new to me, and I was never tired of admiring the tree-crowned scaurs or precipices, where the rich glow of the red sandstone harmonised so well with the autumnal tints of the foliage.

We often bathed in the pure stream of the Jed. My aunt always went with us, and was the merriest of the party; we bathed in a pool which was deep under the high scaur, but sloped gradually from the grassy bank on the other side. Quiet and transparent as the Jed was, it one day came down with irresistible fury, red with the débris of the sandstone scaurs. There had been a thunderstorm in the hills up-stream, and as soon as the river began to rise, the people came out with pitchforks and hooks to catch the hayricks, sheaves of corn, drowned pigs, and other animals that came sweeping past. My cousins and I were standing on the bridge, but my aunt called us off when the water rose above the arches, for fear of the bridge giving way. We made expeditions every day; sometimes we went nutting in the forest; at other times we gathered mushrooms on the grass parks of Stewartfield, where there was a wood of pictur-esque old Scotch firs, inhabited by a colony of rooks. I still kept the habit of looking out for birds, and had the good fortune to see a heron, now a rare bird in the valley of the Jed. Some of us went every day to a spring called the Allerly well,[16] about a quarter of a mile from the manse, and brought a large jug of its sparkling water for dinner. The evenings were cheerful; my aunt sang Scotch songs prettily, and told us stories and legends about Jedburgh, which had been a royal residence in the olden time. She had a tame white and tawny-coloured owl, which we fed every night, and sometimes brought into the drawing-room. The Sun-day evening never was gloomy, though properly observed. We occasionally drank tea with acquaintances, and made visits of a few days to the Rutherfurds° of Edgerton and others; but I was always glad to return to the manse.

My uncle, like other ministers of the Scottish Kirk, was allowed a glebe, which he farmed himself. Besides horses, a cow was kept, which supplied the family with cream and butter, and the skimmed milk was given to the poor; but as the milk became scarce, one woman was deprived, for the time, of her share. Soon after, the cow was taken ill, and my uncle's ploughman, Will, came to him and said, 'Sir, gin you would give that carline Tibby Jones her soup o' milk again, the coo would soon be weel eneugh.' Will was by no means the only believer in witchcraft at that time.

[*2D, 23 bis:* Dr Charters, minister of Wilton near Hawick, was a cousin of my mother's and had been an admirer of her, but as she did not fancy him he remained a bachelor till very late in life when he married a ladylike amiable person of good family nearly of his own age. They had property of their own in the neighbourhood, but they lived in the manse prettily situated on the banks of the Slitterik.[17] I was a particular favourite of both; they invited me to pay them a visit and sent the carriage to Jedburgh for my cousin Janet and me. It was an antiquated affair with a pair of fat, sleek, black horses with long tails, and a coachman who had been in the family time out of mind, yet he was a strict dissenter and would on no account hear his master preach. Dr Charters was a man of high cultivation and taste, he had travelled much in his youth, was a charming companion, grave in his demeanour yet cheerful, and perfectly liberal in his opinions. He took great interest in the education of his parishioners and had a library for the express purpose of lending them books not only on religion, but history, travels and voyages, also Shakespeare, Milton and other poets and was always ready to explain what they did not understand. Mrs Charters had five or six beautiful tortoise-shell coloured cats. One or two were always on her knee and they were very fierce and would not let me touch them, and above all they hated music, for one day when my cousin was singing with rather a loud screamy voice, one of the cats flew at her throat and bit her.]

THREE

Edinburgh – Youthful Studies and Amusements – Politics –
The Theatres of the Time

[My mother's next visit was to the house of her uncle, William
Charters, in Edinburgh. From thence she was enabled to
partake of the advantages of a dancing-school of the period.]

———————————

THEY sent me to Strange's dancing school. Strange himself
was exactly like a figure on the stage; tall and thin, he wore a
powdered wig, with cannons at the ears, and a pigtail.
Ruffles at the breast and wrists, white waistcoat, black silk
or velvet shorts, white silk stockings, large silver buckles,
and a pale blue coat completed his costume. He had a little
fiddle on which he played, called a kit. My first lesson was
how to walk and make a curtsey. 'Young lady, if you visit
the queen you must make three curtsies, lower and lower
and lower as you approach her. So-o-o,' leading me on and
making me curtsey. 'Now, if the queen were to ask you to
eat a bit of mutton with her, what would you say?' Every
Saturday afternoon all the scholars, both boys and girls,
met to practise in the public assembly rooms in George's
Street. It was a handsome large hall with benches rising like
an amphitheatre. Some of the elder girls were very pretty,
and danced well, so these practisings became a lounge for
officers from the Castle, and other young men. We used
always to go in full evening dress. We learnt the *minuet de la
cour*, reels and country dances. Our partners used to give us

gingerbread and oranges. Dancing before so many people was quite an exhibition, and I was greatly mortified one day when ready to begin a minuet, by the dancing-master shaking me roughly and making me hold out my frock properly.

Though kind in the main, my uncle and his wife were rather sarcastic and severe, and kept me down a good deal, which I felt keenly, but said nothing. I was not a favourite with my family at that period of my life, because I was reserved and unexpansive, in consequence of the silence I was obliged to observe on the subjects which interested me. Three Miss Melvilles, friends, or perhaps relatives, of Mrs Charters, were always held up to me as models of perfection, to be imitated in everything, and I wearied of hearing them constantly praised at my expense.

In a small society like that of Edinburgh there was a good deal of scandal and gossip; every one's character and conduct were freely criticised, and by none more than by my aunt and her friends. She used to sit at a window embroidering, where she not only could see every one that passed, but with a small telescope could look into the dressing-room of a lady of her acquaintance, and watch all she did. A spinster lady of good family, a cousin of ours, carried her gossip so far, that she was tried for defamation, and condemned to a month's imprisonment, which she actually underwent in the Tolbooth. She was let out just before the king's birthday, to celebrate which, besides the guns fired at the Castle, the boys let off squibs and crackers in all the streets. As the lady in question was walking up the High Street, some lads in a wynd, or narrow street, fired a small cannon, and one of the slugs with which it was loaded hit her mouth and wounded her tongue. This raised a universal laugh; and no one enjoyed it more than my uncle William, who disliked this somewhat masculine woman.

Whilst at my uncle's house, I attended a school for writing and arithmetic, and made considerable progress in the latter, for I liked it, but I soon forgot it from want of practice.

My uncle and aunt generally paid a visit to the Lyells of Kinnordy, the father and mother of my friend Sir Charles Lyell°, the celebrated geologist, but this time they accepted an invitation from Captain Wedderburn, and took me with them. Captain Wedderburn was an old bachelor, who had left the army and devoted himself to agriculture. Mounted on a very tall but quiet horse, I accompanied my host every morning when he went over his farm, which was chiefly a grass farm. The house was infested with rats, and a masculine old maid, who was of the party, lived in such terror of them, that she had a light in her bedroom, and after she was in bed, made her maid tuck in the white dimity curtains all round. One night we were awakened by violent screams, and on going to see what was the matter, we found Miss Cowe in the middle of the room, bare-footed, in her night-dress, screaming at the top of her voice. Instead of tucking the rats out of the bed, the maid had tucked one in, and Miss Cowe on waking beheld it sitting on her pillow.

There was great political agitation at this time. The corruption and tyranny of the court, nobility, and clergy in France were so great, that when the revolution broke out, a large portion of our population thought the French people were perfectly justified in revolting, and warmly espoused their cause. Later many changed their opinions, shocked, as every one was, at the death of the king and queen, and the atrocious massacres which took place in France. Yet some not only approved of the revolution abroad, but were so disgusted with our maladministration at home, to which they attributed our failure in the war in Holland and elsewhere, that great dissatisfaction and alarm prevailed throughout the country. The violence, on the other hand, of the opposite party was not to be described, – the very name of Liberal was detested.

Great dissensions were caused by difference of opinion in families; and I heard people previously much esteemed accused from this cause of all that was evil. My uncle William and my father were as violent Tories as any.

The Liberals were distinguished by wearing their hair short, and when one day I happened to say how becoming a crop was, and that I wished the men would cut off those ugly pigtails, my father exclaimed, 'By G—, when a man cuts off his queue, the head should go with it.'

[*1D, 31:* The government was alarmed, it was dangerous to mention measures which have now been carried in parliament, and a monument has been raised to the three martyrs, Thelwall°, Hardy° and Horne Tooke° then tried for their opinions and defended by the Honorable Henry [actually 'Thomas'] Erskine° afterwards Lord Chancellor.]

The unjust and exaggerated abuse of the Liberal party made me a Liberal. From my earliest years my mind revolted against oppression and tyranny, and I resented the injustice of the world in denying all those privileges of education to my sex which were so lavishly bestowed on men. My liberal opinions, both in religion and politics, have remained unchanged (or, rather, have advanced) throughout my life, but I have never been a republican. I have always considered a highly-educated aristocracy essential, not only for government, but for the refinement of a people.

[After her winter in Edinburgh, my mother returned to Burntisland. Strange to say, she found there, in an illustrated magazine of fashions, the introduction to the great study of her life.]

———————

I was often invited with my mother to the tea-parties given either by widows or maiden ladies who resided at

Burntisland. A pool of commerce used to be keenly contested till a late hour at these parties, which bored me exceedingly, but I there became acquainted with a Miss Ogilvie, much younger than the rest, who asked me to go and see fancy works she was doing, and at which she was very clever. I went next day, and after admiring her work, and being told how it was done, she showed me a monthly magazine with coloured plates of ladies' dresses, charades, and puzzles. At the end of a page I read what appeared to me to be simply an arithmetical question; but on turning the page I was surprised to see strange looking lines mixed with letters, chiefly X's and Y's, and asked; 'What is that?' 'Oh,' said Miss Ogilvie, 'it is a kind of arithmetic: they call it algebra; but I can tell you nothing about it.' And we talked about other things; but on going home I thought I would look if any of our books could tell me what was meant by algebra.

In Robertson's° *Navigation* I flattered myself that I had got precisely what I wanted; but I soon found that I was mistaken. I perceived, however, that astronomy did not consist in star-gazing,[18] and as I persevered in studying the book for a time, I certainly got a dim view of several subjects which were useful to me afterwards. Unfortunately not one of our acquaintances or relations knew anything of science or natural history; nor, had they done so, should I have had courage to ask any of them a question, for I should have been laughed at. I was often very sad and forlorn; not a hand held out to help me.

My uncle and aunt Charters took a house at Burntisland for the summer, and the Miss Melville I have already mentioned came to pay them a visit. She painted miniatures, and from seeing her at work, I took a fancy to learn to draw, and actually wasted time in copying prints; but this circumstance enabled me to get elementary books on algebra and geometry without asking questions of any one, as will be explained afterwards. The rest of the summer I spent in playing on the piano and learning Greek enough to read Xenophon and part of Herodotus;[19] then we prepared to go to Edinburgh.

My mother was so much afraid of the sea that she never would cross the Firth except in a boat belonging to a certain skipper who had served in the Navy and lost a hand; he had a hook fastened on the stump to enable him to haul ropes. My brother and I were tired of the country, and one sunny day we persuaded my mother to embark. When we came to the shore, the skipper said, 'I wonder that the leddy boats to-day, for though it is calm here under the lee of the land, there is a stiff breeze outside.' We made him a sign to hold his tongue, for we knew this as well as he did. Our mother went down to the cabin and remained silent and quiet for a time; but when we began to roll and be tossed about, she called out to the skipper, 'George! this is an awful storm, I am sure we are in great danger. Mind how you steer; remember, I trust in you!' He laughed, and said, 'Dinna trust in me, leddy; trust in God Almighty.' Our mother, in perfect terror, called out, 'Dear me! is it come to that?' We burst out laughing, skipper and all.

Nasmyth°, an exceedingly good landscape painter had opened an academy for ladies in Edinburgh, a proof of the gradual improvement which was taking place in the education of the higher classes; my mother, very willingly allowed me to attend it. The class was very full. I was not taught to draw, but looked on while Nasmyth painted; then a picture was given me to copy, the master correcting the faults. Though I spoilt canvas, I had made some progress by the end of the season.[20] Mr Nasmyth, besides being a good artist, was clever, well-informed, and had a great deal of conversation. One day I happened to be near him while he was talking to the ladies Douglas about perspective. He said, 'You should study Euclid's Elements of Geometry; the foundation not only of perspective, but of astronomy and all mechanical science.' Here, in the most unexpected manner, I got the information I wanted, for I at once saw that it would help me to understand some parts of Robertson's *Navigation*; but as to going to a bookseller and asking for Euclid the thing was impossible! Besides I did not yet know anything definite about algebra, so no more could be done at that time; but I never lost sight of an object which had interested me from the first.

I rose early, and played four or five hours, as usual, on the piano, and had lessons from Corri°, an Italian, who taught carelessly, and did not correct a habit I had of thumping so as to break the strings; but I learnt to tune a piano and mend the strings, as there was no tuner at Burntisland. Afterwards I got over my bad habit and played the music then in vogue: pieces by Pleyel, Clementi, Steibelt, Mozart, and Beethoven, the last being my favourite to this day.[21] I was sometimes accompanied on the violin by Mr Thomson°, the friend of Burns; more frequently by Stabilini°; but I was always too shy to play before people, and invariably played badly when obliged to do so, which vexed me.

The prejudice against the theatre had been very great in Scotland, and still existed among the rigid Calvinists. One day, when I was fourteen or fifteen, on going into the drawing-room, an old man sitting beside my mother rose and kissed me, saying, 'I am one of your mother's oldest friends.' It was Home°, the author of the tragedy of *Douglas*. He was obliged to resign his living in the kirk for the scandal of having had his play acted in the theatre in Edinburgh, and some of his clerical friends were publicly rebuked for going to see it. Our family was perfectly liberal in all these matters. The first time I had ever been in a theatre I went with my father to see *Cymbeline*. I had never neglected Shakespeare, and when our great tragedians, Mrs Siddons° and her brother, John Kemble°, came for a short time to act in Edinburgh, I could think of nothing else. They were both remarkably handsome, and, notwithstanding the Scotch prejudice, the theatre was crowded every night. It was a misfortune to me that my mother never would go into society during the absence of my father, nor, indeed, at any time, except, perhaps, to a dinner party; but I had no difficulty in finding a chaperone, as we knew many people. I used to go to the theatre in the morning, and ask to see the plan of the house for the evening, that I might know which ladies I could accompany to their boxes. Of course I paid for my place. Our friends were so kind that I saw these great artists, as well as Charles Kemble°, Young°, and Bannister°, in *Hamlet, Macbeth, Othello, Coriolanus, The Gamester,* &c.[22]

It was greatly to the honour of the British stage that all the principal actors, men and women, were of excellent moral character, and much esteemed. Many years afterwards, when Mrs Siddons was an old woman, I drank tea with her, and heard her read Milton and Shakespeare. Her daughter told us to applaud, for she had been so much accustomed to it in the theatre that she could not read with spirit without this expression of approbation.

My mother was pleased with my music and painting, and, although she did not go to the theatre herself, she encouraged me to go. She was quite of the old school with regard to the duties of women, and very particular about her table; and, although we were obliged to live with rigid economy, our food was of the best quality, well dressed, and neatly served, for she could tell the cook exactly what was amiss when anything was badly cooked. She thought besides that some of the comfort of married life depended upon the table, so I was sent to a pastrycook for a short time every day, to learn the art of cookery. I had for companions Miss Moncreiff, daughter of Sir Henry Moncreiff Wellwood°, a Scotch baronet of old family. She was older than I, pretty, pleasing, and one of the belles of the day. We were amused at the time, and afterwards made jellies and creams for little supper parties, then in fashion, though, as far as economy went, we might as well have bought them.

On returning to Burntisland, I played on the piano as diligently as ever, and painted several hours every day. At this time, however, a Mr Craw came to live with us as tutor to my youngest brother, Henry. He had been educated for the kirk, was a fair Greek and Latin scholar, but, unfortunately for me, was no mathematician. He was a simple, good-natured kind of man, and I ventured to ask him about algebra and geometry, and begged him, the first time he went to Edinburgh, to buy me something elementary on these subjects, so he soon brought me *Euclid* and Bonnycastle's *Algebra*, which were the books used in the schools at that time. Now I had got what I so long and earnestly desired. I asked Mr Craw to hear me demonstrate a few problems in the first book of *Euclid*, and then I continued the study alone with courage and assiduity, knowing I was on the right road. Before I began to read algebra I found it necessary to study arithmetic again, having forgotten much of it. I never was expert at addition, for, in summing up a long column of pounds, shillings, and pence, in the family account book, it seldom came out twice the same way. In after life I, of course, used logarithms for the higher branches of science.

I had to take part in the household affairs, and to make and mend my own clothes. I rose early, played on the piano, and painted during the time I could spare in the daylight hours, but I sat up very late reading *Euclid*. The servants, however, told my mother, 'It was no wonder the stock of candles was soon exhausted, for Miss Mary sat up reading till a very late hour;' whereupon an order was given to take away my candle as soon as I was in bed. I had, however, already gone through the first six books of *Euclid*, and now I was thrown on my memory, which I exercised by beginning at the first book, and demonstrating in my mind a certain number of problems every night, till I could nearly go through the whole. My father came home for a short time, and, somehow or other, finding out what I was about, said to my mother, 'Peg, we must put a stop to this, or we shall have Mary in a strait jacket one of these days. There was X., who went raving mad about the longitude!'

In our younger days my brother Sam and I kept various festivals: we burnt nuts, ducked for apples, and observed many other of the ceremonies of Halloween, so well described by Burns, and we always sat up to hail the new year on New Year's Eve. When in Edinburgh we sometimes disguised ourselves as 'guisarts,' and went about with a basket full of Christmas cakes called buns and shortbread, and a flagon of 'het-pint' or posset, to wish our friends a 'Happy New Year.' At Christmas time a set of men, called the Christmas Wakes, walked slowly through the streets during the midnight hours, playing our sweet Scotch airs on flageolets. I remember the sound from a distance fell gently on my sleeping ear, swelled softly, and died away in distance again, a passing breeze of sweet sound. It was very pleasing; some thought it too sad.

My grandfather was intimate with the Boswells° of Balmuto, a bleak place a few miles to the north of Burntisland. Lord Balmuto, a Scotch judge, who was then proprietor, had been a dancing companion of my mother's, and had a son and two daughters, the eldest a nice girl of my age, with whom I was intimate, so I gladly accepted an invitation to visit them at Balmuto. Lord Balmuto was a large coarse-looking man, with black hair and beetling eyebrows. Though not vulgar, he was passionate, and had a boisterous manner. My mother and her sisters gave him the nickname of the 'black bull of Norr'away,' in allusion to the northern position of Balmuto. Mrs Boswell was gentle and lady-like. The son had a turn for chemistry, and his father took me to see what they called the Laboratory. What a laboratory might be I knew not, as I had never heard the word before, but somehow I did not like the look of the curiously-shaped glass things and other apparatus, so when the son put a substance on the table, and took a hammer, his father saying, 'Now you will hear a fine report,' I ran out of the room, saying, 'I don't like reports.' Sure enough there was a very loud report, followed by a violent crash, and on going into the room again, we found that the son had been knocked down, the father was trembling from head to foot, and the apparatus had been smashed to pieces. They had had a narrow escape. Miss Boswell led a dull life, often passing the winter with her mother in that solitary place, Balmuto; and when in Edinburgh, she was much kept down by her father, and associated little with people of her own age and station. The consequence was that she eloped with her drawing-master, to the inexpressible rage and mortification of her father, who had all the Scotch pride of family and pure blood.

[*1D, 41 verso:* The Earl of Rosslyn, who was I believe Lord Lieutenant of Fife at the time, invited my father and mother and me to dine and spend the night but did not mention at what hour they dined. Now my father who had been little ashore of late and was accustomed to early sea hours insisted, in spite of all my mother could say, in setting off so early that though the distance was considerable, we arrived while they were at lunch, or breakfast for anything I know, for we did not dine till eight o'clock. Nothing could be more agreeable or kind than our reception. Lady Rosslyn was very handsome and quite a high bred woman. Dysart is a beautiful place, the weather was fine so we spent the morning in walking on the grounds, There was an agreeable party at dinner so my father and mother enjoyed their visit but I was bored to death because there were no young people. While driving home next morning my mother said, 'You had better take my advice next time I give it; you saw how much too early we were.' 'Pah, pah,' said my father after a little pause, 'who the devil could have believed that anyone was so ridiculously fashionable as to dine at supper time.']

This year we remained longer in the country than usual, and I went to spend Christmas with the Oswalds° of Dunnikeir. The family consisted of a son, a colonel in the army, and three daughters, the youngest about my age, a bold horsewoman. She had talent, became a good Greek and Latin scholar, and was afterwards married to the Earl of Elgin°. More than seventy years after this I had a visit from the Dean of Westminster and Lady Augusta Stanley°, her daughter; a very charming person, who told me about her family, of which I had heard nothing for years. I was very happy to see the Dean, one of the most liberal and distinguished members of the Church of England, and son of my old friend the late Bishop of Norwich.

[*1D, 39:* The other two [daughters] were much older and had seen a great deal of the gay world, they were tall, the youngest rather pretty. The weather was bad and as they walked for exercise in the drawing-room they amused themselves making game of me as I sat at my work. Mrs Oswald came into the room and looking at my work said, 'So you are making a cap in imitation of my daughter's, but you need not take the trouble, for wear what you please, you will never be like her.' I was all my life subject to sick headaches and unfortunately I was seized with one which kept me in bed for a day, and when I came into the drawing-room again, the young ladies laughed and repeated lines from the *Elegant Extracts* about eating too much Christmas cake.[23] It was hard on a timid girl, I inwardly vowed that I never would visit again and rejoiced to return home and go for the rest of the winter to Edinburgh.]

When I returned to Edinburgh Mr Nasmyth was much pleased with the progress I had made in painting, for, besides having copied several landscapes he had lent me,

I had taken the outline of a print and coloured it from a storm I saw at the end of our garden. This picture I still possess.

Dr Blair°, minister of the High Kirk of Edinburgh, the well-known author and professor of Rhetoric and Belles Letters in the University, an intimate friend of my grandfather's, had heard of my turn for painting, and asked my mother to let him see some of my pictures. A few of the best were sent to him, and were returned after a few days accompanied by a long letter from the old gentleman, pointing out what he admired most in each picture. I was delighted with the letter, and not a little vain of the praise.

LETTER FROM DR BLAIR TO MARY FAIRFAX

My dear Miss Fairfax,

This comes to return you a thousand thanks for the pleasure and entertainment I have had from your landscape paintings. I had them placed in the best light I could contrive in my drawing-room, and entertained myself a good while every day looking at them and admiring their beauties, which always grew upon me. I intend to return them to you to-morrow, or rather on the beginning of next week; and as they were taken particular care of, I hope they shall not appear to have suffered any injury.

I have exhibited them to several people, some of whom were excellent judges, whom I brought on purpose to view them – Lady Miller, the Solicitor and Mrs Blair, his lady, Dr Hill, Miss Anne Ker of Nisbet, and a variety of ladies. All joined in praising them highly. The penserosa figure caught the highest admiration of any, from the gracefulness of the figure and attitude, and the boldness and propriety of the scenery. The two morning and evening views – one of Lochness, and the other of Elcho Castle – which make fine companions, and which I always placed together, were also highly admired.

Each of them had their different partizans, and I myself was for a good while undetermined which of them to prefer. At last, I found the placidity of the scene in Elcho Castle, with the cottages among the trees, dwelt most on my imagination, though the gaiety and brightness of the morning sky in the other has also exquisite beauty. On the whole, I am persuaded that your taste and powers of execution in that art are uncommonly great, and that if you go on you must excel highly, and may go what length you please. Landscape painting has been always a great favourite with me; and you have really contributed much to my entertainment. As I thought you might wish to know my sentiments, after your paintings had been a little considered, I was led to write you these lines (in which I assure you there is nothing flattering), before sending back your pieces to you. With best compliments to Lady Fairfax, believe me,

Your obliged and most obedient Servant,

HUGH BLAIR

ARGYLL SQUARE, *11th April (probably) 1796*

A day or two after this a Mrs Ramsay, a rich proud widow, a relation of my mother's, came with her daughter, who was an heiress, to pay us a morning visit. Looking round the room she asked who had painted the pictures hung up on the walls. My mother, who was rather proud of them, said they were painted by me. 'I am glad,' said Mrs Ramsay, 'that Miss Fairfax has any kind of talent that may enable her to win her bread, for everyone knows she will not have a sixpence.' It was a very severe hit, because it was true. Had it been my lot to win my bread by painting, I fear I should have fared badly, but I never should have been ashamed of it; on the contrary, I should have been very proud had I been successful. I must say the idea of making money had never entered my head in any of my pursuits, but I was intensely ambitious to excel in something, for I felt in my own breast that women were capable of taking a higher place in creation than that assigned to them in my early days, which was very low.

Not long after Mrs Ramsay's visit to my mother, Miss Ramsay went to visit the Dons, at Newton Don, a pretty place near Kelso. Miss Ramsay and the three Miss Dons were returning from a long walk; they had reached the park of Newton Don, when they heard the dinner bell ring, and fearing to be too late for dinner, instead of going round, they attempted to cross a brook which runs through the park. One of the Miss Dons stumbled on the stepping-stones and fell into the water. Her two sisters and Miss Ramsay, trying to save her, fell in one after another. The three Miss Dons were drowned, but Miss Ramsay, who wore a stiff worsted petticoat, was buoyed up by it and carried down stream, where she caught by the branch of a tree and was saved. She never recovered the shock of the dreadful scene.

FOUR

Edinburgh Supper Parties – Tour in the Highlands –
Mutiny in the Fleet – Battle of Camperdown

[By this time my mother was grown up, and extremely pretty.
All those who knew her speak of her rare and delicate beauty,
both of face and figure. They called her the 'Rose of Jedwood.'
She kept her beauty to the last day of her life, and was a
beautiful old woman, as she had been a lovely young one. She
used to say, laughing, that 'it was very hard no one ever
thought of painting her portrait so long as she was young
and pretty.' After she became celebrated, various likenesses
were taken of her, by far the best of which are a beautiful bust,
modelled at Rome in 1844 by Mr Lawrence Macdonald°, and
a crayon drawing by Mr James Swinton°, done in London in
1848. My mother always looked considerably younger than her
age; even at ninety, she looked younger than some who were
her juniors by several years. This was owing, no doubt,
principally to her being small and delicate in face and figure,
but also, I think, to the extreme youthfulness and freshness of
both her heart and mind, neither of which ever grew old. It
certainly was not due to a youthful style of dress, for she had
perfect taste in such matters, as well as in other things; and
although no one spent less thought or money on it than she,
my mother was at all times both neatly and becomingly
dressed. She never was careless; and her room, her papers,
and all that belonged to her were invariably in the most
beautiful order. My mother's recollections of this period of
her life are as follows:—]

[*Some of the commentary on Mary Somerville's appearance is given in the drafts in her own words: 1D, 42:* I was now a very pretty girl and much admired, though my mother used to say that her family were like pigs, pretty when young but grew uglier every day. From shyness or timidity I offended one of the acquaintance I had made, for on going to return their visit when at the door I had not the courage to ring the bell and announce myself, but came home vexed and could not even make an apology when we met. I was old enough by this time to be invited with my mother to dinner parties. On one occasion the conversation turned upon an officer who had distinguished himself, and someone asked me if I knew him, I replied very little, I have merely been introduced to him. Whereupon Mr Douglas of Cavers[?] a gentlemanly old man turned sharply round to me and said, 'Young lady you forget the respect due to your sex. You cannot be presented to any man except a sovereign, or a prince of royal blood. All other men, be their age or rank what it may, are presented to you.' I blushed scarlet but I liked and remembered the lesson.]

[*1D, 37:* My teeth were very good, but to my infinite dismay I discovered that a front one was beginning to spoil; as there were no false teeth at that time I expected soon to be toothless and vexed myself about it but it was trifling and remained the same for many years – so much for personal vanity.]

[*1D, 44:* It frequently happened that Madam Billington° and other celebrated singers came to Edinburgh for a short time and sang in the Assembly rooms. On one of these occasions Miss Wardlaw, an elderly maiden lady, asked me to go with her, saying she was to dine out but that she would meet me in the lobby at a certain hour. So I went, sent away my chair and sat down. The crowd was great; numbers of my acquaintances passed and said, 'You are waiting for your chaperone.' At last the room was full and several pieces of music had been performed when a gentleman came out for a lady's shawl and was surprised to see me quite alone. I said that I was waiting for Miss Wardlaw. 'She has been in the room more than an hour, let me take you to her.' 'By no means,' I said, 'I have not courage to go into the room, but do me the kindness to call a chair.' So I went home. I was not in the room next day when Miss Wardlaw came to make an apology but when I met her she said, 'I thought your mother would have torn my eyes out, she was so angry; the dinner party was sooner over than I expected so I went into the room and forgot you altogether.'

There was a great deal of beauty in Edinburgh at that time but no one was to be compared with Lady Charlotte Campbell, daughter of the Duke of Argyle, married to Colonel John Campbell of Shawfield who was as handsome for a man as she was for a woman. I do not remember ever having seen a more distinguished or beautiful woman. She knew it and sometimes dressed fantastically but she was by no means without talent. Dress was far less expensive then than it is now, for it was not thought necessary to appear in a different dress every evening. Had that been the case, I could not have gone into society at all. My morning dresses, which I made myself from patterns lent to me by my friends, consisted of white cambric muslin or printed cotton; at dinner parties I wore India muslin and at balls India muslin over white or rose colour satin, and a fall of broad and very fine French lace round the bosom. I usually had my hair plain but feathers were much in fashion and I cannot help laughing as I write to think that I sometimes appeared with three high ostriches' feathers like the Prince of Wales's crest above my forehead either all white or with a scarlet one in the middle. But such was the mode.]

[1D, 45 verso: I was intimate in the family of a Mrs Wilson, a widow lady who had a son and three daughters, one remarkably pretty, all agreeable and very gay, going out a great deal. Mrs Wilson was a sensible good woman. She had what I believe is called a wall eye: at least it was white and very ugly. Her family were much attached to her, and insisted on having her portrait by an artist who was capricious but very clever. On one occasion when asked to paint a lady's portrait he said yellow paint was so expensive that he could not afford to do it at the ordinary price. When he saw Mrs Wilson he said he would only paint her in profile. She said, 'My children love me notwithstanding my wall eye and the picture must be done such as I am or not at all.' The girls and I used to walk together sometimes accompanied by their brother who was some years older than any of us and had been a student at the University of Glasgow. He had been a good Greek and Latin scholar, wrote pretty verses, was very clever and very eccentric. He disappeared occasionally; he was fond of sailing and I believe he made a voyage as a common sailor; he once joined a company of strolling players in Ireland.

In one of his excursions he was living at a small inn at Windermere when two gentlemen and pretty girl daughter of one of them arrived. The landlady was in distress for want of a waiter, and Wilson° offered to wait on them. While at dinner one of the gentlemen quoted a Latin author, when Wilson said you are mistaken it is so and so – the gentleman said nothing at the time, but took an opportunity before going away to tell him he had suspected he was acting a part.

Some years afterwards I met with my old companion John Wilson at Windermere,[24] now a married man living in a house he had built on a hill above the lake. He had quite a fleet of boats and wore the dress of a common sailor. A traveller said, 'My lad, who does that pretty boat belong to?' 'It belongs to the man who lives in that eastern?-looking house on the hill; and this boat to the same, and this.' [three indecipherable words] 'What a strange sort of fellow he must [be].'

'Oh,' said Wilson, 'if you knew him as well as I do, you would have reason to say so.'

When I went to London, I lost sight of my old companion, and was not a little amused, but by no means surprised, to hear that he was elected professor of moral philosophy in the University of Edinburgh. He was much esteemed and though chiefly occupied with his lectures, he published the *Isle of Palms* and other poems. I think he also wrote in *Blackwood's Magazine*.]

At that time Edinburgh was really the capital of Scotland: most of the Scotch families of distinction spent the winter there, and we had numerous acquaintances who invited me to whatever gaiety was going on. As my mother refused to go into society when my father was at sea, I had to find a chaperone; but I never was at a loss, for we were somehow related to the Erskine° family, and the Countess of Buchan, an amiable old lady, was always ready to take charge of me.

It was under Lady Buchan's care that I made my first appearance at a ball, and my first dancing-partner was the late Earl of Minto, then Mr Gilbert Elliot°, with whom I was always on very friendly terms, as well as with his family. Many other ladies were willing to take charge of me, but a chaperone was only required for the theatre, and concerts, and for balls in the public assembly rooms; at private balls the lady of the house was thought sufficient. Still, although I was sure to know everybody in the room, or nearly so, I liked to have some one with whom to enter and to sit beside. Few ladies kept carriages, but went in sedan chairs, of which there were stands in the principal streets. Ladies were generally attended by a man-servant, but I went alone, as our household consisted of two maid-servants only. My mother knew, however, that the Highlanders who carried me could be trusted. I was fond of dancing, and never

without partners, and often came home in bright daylight.
The dances were reels, country dances, and sometimes Sir
Roger de Coverley.

[At this period, although busily engaged in studying painting
at Nasmyth's academy, practising the piano five hours a day,
and pursuing her more serious studies zealously, my mother
went a good deal into society, for Edinburgh was a gay,
sociable place, and many people who recollect her at that
time, and some who were her dancing-partners, have told me
she was much admired, and a great favourite. They said she
had a graceful figure, below the middle size, a small head, well
set on her shoulders, a beautiful complexion, bright, intelligent
eyes, and a profusion of soft brown hair. Besides the various
occupations I have mentioned, she made all her own dresses,
even for balls. These, however, unlike the elaborate productions of our day, were simply of fine India muslin, with a little
Flanders lace. She says of her life in Edinburgh:—]

Girls had perfect liberty at that time in Edinburgh; we
walked together in Princes Street, the fashionable prome-
nade, and were joined by our dancing-partners. We occasionally gave little supper parties, and presented these
young men to our parents as they came in. At these
meetings we played at games, danced reels, or had a little
music – never cards. After supper there were toasts, sentiments, and songs. There were always one or two hot dishes,
and a variety of sweet things and fruit. Though I was much
more at ease in society now, I was always terribly put out
when asked for a toast or a sentiment. Like other girls, I did
not dislike a little quiet flirtation; but I never could speak
across a table, or take a leading part in conversation. This
diffidence was probably owing to the secluded life I led in
my early youth. At this time I gladly took part in any gaiety

that was going on, and spent the day after a ball in idleness and gossiping with my friends; but these were rare occasions, for the balls were not numerous, and I never lost sight of the main object of my life, which was to prosecute my studies. So I painted at Nasmyth's, played the usual number of hours on the piano, worked and conversed with my mother in the evening; and as we kept early hours, I rose at day-break, and after dressing, I wrapped myself in a blanket from my bed on account of the excessive cold – having no fire at that hour – and read algebra or the classics till breakfast time. I had, and still have, determined perseverance, but I soon found that it was in vain to occupy my mind beyond a certain time. I grew tired and did more harm than good; so, if I met with a difficult point, for example, in algebra, instead of poring over it till I was bewildered, I left it, took my work or some amusing book, and resumed it when my mind was fresh. Poetry was my great resource on these occasions, but at a later period I read novels, *The Old English Baron, The Mysteries of Udolpho, A Romance of the Forest,* &c.[25] I was very fond of ghost and witch stories, both of which were believed in by most of the common people and many of the better educated. I heard an old naval officer say that he never opened his eyes after he was in bed. I asked him why? and he replied, 'For fear I should see something!' Now I did not actually believe in either ghosts or witches, but yet, when alone in the dead of the night, I have been seized with a dread of, I know not what. Few people will now understand me if I say I was *eerie*, a Scotch expression for superstitious awe. I have been struck, on reading the life of the late Sir David Brewster, with the influence the superstitions of the age and country had on both learned and unlearned. Sir David was one of the greatest philosophers of the day. He was only a year younger than I; we were both born in Jedburgh, and both were influenced by the superstitions of our age and country in a similar manner, for he confessed that, although he did not believe in ghosts, he was *eerie* when sitting up to a late hour in a lone house that was haunted. This is a totally different thing from believing in spirit-rapping, which I scorn.

We returned as usual to Burntisland, in spring, and my father, who was at home, took my mother and me a tour in the Highlands. I was a great admirer of Ossian's poems, and viewed the grand and beautiful scenery with awe; and my father, who was of a romantic disposition, smiled at my enthusiastic admiration of the eagles as they soared above the mountains. These noble birds are nearly extirpated; and, indeed, the feathered tribes, which were more varied and numerous in Britain than in any part of Europe, will soon disappear. They will certainly be avenged by the insects.

On coming home from the journey I was quite broken-hearted to find my beautiful goldfinch, which used to draw its water so prettily with an ivory cup and little chain, dead in its cage. The odious wretches of servants, to whose care I trusted it, let it die of hunger. My heart is deeply pained as I write this, seventy years afterwards.

[*1D, 47 verso:* The Fife county races were held at Dunfermline and Mrs Wemyss of Cuttle Hill, married to a coarse hard drinking man of good family and fortune, was kind enough to take me to them. She was a witty agreeable woman and a pleasant person for a shy girl to go with, for I still became shy when placed in a new position. I had been at Leith races which were very gay and pretty. At spring tide the sea along the coast of Leith retires to a great distance, leaving the sand hard and dry for the race. On this occasion the course was turf and although the scene was less brilliant and the horses probably not so good, I was delighted and enjoyed the balls which took place on the alternate nights exceedingly because I was well dressed and had plenty of partners. The town was so crowded that we girls had to sleep two in a room. We generally made little parties on the quiet evenings to talk matters over. One night they assembled in the room where I was; we sat up late and were criticising our partners, when we were startled by a loud knock on the wainscot, when a female voice called out, 'Take care what you say of your beaux, young ladies, for I hear every word.' It was Mary Lady Clerk, a person well known in Edinburgh. We thought it so ladylike that we thanked her next day.]

In Fifeshire, as elsewhere, political opinions separated friends and disturbed the peace of families; discussions on political questions were violent and dangerous on account of the hard drinking then so prevalent. [*1D, 47 verso:* Not long after the races, but I forget exactly when, a dispute arose at a club in Dunfermline between Sir Alexander Boswell of Affleck, and Mr Stuart of Dunearne, both young men – a challenge was sent, a duel was fought and Sir Alexander was killed on the spot. Mr Stuart fled, escaped to the United States where he remained for some years; when he returned it was scarcely possible to recognise him so much had that fatal event distressed him. The gossips in Fife especially the old ladies at Burntisland had selected Mr Stuart as a match for me, but there never was any reason.][26] At this time the oppression and cruelty committed in Great Britain were almost beyond endurance. Men and women were executed for what at the present day would only have been held to deserve a few weeks' or months' imprisonment.[27] Every liberal opinion was crushed, men were entrapped into the army by promises which were never kept, and press-gangs tore merchant seamen from their families, and forced them to serve in the navy, where they were miserably provided for. The severity of discipline in both services amounted to torture. Such was the treatment of the brave men on whom the safety of the nation depended! They could bear it no longer; a mutiny broke out in the fleet which had been cruising off the Texel to watch the movements of a powerful Dutch squadron.[28] The men rose against their officers, took the command, and ship after ship returned to England, leaving only a frigate and the *Venerable*, commanded by Admiral Duncan°, with my father as his flag-captain. To deceive the Dutch, they continued to make signals, as if the rest of the fleet were in the offing, till they could return to England; when, without delay, Admiral Duncan and my father went alone on board each ship, ordered the men to arrest the ringleaders, which was done, and the fleet immediately returned to its station off the Texel. At last, on the morning of the 11th October, 1797, the Dutch fleet came out in great force, and formed in line of battle; that is, with their broadsides towards our ships. Then Admiral Duncan said to my father, 'Fairfax, what shall we do?' – 'Break their line, sir, and draw up on the other side, where they will not be so well prepared.' – 'Do it, then, Fairfax.' So my father signalled accordingly. The circumstances of the battle, which was nobly fought on both sides, are historical.[29] Nine ships of the line and two frigates were taken, and my father was sent home to announce the victory to the Admiralty. The rejoicing was excessive; every town and village was illuminated; and the administration, relieved from the fear of a revolution, continued more confidently its oppressive measures.

When Admiral Duncan came to London, he was made a Baron, and afterwards Earl of Camperdown; and, by an unanimous vote of the House of Commons, he received a pension or a sum of money, I forget which; my father was knighted, and made Colonel of Marines. Earl Spencer was First Lord of the Admiralty at the time, and Lady Spencer said to my father, 'You ask for the promotion of your officers, but you never have asked a reward for yourself.' He replied, 'I leave that to my country.' But his country did nothing for him; and at his death my mother had nothing to live upon but the usual pension of an Admiral's widow, of seventy-five pounds a year. Our friends, especially Robert Ferguson°, junior, of Raith, made various attempts to obtain an addition to it; but it was too late: Camperdown was forgotten.

I remember one morning going to Lord Camperdown's house in Edinburgh with my mother, to see a very large painting, representing the quarter-deck of the *Venerable*, Admiral Duncan, as large as life, standing upright, and the Dutch Admiral, De Winter, presenting his sword to my father. Another representation of the same scene may be seen among the numerous pictures of naval battles which decorate the walls of the great hall at Greenwich Hospital.[30] Many years afterwards I was surprised to see an engraving of this very picture in the public library at Milan. I did not know that one existed.

At a great entertainment given to Lord Duncan by the East India Company, then in great power, the President asked my father, who sat at his left hand, if he had any relation in India? He replied, 'My eldest son is in the Company's military service.' 'Then,' said the President, 'he shall be a Writer, the highest appointment in my power to bestow.' I cannot tell how thankful we were; for, instead of a separation of almost a lifetime, it gave hopes that my brother might make a sufficient fortune in a few years to enable him to come home. There was a great review of the troops at Calcutta, under a burning sun; my brother returned to the barracks, sun-struck, where he found his appointment, and died that evening, at the age of twenty-one.

[*1D, 52: here there are in the first draft two rows of dots after the death of her brother.*]

[My mother has often told us of her heart-broken parting with this brother on his going to India. It was then almost for a lifetime, and he was her favourite brother, and the companion of her childhood. He must have been wonderfully handsome, judging from a beautifully-painted miniature which we have of him.]

Public events became more and more exciting every day, and difficulties occurred at home. There had been bad harvests, and there was a great scarcity of bread; the people were much distressed, and the manufacturing towns in England were almost in a state of revolution; but the fear of invasion kept them quiet. I gloried in the brilliant success of our arms by land and by sea; and although I should have been glad if the people had resisted oppression at home, when we were threatened with invasion, I would have died to prevent a Frenchman from landing on our coast. No one can imagine the intense excitement which pervaded all ranks at that time. Every one was armed, and, notwithstanding the alarm, we could not but laugh at the awkward, and often ridiculous, figures of our old acquaintances, when at drill in uniform. At that time I went to visit my relations at Jedburgh. Soon after my arrival, we were awakened in the middle of the night by the Yeomanry entering the town at full gallop. The beacons were burning on the top of the Cheviots and other hills, as a signal that the French had landed. When day came, every preparation was made; but it was a false alarm.

The rapid succession of victories by sea and land was intensely exciting. We always illuminated our house, and went to the rocky bank in our southern garden to see the illumination of Edinburgh, Leith, and the shipping in the Roads, which was inexpressibly beautiful, though there was no gas in those times. It often happened that balls were given by the officers of the ships of war that came occasionally to Leith Roads, and I was always invited, but never allowed to go; for my mother thought it foolish to run the risk of crossing the Firth, a distance of seven miles, at a late hour, in a small open boat and returning in the morning, as the weather was always uncertain, and the sea often rough from tide and wind. On one occasion, my father was at home, and, though it was blowing hard, I thought he would not object to accepting the invitation; but he said, 'Were it a matter of duty, you should go, even at the risk of your life, but for a ball, certainly not.'

We were as poor as ever, even more so; for my father was led into unavoidable expenses in London; so, after all the excitement, we returned to our more than usually economical life. No events worth mentioning happened for a long time. I continued my diversified pursuits as usual; had they been more concentrated, it would have been better; but there was no choice; for I had not the means of pursuing any one as far as I could wish, nor had I any friend to whom I could apply for direction or information. I was often deeply depressed at spending so much time to so little purpose.

FIVE

First Marriage (1804) – Widowhood – Studies –
Second Marriage

[Mr Samuel Greig was a distant relation of the Charters family. His father°, an officer in the British navy, had been sent by our government, at the request of the Empress Catherine, to organise the Russian navy. Mr Greig came to the Firth of Forth on board a Russian frigate, and was received by the Fairfaxes at Burntisland with Scotch hospitality, as a cousin. He eventually married my mother: not, however, until he had obtained the Russian consulship, and settled permanently in London, for Russia was then governed in the most arbitrary and tyrannical manner, and was neither a safe nor a desirable residence, and my grandfather only gave his consent to the marriage on this condition. My mother says:—]

———————————

MY cousin, Samuel Greig, commissioner of the Russian navy, and Russian consul for Britain, came to pay us a visit, and ultimately became my husband. Fortune I had none, and my mother could only afford to give me a very moderate trousseau, consisting chiefly of fine personal and household linen. When I was going away she gave me twenty pounds to buy a shawl or something warm for the following winter. I knew that the President of the Academy of Painting, Sir Martin Archer Shee°, had painted a portrait of my father immediately after the battle of Camperdown, and I went to see it. The likeness pleased me, –

the price was twenty pounds; so instead of a warm shawl I
bought my father's picture, which I have since given to my
nephew, Sir William George Fairfax. [*1D, 53:* I never
repented, though I suffered for it. My husband had a
gig which he drove to the City where he was engaged the
whole day, and on coming home late in the evening used
frequently to take me to drive. On these occasions I
suffered severely from the cold as winter came on having
only a small scarf; for although I could ask money for the
household, I could not ask it for myself.] My husband's
brother, Sir Alexis Greig°, who commanded the Russian
naval force in the Black Sea for more than twenty years,
came to London about this time, and gave me some furs,
which were very welcome. Long after this, I applied to Sir
Alexis, at the request of Dr Whewell°, Master of Trinity
College, Cambridge, and through his interest an order was
issued by the Russian Government for simultaneous observations to be made of the tides on every sea-coast of the
empire.

LETTER FROM DR WHEWELL TO
MRS SOMERVILLE

UNIVERSITY CLUB, *Jan. 5, 1838*

MY DEAR MRS SOMERVILLE,

I enclose a memorandum respecting tide observations, to
which subject I am desirous of drawing the attention of the
Russian Government. Nobody knows better than you do how
much remains to be done respecting the tides, and what
important results any advance in that subject would have. I
hope, through your Russian friends, you may have the means
of bringing this memorandum to the notice of the administration of their navy, so as to lead to some steps being taken, in
the way of directing observations to be made. The Russian
Government has shown so much zeal in promoting science,

that I hope it will not be difficult to engage them in a kind of research so easy, so useful practically, and so interesting in its theoretical bearing.

Believe me, dear Mrs Somerville,
Very faithfully yours,
W. WHEWELL

My husband had taken me to his bachelor's house in London, which was exceedingly small and ill ventilated. I had a key of the neighbouring square, where I used to walk. I was alone the whole of the day, so I continued my mathematical and other pursuits, but under great disadvantages; for although my husband did not prevent me from studying, I met with no sympathy whatever from him, as he had a very low opinion of the capacity of my sex, and had neither knowledge of nor interest in science of any kind. I took lessons in French, and learnt to speak it so as to be understood. I had no carriage, so went to the nearest church; but, accustomed to our Scotch Kirk, I never could sympathise with the coldness and formality of the service of the Church of England. However, I thought it my duty to go to church and join where I could in prayer with the congregation.

[1D, 55: The members of the Russian legation came frequently to see us, but as they were all unmarried I had no female society. Baron Nicolai, the secretary, Mr Greig and I once spent a day at Windsor and went in the evening to see George III, the Queen and royal family taking their usual walk on the terrace of the castle. The princes and princesses were fine looking merry young people, the whole party talking frankly to everyone they knew.]

There was no Italian opera in Edinburgh; the first time I went to one was in London as chaperone to Countess Catharine Woronzow°, afterwards Countess of Pembroke, who was godmother to my eldest son. I sometimes spent the evening with her, and occasionally dined at the embassy; but went nowhere else till we became acquainted with the family of Mr Thomson Bonar, a rich Russian merchant, who lived in great luxury at a beautiful villa at Chiselhurst, in the neighbourhood of London, which has since become the refuge of the ex-Emperor Napoleon the Third° and the Empress Eugénie. The family consisted of Mr and Mrs Bonar, – kind, excellent people, – with two sons and a daughter, all grown up. We were invited from time to time to spend ten days or a fortnight with them, which I enjoyed exceedingly. I had been at a riding school in Edinburgh, and rode tolerably, but had little practice, as we could not afford to keep horses. On our first visit, Mrs Bonar asked me if I would ride with her, as there was a good lady's horse to spare, but I declined. Next day I said, 'I should like to ride with you.' 'Why did you not go out with me yesterday?' she asked. 'Because I had heard so much of English ladies' riding, that I thought you would clear all the hedges and ditches, and that I should be left behind lying on the ground.' I spent many pleasant days with these dear good people; and no words can express the horror I felt when we heard that they had been barbarously murdered in their bedroom. The eldest son and daughter had been at a ball somewhere near, and on coming home they found that one of the men-servants had dashed out the brains of both their parents with a poker. The motive remains a mystery to this day, for it was not robbery.

[After three years of married life, my mother returned to her father's house in Burntisland, a widow, with two little boys. The youngest died in childhood. The eldest was Woronzow Greig°, barrister-at-law, late Clerk of the Peace for Surrey. He died suddenly in 1865, to the unspeakable sorrow of his family, and the regret of all who knew him.]

[*1D, 56:* According to the plan I have laid down I pass over all family and domestic occurrences. I shall merely state, that after three years of married life, I returned to my father's house a widow with two sons, one at the breast. I was much out of health, my complexion very pure and pale and I wore a widow's cap; an old gentleman whom I had long known said my face was like the back of a silver spoon.]

I was much out of health after my husband's death, and chiefly occupied with my children, especially with the one I was nursing; but as I did not go into society, I rose early, and, having plenty of time, I resumed my mathematical studies. By this time I had studied plane and spherical trigonometry, conic sections, and Ferguson's *Astronomy*.[31] I think it was immediately after my return to Scotland that I attempted to read Newton's° *Principia*. I found it extremely difficult, and certainly did not understand it till I returned to it some time after, when I studied that wonderful work with great assiduity, and wrote numerous notes and observations on it. I obtained a loan of what I believe was called the Jesuit's edition, which helped me. At this period mathematical science was at a low ebb in Britain; reverence for Newton had prevented men from adopting the 'Calculus,' which had enabled foreign mathematicians to carry astronomical and mechanical science to the highest perfection. Professors Ivory° and De Morgan° had adopted the 'Calculus'; but several years elapsed before Mr Herschel° and Mr Babbage° were joint-editors with Professor Peacock° in publishing an abridged translation of Lacroix's° *Treatise on the Differential and Integral Calculus*. I became acquainted with Mr Wallace°, who was, if I am not mistaken, mathematical teacher of the Military College at Marlow, and editor of a mathematical journal published there. I had solved some of the problems contained in it and sent them to him, which led to a correspondence, as Mr Wallace sent me his own solutions in return. Mine were sometimes right and sometimes wrong, and it occasionally happened that we solved the same problem by different methods. At last I succeeded in solving a prize problem! It was a diophantine problem, and I was awarded a silver medal cast on purpose with my name, which pleased me exceedingly.

Mr Wallace was elected Professor of Mathematics in the University of Edinburgh, and was very kind to me. When I told him that I earnestly desired to go through a regular course of mathematical and astronomical science, even including the highest branches, he gave me a list of the requisite books, which were in French, and consisted of Francœur's pure *Mathematics*, and his *Elements of Mechanics*, Lacroix's *Algebra*, and his large work on the *Differential and Integral Calculus*, together with his work on *Finite Differences and Series*, Biot's° *Analytical Geometry and Astronomy*, Poisson's° *Treatise on Mechanics*, Lagrange's° *Theory of Analytical Functions*, Euler's *Algebra*, Euler's *Isoperimetrical Problems* (in Latin), Clairault's *Figure of the Earth*, Monge's *Application of Analysis to Geometry*, Callet's *Logarithms*, Laplace's° *Mécanique Céleste*, and his *Analytical Theory of Probabilities*, &c., &c., &c.[32]

I was thirty-three years of age when I bought this excellent little library. I could hardly believe that I possessed such a treasure when I looked back on the day that I first saw the mysterious word 'Algebra,' and the long course of years in which I had persevered almost without hope. It taught me never to despair. I had now the means, and pursued my studies with increased assiduity; concealment was no longer possible, nor was it attempted. I was considered eccentric and foolish, and my conduct was highly disapproved of by many, especially by some members of my own family, as will be seen hereafter. They expected me to entertain and keep a gay house for them, and in that they were disappointed. As I was quite independent, I did not care for their criticism.

A great part of the day I was occupied with my children; in the evening I worked, played piquet with my father, or played on the piano, sometimes with violin accompaniment.

[*1D, 59–61:* In Spring we went to Burntisland which I found sadly changed. Enormous shoals of herrings had come up the Firth, the very sea was rippled by them. They were pursued by flocks of marine birds and whales were seen spouting in various directions, the scene was animated and interesting but the primitive simplicity of the little town was gone. Multitudes of strangers had come to profit by the fishery and speculators built ugly brick houses on the Links for salting and smoking the fish. The fields in the vicinity were manured with the offal and the fish themselves; the air was tainted, the place became uninhabitable and our house and gardens were sold. The following summer we hired a small solitary house on an undulating pasture land between Burntisland and Kinghorn. On entering it I observed that the wall was rent from top to bottom, and was not at all pleased to hear that it was the effect of lightning, being aware that a place once struck was often liable to be struck again. However, I was in greater danger a few days after from a very different cause. My father generally went out with his gun or fishing rod to a lake at a little distance, and as my mother seldom went further than the garden, I resumed my wandering habit and often went in search of plants or merely for a walk on the undulating pasture land. I was not afraid of cattle till one day while heedlessly passing a herd of them I heard a loud bellowing and on looking round I saw a bull pawing the ground and coming towards me. I turned back and went to the top of an undulation and then ran down the other side hoping that when out of sight the bull would return to the herd, but I was no sooner at the bottom than I saw him on the top in full chase. I ran up the next undulation as the animal ran down the preceding, and he continued to pursue me for more than a quarter of a mile till I arrived half dead with fear and fatigue at our own door.]

This was the most brilliant period of *The Edinburgh Review*;[33] it was planned and conducted with consummate talent by a small society of men of the most liberal principles. Their powerful articles gave a severe and lasting blow to the oppressive and illiberal spirit which had hitherto prevailed. I became acquainted with some of these illustrious men, and with many of their immediate successors. I then met Henry Brougham°, who had so remarkable an influence on my future life. His sister had been my early companion, and while visiting her I saw her mother – a fine, intelligent old lady, a niece of Robertson the historian. I had seen the Rev. Sydney Smith°, that celebrated wit and able contributor to the *Review*, at Burntisland, where he and his wife came for sea-bathing. Long afterwards we lived on the most friendly terms till their deaths. Of that older group no one was more celebrated than Professor Playfair°. He knew that I was reading the *Mécanique Céleste*, and asked me how I got on? I told him that I was stopped short by a difficulty now and then, but I persevered till I got over it. He said, 'You would do better to read on for a few pages and return to it again, it will then no longer seem so difficult.' I invariably followed his advice and with much success.

Professor Playfair was a man of the most varied accomplishments and of the highest scientific distinction. He was an elderly man when I first became acquainted with him, by no means good-looking, but with a benevolent expression, somewhat concealed by the large spectacles he always wore. His manner was gravely cheerful; he was perfectly amiable, and was both respected and loved, but he could be a severe though just critic. He liked female society, and, philosopher as he was, marked attention from the sex obviously flattered him. [*2D, 57 in margin:* Mrs Apreece, afterwards Lady Davy°, did her best to captivate him and while out walking, she made him tie her shoe string which amused the Edinburgh gossips.]

I had now read a good deal on the higher branches of mathematics and physical astronomy, but as I never had been taught, I was afraid that I might imagine that I understood the subjects when I really did not; so by Professor Wallace's advice I engaged his brother to read with me, and the book I chose to study with him was the *Mécanique Céleste*. Mr John Wallace was a good mathematician, but I soon found that I understood the subject as well as he did. I was glad, however, to have taken this resolution, as it gave me confidence in myself and consequently courage to persevere. We had advanced but little in this work when my marriage with my cousin, William Somerville° (1812), put an end to scientific pursuits for a time.

SIX

Somerville Family – Dr Somerville's Character – Letters –
Journey to the Lakes – Death of Sir William Fairfax –
Reminiscences of Sir Walter Scott

[With regard to my father's family, I cannot do better than quote what my grandfather, the Rev. Thomas Somerville, says in his *Life and Times*: – 'I am a descendant of the ancient family of Somerville of Cambusnethan, which was a branch of the Somervilles of Drum, ennobled in the year 1424. Upon the death of George Somerville, of Corhouse, fifty years ago, I became the only male representative of the family.' There is a quaint old chronicle, entitled 'Memorie of the Somervilles,' written by James, eleventh Lord Somerville, who died in 1690, which was printed for private distribution, and edited by Sir Walter Scott, and gives ample details of all the branches of our family. Although infinitely too prolix for our nineteenth century ideas, it contains many curious anecdotes and pictures of Scottish life.

My father was the eldest son of the minister of Jedburgh, and until his marriage with my mother, had lived almost entirely abroad and in our colonies. It was always a subject of regret to my mother that my father never could be induced to publish an account of his important travels in South Africa, for which he had ample materials in the notes he brought home, many of which we still possess. Without being very deeply learned on any one special subject, he was generally well-informed, and very intelligent. He was an excellent classical scholar, and could repeat long passages from Horace and other authors. He had a lively interest in all branches of natural history, was a

good botanist and mineralogist, and could take note of all the
strange animals, plants, or minerals he saw in his adventurous
journeys in the countries, now colonised, but then the hunt-
ing-grounds of Caffres[34] and other uncivilised tribes. He was
the first white man who penetrated so far into the country, and
it was not without great risk. Indeed, on one occasion he was
sentenced to death by a Caffre chief, and only saved by the
interposition of the chief's mother.

My father's style in writing English was singularly pure and
correct, and he was very fastidious on this topic – a severe
critic, whether in correcting the children's lessons or in reading over the last proof sheets of my mother's works previous to
their publication. These qualities would have fitted him very
well to write the history of his travels, but he disliked the
trouble of it, and, never having the slightest ambition on his
own account, he let the time for publication slip by. Others
travelled over the country he first explored, and the novelty
was at an end. He was far happier in helping my mother in
various ways, searching the libraries for the books she required, indefatigably copying and recopying her manuscripts,
to save her time. No trouble seemed too great which he
bestowed upon her; it was a labour of love. My father was
most kindhearted, and I have often heard my mother say how
many persons he had assisted in life, and what generous
actions he had done, many of them requited with ingratitude,
and with betrayal of confidence. From the way my mother
speaks of their life, it can be seen how happy was their marriage
and how much sympathy there was between them. Speaking of
his son's marriage with my mother, the Rev. Dr Somerville
says, in his *Life and Times* page 390: 'To myself this connection
was on every account peculiarly gratifying. Miss Fairfax had
been born and nursed in my house; her father being at that
time abroad on public service. She afterwards often resided in
my family, was occasionally my scholar, and was looked upon
by me and my wife as if she had been one of our own children.
I can truly say, that next to them she was the object of our most

tender regard. Her ardent thirst for knowledge, her assiduous application to study, and her eminent proficiency in science and the fine arts, have procured her a celebrity rarely obtained by any of her sex. But she never displays any pretensions to superiority, while the affability of her temper, and the gentleness of her manners afford constant sources of gratification to her friends. But what, above all other circumstances, rendered my son's choice acceptable to me, was that it had been the anxious, though secret, desire of my dear wife.' I have already said that this esteem and affection of her father-in-law was warmly responded to by my mother. The following letter from her to him shows it vividly:—]

LETTER FROM MRS SOMERVILLE TO THE REV. DR SOMERVILLE

EDINBURGH, *1st June, 1812*

MY DEAR SIR,

I have this moment been gratified and delighted with your excellent and affectionate letter; the intercourse we have so long enjoyed has always been a source of the purest pleasure to me, and the kind interest you have taken from my infancy in my welfare was at all times highly flattering, and much valued; but now that the sacred name of Father is added, nothing is wanting to complete my happiness; and you may rest assured that William is not more anxious to hasten our visit to Jedburgh than I am . . . With the affectionate love of all here,
I remain your ever most affectionate daughter,
MARY SOMERVILLE

P.S. – I am much flattered by the Latin quotation, and feel happy that your instructions have enabled me to read it.

[I will now proceed with the extracts from my mother's *Recollections*:—]

My husband had been present at the taking of the Cape of Good Hope, and was sent by the authorities to make a treaty with the savage tribes on the borders of the colony, who had attacked the Boors, or Dutch farmers, and carried off their cattle. In this journey he was furnished with a waggon and accompanied by Mr Danicll°, a good artist, who made drawings of the scenery, as well as of the animals and people. The savage tribes again became troublesome, and in a second expedition my cousin was only accompanied by a faithful Hottentot as interpreter.[35] They were both mounted, and each led a spare horse with such things as were absolutely necessary, and when they bivouacked where, for fear of the natives, they did not dare light a fire to keep off the wild beasts, one kept watch while the other slept. After many adventures and dangers, my husband reached the Orange River, and was the first white man who had ever been in that part of Africa. He afterwards served in Canada and in Sicily at the head of the medical staff, under his friend General Sir James Craig°. On returning to England he generally lived in London, so that he was seldom with his family, with whom he was not a favourite on account of his liberal principles, the very circumstance that was an attraction to me. He had lived in the world, was extremely handsome, had gentlemanly manners, spoke good English, and was emancipated from Scotch prejudices.

I had been living very quietly with my parents and children, so until I was engaged to my cousin I was not aware of the extreme severity with which my conduct was criticised by his family, and I have no doubt by many others; for as soon as our engagement was known I received a most impertinent letter from one of his sisters, who was unmarried, and younger than I, saying, she 'hoped I would give up my foolish manner of life and studies, and make a respectable and useful wife to her brother.' I was extremely indignant. My husband was still more so, and wrote a severe and angry letter to her; none of the family dared to interfere again. I lived in peace with her, but there was a coldness and reserve between us ever after. I forgot to mention that during my widowhood I had several offers of marriage. One of the persons whilst he was paying court to me, sent me a volume of sermons with the page ostentatiously turned down at a sermon on the Duties of a Wife, which were expatiated upon in the most illiberal and narrow-minded language. I thought this as impertinent as it was premature; sent back the book and refused the proposal. [*2D, pinned to the foot of 57 in MS's hand:* It was the fashion of a set of ladies such as Mrs Hannah More°, Mrs Elizabeth Hamilton° and Mrs Grant° of Laggan to write on female education. I detested their books for they imposed such restraints and duties that they seemed to have been written to please men.]

My uncle, the Rev. Dr Somerville, was delighted with my marriage with his son, for he was liberal, and sincerely attached to me. We were married by his intimate friend, Sir Henry Moncreiff Wellwood, and set off for the lakes in Cumberland. My husband's second sister, Janet, resolved to go with us, and she succeeded through the influence of my aunt, now my mother-in-law – a very agreeable, but bold, determined person, who was always very kind and sincerely attached to me. We were soon followed by my cousin, Samuel Somerville° and his wife. We had only been a day or two in the little inn at Lowood when he was taken ill of a fever, which detained us there for more than a month. During his illness he took a longing for currant jelly, and here my cookery was needed; I made some that was excellent, and I never can forget the astonishment expressed at my being able to be so useful.

Somerville and I proceeded to London; and we managed to obtain a good position near Temple Bar to see the Emperor of Russia, the King of Prussia and his sons, Blücher, Platoff, the Hetman of the Cossacks, &c., &c.,

enter the City.[36] There was a brilliant illumination in the evening, and great excitement. We often saw these noted persons afterwards, but we did not stay long in London, as my husband was appointed head of the Army Medical Department in Scotland, so we settled in Edinburgh. As he was allowed to have a secretary, he made choice of Donald Finlayson, a young man of great learning and merit, who was to act as tutor to my son, Woronzow Greig, then attending the High School, of which Mr Pillans° was master. Mr Finlayson was a remarkably good Greek scholar, and my husband said, 'Why not take advantage of such an opportunity of improvement?' So I read Homer for an hour every morning before breakfast. Mr Finlayson joined the army as surgeon, and distinguished himself by his courage and humanity during the battle of Waterloo; but he was lost in the march of the army to Paris, and his brother George, after having sought for him in vain, came to live with us in his stead. He excelled in botany, and here again, by my husband's advice, I devoted a morning hour to that science, though I was nursing a baby at the time. I knew the vulgar name of most of the plants that Mr Finlayson° had gathered, but now I was taught systematically, and afterwards made a herbarium, both of land plants and fuci. This young man's hopeful career was early arrested by his love of science, for he died of jungle fever in Bengal, caught while in search of plants.

Professor Playfair was now old, and resigned his chair, which Mr Leslie° was perfectly competent to fill on account of his acknowledged scientific acquirements; but, being suspected of heretical opinions, his appointment was keenly opposed, especially on the part of the clergy, and a violent contest arose, which ended in his favour. We became acquainted with him and liked him. He was a man of original genius, full of information on a variety of subjects, agreeable in conversation and good natured, but with a singular vanity as to personal appearance.

Though one of the coarsest looking men I ever knew, he talked so much of polish and refinement that it tempted Mr William Clerk°, of Eldin, to make a very clever clay model of his ungainly figure. The professor's hair was grey, and he dyed it with something that made it purple; and, as at that time the art was not brought to its present perfection, the operation was tedious and only employed at intervals, so that the professor's hair was often white at the roots and dark purple at the extremities. He was always falling in love, and, to Somerville's inexpressible amusement, he made me his decoy duck, inviting me to see some experiments, which he performed dexterously; at the same time telling me to bring as many young ladies as I chose, especially Miss—, for he was sure she had a turn for science. He was unfortunate in his aspirations, and remained a bachelor to the end of his life.

It was the custom in Edinburgh, especially among the clergy, to dine between the morning and evening service on Sundays, and to sup at nine or ten o'clock. In no family were these suppers more agreeable or cheerful than in that of Sir Henry Moncreiff Wellwood, minister of the West Kirk. There were always a few of the friends of Sir Henry and Lady Moncreiff present, and we were invited occasionally. There was a substantial hot supper of roasted fowls, game, or lamb, and afterwards a lively, animated conversation on a variety of subjects, without a shade of austerity, though Sir Henry was esteemed an orthodox preacher.

There was an idiot in Edinburgh, the son of a respectable family, who had a remarkable memory. He never failed to go to the Kirk on Sunday, and on returning home could repeat the sermon word for word, saying, Here the minister coughed, Here he stopped to blow his nose. During the tour we made in the Highlands we met with another idiot who knew the Bible so perfectly that if you asked him where such a verse was to be found, he could tell without hesitation, and repeat the chapter. The common people in Scotland at that time had a kind of serious compassion for these harmless idiots, because 'the hand of God was upon them.'

The wise as well as the foolish are sometimes endowed with a powerful memory. Dr Gregory°, an eminent Edinburgh physician, one of the cleverest and most agreeable men I ever met with, was a remarkable instance of this. He wrote and spoke Latin fluently, and Somerville, who was a good Latinist, met with a Latin quotation in some book he was reading, but not knowing from whence it was taken, asked his friend Dr Gregory. 'It is forty years since I read that author,' said Dr Gregory, 'but I think you will find the passage in the middle of such a page.' Somerville went for the book, and at the place mentioned there it was.

[*1D, 66b:* George IV had been handsome when young and vain of his good looks, he was fond of eating, lived luxuriously, and the dissipated life he led told so much on him as he advanced in years that he became fat, red faced and bloated which annoyed him so much that he consulted Dr Gregory then in the highest repute. 'What shall I take?' 'Nothing, Sir, I recommend your Majesty to follow the advice which that renowned physician Don Tirteafuera gave to — in *Don Quixote.*' The king neither liked nor followed the advice.][37]

I had the grief to lose my dear father at this time. He had served sixty-seven years in the British Navy, and must have been twice on the North American station, for he was present at the taking of Quebec by General Wolfe, in 1759,[38] and afterwards during the War of Independence. After the battle of Camperdown he was made a Colonel of Marines, and died, in 1813, Vice-Admiral of the Red.

Geology, which has now been so far advanced as a science, was still in its infancy. Professor Playfair and Mr Hugh

Miller° had written on the subject; and in my gay young days, when Lady Helen Hall was occasionally my chaper-one, I had heard that Sir James Hall° had taken up the subject, but I did not care about it; I am certain that at that time I had never heard the word 'geology.' I think it was now, on going with Somerville to see the Edinburgh Museum, that I recognised the fossil plants I had seen in the coal limestone on the sands at the Links of Burntis-land. Ultimately geology became a favourite pursuit of ours, but then minerals were the objects of our joint study. Mineralogy had been much cultivated on the Continent by this time, especially in Germany. It had been established as a science by Werner°, who was educated at an institution near the silver mines of Freiburg, where he afterwards lectured on the properties of crystals, and had many pupils. In one of our tours on the Continent, Somerville and I went to see these silver mines and bought some specimens for our cabinet. The French took up the subject with great zeal, and the Abbé Haüy's° work became a standard book on the science. Cabinets of minerals had been established in the principal cities of Great Britain, professors were appointed in the universities, and collections of minerals were not uncommon in private houses. While quite a girl, I went with my parents to visit the Fergusons° of Raith, near Kirkcaldy, and there I saw a magnificent collection of minerals, made by their son while abroad. It contained gems of great value and crystallised specimens of precious and other metals, which surprised and interested me; but seeing that such valuable things could never be obtained by me, I thought no more about them. In those early days I had every difficulty to contend with; now, through the kindness and liberal opinions of my husband, I had every encouragement. He took up the study of mineralogy with zeal, and I heartily joined with him. We made the acquain-tance of Professor Jameson°, a pupil of Werner's, whose work on mineralogy was of great use to us. We began to form a cabinet of minerals, which, although small, were good of their kind. We were criticised for extravagance, and, no doubt I had the lion's share of blame; but more of minerals hereafter.

Abbotsford is only twelve miles distant from Jedburgh, and my father-in-law, Dr Somerville, and Sir Walter Scott had been intimate friends for many years, indeed through life. The house at Abbotsford was at first a mere cottage, on the banks of the Tweed; my brother-in-law, Samuel, had a villa adjacent to it, and John, Lord Somerville, had a house and property on the opposite bank of the river, to which he came every spring for salmon fishing. He was a handsome, agreeable man, had been educated in England, and as he thought he should never live in Scotland, he sold the family estate of Drum, within five miles of Edinburgh, which he afterwards regretted, and bought the property on the Tweed he then inhabited.

There was great intimacy between the three families, and the society was often enlivened by Adam Ferguson° and Willie Clerk, whom we had met with at Raith. I shall never forget the charm of this little society, especially the supper-parties at Abbotsford, when Scott was in the highest glee, telling amusing tales, ancient legends, ghost and witch stories. Then Adam Ferguson would sing the 'Laird of Cockpen,' and other comic songs, and Willie Clerk amused us with his dry wit. When it was time to go away all rose, and, standing hand-in-hand round the table, Scott taking the lead, we sang in full chorus,

> Weel may we a' be,
> Ill may we never see;
> Health to the king
> And the gude companie.

At that time no one knew who was the author of the *Waverley Novels*. There was much speculation and curiosity on the subject. While talking about one which had just been published, my son Woronzow said, 'I knew all these stories long ago, for Mr Scott writes on the dinner-table. When he has finished, he puts the green-cloth with the papers in a corner of the dining-room; and when he goes out, Charlie Scott and I read the stories.' My son's tutor was the original of Dominie Sampson in *Guy Mannering*.[39] The *Memorie of the Somervilles* was edited by Walter Scott, from an ancient and very quaint manuscript found in the archives of the family, and from this he takes passages which he could not have found elsewhere. Although the work was printed it was never published, but copies were distributed to the different members of the family. One was of course given to my husband.

The Burning of the Water, so well described by Walter Scott in *Guy Mannering*, we often witnessed.[40] The illumination of the banks of the river, the activity of the men striking the salmon with the 'leisters,' and the shouting of the people when a fish was struck, was an animated, and picturesque, but cruel scene.

Sophia Scott, afterwards married to Mr Lockhart°, editor of *The Quarterly Review*, was the only one of Sir Walter's family who had talent. She was not pretty, but remarkably engaging and agreeable, and possessed her father's joyous disposition as well as his memory and fondness for ancient Border legends and poetry. Like him, she was thoroughly alive to peculiarities of character, and laughed at them good-naturedly. She was not a musician, had little voice, but she sang Scotch songs and translations from the Gaelic with, or without, harp accompaniment; the serious songs with so much expression, and the merry ones with so much spirit, that she charmed everybody. The death of her brothers and of her father, to whom she was devotedly attached, cast a shade over the latter part of her life. Mr Lockhart was clever and an able writer, but he was too sarcastic to be quite agreeable; however, we were always on the most friendly terms. He was of a Lanarkshire family and distantly related to Somerville. After the death of his wife and sons, Lockhart fell into bad health and lost much of his asperity.

Scott was ordered to go abroad for relaxation. Somerville and I happened to be at the seaport where he embarked, and we went to take leave of him. He kissed me, and said, 'Farewell, my dear; I am going to die abroad like other British novelists.' Happy would it have been if God had so willed it, for he returned completely broken down; his hopes were blighted, his sons dead, and his only remaining descendant was a grand-daughter, daughter of Mrs Lockhart. She married Mr James Hope°, and soon died, leaving an only daughter, the last descendant of Sir Walter Scott. Thus the 'Merry, merry days that I have seen,' ended very sadly.

When at Jedburgh, I never failed to visit James Veitch°, who was Laird of Inchbonny, a small property beautifully situated in the valley of the Jed, at a short distance from the manse. He was a ploughwright, a hard-working man, but of rare genius, who taught himself mathematics and astronomy in the evenings with wonderful success, for he knew the motions of the planets, calculated eclipses and occultations, was versed in various scientific subjects, and made excellent telescopes, of which I bought a very small one; it was the only one I ever possessed. Veitch was handsome, with a singularly fine bald forehead and piercing eyes, that quite looked through one. He was perfectly aware of his talents, shrewd, and sarcastic. His fame had spread, and he had many visits, of which he was impatient, as it wasted his time. He complained especially of those from ladies not much skilled in science, saying, 'What should they do but ask silly questions, when they spend their lives in doing naething but spatting muslin?' Veitch was strictly religious and conscientious, observing the Sabbath day with great solemnity; and I had the impression that he was stern to his wife, who seemed to be a person of intelligence, for I remember seeing her come from the washing-tub to point out the planet Venus while it was still daylight.

The return of Halley's comet, in 1835, exactly at the computed time, was a great astronomical event, as it was the first comet of long period clearly proved to belong to our system. I was asked by Mr John Murray° to write an article on the subject for *The Quarterly Review*.[41] After it was published, I received a letter from James Veitch, reproaching me for having mentioned that a peasant in Hungary was the first to see Halley's comet, and for having omitted to say that, 'a peasant at Inchbonny was the first to see the comet of 1811, the greatest that had appeared for a century.' I regretted, on receiving this letter, that I either had not known, or had forgotten the circumstance. Veitch has been long dead, but I avail myself of this opportunity of making the *amende honorable* to a man of great mental power and acquirements who had struggled through difficulties, un-aided, as I have done myself.

LETTER FROM JAMES VEITCH TO MRS SOMERVILLE

INCHBONNY, *12th October, 1836*

DEAR MADAM,

I saw in the Quarterly review for December 1835 page 216 that the comet 1682 was discovered by a Peasent, George Palitzch residing in the neighbourhood of Dresden on the 25th of December 1758 with a small Telescope. But no mention is made of the Peasent at Inchbonny who first discovered the beautiful comet 1811. You will remember when Dr. Wollaston° was at Inchbonny I put a difficult question to him that I could not solve about the focal distance of optic glasses when the Dr. got into a passion and said: Had he problems in his pocket ready to pull out in every occasion? and with an angry look at me said, You pretend to be the first that discovered the comet altho' it has been looked for by men of science for some time back. Now I never heard of such a thing and you will perhaps know something about it as the Dr. would not be mistaken. After we got acquainted, the Dr. was a warm friend of mine and I have often regretted that I had not improved the opportunity I had when he was here on many things he was master of. What ever others had known or expected I knew nothing about, But I know this, that on the 27th of August 1811 I first saw it in the NNW. part of the Heavens nigh the star marked 26 on the shoulder of the little Lion and continued treacing its path among the fixed stars until it dissapeared and it was generally admitted that I had discovered it four days before any other person in Britain. However Mr. Thomas Dick on the Diffusion of Knowledge page 101 and 102 has made the following observation 'The splendid comet which appeared in our hemisphere in 1811 was first discovered in this country by a sawer. The name of this Gentleman is Mr. Veitch and I believe he resides in the neighbourhood of Kelso who with a Reflecting telescope of his own construction and from his sawpit as an observatory, descried that celestial visitant before it had been noticed by any other astronomer in North Britain.'[42] A strange story – a sawer and a gentleman; and what is stranger still Mr. Baily° would not have any place but the sawpit for his observatory on the 15th May last. I am sorry to say with all the improvement and learning that we can bost of in the present day Halley's comet the predictions have not been fulfilled, either with respect to time or place. Thus on the 10 October, at 50 minutes past 5 in the evening the Right ascension of the comet was $163° 37'$, with $63° 38'$ of north declination but by the nautical almanac for the 10 October its right ascension ought to have been $225° 2' 6$, and its declination $29° 33'$. Hence the difference is no less than $61°$ in Right ascension and $34°$ in declination. When you have time, write me.

Dear Madam, I remain,

Yours sincerely,

JAMES VEITCH

Sir David Brewster was many years younger than James Veitch; in his early years he assisted his father in teaching the parish-school at Jedburgh, and in the evenings he went to Inchbonny to study astronomy with James Veitch, who always called him Davie. They were as much puzzled about the meaning of the word parallax[43] as I had been with regard to the word 'algebra,' and only learnt what it meant when Brewster went to study for the kirk in Edinburgh. They were both very devout; nevertheless, Brewster soon gave up the kirk for science, and he devoted himself especially to optics, in which he made so many discoveries. Sir David was of ordinary height, with fair or sandy-coloured hair and blue eyes. He was by no means good-looking, yet with a very pleasant, amiable expression; in conversation he was cheerful and agreeable when quite at ease, but of a timid, nervous, and irritable temperament, often at war with his fellow-philosophers upon disputed subjects, and extremely jealous upon priority of discovery. I was much indebted to Sir David, for he reviewed my book on the *Connexion of the Physical Sciences*, in the April number of *The Edinburgh Review* for 1834, and the *Physical Geography* in the April number of *The North British Review*, both favourably.

SEVEN

Life in Hanover Square – Visit to France – Arago – Cuvier – Rome

[My father was appointed, in 1816, a member of the Army Medical Board, and it became necessary for him to reside in London. He and my mother accordingly wished farewell to Scotland, and proceeded to take up their residence in Hanover Square. My mother preserved the following recollections of this journey:—]

———————————

ON our way we stopped a day at Birmingham, on purpose to see Watt and Boulton's manufactory of steam engines at Soho. Mr Boulton showed us everything.[44] The engines, some in action, although beautifully smooth, showed a power that was almost fearful. Since these early forms of the steam engine I have lived to see this all but omnipotent instrument change the locomotion of the whole civilised world by sea and by land.

[*1D, 74:* There is now a railway over the top of Mont Cenis, and a tunnel seven miles long through the Alps will be opened in a few years, so notwithstanding the wisdom of Solomon there is a good deal new under the sun.[45] I wonder what will be discovered and done before the year 1968. What is left to do? Perhaps to fly if they can carry a point of resistance aloft in a balloon the Mr Glaisher° of that day may become acquainted with 'the man i' the moon and his dog and his bush.']

Soon after our arrival in London we became acquainted
with the illustrious family of the Herschels, through the
kindness of our friend Professor Wallace, for it was by his
arrangement that we spent a day with Sir William° and
Lady Herschel, at Slough. Nothing could exceed the kindness of Sir William. He made us examine his celebrated
telescopes, and explained their mechanism; and he showed
us the manuscripts which recorded the numerous astronomical discoveries he had made. They were all arranged
in the most perfect order, as was also his musical library, for
that great genius was an excellent musician. Unfortunately,
his sister, Miss Caroline Herschel°, who shared in the
talents of the family, was abroad, but his son, afterwards
Sir John, my dear friend for many years, was at home, quite
a youth. It would be difficult to name a branch of the
physical sciences which he has not enriched by important
discoveries. He has ever been a dear and valued friend to
me, whose advice and criticism I gratefully acknowledge.

I took lessons twice a week from Mr Glover°, who painted
landscapes very prettily, and I liked him on account of his
kindness to animals, especially birds, which he tamed so
that they flew before him when he walked, or else sat on the
trees, and returned to him when he whistled. I regret now
that I ever resumed my habit of painting in oil; water-
colours are much better suited to an amateur, but as I had
never seen any that were good, I was not aware of their
beauty. [*1D, 82:* Now some ladies draw like first rate artists,
and hundreds of girls sketch beautifully. Water-colours
have an advantage in this respect, that the real light is
reflected through the colour from the surface of the paper
which gives a brilliancy only to be attained in oil by
contrast.]

I also took lessons in mineralogy from Mrs Lowry°, a
Jewess, the wife of an eminent line engraver, who had a
large collection of minerals, and in the evening Somerville

and I amused ourselves with our own, which were not numerous.

Our house in Hanover Square was within a walking distance of many of our friends, and of the Royal Institution in Albemarle Street, where I attended the lectures, and Somerville frequently went with me.[46] The discoveries of Sir Humphry Davy° made this a memorable epoch in the annals of chemical science. At this time there was much talk about the celebrated Count Rumford's° steam kitchen,[47] by which food was to be cooked at a very small expense of fuel. It was adopted by several people, and among others by Naldi°, the opera singer, who invited some friends to dine the first day it was to be used. Before dinner they all went to see the new invention, but while Naldi was explaining its structure, it exploded and killed him on the spot. By this sad accident his daughter, a pretty girl and a good singer, was left destitute. A numerously-attended concert was given for her benefit, at which Somerville and I were present. She was soon after engaged to sing in Paris, but ultimately married the Comte de Sparre, a French gentleman, and left the stage.

When MM. Arago° and Biot came to England to continue the French arc of the meridian through Great Britain, they were warmly received by the scientific men in London, and we were always invited to meet them by those whom we knew. They had been told of my turn for science, and that I had read the works of Laplace. Biot expressed his surprise at my youth.

One summer Somerville proposed to make a tour in Switzerland, so we set off, and on arriving at Chantilly we were told that we might see the château upon giving our cards to the doorkeeper. On reading our name, Mademoiselle de Rohan came to meet us, saying that she had been at school in England with a sister of Lord Somerville's, and was glad to see any of the family. She presented us to the

Prince de Condé°, a fine-looking old man, who received us very courteously, and sent the lord-in-waiting to show us the grounds, and especially the stables, the only part of the castle left in its regal magnificence after the Revolution. The Prince and the gentleman who accompanied us wore a gaudy uniform like a livery, which we were told was the Chantilly uniform, and that at each palace belonging to the Prince there was a different uniform worn by him and his court.

[*1D, 83–84:* At Chantilly I bought a very handsome black lace dress which I wore over white or rose coloured satin. I could afford to buy good things, for variety was not the fashion as it is now; but I was never extravagant. I must confess that I was fond of dress and had such good taste that my cousins and companions copied my style of dress so closely that I was sometimes provoked.]

At Paris we were received with the kindest hospitality by M. and Madame Arago. I liked her much, she was so gentle and ladylike; he was tall and good-looking, with an animated countenance and black eyes. His character was noble, generous, and singularly energetic; his manners lively and even gay. He was a man of very general information, and, from his excitable temperament, he entered as ardently into the politics and passing events of the time as into science, in which few had more extensive knowledge. On this account I thought his conversation more brilliant than that of any of the French savants with whom I was acquainted. They were living at the Observatory, and M. Arago showed me all the instruments of that magnificent establishment in the minutest detail, which was highly interesting at the time, and proved more useful to me than I was aware of. M. Arago made us acquainted with the Marquis de Laplace, and the Marquise, who was quite an *élégante*. The Marquis was not tall, but thin, upright, and rather formal. He was distinguished in his manners, and I thought there was a little of the courtier in them, perhaps from having been so much at the court of the Emperor Napoleon, who had the highest regard for him. Though incomparably superior to Arago in mathematics and astronomical science, he was inferior to him in general acquirements, so that his conversation was less varied and popular. We were invited to go early and spend a day with them at Arcœuil, where they had a country house. M. Arago had told M. de Laplace that I had read the *Mécanique Céleste*, so we had a great deal of conversation about astronomy and the calculus, and he gave me a copy of his *Système du Monde* with his inscription, which pleased me exceedingly. I spoke French very badly, but I was less at a loss on scientific subjects, because almost all my books on science were in French. The party at dinner consisted of MM. Biot, Arago, Bouvard°, and Poisson. I sat next M. de Laplace, who was exceedingly kind and attentive. In such an assemblage of philosophers I expected a very grave and learned conversation. But not at all! Everyone talked in a gay, animated, and loud key, especially M. Poisson, who had all the vivacity of a Frenchman. Madame Biot, from whom we received the greatest attention, made a party on purpose, as she said, to show us, '*les personnes distinguées.*' Madame Biot was a well-educated woman, and had made a translation from the German of a work, which was published under the name of her husband. The dinner was very good, and Madame Biot was at great pains in placing every one. Those present were Monsieur and Madame Arago, Monsieur and Madame Poisson, who had only been married the day before, and Baron Humboldt°. The conversation was lively and entertaining.

The consulate and empire of the first Napoleon was the most brilliant period of physical astronomy in France. Lagrange, who proved the stability of the solar system, Laplace, Biot, Arago, Bouvard, and afterwards Poinsot, formed a perfect constellation of undying names; yet the French had been for many years inferior to the English in practical astronomy. The observations made at Greenwich by Bradley°, Maskelyne°, and Pond°, have been so admirably continued under the direction of the present Astronomer Royal, Mr Airy°, the first practical astronomer in Europe, that they have furnished data for calculating the astronomical tables both in France and England.

The theatre was at this time very brilliant in Paris. We saw Talma°, who was considered to be the first tragedian of the age in the character of Tancrède. I admired the skill with which he overcame the disagreeable effect which the rhyme of the French tragedies has always had on me. Notwithstanding his personal advantages, I thought him a great artist, though inferior to John Kemble. I am afraid my admiration of Shakespeare, my want of sympathy with the artificial style of French tragedy, and perhaps my youthful remembrance of our great tragedian Mrs Siddons, made me unjust to Mademoiselle Duchênois°, who, although ugly, was certainly an excellent actress and a favourite of the public. I was so fond of the theatre that I enjoyed comedy quite as much as tragedy, and was delighted with Mademoiselle Mars°, whom we saw in *Tartuffe*. Some years later I saw her again, when, although an old woman, she still appeared handsome and young upon the stage, and was as graceful and lively as ever.

Soon after our dinner party at Arcœuil, we went to pay a morning visit to Madame de Laplace. It was late in the day; but she received us in bed elegantly dressed. I think the curtains were of muslin with some gold ornaments, and the coverlet was of rich silk and gold. It was the first time that I had ever seen a lady receive in that manner. Madame de Laplace was lively and agreeable; I liked her very much.

We spent a most entertaining day with M. and Madame Cuvier° at the Jardin des Plantes,[48] and saw the Museum, and everything in that celebrated establishment. On returning to the house, we found several people had come to spend the evening, and the conversation was carried on with a good deal of spirit; the Countess Albrizzi°, a Venetian lady, of high acquirements, joined in it with considerable talent and animation. Cuvier had a very remarkable countenance, not handsome, but agreeable, and his manner was pleasing and modest, and his conversation very interesting. Madame de Staël° having died lately, was much discussed. She was much praised for her good-nature, and for the brilliancy of her conversation. They agreed, that the energy of her character, not old age, had worn her out. Cuvier said, the force of her imagination misled her judgment, and made her see things in a light different from all the world. As a proof of this, he mentioned that she makes Corinne lean on a marble lion which is on a tomb in St Peter's, at Rome, more than twenty feet high.[49] Education was very much discussed. Cuvier said, that when he was sent to inspect the schools at Bordeaux and Marseilles, he found very few of the scholars who could perform a simple calculation in arithmetic; as to science, history, or literature, they were unknown, and the names of the most celebrated French philosophers, famed in other countries, were utterly unknown to those who lived in the provinces. M. Biot had written home, that he had found in Aberdeen not one alone, but many, who perfectly understood the object of his journey, and were competent to converse with him on the subject. Cuvier said such a circumstance constituted one of the striking differences between France and England; for in France science was highly cultivated, but confined to the capital. It was at M. Cuvier's that I first met Mr Pentland°, who made a series of physical and geological observations on the Andes of Peru. I was residing in Italy when I published my *Physical Geography*, and Mr Pentland kindly undertook to carry the book through the press for me. From that time he has been a steady friend, ever ready to get me information, books, or anything I wanted. We became acquainted also with M. Gay-Lussac°, who lived in the Jardin des Plantes,

and with Baron Larrey°, who had been at the head of the
medical department of the army in Egypt under the first
Napoleon.

At Paris I equipped myself in proper dresses, and we
proceeded by Fontainebleau to Geneva, where we found
Dr Marcet°, with whom my husband had already been
acquainted in London. I, for the first time, met Mrs
Marcet°, with whom I have ever lived on terms of affectionate friendship. So many books have now been published for young people, that no one at this time can duly
estimate the importance of Mrs Marcet's scientific works.
To them is partly owing that higher intellectual education
now beginning to prevail among the better classes in
Britain. They produced a great sensation, and went
through many editions. Her *Conversations on Chemistry*,
first opened out to Faraday's° mind that field of science
in which he became so illustrious, and at the height of his
fame he always mentioned Mrs Marcet with deep reverence.

Through these kind friends we became acquainted with
Professors De Candolle°, Prévost°, and De la Rive°. Other
distinguished men were also presented to us; among these
was Mr Sismondi°, author of the *History of the Italian
Republics'*. Madame Sismondi was a Miss Allen, of a family
with whom we were very intimate.

[Some time after her return to England, my mother, desirous of continuing the study of botany, in which she had
already attained considerable proficiency, wrote to M. De
Candolle, asking his advice, and he sent her the following
reply:—]

LETTER FROM M. DE CANDOLLE TO
MRS SOMERVILLE

LONDRES, *5 Juin, 1819*

MADAME,

Vous avez passé les premières difficultés de l'étude des plantes et vous me faites l'honneur de me consulter sur les moyens d'aller en avant; connaissant votre goût et votre talent pour les sciences les plus relevées je ne craindrai point de vous engager à sortir de la Botanique élémentaire et à vous élever aux considérations et aux études qui en font une science susceptible d'idées générales, d'applications aux choses utiles et de liaison avec les autres branches des connaissances humaines. Pour cela il faut étudier non plus seulement la nomenclature et l'échafaudage artificiel qui la soutient, mais les rapports des plantes entre elles et avec les élémens extérieures, ou en d'autres termes, la classification naturelle et la Physiologie.

Pour l'un et l'autre de ces branches de la science il est nécessaire en premier lieu de se familiariser avec la structure des plantes considérée dans leur caractère exacte. Vous trouverez un précis abrégé de ces caractères dans le 1er vol. de la Flore française; vous le trouverez plus développé et accompagné de planches dans les Elémens de Botanique de Michel. Quant à la structure du fruit qui est un des points les plus difficiles et les plus importans, vous allez avoir un bon ouvrage traduit et augmenté par un de vos jeunes et habiles compatriotes, Mr. Lindley – c'est l'analyse du fruit de M. Richard. La traduction vaudra mieux que l'original. Outre ces lectures, ce qui vous apprendra surtout la structure des plantes, c'est de les analyser et de les décrire vous-même d'après les termes techniques; ce travail deviendrait pénible et inutile à faire sur un grand nombre de plantes, et il vaut mieux ne le faire que sur un très petit nombre d'espèces choisies dans des classes très distinctes. Quelques descriptions faites aussi complètes qu'il vous sera possible vous apprendra plus que tous les livres.

Dès que vous connaîtrez bien les organes et concurremment avec cette étude vous devrez chercher à prendre une idée de la classification naturelle. Je crains de vous paraître présomptueux en vous engageant à lire d'abord sous ce point de vue ma Théorie élémentaire. Après ces études on à peu près en même temps pour profiter de la saison, vous ferez bien de rapporter aux ordres naturels toutes les plantes que vous aurez recueillies. La lecture des caractères des familles faites la plante à la main et l'acte de ranger vos plantes en familles vous feront connaître par théorie et par pratique ces groupes naturels. Je vous engage dans cette étude, surtout en le commencement, à ne donner que peu d'attention au système général qui lie les familles, mais beaucoup à la connaissance de la physionomie qui est propre à chacune d'elles. Sous ce point de vue vous pourrez trouver quelque intérêt à lire – 1° les Tableaux de la Nature de M. de Humboldt; 2° mon essai sur les propriétés des plantes comparées avec leurs formes extérieures; 3° les remarques sur la géographie botanique de la Nouvelle Hollande et de l'Afrique, insérés par M. Robt. Brown° à la fin du voyage de Flinders° et de l'expedition au Congo.

Quant à l'étude de la Physiologie ou de la connaissance des végétaux considérés comme êtres vivans, je vous engage à lire les ouvrages dans l'ordre suivant: Philibert, Elémens de Bot. et de Phys., 3 vols.; la 2de partie des principes élémentaires de la Bot. de la Flore française. Vous trouverez la partie anatomique dans l'ouvrage de Mirbel; la partie chimique dans les recherches chimiques sur la Veget. de T. de Saussure; la partie statique dans la statique des végétaux de Hales, &c. &c. Mais je vous engage surtout à voir par vous-même les plantes à tous leurs ages, à suivre leur végétation, à les décrire en détail, en un mot à vivre avec elles plus qu'avec les livres.

Je désire, madame, que ces conseils puissent vous engager à suivre l'étude des plantes sous cette direction qui je crois en relève beaucoup l'importance et l'intérêt. Je m'estimerai heureux si en vous l'indiquant je puis concourir à vos succès futures et à vous initier dans une étude que j'ai toujours regardé comme une de celles qui peut le plus contribuer au bonheur journalier.

Je vous prie d'agréer mes hommages empressés.

DE CANDOLLE

———————————

We had made the ordinary short tour through Switzerland, and had arrived at Lausanne on our way home, when I was taken ill with a severe fever which detained us there for many weeks. I shall never forget the kindness I received from two Miss Barclays°, Quaker ladies, and a Miss Fotheringham, who, on hearing of my illness, came and sat up alternate nights with me, as if I had been their sister. [*1D, 91:* One day while still very weak, etc. I was unconsciously singing in a low feeble voice 'Angels ever bright and fair' when Somerville came into the room thinking I was delirious, 'Oh no,' I said, 'I was only thinking of Handel's music and Mrs Kater's sweet voice.' I recovered very slowly, and was annoyed at having my hair cut off, but enough was left in front to make flat curls, then the mode.]

The winter was now fast approaching, and Somerville thought that in my weak state a warm climate was necessary; so we arranged with our friends, the Miss Barclays, to pass the Simplon together. We parted company at Milan, but we renewed our friendship in London.

[*1D, 91:* We had a letter of introduction from a Milanese lady who happened to be out of town but she lent us the key of her opera box. The servant who brought the key asked if I wished the lamp to be lighted, I said yes not in the least aware that it was a signal that the lady received her male friends, so as I knew nobody, nobody came.]

We went to Monza, and saw the iron crown;[50] and there I found the Magnolia grandiflora, which hitherto I had only known as a greenhouse plant, rising almost into a forest tree.

At Venice we renewed our acquaintance with the Countess Albrizzi, who received every evening. It was at these receptions that we saw Lord Byron°, but he would not make the acquaintance of any English people at that time. When he came into the room I did not perceive his lameness, and thought him strikingly like my brother Henry, who was remarkably handsome. I said to Somerville, 'Is Lord Byron like anyone you know?' 'Your brother Henry, decidedly.' Lord Broughton, then Sir John Cam Hobhouse°, was also present.

At Florence, I was presented to the Countess of Albany°, widow of Prince Charles Edward Stuart the Pretender. She was then supposed to be married to Alfieri° the poet, and had a kind of state reception every evening. I did not like her, and never went again. Her manner was proud and insolent. 'So you don't speak Italian; you must have had a very bad education, for Miss Clephane Maclane° there [who was close by] speaks both French and Italian perfectly.' So saying, she turned away, and never addressed another word to me. That evening I recognised in Countess Moretti my old friend Agnes Bonar. Moretti was of good family; but, having been banished from home for political opinions, he taught the guitar in London for bread, and an attachment was formed between him and his pupil. After the murder of her parents, they were both persecuted with the most unrelenting cruelty by her brother. They escaped to Milan where they were married.

I was still a young woman; but I thought myself too old to learn to speak a foreign language, consequently I did not try. I spoke French badly; and now, after several years' residence in Italy, although I can carry on a conversation fluently in Italian, I do not speak it well. [*1D, 94–95:* I never attempted to write either French or Italian and being an almost uneducated Scotch woman I had much trouble in writing English, especially at first, and never was aware of any errors till I saw them printed in my proof sheets; especially the use of 'shall' and 'will', 'could' and 'should', 'these' and 'those'; yet I was complemented on the English in some of my books by the Rev. Sydney Smith one of the best writers of the day. As for spelling I am very bad at it, even now, that I am writing in extreme old age. On comparing notes with my dear old friend, Joanna Baillie° the poetess, who agreed with me in points much more important than that of spelling, we were not a little amused to find that in writing a letter we made use of words we could spell, not those we should have used in conversation. In writing for the press I generally consulted a dictionary, sometimes when lazy I trust to the compositor for spelling, always for pointing. But my MSS are well written and easy to read, but my hand shakes sadly now, especially when I first begin to write in the morning.]

[When my mother first went abroad, she had no fluency in talking French, although she was well acquainted with the literature. To show how, at every period of her life, she missed no opportunity of acquiring information or improvement, I may mention that many years after, when we were spending a summer in Siena, where the language is spoken with great purity and elegance, she engaged a lady to converse in Italian with her for a couple of hours daily. By this means she very soon became perfectly familiar with the language, and could keep up conversation in Italian without difficulty. She never cared to write in any language but English. Her style has been reckoned particularly clear and good, and she was complimented on it by various competent judges, although she herself was always diffident about her writings, saying she was only a self-taught, uneducated Scotchwoman, and feared to use Scotch idioms inadvertently. In speaking she had a very decided but pleasant Scotch accent, and when aroused and excited, would often unconsciously use not only native idioms, but quaint old Scotch words. Her voice was soft and low, and her manner earnest.]

[*1D, 96:* During our tour we had seen the pictures in the Louvre, Brera,[51] at Venice, Parma, and now those in the Uffizi and Pitti palace at Florence. I was bewildered by the number of pictures I had seen in such rapid succession, and being totally ignorant of the highest branch of art, my admiration of them was merely an instinctive feeling of their beauty. Ignorant as I was I could not fail to perceive a vast difference in the character and style of the pictures, but even now after having lived so many years in Italy, were I called upon to name the artists, I should make many mistakes. It has required long cultivation to make me appreciate the exquisite sentiment expressed in frescoes and pre-Raphaelite pictures.]

On our way to Rome, where we spent the winter of 1817, it was startling to see the fine church of Santa Maria degli Angeli, below Assisi, cut in two; half of the church and half of the dome above it were still entire; the rest had been thrown down by the earthquake which had destroyed the neighbouring town of Foligno,[52] and committed such ravages in this part of Umbria. [*1D, 97:* We travelled slowly enjoying the scenery so we had time to collect specimens of a flora entirely new to me and I stopped the carriage frequently to gather flowers a pleasure we are now deprived of by railway travelling. The journey would have been delightful but for the dirtiness of the hotels which was a real distress to us nor was it less at Rome.]

At that time I might have been pardoned if I had described St Peter's, the Vatican, and the innumerable treasures of art and antiquity at Rome; but now that they are so well known it would be ridiculous and superfluous. Here I gained a little more knowledge about pictures; but I preferred sculpture, partly from the noble specimens of Greek art I saw in Paris and Rome, and partly because I was such an enthusiast about the language and everything belonging to ancient Greece. During this journey I was highly gratified, for we made the acquaintance of Thorwaldsen° and Canova°. Canova was gentle and amiable, with a beautiful countenance, and was an artist of great reputation. Thorwaldsen had a noble and striking appearance, and had more power and originality than Canova. His bas-reliefs were greatly admired. I saw the one he made of Night in the house of an English lady, who had a talent for modelling, and was said to be attached to him. We were presented to Pope Pius the Seventh°; a handsome, gentlemanly, and amiable old man. He received us in a summerhouse in the garden of the Vatican. He was sitting on a sofa, and made me sit beside him. His manners were simple and very gracious; he spoke freely of what he had suffered in France. He said, 'God forbid that he should bear ill-will to any one; but the journey and the cold were trying to an old man, and he was glad to return to a warm climate and to his own country.' When we took leave, he said to me, 'Though a Protestant, you will be none the worse for an old man's blessing.' Pius the Seventh was loved and respected; the people knelt to him as he passed. Many years afterwards we were presented to Gregory the Sixteenth°, a very commonlooking man, forming a great contrast to Pius the Seventh.

I heard more good music during this first visit to Rome than I ever did after; for besides that usual in St Peter's, there was an Academia every week, where Marcello's° Psalms were sung in concert by a number of male voices, besides other concerts, private and public. We did not make the acquaintance of any of the Roman families at this time; but we saw Pauline Borghese, sister of the Emperor Napoleon, so celebrated for her beauty, walking on the Pincio every afternoon. Our great geologist, Sir Roderick Murchison°, with his wife, were among the

English residents at Rome. At that time he hardly knew one stone from another. He had been an officer in the Dragoons, an excellent horseman, and a keen fox-hunter. Lady Murchison, – an amiable and accomplished woman, with solid acquirements which few ladies at that time possessed – had taken to the study of geology; and soon after her husband began that career which has rendered him the first geologist of our country. It was then that a friendship began between them and us, which will only end with life. Mrs Fairfax, of Gilling Castle, and her two handsome daughters were also at Rome. She was my namesake – Mary Fairfax – and my valued friend till her death. Now, alas! many of these friends are gone.

There were such troops of brigands in the Papal States, that it was considered unsafe to go outside the gates of Rome. They carried off people to the mountains, and kept them till ransomed; sometimes even mutilated them, as they do at the present day in the kingdom of Naples. Lucien Bonaparte° made a narrow escape from being carried off from his villa, Villa Ruffinella, near Frascati. When it could be proved that brigands had committed murder, they were confined in prisons in the Maremma, at Campo Morto, where fever prevails, and where they were supposed to die of malaria. I saw Gasperone, the chief of a famous band, in a prison at Civita Vecchia; he was said to be a relative of Cardinal Antonelli°, both coming from the brigand village of Sonnino, in the Volscian mountains. In going to Naples our friends advised us to take a guard of soldiers; but these were suspected of being as bad, and in league with the brigands. So we travelled post without them; and though I foolishly insisted on going round by the ruins of ancient Capua, which was considered very unsafe, we arrived at Naples without any encounter. Here we met with the son and daughter of Mr Smith°, of Norwich, a celebrated leader in the anti-slavery question. This was a bond of interest between his family and me; for when I was a girl I took the anti-slavery cause so warmly to heart that I would not take sugar in my tea, or indeed taste anything with sugar in it. I was not singular in this for my cousins and many of my acquaintances came to the same resolution. How long we kept it I do not remember. Patty Smith and I became great friends, and I knew her sisters; but only remember her niece Florence Nightingale° as a very little child. My friend Patty was liberal in her opinions, witty, original, an excellent horsewoman, and drew cleverly; but from bad health she was peculiar in all her habits. She was a good judge of art. Her father had a valuable collection of pictures of the ancient masters; and I learnt much from her with regard to paintings and style in drawing. We went to see everything in Naples and its environs together, and she accompanied Somerville and me in an expedition to Pæstum[53], where we made sketches of the temples. At Naples we bought a beautiful cork model of the Temple of Neptune, which was placed on our mineral cabinet on our return to London. A lady who came to pay me a morning visit asked Somerville what it was; and when he told her, she said, 'How dreadful it is to think that all the people who worshipped in that temple are in eternal misery, because they did not believe in our Saviour.' Somerville asked, 'How could they believe in Christ when He was not born till many centuries after?' I am sure she thought it was all the same.

There had been an eruption of Vesuvius just before our arrival at Naples, and it was still smoking very much; however, we ascended it, and walked round the crater, running and holding a handkerchief to our nose as we passed through the smoke, when the wind blew it to our side. The crater was just like an empty funnel, wide at the mouth, and narrowing to a throat. The lava was hard enough to bear us; but there were numerous *fumeroles*, or red-hot chasms, in it, which we could look into. Somerville bought a number of crystals from the guides, and went repeatedly to Portici afterwards to complete our collection of volcanic minerals.

They were excavating busily at Pompeii; at that time, and in one of our many excursions there Somerville bought from one of the workmen a bronze statuette of Minerva, and a very fine *rosso antico* Terminus, which we contrived to smuggle into Naples; and it now forms part of a small but excellent collection of antiques which I still possess. The excavations at that period were conducted with little regularity or direction, and the guides were able to carry on a contraband trade as mentioned. Since the annexation of the Neapolitan provinces to the kingdom of Italy, the Cavaliere Fiorelli° has organised the system of excavations in the most masterly manner, and has made many interesting discoveries. About one-third of the town has been excavated since it was discovered till the present day.

[*1D, 104–5:* During the whole of this journey I bitterly regretted having devoted my life exclusively to science and the dead instead of the living languages. Although my husband spoke for me, I felt myself an incumbrance in foreign society consequently I spoke little. I should have been in high estimation among the Persians who say of their women, 'To speak little is silver, not to speak at all is gold.' I am now deaf also and unable to join in the general conversation even when in my native tongue but I thank God that my sight and intelligence are still unimpaired. I had reason lately to be glad I was deaf for there had been a violent thunderstorm during the night, I heard it not, and slept soundly, but I am not so much afraid as I used to be.]

In passing through Bologna, we became acquainted with the celebrated Mezzofanti°, afterwards Cardinal. He was a quiet-looking priest; we could not see anything in his countenance that indicated talent, nor was his conversation remarkable; yet he told us that he understood fifty-two languages. He left no memoir at his death; nor did he ever trace any connection between these languages; it was merely an astonishing power, which led to nothing, like that of a young American I lately heard of, who could play eleven games at chess at the same time, without looking at any chess-board.

EIGHT

Education of Daughters – Dr Wollaston – Dr Young –
The Herschels

[*1D, 39:* Immediately on returning home we went to Scotland, and after remaining some weeks with my father-in-law, we went to Fifeshire to visit Mr and Mrs Ferguson at Raith with whom we had always been on the terms of strictest friendship and never came to Scotland without keeping some time with them at Mrs Ferguson's paternal homes of Biel and Archerfield in East Lothian, all magnificent places endeared to me by the affectionate kindness of their proprietors. I still have a view of the Bass Rock and the islands at the mouth of the Firth of Forth which I painted from a sketch I made at Archerfield.]

When we returned to Hanover Square, I devoted my morning hours, as usual, to domestic affairs, but now my children occupied a good deal of my time. Although still very young, I thought it advisable for them to acquire foreign languages; so I engaged a French nursery-maid, that they might never suffer what I had done from ignorance of modern languages. I besides gave them instruction in such things as I was capable of teaching, and which were suited to their age.

It was a great amusement to Somerville and myself to arrange the minerals we had collected during our journey. [*1D, 108:* I made little pasteboard trays for our minerals, and we had small wooden cups turned, in the centre of which our crystals were mounted on pedestals of wax for many especially the diamonds were very small.] Our cabinet was now very rich. Some of our specimens we had bought; our friends had given us duplicates of those they possessed; and George Finlayson, who was with our troops in Ceylon, and who had devoted all his spare time to the study of the natural productions of the country, sent us a valuable collection of crystals of sapphire, ruby, oriental topaz, amethyst, &c., &c. Somerville used to analyse minerals with the blowpipe, which I never did. One evening, when he was so occupied, I was playing the piano, when suddenly I fainted; he was very much startled, as neither I nor any of our family had ever done such a thing. When I recovered, I said it was the smell of garlic that had made me ill. The truth was, the mineral contained arsenic, and I was poisoned for the time by the fumes.

At this time we formed an acquaintance with Dr Wollaston, which soon became a lasting friendship. He was gentlemanly, a cheerful companion, and a philosopher; he was also of agreeable appearance, having a remarkably fine, intellectual head. He was essentially a chemist, and discovered palladium; but there were few branches of science with which he was not more or less acquainted. He made experiments to discover imponderable matter; I believe, with regard to the ethereal medium. Mr Brand°, of the Royal Institution, enraged him by sending so strong a current of electricity through a machine he had made to prove electro-magnetic rotation, as to destroy it. His characteristic was extreme accuracy, which particularly fitted him for giving that precision to the science of crystallography which it had not hitherto attained. By the invention of the goniometer[54] which bears his name, he was enabled to measure the angle formed by the faces of a crystal by means of the reflected images of bright objects seen in them. We bought a goniometer, and Dr Wollaston, who often dined with us, taught Somerville and me how to use it, by measuring the angles of many of our crystals during the evening. I learnt a great deal on a variety of subjects besides crystallography from Dr Wollaston, who, at his death, left me a collection of models of the forms of all the natural crystals then known.

Though still occasionally occupied with the mineral productions of the earth, I became far more interested in the formation of the earth itself. Geologists had excited public attention, and had shocked the clergy and the more scrupulous of the laity by proving beyond a doubt that the formation of the globe extended through enormous periods of time. The contest was even more keen then than it is at the present time about the various races of pre-historic men. It lasted very long, too; for after I had published my work on Physical Geography, I was preached against by name in York Cathedral. Our friend Dr Buckland°, committed himself by taking the clerical view in his 'Bridgewater Treatise;[55] but facts are such stubborn things, that he was obliged to join the geologists at last. He and Mrs Buckland invited Somerville and me to spend a week with them in Christchurch College, Oxford. Mr and Mrs Murchison were their guests at the same time. Mr Murchison (now Sir Roderick) was then rising rapidly to the pre-eminence he now holds as a geologist. We spent every day in seeing some of the numerous objects of interest in that celebrated university, venerable for its antiquity, historical records, and noble architecture.

Somerville and I used frequently to spend the evening with Captain and Mrs Kater°. [*1D, 113 verso:* Captain Kater was very agreeable and plausible in society but of a stern and severe character at home. Mrs Kater was truly amiable, sensible, and of great assistance to her husband in doing his calculations and copying for him, though she had work enough in educating her children.] Dr Wollaston, Dr Young°, and others were generally of the party; sometimes we had music, for Captain and Mrs Kater sang very prettily. All kinds of scientific subjects were discussed, experiments tried and astronomical observations made in a little garden in front of the house. One evening we had been trying the power of a telescope in separating double stars till about two in the morning; on our way home we saw a light in Dr Young's window, and when Somerville rang the bell, down came the doctor himself in his dressing-gown, and said, 'Come in; I have something curious to show you.' Astronomical signs are frequently found on ancient Egyptian monuments, and were supposed to have been employed by the priests to record dates. Now Dr Young had received a papyrus from Egypt, sent to him by Mr Salt, who had found it in a mummy-case; and that very evening he had proved it to be a horoscope of the age of the Ptolemies, and had determined the date from the configuration of the heavens at the time of its construction. Dr Young had already made himself famous by the interpretation of hieroglyphic characters on a stone which had been brought to the British Museum from Rosetta in Egypt. On that stone there is an inscription in hieroglyphics, the sacred symbolic language of the early Egyptians; another in the Enchorial or spoken language of that most ancient people, and a mutilated inscription in Greek. By the aid of some fragments of papyri Dr Young discovered that the Enchorial language is alphabetical, and that nine of its letters correspond with ours; moreover, he discovered such a relation between the Enchorial and the hieroglyphic inscription that he interpreted the latter and published his discoveries in the years 1815 and 1816.

M. Champollion°, who had been on the same pursuit, examined the fine collection of papyri in the museum at Turin, and afterwards went to Egypt to pursue his studies on hieroglyphics, to our knowledge of which he contributed greatly. It is to be regretted that one who had brought that branch of science to such perfection should have been so ungenerous as to ignore the assistance he had received from the researches of Dr Young. When the Royal Institution was first established, Dr Young lectured on natural philosophy. He proved the undulatory theory of light by direct experiment, but as it depended upon the hypothesis of an ethereal medium, it was not received in England, the more so as it was contrary to Newton's theory. The French *savants* afterwards did Young ample justice. The existence of the ethereal medium is now all but proved, since part of the corona surrounding the moon during a total solar eclipse is polarised – a phenomenon depending on matter. Young's Lectures, which had been published, were a mine of riches to me. He was of a Quaker family; but although he left the Society of Friends at an early age, he retained their formal precision of manner to the last. He was of a kindly disposition, and his wife and her sisters, with whom I was intimate, were much attached to him. Dr Young was an elegant and critical scholar at a very early age; he was an astronomer, a mathematician, and there were few branches of science in which he was not versed. When young, his Quaker habits did not prevent him from taking lessons in music and dancing. I have heard him accompany his sister-in-law with the flute, while she played the piano. When not more than sixteen years of age he was so remarkable for steadiness and acquirements that he was engaged more as a companion than tutor to young Hudson Gurney°, who was nearly of his own age. One spring morning Young came to breakfast in a bright green coat, and said in explanation of his somewhat eccentric costume for one who had been a Quaker, that it was suitable to the season. One day, on returning from their ride, Gurney leaped his horse over the stableyard gate. Young, trying to do the same, was thrown; he got up, mounted, and made a second attempt with no better success; the third time he kept his seat, then quietly dismounting, he said, 'What one man can do, another may.'

One bright morning Dr Wollaston came to pay us a visit in Hanover Square, saying, 'I have discovered seven dark lines crossing the solar spectrum, which I wish to show you;' then, closing the window-shutters so as to leave only a narrow line of light, he put a small glass prism into my hand, telling me how to hold it. I saw them distinctly. I was among the first, if not the very first, to whom he showed these lines, which were the origin of the most wonderful series of cosmical discoveries, and have proved that many of the substances of our globe are also constituents of the sun, the stars, and even of the nebulæ. Dr Wollaston gave me the little prism, which is doubly valuable, being of glass manufactured at Munich by Fraunhofer°, whose table of dark lines has now become the standard of comparison in that marvellous science, the work of many illustrious men, brought to perfection by Bunsen° and Kirchhoff°.

[*1D, 120–1:* Several unsuccessful attempts had been made in Italy to ascertain whether the most refrangible rays of the solar spectrum possess a magnetic power. Why I thought experiments might succeed in England I cannot tell, but I made the trial aided by a very delicate test which my kind friend Sir John Herschel made for me – I imagined I had succeeded or I should not have published my experimentation in the transactions of the Royal Society of which I am heartily ashamed as I think I must have been mistaken.[56] I am still more ashamed of my presumption in having sent a copy to the Marquis de Laplace, who very good-naturedly thanked me for it in a letter he wrote introducing M. Bouvard the astronomer and *savant. 2D adds*: Since then I have committed all copies to the flames.]

Sir William Herschel had discovered that what appeared to be single stars were frequently two stars in such close approximation that it required a very high telescopic power to see them separately, and that in many of these one star was revolving in an orbit round the other. Sir James South° established an observatory at Camden Hill, near Kensington, where he and Sir John Herschel united in observing the double stars and binary systems with the view of affording further data for improving our knowledge of their movements. In each two observations are requisite, namely, the distance between the two stars, and the angle of position, that is, the angle which the meridian or a parallel to the equator makes with the lines joining the two stars. These observations were made by adjusting a micrometer to a very powerful telescope, and were data sufficient for the determination of the orbit of the revolving star, should it be a binary system. I have given an account of this in the *Connexion of the Physical Sciences*, so I shall only mention here that in one or two of the binary systems the revolving star has been seen to make more than one revolution, and that the periodical times and the elliptical elements of a great many other orbits have been calculated, though they are more than 200,000 times farther from the sun than we are.

After Sir John Herschel was married, we paid him a visit at Slough; fortunately, the sky was clear, and Sir John had the kindness to show me many nebulæ and clusters of stars which I had never seen to such advantage as in his 20 ft. telescope. I shall never forget the glorious appearance of Jupiter as he entered the field of that instrument.

For years the British nation was kept in a state of excitement by the Arctic voyages of our undaunted seamen in quest of a north-west passage from the Atlantic to the Pacific Ocean. The idea was not new, for a direct way to our Eastern possessions had been long desired. On this occasion the impulse was given by William Scoresby°, captain of a whaler who had sailed on the east coast of Greenland as high as the 80th parallel of latitude, and for two successive seasons had found that the sea between Greenland and Spitzbergen was free of ice for 18,000 square miles – a circumstance which had not occurred before in the memory of man. Scoresby was of rare genius, well versed in science, and of strict probity. When he published this discovery, the Admiralty, in the year 1818, sent off two expeditions, one under the command of Captains Franklin° and Buchan to the east of Greenland, and another under Captains Ross° and Parry° to Baffin Bay. Such was the beginning of a series of noble adventures, now the province of history.

I had an early passion for everything relating to the sea, and when my father was at home I never tired asking him questions about his voyages and the dangers to which he had been exposed. Now, when I knew something of nautical science, I entered with enthusiasm into the spirit of these Arctic voyages; nor was my husband less interested. We read Scoresby's whaling voyages with great delight, and we made the acquaintance of all the officers who had been on these northern expeditions.

Sir Edward Parry, who had brought us minerals and seeds of plants from Melville Island, invited us to see the ships prepared for his third voyage, and three years' residence in the Arctic seas. It is impossible to describe how perfectly everything was arranged: experience had taught them what was necessary for such an expedition. On this occasion I put in practice my lessons in cookery by making a large quantity of orange marmalade for the voyage. When, after three years, the ships returned, we were informed that the name of Somerville had been given to an island so far to the north that it was all but perpetually covered with ice and snow. Notwithstanding the sameness which naturally prevails in the narratives of these voyages, they are invested with a romantic interest by the daring bravery displayed, and by the appalling difficulties overcome. The noble endeavour of Lady Franklin to save her gallant husband, and the solitary voyage of Sir Leopold McClintock in a small yacht in search of his lost friend, form the touching and sad termination to a very glorious period of maritime adventure. More than fifty years after these events I renewed my acquaintance with Lady Franklin. She and her niece came to see me at Spezia on their way to Dalmatia. She had circumnavigated the globe with her husband when he was Governor in Australia. After his loss she and her niece had gone round the world a second time, and she assured me that although they went to Japan and China (less known at that time than they are now), they never experienced any difficulty. Seeing ladies travelling alone, people were always willing to help them. The French sent a Polar expedition under Captain Gaimard° in the years 1838 and 1839; and the United States of North America took an active part in Arctic exploration. Whether Dr Kane's discovery of an open polar ocean will ever be verified is problematical; at all events, the deplorable fate of Sir John Franklin has put a stop to the chance of it for the present; yet it is a great geographical question which we should all like to see decided.

Captain Sabine°, of the Artillery (now General Sir Edward Sabine, President of the Royal Society), was appointed to accompany the first expedition under Captains Ross and Parry on account of his high scientific acquirements. The observations made during the series of Arctic voyages on the magnetism of the earth, combined with an enormous mass of observations made by numerous observers in all parts of the globe by sea and by land, have enabled Sir Edward Sabine, after a labour of nearly fifty years, to complete his marvellous system of terrestrial magnetism in both hemispheres. During that long period a friendship has lasted between Sir Edward and me. He has uniformly sent me copies of all his works; to them I chiefly owe what I know on the subject, and quite recently I have received his latest and most important publication. Sir Edward married a lady of talent and scientific acquirements. She translated *Cosmos* from the German, and assisted and calculated for her husband in his laborious work.

I do not remember the exact period, but I think it was subsequent to the Arctic voyages, that the theory was discovered of those tropical hurricanes which cause such devastation by sea and land. Observations are now made on barometric pressure, and warnings are sent to our principal seaports by telegraph, as well as along both sides of the Channel; but notwithstanding numerous disastrous ship-wrecks occur every winter on our dangerous coasts. They were far more numerous in my younger days. Life-boats were not then invented; now they are stationed on almost every coast of Great Britain, and on many continental shores. The readiness with which they are manned, and the formidable dangers encountered to save life, show the gallant, noble character of the sailor.

[*1D, 132–3, it is difficult to know where to place this passage since it jumps about in time, but it seems a pity to lose it:* The reports brought from time to time of the crimes committed in our West Indian Colonies had filled every one with horror for a long time and at last raised such universal indignation that a large sum was voted by parliament to indemnify the slave proprietors and slavery was declared to be illegal in Great Britain and her colonies, a decision that was received with acclamation [1834]. The recent emancipation of slaves in the United States [1865] is a noble deed even though bought with the price of blood.

Somerville and I were intimate with those members of the Clapham Common Society[57] who were the principal leaders in this important movement, especially Sir Robert Inglis at whose house we met with Mr Wilberforce, Mr Macaulay, Mr Henry Thornton and others of the anti-slavery party. The Quakers took up the cause with warmth, and we were on friendly terms with many of them, the Barclays, the Gurneys and Mrs Fry highly esteemed for the merciful amelioration she effected in the severity of prison discipline at home and abroad which amounted to cruelty.

The atrocities of the French had raised a rebellion among the slaves in Haiti, the revenge was fearful and in the various revolutions which occurred a black queen and her two daughters took refuge in London. My friend Patty Smith, daughter of Mr William Smith member, I believe, for Norwich, asked me if I should like to be presented to the Queen, 'By all means,' I said, 'but tell me what kind of people they are.' 'Very respectable, submitting with a good grace to the change in their condition: when I went to wait upon her Majesty yesterday, she and her daughters were busy starching and ironing their ruffs.' Somerville invited a black man to a little party I had one evening. He was either Count Limonade or Marmalade – I forget which, There was a good deal of laughing at the title.]

NINE

*Society in London – Coronation of George IV – Letter
to Dr Somerville*

WE went frequently to see Mr Babbage while he was making
his Calculating-machines. He had a transcendent intellect,
unconquerable perseverance, and extensive knowledge on
many subjects, besides being a first-rate mathematician. I
always found him most amiable and patient in explaining the
structure and use of the engines. The first he made could
only perform arithmetical operations. Not satisfied with
that, Mr Babbage constructed an analytical engine, which
could be so arranged as to perform all kinds of mathematical
calculations, and print each result.

Nothing has afforded me so convincing a proof of the
unity of the Deity as these purely mental conceptions of
numerical and mathematical science which have been by
slow degrees vouchsafed to man, and are still granted in
these latter times by the differential calculus,[58] now superseded by the higher algebra, all of which must have existed
in that sublimely omniscient Mind from eternity.

Many of our friends had very decided and various
religious opinions, but my husband and I never entered
into controversy; we had too high a regard for liberty of
conscience to interfere with any one's opinions, so we have
lived on terms of sincere friendship and love with people
who differed essentially from us in religious views, and in
all the books which I have written I have confined myself
strictly and entirely to scientific subjects, although my
religious opinions are very decided.

Timidity of character, probably owing to early education, had a great influence on my daily life; for I did not assume my place in society in my younger days; and in argument I was instantly silenced, although I often knew, and could have proved, that I was in the right. The only thing in which I was determined and inflexible was in the prosecution of my studies. They were perpetually interrupted, but always resumed at the first opportunity. No analysis is so difficult as that of one's own mind, but I do not think I err much in saying that perseverance is a characteristic of mine.

Somerville and I were very happy when we lived in Hanover Square. We were always engaged in some pursuit, and had good society. General society was at that time brilliant for wit and talent. The Rev. Sydney Smith, Rogers°, Thomas Moore°, Campbell°, the Hon. William Spencer°, Macaulay°, Sir James Mackintosh°, Lord Melbourne°, &c., &c., all made the dinner-parties very agreeable. The men sat longer at table than they do now, and, except in the families where I was intimate, the conversation of the ladies in the drawing-room, when we came up from dinner, often bored me. I disliked routs exceedingly, and should often have sent an excuse if I had known what to say. After my marriage I did not dance, for in Scotland it was thought highly indecorous for a married woman to dance. Waltzing, when first introduced, was looked upon with horror, and even in England it was then thought very improper.

One season I subscribed to the Concerts of Ancient Music, established by George the Third. They seemed to be the resort of the aged; a young face was scarcely to be seen. The music was perfect of its kind, but the whole affair was very dull. The Philharmonic Concerts were excellent for scientific musicians, and I sometimes went to them; but for my part I infinitely preferred hearing Pasta°, Malibran°, and Grisi°, who have left the most vivid impression on my mind, although so different from each other. Somerville enjoyed a comic opera exceedingly, and so did I; and at that time Lablache° was in the height of his fame. When Somerville and I made the tour in Italy already mentioned, we visited Catalani° (then Madame Valbarèque) in a villa near Florence, to which she retired in her old age. She, however, died in Paris, of cholera, some years later.

Somerville liked the theatre as much as I did; so we saw all the greatest actors of the day, both in tragedy and comedy, and the English theatre was then excellent. Young, who was scarcely inferior to John Kemble, Macready°, Kean°, Liston°, &c., and Miss O'Neill°, who after a short brilliant career entered into domestic life on her marriage with Sir William Becher, were all at the height of their fame. It was then I became acquainted with Lady Becher, who was so simple and natural that no one could have discovered she had ever been on the stage. A very clever company of French comedians acted in a temporary theatre in Tottenham Court Road, where we frequently went with a party of friends, and enjoyed very pleasant evenings. I think my fondness for the theatre depended to a certain degree on my silent disposition; for unless among intimate friends, or when much excited, I was startled at the sound of my own voice in general conversation, from the shyness which has haunted me through life, and starts up occasionally like a ghost in my old age. At a play I was not called upon to make any exertion, but could enjoy at my ease an intellectual pleasure for the most part far superior to the general run of conversation.

Among many others, we were intimate with Dr and Mrs Baillie and his sisters. Joanna was my dear and valued friend to the end of her life. When her tragedy of *Montfort*[59] was to be brought on the stage, Somerville and I, with a large party of her relations and friends, went with her to the theatre. The play was admirably acted, for Mrs Siddons and her brother John Kemble performed the principal parts. It was warmly applauded by a full house, but it was never acted again. Some time afterwards *The Family Legend*, founded on a Highland story, had better success in Edinburgh; but Miss Baillie's plays, though highly poetical, are not suited to the stage. Miss Mitford° was more successful, for some of her plays were repeatedly acted. She excelled also as a writer. *Our Village* is perfect of its kind; nothing can be more animated than her description of a game of cricket. I met with Miss Austen's novels at this time, and thought them excellent, especially *Pride and Prejudice*. It certainly formed a curious contrast to my old favourites, the Radcliffe novels and the ghost stories; but I had now come to years of discretion.

Among my Quaker friends I met with that amiable but eccentric person Mrs Opie°. Though a 'wet' Quakeress, she continued to wear the peculiar dress. I was told that she was presented in it at the Tuileries, and astonished the French ladies. We were also acquainted with Mrs Fry°, a very different person, and heard her preach. Her voice was fine, her delivery admirable, and her prayer sublime. We were intimate with Mr (now Sir Charles) Lyell, who, if I mistake not, first met with his wife at our house, where she was extremely admired as the beautiful Miss Horner. Until we lost all our fortune, and went to live at Chelsea, I used to have little evening parties in Hanover Square.

I was not present at the coronation of George the Fourth;[60] but I had a ticket for the gallery in Westminster Hall, to see the banquet. Though I went very early in the morning, I found a wonderful confusion. I showed my ticket of admission to one official person after another; the answer always was 'I know nothing about it.' At last I got a good place near some ladies I knew; even at that early hour the gallery was full. Some time after the ceremony in the Abbey was over, the door of the magnificent hall was thrown open,

and the king entered in the flowing curls and costume of
Henry the Eighth, and, imitating the jaunty manner of that
monarch, walked up the hall and sat down on the throne at
its extremity. The peeresses had already taken their seats
under the gallery, and the king was followed by the peers,
and the Knights of the Garter, Bath, Thistle, and St
Patrick, all in their robes. After every one had taken his
seat, the Champion, on his horse, both in full armour, rode
up the hall, and threw down a gauntlet before the king,
while the heralds proclaimed that he was ready to do battle
with any one who denied that George the Fourth was the
liege lord of these realms. Then various persons presented
offerings to the king in right of which they held their estates.
One gentleman presented a beautiful pair of falcons in their
hoods. While this pageantry and noise was at its height,
Queen Caroline demanded to be admitted. There was a
sudden silence and consternation, – it was like the 'handwriting on the wall!' The sensation was intense. At last the
order was given to refuse her admittance; the pageantry was
renewed, and the banquet followed. The noise, heat, and
vivid light of the illumination of the hall gave me a racking
headache; at last I went out of the gallery and sat on a stair,
where there was a little fresh air, and was very glad when all
was over. Years afterwards I was present in Westminster
Abbey at the coronation of our Queen, then a pretty young
girl of eighteen. Placed in the most trying position at that
early age, by her virtues, both public and private, she has
endeared herself to the nation beyond what any sovereign
ever did before.

[*1D, 144–5:* Somerville and I were on a visit to my mother
when George the Fourth came to Edinburgh. No sovereign
had been in our capital since James the Sixth mounted the
British throne. The Scotch were highly gratified with this
visit of their king. Richly decorated apartments were prepared for him in the ancient Palace of Holyrood and he was
received with enthusiasm. Now Holyrood and its pictur-

esque park are restored to regal splendour by Queen Victoria who has won the hearts of her Scotch subjects by coming annually to reside among them.

In my younger days I often saw the Duc d'Artois, afterwards Charles X°, walking about in Edinburgh on the Sundays. He had taken refuge in Holyrood during the French Revolution. It was an asylum and being in debt, he could not go out on any other day. I remember dining in company with [. . .] one of his suite who asked me in bad English what faith I was of, the lady of the house seeing me very much embarrassed and shy, good-naturedly said, she is too young to know anything about different faiths which was quite true; she had invited me merely that I might hear French spoken though I could not speak it myself. But to return from this digression.]

I, who had so many occupations and duties at home, soon tired of the idleness and formality of visiting in the country. I made an exception, however, in favour of an occasional visit to Mr Sotheby°, the poet, and his family in Epping Forest, of which, if I mistake not, he was deputy-ranger; at all events, he had a pretty cottage there where he and his family received their friends with kind hospitality. He spent part of the day in his study, and afterwards I have seen him playing cricket with his son and grandson, with as much vivacity as any of them. The freshness of the air was quite reviving to Somerville and me; and our two little girls played in the forest all the day.

We also gladly went for several successive years to visit Sir John Saunders Sebright° at Beechwood Park, Hertfordshire. Dr Wollaston generally travelled with us on these occasions, when we had much conversation on a variety of subjects, scientific or general. He was remarkably acute in his observations on objects as we passed them. 'Look at that ash tree; did you ever notice that the branches of the ash tree are curves of double curvature?' There was a comet visible at the time of one of these little journeys. Dr Wollaston had made a drawing of the orbit and its elements; but, having left it in town, he described the lines so accurately without naming them, that I remarked at once, 'That is the curtate or perihelion distance,'[61] which pleased him greatly, as it showed how accurate his description was. He was a chess-player, and, when travelling alone, he used to carry a book with diagrams of partially-played games, in which it is required to give checkmate in a fixed number of moves. He would study one of them, and then, shutting the book, play out the game mentally.

Although Sir John was a keen sportsman and fox-hunter in his youth, he was remarkable for his kindness to animals and for the facility with which he tamed them. He kept terriers, and his pointers were first rate, yet he never allowed his keepers to beat a dog, nor did he ever do it himself; he said a dog once cowed was good for nothing ever after. He trained them by tying a string to the collar and giving it a sharp pull when the dog did wrong, and patting him kindly when he did right. In this manner he taught some of his non-sporting dogs to play all sorts of tricks, such as picking out the card chosen by any spectator from a number placed in a circle on the floor, the signal being one momentary glance at the card, &c., &c. Sir John published a pamphlet on the subject, and sent copies of it to the sporting gentlemen and keepers in the county, I fear with little effect; men are so apt to vent their own bad temper on their dogs and horses.

At one of the battues at Beechwood, Chantrey° killed two woodcocks at one shot. Mr Hudson Gurney some time after saw a brace of woodcocks carved in marble in Chantrey's studio; Chantrey told him of his shot and the difficulty of finding a suitable inscription, and that it had been tried in Latin and even Greek without success. Mr Gurney said it should be very simple, such as:—

Driven from the north, where winter starved them,
Chantrey first shot, and then he carved them.

Beechwood was one of the few places in Great Britain in
which hawking was kept up. The falcons were brought from
Flanders, for, except in the Isle of Skye, they have been
extirpated in Great Britain, like many other of our fine
indigenous birds. Sir John kept fancy pigeons of all breeds.
He told me he could alter the colour of their plumage in
three years by cross-breeding, but that it required fully six
to alter the shape of the bird.

At some house where we were dining in London, I forget
with whom, Ugo Foscolo°, the poet, was one of the party.
He was extremely excitable and irritable, and when some
one spoke of a translation of Dante as being perfect,
'Impossible,' shouted Foscolo, starting up in great excitement, at the same time tossing his cup full of coffee into the
air, cup and all, regardless of the china and the ladies'
dresses. He died in England, I fear in great poverty. He was
a most distinguished classical scholar as well as poet. His
remains have been brought to Italy within these few years,
and interred in Santa Croce, in Florence.

I had a severe attack of what appeared to be cholera, and
during my recovery Mrs Hankey very kindly lent us her villa
at Hampstead for a few weeks. There I went with my
children, Somerville with some friends always coming to
dinner on the Sundays. On one of these occasions there was
a violent thunderstorm, and a large tree was struck not far
from the house. We all went to look at the tree as soon as
the storm ceased, and found that a large mass of wood was
scooped out of the trunk from top to bottom. I had
occasion in two other instances to notice the same effect.
Dr Wollaston lent me a sextant and artificial horizon; so I
amused myself taking the altitude of the sun, the conse-

quence of which was that I became as brown as a mulatto, [*1D, 152:* but I was too anxious to learn something of practical astronomy to care for that as I knew it was temporary. I was still very good looking and was aware of it, and notwithstanding my love of science I liked to be admired and dressed to look well but never younger than my age.]

TEN

Death of Margaret Somerville – Letter from Mrs Somerville to the Rev. Dr Somerville – Life at Chelsea – The Napiers – Maria Edgeworth – Tour in Germany

OUR happy and cheerful life in Hanover Square came to a sad end. The illness and death of our eldest girl threw Somerville and me into the deepest affliction. She was a child of intelligence and acquirements far beyond her tender age.[62]

[The long illness and death of this young girl fell very heavily on my mother, who by this time had lost several children. The following letter was written by her to my grandfather on this occasion. It shows her steadfast faith in the mercy and goodness of God, even when crushed by almost the severest affliction which can wring a mother's heart:—]

MRS SOMERVILLE TO THE REV. DR SOMERVILLE

LONDON, *October, 1823*

MY DEAR FATHER,

I never was so long of writing to you, but when the heart is breaking it is impossible to find words adequate to its relief. We are in deep affliction, for though the first violence of grief has subsided, there has succeeded a calm sorrow not less painful, a feeling of hopelessness in this world which only finds comfort in the prospect of another, which longs for the consummation of all things that we may join those who have gone before. To return to the duties of life is irksome, even to those duties which were a delight when the candle of the Lord shone upon us. I do not arraign the decrees of Providence, but even in the bitterness of my soul I acknowledge the wisdom and goodness of God, and endeavour to be resigned to His will. It is ungrateful not to remember the many happy years we have enjoyed, but that very remembrance renders our present state more desolate and dreary – presenting a sad contrast. The great source of consolation is in the mercy of God and the virtues of those we lament; the full assurance that no good disposition can be lost but must be brought to perfection in a better world. Our business is to render ourselves fit for that blessed inheritance that we may again be united to those we mourn.

Your affectionate daughter,

MARY SOMERVILLE

Somerville still held his place at the army medical board, and was now appointed physician to Chelsea Hospital; so we left our cheerful, comfortable house and went to reside in a government house in a very dreary and unhealthy situation, far from all our friends, which was a serious loss to me, as I was not a good walker, and during the whole time I lived at Chelsea I suffered from sick headaches. Still we were very glad of the appointment, for at this time we lost almost the whole of our fortune, through the dishonesty of a person in whom we had the greatest confidence.[63]

All the time we lived at Chelsea we had constant intercourse with Lady Noel Byron° and Ada, who lived at Esher, and when I came abroad I kept up a correspondence with both as long as they lived. Ada was much attached to me, and often came to stay with me. It was by my advice that she studied mathematics. She always wrote to me for an explanation when she met with any difficulty. Among my papers I lately found many of her notes, asking mathematical questions. Ada Byron° married Lord King, afterwards created Earl of Lovelace, a college companion and friend of my son.

Somerville had formed a friendship with Sir Henry Bunbury when he had a command in Sicily, and we went occasionally to visit him at Barton in Suffolk. I liked Lady Bunbury° very much; she was a niece of the celebrated Charles Fox, and had a turn for natural history. I had made a collection of native shells at Burntisland, but I only knew their vulgar names; now I learnt their scientific arrangement from Lady Bunbury. Her son, Sir Charles Bunbury, is an authority for fossil botany. The first Pinetum I ever saw was at Barton, and in 1837 I planted a cedar in remembrance of one of our visits.

Through Lady Bunbury we became intimate with all the members of the illustrious family of the Napiers, as she was sister of Colonel, afterwards General Sir William Napier, author of the *History of the Peninsular War*. One day Colonel Napier, who was then living in Sloane Street, introduced Somerville and me to his mother, Lady Sarah Napier. Her manners were distinguished, and though totally blind, she still had the remains of great beauty; her hand and arm, which were exposed by the ancient costume she wore, were most beautiful still. The most sincere friendship existed between Richard Napier and his wife and me through life; I shall never forget their kindness to me at a time when I was in great sorrow. All the brothers are now gone. Richard and his wife were long in bad health, and he was nearly blind; but his wife never knew it, through the devoted attachment of Emily Shirriff, daughter of Admiral Shirriff, who was the comfort and consolation of both to their dying day.

Maria Edgeworth° came frequently to see us when she was in England. She was one of my most intimate friends, warm-hearted and kind, a charming companion, with all the liveliness and originality of an Irishwoman. For seventeen years I was in constant correspondence with her. The cleverness and animation as well as affection of her letters I cannot express; certainly women are superior to men in letter-writing.

[The following is an extract from a letter from Maria Edgeworth to a friend concerning my mother:—

MARIA EDGEWORTH TO MISS . . .

BEECHWOOD PARK, *January 17th, 1822*

We have spent two days pleasantly here with Dr Wollaston, our own dear friend Mrs Marcet, and the Somervilles. Mrs Somerville is the lady who, Laplace says, is the only woman who understands his works. She draws beautifully, and while her head is among the stars her feet are firm upon the earth.

Mrs Somerville is little, slightly made, fairish hair, pink colour, small, grey, round, intelligent, smiling eyes, very pleasing countenance, remarkably soft voice, strong, but well-bred Scotch accent; timid, not disqualifying timid, but naturally modest, yet with a degree of self-possession through it which prevents her being in the least awkward, and gives her all the advantage of her understanding, at the same time that it adds a prepossessing charm to her manner and takes off all dread of her superior scientific learning.]

While in London I had a French maid for my daughters, and on coming to Chelsea I taught them a little geometry and algebra, as well as Latin and Greek, and, later, got a master for them, that they might have a more perfect knowledge of these languages than I possessed. Keenly alive to my own defects, I was anxious that my children should never undergo the embarrassment and mortification I had suffered from ignorance of the common European languages. I engaged a young German lady, daughter of Professor Becker°, of Offenbach, near Frankfurt, as governess, and was most happy in my choice; but after being with us for a couple of years, she had a very bad attack of fever, and was obliged to return home. She was replaced by a younger sister, who afterwards married Professor Trendelenburg°, Professor of Philosophy at the University of Berlin. Though both these sisters were quite young, I had the most perfect confidence in them, from their strict conscientiousness and morality. They were well educated, ladylike, and so amiable, that they gained the friendship of my children and the affection of us all. [*1D, 155:* My daughters became excellent linguists and wrote when necessary for me, as I never attempted to write any language but English. They showed a very decided taste for music at an early age and became good musicians which was more owing to their own industry and talent than to teaching.]

As we could with perfect confidence leave the children to Miss Becker's care, Sir James Mackintosh, Somerville and I made an excursion to the Continent. We went to Brussels, and what lady can go there without seeing the lace manufactory? I saw, admired, – and bought none! We were kindly received by Professor Quetelet°, whom we had previously known, and who never failed to send me a copy of his valuable memoirs as soon as they were published. I have uniformly met with the greatest kindness from scientific men at home and abroad. If any of them are alive when this record is published, I beg they will accept of my gratitude. Of those that are no more I bear a grateful remembrance.

The weather was beautiful when we were at Brussels, and in the evening we went to the public garden. It was crowded with people, and very gay. We sat down, and amused ourselves by looking at them as they passed. Sir James was a most agreeable companion, intimate with all the political characters of the day, full of anecdote and historical knowledge. That evening his conversation was so brilliant that we forgot the time, and looking around found that everybody had left the garden, so we thought we might as well return to the hotel; but on coming to the iron-barred gate we found it locked. Sir James and Somerville begged some of those that were passing to call the keeper of the park to let us out; but they said it was impossible, that we must wait till morning. A crowd assembled laughing and mocking, till at last we got out through the house of one of the keepers of the park.

At Bonn we met with Baron Humboldt, and M. Schlegel°, celebrated for his translation of Shakespeare. On going up the Rhine, Sir James knew the history of every place and of every battle that had been fought. A professor of his acquaintance in one of the towns invited us to dinner, and I was astonished to see the lady of the house going about with a great bunch of keys dangling at her side, assisting in serving up the dinner, and doing all the duty of carving, her husband taking no part whatever in it. I was annoyed that we had given so much trouble by accepting the invitation. In my younger days in Scotland, a lady might make the pastry and jelly or direct in the kitchen; but she took no part in cooking or serving up the dinner, and never rose from the table till the ladies went to the drawing-room. However, as we could not afford to keep a regular cook, an ill-dressed dish would occasionally appear, and then my father would say, 'God sends food, but the devil sends cooks.'

In our tour through Holland, Somerville was quite at home, and amused himself talking to the people, for he had learnt the Dutch language at the Cape of Good Hope. We admired the pretty quaint costumes of the women; but I was the only one who took interest in the galleries. Many of the pictures of the Dutch school are very fine; but I never should have made a collection exclusively of them as was often done at one time in England. Lord Granville° was British Minister at the Hague, and dining at the Embassy one day we met with a Mrs—, who, on hearing one of the attachés addressed as Mr Abercromby, said, 'Pray, Lord Granville, is that a son of the great captain whom the Lord slew in the land of Egypt?'[64]

I never met with Madame de Staël but heard a great deal about her during this journey from Sir James Mackintosh, who was very intimate with her. At that time the men sat longer at table after dinner than they do now; and on one occasion, at a dinner party at Sir James's house, when Lady Mackintosh and the ladies returned to the drawing-room, Madame de Staël who was exceedingly impatient of women's society, would not deign to enter into conversation with any of the ladies, but walked about the room; then suddenly ringing the bell, she said, 'Ceci est insupportable!' and when the servant appeared, she said: 'Tell your master to come upstairs directly; they have sat long enough at their wine.'

ELEVEN

*Letter from Lord Brougham – Writes 'Mechanism of
the Heavens' – Anecdote of the Roman Improvisatrice –
Letters from Sir John Herschel and Professor Whewell –
Elected Hon. Member of the Royal Astronomical Society –
Notice in the Académie des Sciences, and Letter from M. Biot –
Pension – Letter from Sir Robert Peel – Begins to Write 'On the
Connexion of the Physical Sciences' – Visit to Cambridge –
Letters from Professor Sedgwick and Laplace*

AFTER my mother's return home my father received the
following letter from Lord Brougham, which very impor-
tantly influenced the further course of my mother's life. It is
dated March 27th, 1827:—

LETTER FROM LORD BROUGHAM TO
DR SOMERVILLE

MY DEAR SIR,

I fear you will think me very daring for the design I have
formed against Mrs. Somerville, and still more for making
you my advocate with her: through whom I have every hope
of prevailing. There will be sent to you a prospectus, rules,
and a preliminary treatise of our Society for Diffusing Useful
Knowledge, and I assure you I speak without any flattery
when I say that of the two subjects which I find it most
difficult to see the chance of executing, there is one, which –
unless Mrs. Somerville will undertake – none else can, and it
must be left undone, though about the most interesting of the
whole, I mean an account of the Mécanique Céleste; the

other is an account of the Principia, which I have some hopes
of at Cambridge. The kind of thing wanted is such a description of that divine work as will both explain to the unlearned
the sort of thing it is – the plan, the vast merit, the wonderful
truths unfolded or methodized – and the calculus by which all
this is accomplished, and will also give a somewhat deeper
insight to the uninitiated. Two treatises would do this. No
one without trying it can conceive how far we may carry
ignorant readers into an understanding of the depths of
science, and our treatises have about 100 to 800 pages of
space each, so that one might give the more popular view, and
another the analytical abstracts and illustrations. In England
there are now not twenty people who know this great work,
except by name: and not a hundred who know it even by
name. My firm belief is that Mrs. Somerville could add two
cyphers to each of those figures. Will you be my counsel in
this suit? Of course our names are concealed, and no one of
our council but myself needs to know it.

Yours ever most truly,

H. BROUGHAM

[My mother in alluding to the above says:—]

This letter surprised me beyond expression. I thought Lord
Brougham must have been mistaken with regard to my
acquirements, and naturally concluded that my self-ac-
quired knowledge was so far inferior to that of the men
who had been educated in our universities that it would be
the height of presumption to attempt to write on such a
subject, or indeed on any other. A few days after this Lord
Brougham came to Chelsea himself, and Somerville joined
with him in urging me at least to make the attempt. I said,
'Lord Brougham, you must be aware that the work in
question never can be popularised, since the student must

at least know something of the differential and integral calculi, and as a preliminary step I should have to prove various problems in physical mechanics and astronomy. Besides, Laplace never gives diagrams or figures, because they are not necessary to persons versed in the calculus, but they would be indispensable in a work such as you wish me to write. I am afraid I am incapable of such a task: but as you both wish it so much, I shall do my very best upon condition of secrecy, and that if I fail the manuscript shall be put into the fire.' Thus suddenly and unexpectedly the whole character and course of my future life was changed.

I rose early and made such arrangements with regard to my children and family affairs that I had time to write afterwards; not, however, without many interruptions. A man can always command his time under the plea of business, a woman is not allowed any such excuse. At Chelsea I was always supposed to be at home, and as my friends and acquaintances came so far out of their way on purpose to see me, it would have been unkind and un-generous not to receive them. Nevertheless, I was some-times annoyed when in the midst of a difficult problem some one would enter and say, 'I have come to spend a few hours with you.' However, I learnt by habit to leave a subject and resume it again at once, like putting a mark into a book I might be reading; this was the more necessary as there was no fire-place in my little room, and I had to write in the drawing-room in winter. Frequently I hid my papers as soon as the bell announced a visitor, lest anyone should discover my secret.

[My mother had a singular power of abstraction. When occupied with some difficult problem, or even a train of thought which deeply interested her, she lost all consciousness of what went on around her, and became so entirely absorbed that any amount of talking, or even practising scales and *solfeggi*, went on without in the least disturbing her. Sometimes a song or a strain of melody would recall her to a sense of the present, for she was passionately fond of music. A curious instance of this peculiarity of hers occurred at Rome, when a large party were assembled to listen to a celebrated improvisatrice. My mother was placed in the front row, close to the poetess, who, for several stanzas, adhered strictly to the subject which had been given to her. What it was I do not recollect, except that it had no connection with what followed. All at once, as if by a sudden inspiration, the lady turned her eyes full upon my mother, and with true Italian vehemence and in the full musical accents of Rome, poured forth stanza after stanza of the most eloquent panegyric upon her talents and virtues, extolling them and her to the skies. Throughout the whole of this scene, which lasted a considerable time, my mother remained calm and unmoved, never changing countenance, which surprised not only the persons present but ourselves, as we well knew how much she disliked any display or being brought forward in public. The truth was, that after listening for a while to the improvising, a thought struck her connected with some subject she was engaged in writing upon at the time and so entirely absorbed her that she heard not a word of all that had been declaimed in her praise, and was not a little surprised and confused when she was complimented on it. I call this, advisedly, a power of hers, for although it occasionally led her into strange positions, such as the one above mentioned, it rendered her entirely independent of outward circumstances, nor did she require to isolate herself from the family circle in order to pursue her studies. I have already mentioned that when we were very young she taught us herself for a few hours daily; when our lessons were over we always remained in the room with her, learning grammar, arithmetic, or some such plague of childhood. Any one who has plunged into the mazes of the higher branches of mathematics or other abstruse science, would probably feel no slight degree of irritation on being interrupted at a critical moment when the solution was almost within his grasp, by some childish question about tense or gender, or how much seven times seven made. My mother was never impatient, but explained our little difficulties quickly and kindly, and returned calmly to her own profound thoughts. Yet on occasion she could show both irritation and impatience – when we were stupid or inattentive, neither of which she could stand. With her clear mind she darted at the solution, sometimes forgetting that we had to toil after her laboriously step by step. I well remember her slender white hand pointing impatiently to the book or slate – 'Don't you see it? there is no difficulty in it, it is quite clear.' Things were so clear to her! I must here add some other recollections by my mother of this very interesting portion of her life.]

I was a considerable time employed in writing this book, but I by no means gave up society, which would neither have suited Somerville nor me. We dined out, went to evening parties, and occasionally to the theatre. As soon as my work was finished I sent the manuscript to Lord Brougham, requesting that it might be thoroughly examined, criticised and destroyed according to promise if a failure. I was very nervous while it was under examination, and was equally surprised and gratified that Sir John Herschel, our greatest astronomer, and perfectly versed in the calculus, should have found so few errors. The letter he wrote on this occasion made me so happy and proud that I have preserved it.

LETTER FROM SIR JOHN HERSCHEL TO MRS SOMERVILLE

Dear Mrs Somerville,

I have read your manuscript with the greatest pleasure, and will not hesitate to add, (because I am sure you will believe it sincere,) with the highest admiration. Go on thus, and you will leave a memorial of no common kind to posterity; and, what you will value far more than fame, you will have accomplished a most useful work. What a pity that Laplace has not lived to see this illustration of his great work! You will only, I fear, give too strong a stimulus to the study of abstract science by this performance.

I have marked as somewhat obscure a part of the illustration of the principle of virtual velocities . . . Will you look at this point again? I have made a trifling remark in page 6, but it is a mere matter of metaphysical nicety, and perhaps hardly worth pencilling your beautiful manuscript for.

Ever yours most truly,
J. HERSCHEL

[In publishing the following letter, I do not consider that I am infringing on the rule I have followed in obedience to my mother's wishes, that is, to abstain from giving publicity to all letters which are of a private and confidential character. This one entirely concerns her scientific writings, and is interesting as showing the confidence which existed between Sir John Herschel and herself. This great philosopher was my mother's truest and best friend, one whose opinion she valued above all others, whose genius and consummate talents she admired, and whose beautiful character she loved with an intensity which is better shown by some extracts from her letters to be given presently than by anything I can say. This deep regard on her part he returned with the most chivalrous respect and admiration. In any doubt or difficulty it was his advice she sought, his criticism she submitted to; both were always frankly given without the slightest fear of giving offence, for Sir John Herschel well knew the spirit with which any remarks of his would be received.]

FROM SIR JOHN HERSCHEL TO
MRS SOMERVILLE

SLOUGH, *Feb. 23rd, 1830*

MY DEAR MRS SOMERVILLE,

. . . As you contemplate separate publication, and as the attention of many will be turned to a work from *your* pen who will just possess quantum enough of mathematical knowledge to be able to read the first chapter without being able to follow you into its application, and as these, moreover, are the very people who will think themselves privileged to criticise and use their privilege with the least discretion, I cannot recommend too much clearness, fulness, and order in the *exposé* of the principles. Were I you, I would devote to this first part at least double the space you have done. Your familiarity with the results and formulæ has led you into what is extremely natural in such a case – a somewhat hasty passing over what, to a beginner, would prove insuperable difficulties; and if I may so express it, a sketchiness of outline (as a painter you will understand my meaning, and what is of more consequence, see how it is to be remedied).

You have adopted, I see, the principle of virtual velocity, and the principle of d'Alembert°, rather as separate and independent principles to be used as instruments of investigation than as convenient theories, flowing themselves from the general law of force and equilibrium, to be first *proved* and then remembered as compact statements in a form fit for use. The demonstration of the principle of virtual velocities is so easy and direct in Laplace that I cannot imagine anything capable of rendering it plainer than he has done. But a good deal more explanation of what *is* virtual velocity, &c., would be advantageous – and virtual velocities should be kept quite distinct from the arbitrary variations represented by the sign δ.

With regard to the *principle of d'Alembert* – take my advice and explode it altogether. It is the most awkward and involved statement of a plain dynamical equation that ever puzzled student. I speak feelingly and with a sense of irritation at the whirls and vortices it used to cause in my poor head when first I entered on this subject in my days of studentship. I know not a single case where its application does not create obscurity – nay *doubt*. Nor can a case ever occur where any such principle is called for. The general law that the change of motion is proportional to the moving force and takes place in its direction, provided we take care always to regard the *reaction* of curves, surfaces, obstacles, &c., as so many real moving forces of (for a time) unknown magnitude, will always help us out of any dynamical scrape we may get into. Laplace, page 20, Méc. Cél. art. 7, is a little obscure here, and in deriving his equation (*f*) a page of explanation would be well bestowed.

One thing let me recommend, if you use as principles either this, or that of virtual velocities, or any other, state them broadly and in general terms . . .

You will think me, I fear, a rough critic, but I think of Horace's *good critic*,

> Fiet Aristarchus: nec dicet, cur ego amicum
> Offendam in nugis? Hæ nugæ seria ducent
> In mala,

and what we can both now laugh at, and you may, if you like, burn as nonsense (I mean these remarks), would come with a very different kind of force from some sneering reviewer in the plenitude of his triumph at the detection of a slip of the pen or one of those little inaccuracies which *humana parum cavit natura*[65] . . .

Very faithfully yours,
J. HERSCHEL

[About the same time my father received a letter from Dr Whewell, afterwards Master of Trinity College, Cambridge, dated 2nd November, 1831, in which he says:—]

I beg you to offer my best thanks to Mrs. Somerville for her kind present. I shall have peculiar satisfaction in possessing it as a gift of the author, a book which I look upon as one of the most remarkable which our age has produced, which would be highly valuable from anyone, and which derives a peculiar interest from its writer. I am charged also to return the thanks of the Philosophical Society here for the copy presented to them. I have not thought it necessary to send the official letter containing the acknowledgment, as Mrs. Somerville will probably have a sufficient collection of specimens of such character. I have also to thank her on the part of our College for the copy sent to the library. I am glad that our young mathematicians in Trinity will have easy access to the book, which will be very good for them as soon as they can read it. When Mrs. Somerville shows herself in the field which we mathematicians have been labouring in all our lives, and puts us to shame, she ought not to be surprised if we move off to other ground, and betake ourselves to poetry. If the fashion of 'commendatory verses' were not gone by, I have no doubt her work might have appeared with a very pretty collection of well-deserved poetical praises in its introductory pages. As old customs linger longest in places like this, I hope she and you will not think it quite extravagant to send a single sonnet on the occasion.

Believe me,

Faithfully yours,

W. WHEWELL

TO MRS SOMERVILLE,

ON HER 'MECHANISM OF THE HEAVENS'

Lady, it was the wont in earlier days
When some fair volume from a valued pen,
Long looked for, came at last, that grateful men
Hailed its forthcoming in complacent lays:
As if the Muse would gladly haste to praise

That which her mother, Memory, long should keep
Among her treasures. Shall such usage sleep
With us, who feel too slight the common phrase
For our pleased thoughts of you, when thus we find
That dark to you seems bright, perplexed seems plain,
Seen in the depths of a pellucid mind,
Full of clear thought, pure from the ill and vain
That cloud the inward light? An honoured name
Be yours; and peace of heart grow with your growing fame.

[Professor Peacock, afterwards Dean of Ely, in a letter, dated February 14th, 1832, thanked my mother for a copy of the *Mechanism of the Heavens*.]

LETTER FROM PROFESSOR PEACOCK TO MRS SOMERVILLE

I consider it to be a work which will contribute greatly to the extension of the knowledge of physical astronomy, in this country, and of the great analytical processes which have been employed in such investigations. It is with this view that I consider it to be a work of the greatest value and importance. Dr Whewell and myself have already taken steps to introduce it into the course of our studies at Cambridge, and I have little doubt that it will immediately become an essential work to those of our students who aspire to the highest places in our examinations.

[On this my mother remarks:—]

———————

I consider this as the highest honour I ever received, at the time I was no less sensible of it, and was most grateful. I was surprised and pleased beyond measure to find that my book should be so much approved of by Dr Whewell, one of the most eminent men of the age for science and literature; and by Professor Peacock, a profound mathematician, who with Herschel and Babbage had, a few years before, first introduced the calculus as an essential branch of science into the University of Cambridge.

In consequence of this decision the whole edition of the *Mechanism of the Heavens*, amounting to 750 copies, was sold chiefly at Cambridge, with the exception of a very few which I gave to friends; but as the preface was the only part of the work that was intelligible to the general reader, I had some copies of it printed separately to give away.

I was astonished at the success of my book; all the reviews of it were highly favourable; I received letters of congratulation from many men of science. I was elected an honorary member of the Royal Astronomical Society at the same time as Miss Caroline Herschel. To be associated with so distinguished an astronomer was in itself an honour. Mr De Morgan, to whom I am indebted for many excellent mathematical works, was then secretary of the society, and announced to us the distinction conferred. The council of the Society ordered that a copy of the 'Greenwich Observations' should be regularly sent to me.

[The *Académie des Sciences* elected my mother's old friend M. Biot to draw up a report upon her *Mechanism of the Heavens*, which he did in the most flattering terms, and upon my mother writing to thank him, replied as follows:—]

FROM M. BIOT TO MRS SOMERVILLE

MADAME,

Revenu de Lyon depuis quelques jours, j'ai trouvé à Paris les deux lettres dont vous avez daigné m'honorer, et j'ai reçu également l'exemplaire de votre ouvrage que vous avez bien voulu joindre à la dernière. C'est être mille fois trop bonne,

Madame, que de me remercier encore de ce qui m'a fait tant de plaisir. En rendant compte de cet étonnant Traité, je remplissais d'abord un devoir, puisque l'Académie m'avait chargé de le lire pour elle; mais ce devoir m'offrait un attrait que vous concevriez facilement, s'il vous était possible de vous rappeler l'admiration vive et profonde que m'inspira il y a longtems l'union si extraordinaire de tous les talens et de toutes les grâces, avec les connaissances sevères que nous autres hommes avions la folie de croire notre partage exclusif. Ce qui me charma alors, Madame, je n'ai pas cessé depuis de m'en souvenir; et des rapports d'amitié qui me sont bien chers, ont encore, à votre insçu, fortifié ces sentimens. Jugez donc, Madame, combien j'étais heureux d'avoir à peindre ce que je comprenais si bien, et ce que j'avais vu avec un si vif intérêt. Le plus amusant pour moi de cette rencontre, c'était de voir nos plus graves confrères, par exemple, Lacroix et Legendre, qui certes ne sont pas des esprits légers, ni galans d'habitude, ni faciles à émouvoir, me gourmander, comme ils le faisaient à chaque séance, de ce que je tardais tant à faire mon rapport, de ce que j'y mettais tant d'insouciance et si peu de grâce; enfin, Madame, c'était une conquête intellectuelle complète. Je n'ai pas manqué de raconter cette circonstance comme un des fleurons de votre couronne. Je me suis ainsi acquitté envers eux; et quant à vous, Madame, d'après la manière dont vous parlez vous-même de votre ouvrage, j'ai quelque espérance de l'avoir présenté sous le point de vue où vous semblez l'envisager. Mais, en vous rendant ce juste et sincère hommage et en l'insérant au Journal des Savans, je n'ai pas eu la précaution de demander qu'on m'en mit à part; aujourd'hui que la collection est tirée je suis aux regrets d'avoir été si peu prévoyant. Au reste, Madame, il n'y a rien dans cet extrait que ce que pensent tous ceux qui vous connaissent, ou même qui ont eu une seule fois le bonheur de vous approcher. Vos amis trouveront que j'ai exprimé bien faiblement les charmes de votre esprit et de votre caractère; charmes qu'ils doivent apprécier d'autant mieux qu'ils en jouissent plus souvent; mais vous, Madame, qui êtes indulgente, vous pardonnerez la faiblesse d'un portrait qui n'a pu être fait que de souvenir.

J'ai l'honneur d'être, avec le plus profond respect,

Madame,

Votre très humble et très obéissant serviteur,

BIOT

It was unanimously voted by the Royal Society of London, that my bust should be placed in their great Hall, and Chantrey was chosen as the sculptor. Soon after it was finished, Mr Potter, a great ship-builder at Liverpool, who had just completed a fine vessel intended for the China and India trade, wrote to my friend, Sir Francis Beaufort°, hydrographer of the Royal Navy, asking him if I would give him permission to call her the *Mary Somerville*, and to have a copy of my bust for her figure-head. I was much gratified with this, as might be expected. The *Mary Somerville* sailed, but was never heard of again; it was supposed she had foundered during a typhoon in the China Sea.

I was elected an honorary member of the Royal Academy at Dublin, of the Bristol Philosophical Institution, and of the Société de Physique et d'Histoire Naturelle of Geneva, which was announced to me by a very gratifying letter from Professor Prevost.

Our relations and others who had so severely criticised and ridiculed me, astonished at my success, were now loud in my praise. The warmth with which Somerville entered into my success deeply affected me; for not one in ten thousand would have rejoiced at it as he did, but he was of a generous nature, far above jealousy, and he continued through life to take the kindest interest in all I did.

I now received the following letter from Sir Robert Peel°, informing me in the handsomest manner that he had advised the King to grant me a pension of £200 a year –

LETTER FROM SIR ROBERT PEEL TO
MRS SOMERVILLE

WHITEHALL GARDENS,
March, 1835

MADAM,

In advising the Crown in respect to the grant of civil pensions, I have acted equally with a sense of public duty and on the impulse of my own private feelings in recognising among the first claims on the Royal favour those which are derived from eminence in science and literature.

In reviewing such claims, it is impossible that I can overlook those which you have established by the successful prosecution of studies of the highest order, both from the importance of the objects to which they relate, and from the faculties and acquirements which they demand.

As my object is a public one, to encourage others to follow the bright example which you have set, and to prove that great scientific attainments are recognised among public claims, I prefer making a direct communication to you, to any private inquiries into your pecuniary circumstances, or to any proposal through a third party. I am enabled to advise His Majesty to grant to you a pension on the civil list of two hundred pounds per annum; and if that provision will enable you to pursue your labours with less of anxiety, either as to the present or the future, I shall only be fulfilling a public duty, and not imposing upon you the slightest obligation, by availing myself of your permission to submit such a recommendation to the King.

I have the honour to be,
Madam, with the sincerest respect,
ROBERT PEEL

I was highly pleased, but my pleasure was of short duration, for the very next day a letter informed us that by the treachery of persons in whom we trusted, the last remains of our capital were lost. By the kindness of Lord John Russell°, when he was Prime Minister, a hundred a year was added to my pension, for which I was very grateful.

[*1D, 168–9:* In the climax of my great success, the approbation of some of the first scientific men of the age and of the public in general I was highly gratified, but much less elated than might have been expected, for although I had recorded in a clear point of view some of the most refined and difficult analytical processes and astronomical discoveries, I was conscious that I had never made a discovery myself, that I had no originality. I have perseverance and intelligence but no genius. That spark from heaven is not granted to the sex, we are of the earth, earthy, whether higher powers may be allotted to us in another state of existence, God knows, original genius in science at least is hopeless in this. (*scored out:* At all events it has not yet appeared in the higher branches of science.)

Soon after the *Mechanism of the Heavens* was published we were at a large party in Lansdown House when a celebrated physician who often presided at scientific meetings and wrote clever articles in the reviews, came to me with a grave face and said, 'It is a pity you published that book, you have made a sad mistake with regard to the effect of air in falling bodies in the very beginning of the book which vitiates all the rest, I am sorry for you,' and he walked away. I was thunder struck and fairly lost my head or I should at once have seen that he was speaking nonsense, besides I might have been certain that neither Mr Herschel nor Lord Brougham would have overlooked so gross an error, but I was confused and spent a very unhappy evening. This was not the only attack my book met with; a Mr Buller°, member for some place I have forgotten in the West of England, spoke of it in the House of Commons with sovereign contempt. I was much more annoyed than I ought to have been for he showed that he was totally ignorant of the state of science. *2D has a marginal note in MS's hand to say that this may stay.*]

After the *Mechanism of the Heavens* was published, I was thrown out of work, and now that I had got into the habit of writing I did not know what to make of my spare time. Fortunately the preface of my book furnished me with the means of active occupation, for in it I saw such mutual dependence and connection in many branches of science, that I thought the subject might be carried to a greater extent.

There were many subjects with which I was only partially acquainted, and others of which I had no previous knowledge, but which required to be carefully investigated, so I had to consult a variety of authors, British and foreign. Even the astronomical part was difficult, for I had to translate analytical formulæ into intelligible language, and to draw diagrams illustrative thereof, and this occupied the first seven sections of the book. I should have been saved much trouble had I seen a work on the subject by Mr Airy, Astronomer Royal, published subsequently to my book.

My son, Woronzow Greig, had been educated at Trinity College, Cambridge, and was travelling on the Continent, when Somerville and I received an invitation from the Principal, Dr Whewell, to visit the University. Mr Airy, then astronomer at Cambridge, now Astronomer Royal at Greenwich, and Mrs Airy kindly wished us to be their guests: but as the Observatory was at some distance from Cambridge, it was decided that we should have an apartment in Trinity College itself; an unusual favour where a lady is concerned. Mr Sedgwick°, the geologist, made the arrangements, received us, and we spent the first day at dinner with him. He is still alive – one of my few coevals – either in Cambridge or England. The week we spent in Cambridge, receiving every honour from the heads of the university, was a period of which I have ever borne a proud and grateful remembrance.

[Professor Sedgwick wrote as follows to my father:—]

FROM PROFESSOR SEDGWICK TO DR SOMERVILLE

TRINITY COLLEGE, *April, 1834*

MY DEAR SOMERVILLE,

Your letter delighted us. I have ordered dinner on Thursday at 6½ and shall have a small party to welcome you and Mrs Somerville. In order that we may not have to fight for you, we have been entering on the best arrangements we can think of. On Tuesday you will, I hope, dine with Peacock; on Wednesday with Whewell: on Thursday at the Observatory. For Friday, Dr. Clarke°, our Professor of Anatomy, puts in a claim. For the other days of your visit we shall, D.V., find ample employment. A four-poster bed now (a thing utterly out of our regular monastic system) will rear its head for you and Madame in the chambers immediately below my own; and your handmaid may safely rest her bones in a small inner chamber. Should Sheepshanks return, we can stuff him into a lumber room of the observatory; but of this there is no fear as I have written to him on the subject, and he has no immediate intention of returning. You will of course drive to the great gate of Trinity College, and my servant will be in waiting at the Porter's lodge to show you the way to your academic residence. We have no cannons at Trinity College, otherwise we would fire a salute on your entry; we will however give you the warmest greeting we can. Meanwhile give my best regards to Mrs. S.

And believe me most truly yours,

A. SEDGWICK

Laplace had a profound veneration for Newton; he sent me a copy of his *Système du Monde*, and a letter, dated 15th

August, 1824, in which he says; 'Je publie successivement les divers livres du cinquième livre qui doit terminer mon traité de *Mécanique Céleste*, et dans cela je donne l'analyse historique des recherches des géomètres sur cette matière, cela m'a fait relire avec une attention particulière l'ouvrage si incomparable des principes mathématiques de la philosophie naturelle de Newton, qui contient le germe de toutes ses recherches. Plus j'ai étudié cet ouvrage plus il m'a paru admirable, en me transportant surtout à l'époque où il a été publié. Mais en même tems que je sens l'élégance de la méthode synthétique suivant laquelle Newton a présenté ses découvertes, j'ai reconnu l'indispensable nécessité de l'analyse pour approfondir les questions très difficiles que Newton n'a pu qu'effleurer par la synthèse. Je vois avec un grand plaisir vos mathématiciens se livrer maintenant à l'analyse et je ne doute point qu'en suivant cette méthode avec la sagacité propre à votre nation ils ne seront conduits à d'importantes découvertes.'[66]

Newton himself was aware that by the law of gravitation the stability of the solar system was endangered. The power of analysis alone enabled Lagrange to prove that all the disturbances arising from the reciprocal attraction of the planets and satellites are periodical, whatever the length of the periods may be, so that the stability of the solar system is insured for unlimited ages. The perturbations are only the oscillations of that immense pendulum of Eternity which beats centuries as ours beats seconds.

Laplace, and all the great mathematicians of that period, had scarcely passed away when the more powerful Quaternion system began to dawn.[67]

TWELVE

Paris – Arago, Lafayette, MM. Bouvard, Poisson, Lacroix, &c., Marquise de Laplace, Dupin, F. Cooper – Legitimiste Society – Majendie – Visit Baron Louis – Letter from Lafayette

MY health was never good at Chelsea, and as I had been working too hard, I became so ill, that change of air and scene were thought absolutely necessary for me. We went accordingly to Paris; partly, because it was near home, as Somerville could not remain long with us at a time, and, partly, because we thought it a good opportunity to give masters to the girls, which we could not afford to do in London. When we arrived, I was so weak, that I always remained in bed writing till one o'clock, and then, either went to sit in the Tuileries gardens, or else received visits. All my old friends came to see me, Arago the first. He was more engaged in politics than science, and as party spirit ran very high at that time, he said he would send tickets of admission to the Chambers every time there was likely to be an *orage*.[68] When I told him what I was writing, he gave me some interesting memoirs, and lent me a mass of manuscripts, with leave to make extracts, which were very useful to me. General de Lafayette° came to town on purpose to invite Somerville and me to visit him at La Grange, where we found him living like a patriarch, surrounded by his family to the fourth generation. He was mild, highly distinguished, and noble in his manners; his conversation was exceedingly interesting, as he readily spoke of the Revolution in which he had taken so active a part. Among other anecdotes, he mentioned, that he had sent the principal key of the Bastile to General Washington, who kept it under a glass case. He was much interested to hear that I could, in some degree, claim a kind of relationship with Washington, whose mother was a Fairfax. Baron Fairfax, the head of the family, being settled in America, had joined the independent party at the Revolution.[69]

The two daughters of Lafayette, who had been in prison with him at Olmütz, were keen politicians, and discussed points with a warmth of gesticulation which amused Somerville and me, accustomed to our cold still manners. The grand-daughters, Mesdames de Rémusat and de Corcelles, were kind friends to me all the time I was in Paris.

M. Bouvard, whom we had known in London, was now Astronomer Royal of France, and he invited us to dine with him at the Observatory. The table was surrounded by *savants*, who complimented me on the *Mechanism of the Heavens*. I sat next M. Poisson, who advised me in the strongest manner to write a second volume, so as to complete the account of Laplace's works; and he afterwards told Somerville that there were not twenty men in France who could read my book. M. Arago, who was of the party, said he had not written to thank me for my book, because he had been reading it, and was busy preparing an account of it for the Journal of the Institute. At this party, I made the acquaintance of the celebrated astronomer, M. Pontécoulant°, and soon after, of M. Lacroix to whose works I was indebted for my knowledge of the highest branches of mathematics. M. Prony°, and M. Poinsot°, came to visit me, the latter, an amiable and gentlemanly person; both gave me a copy of their works.

We had a long visit from M. Biot, who seemed really glad to renew our old friendship. He was making experiments on light, though much out of health; but when we dined with him and Madame Biot, he forgot for the time his bad health, and resumed his former gaiety. They made us promise to visit them at their country-house when we returned to England, as it lay on our road.

To my infinite regret, Laplace had been dead some time; the Marquise was still at Arcœuil, and we went to see her. She received us with the greatest warmth, and devoted herself to us the whole time we were in Paris. As soon as she came to town, we went to make a morning visit; it was past five o'clock; we were shown into a beautiful drawing-room, and the man-servant, without knocking at the door, went into the room which was adjacent, and we heard her call out, 'J'irai la voir! j'irai la voir!' and when the man-servant came out, he said, 'Madame est désolée, mais elle est en chemise.' Madame de Laplace was exceedingly agreeable, the life of every party, with her cheerful gay manner. She was in great favour with the Royal Family, and was always welcome when she went to visit them in an evening. She received once a week, and her grand-daughter, only nineteen, lovely and graceful, was an ornament to her parties. She was already married to M. de Colbert°, whose father fell at Corunna.

No one was more attentive to me than Dr Milne-Edwards°, the celebrated natural historian. He was the first Englishman who was elected a member of the Institute. I was indebted to him for the acquaintance of MM. Ampère° and Becquerel°. I believe Dr Edwards was at that time writing on Physiology, and, in conversation, I happened to mention that the wild ducks in the fens, at Lincolnshire, always build their nests on high tufts of grass, or reeds, to save them from sudden floods; and that Sir John Sebright had raised wild ducks under a hen, which built their nests on tufts of grass as if they had been in the fens. Dr Edwards begged of me to inquire for how many generations that instinct lasted.

Monsieur and Madame Gay Lussac lived in the Jardin des Plantes. Madame was only twenty-one, exceedingly pretty, and well-educated; she read English and German, painted prettily, and was a musician. She told me it had been computed, that if all the property in France were equally divided among the population, each person would have 150 francs a year, or four sous per day; so that if anyone should spend eight sous a day, some other person would starve.

The Duchesse de Broglie, Madame de Staël's daughter, called, and invited us to her receptions, which were the most brilliant in Paris. Every person of distinction was there, French or foreign, generally four or five men to one woman. The Duchess was a charming woman, both handsome and amiable, and received with much grace. The Duke° was, then, Minister for Foreign Affairs. They were remarkable for their domestic virtues, as well as for high intellectual cultivation. The part the Duke took in politics is so well known, that I need not allude to it here.

At some of these parties I met with Madame Charles Dupin°, whom I liked much. When I went to return her visit, she received us in her bedroom. She was a fashionable and rather elegant woman, with perfect manners. She invited us to dinner to meet her brother-in-law, the President of the Chamber of Deputies. He was animated and witty, very fat, and more ugly than his brother, but both were clever and agreeable. The President invited me to a very brilliant ball he gave, but as it was on a Sunday I could not accept the invitation. We went one evening with Madame Charles Dupin to be introduced to Madame de Rumford. Her first husband, Lavoisier°, the chemist, had been guillotined at the Revolution, and she was now a widow, but had lived long separated from her second husband. She was enormously rich, and had a magnificent palace, garden, and conservatory, in which she gave balls and concerts. At all the evening parties in Paris the best bedroom was lighted up for reception like the other rooms. Madame de Rumford was capricious and ill-tempered; however, she received me very well, and invited me to meet a very large party at dinner. Mr Fenimore Cooper°, the American novelist, with his wife and daughter, were among the guests. I found him extremely amiable and agreeable, which surprised me, for when I knew him in England he was so touchy that it was difficult to converse with him without giving him offence. He was introduced to Sir Walter Scott by Sir James Mackintosh, who said, in presenting him, 'Mr Cooper, allow me to introduce you to your great forefather in the art of fiction'; 'Sir,' said Cooper, with great asperity, 'I have no forefather.' Now, though his manners were rough, they were quite changed. We saw a great deal of him, and I was frequently in his house, and found him perfectly liberal; so much so, that he told us the faults of his country with the greatest frankness, yet he was the champion of America, and hated England.

None were kinder to us than Lord and Lady Granville. Lady Granville invited us to all her parties; and when Somerville was obliged to return to England, she assured him that in case of any disturbance, we should find a refuge in the Embassy. I went to some balls at the Tuileries with Madame de Lafayette Lasteyrie and her sister. The Queen Amélie° was tall, thin, and very fair, not pretty, but infinitely more regal than Adelaide°, Queen of England, at that time. The Royal Family used to walk about in the streets of Paris without any attendants.

Sir Sidney Smith° was still in Paris trying to renew the order of the Knights Templars. Somerville and I went with him one evening to a reception at the Duchesse d'Abrantès°, widow of Junot. She was short, thick, and not in the least distinguished-looking, nor in any way remarkable. I had met her at the Duchesse de Broglie's, where she talked of Junot as if he had been in the next room. Sir Sidney was quite covered with stars and crosses, and I was amused with the way he threw his cloak back to display them as he handed me to the carriage.

I met with Prince Kosloffsky° everywhere; he was the

fattest man I ever saw, a perfect Falstaff. However, his intellect was not smothered, for he would sit an hour with me talking about mathematics, astronomy, philosophy, and what not. He was banished from Russia, and as he had been speaking imprudently about politics in Paris, he was ordered to go elsewhere; still, he lingered on, and was with me one morning when Pozzo di Borgo°, the Russian Ambassador called. Pozzo di Borgo said to me, 'Are you aware that Prince Kosloffsky has left Paris?' 'Oh yes,' I said, 'I regret it much.' He took the hint, and went away directly.

I had been hitherto entirely among the Liberal set. How it came that I was invited to dine with M. Héricourt de Thury°, I do not remember. M. de Thury was simple in his manners, and full of information; he had been Director of the Mines under Napoleon, and had charge of the Public Buildings under Louis XVIII and Charles X, but resigned his charges at the Revolution of July. At this time the Duchesse de Berry° was confined in the citadel of Blaye. She had a strong party in Paris, who furiously resented the treatment she met with. M. de Thury was a moderate Légitimiste, but Madame was ultra. When I happened to mention that we had been staying with Lafayette, at La Grange, she was horrified, and begged of me not to talk politics, or mention where we had been, or else some of her guests would leave the room. The ladies of that party would not dance or go to any gay party; they had a part of the theatre reserved for themselves; they wore high dark dresses with long sleeves, called 'Robes de Résistance,' and even the Légitimiste newspapers appeared with black edges. They criticised those who gave balls, and Lady Granville herself did not escape their censure. The marriage of the Duchesse de Berry to the Marchese Lucchesi Palli made an immense sensation; it was discussed in the salons in a truly French manner; it was talked of in the streets; the 'Robes de Résistance' were no longer worn, and the Légitimiste newspapers went out of mourning.

All parties criticised the British Administration in Ireland. A lady sitting by me at a party said, 'No wonder so many English prefer France to so odious a country as England, where the people are oppressed, and even cabbages are raised in hot-beds.' I laughed, and said, 'I like England very well, for all that.' An old gentleman, who was standing near us, said, 'Whatever terms two countries may be on, it behoves us individuals to observe good manners;' and when I went away, this gentleman handed me to the carriage, though I had never seen him before.

The Marquise de Laplace was commissioned by Dr Majendie° to invite me to meet her and Madame Gay Lussac at dinner. I was very unwilling to go: for I detested the man for his wanton cruelties, but I found I could not refuse on account of these ladies. There was a large party of *savants*, agreeable and gentlemanly; but Majendie himself had the coarsest manners; his conversation was horridly professional; many things were said and subjects discussed not fit for women to hear. What a contrast the refined and amiable Sir Charles Bell° formed with Majendie! Majendie and the French school of anatomy made themselves odious by their cruelty, and failed to prove the true anatomy of the brain and nerves, while Sir Charles Bell did succeed, and thus made one of the greatest physiological discoveries of the age without torturing animals, which his gentle and kindly nature abhorred. To Lady Bell I am indebted for a copy of her husband's Life. She is one of my few dear and valued friends who are still alive.

While in Paris, I lost my dear mother. She died at the age of ninety, attended by my brother Henry. She was still a fine old lady, with few grey hairs. The fear of death was almost hereditary in the Charters family, and my mother possessed it in no small degree; yet when it came, she was perfectly composed and prepared for it. I have never had that fear;

may God grant that I may be as calm and prepared as she was.

I was in better health, but still so delicate that I wrote in bed till one o'clock. The *Connexion of the Physical Sciences* was a tedious work, and the proof sheets had to be sent through the Embassy.

M. Arago told me that David°, the sculptor, wished to make a medallion of me; so he came and sat an hour with me, and pleased me by his intelligent conversation and his enthusiasm for art. A day was fixed, and he took my profile on slate with pink wax, in a wonderfully short time. He made me a present of a medallion in bronze, nicely framed, and two plaster casts for my daughters.

I frequently went to hear the debates in the Chambers, and occasionally took my girls, as I thought it was an excellent lesson in French. As party spirit ran very high, the scenes that occurred were very amusing. A member, in the course of his speech, happening to mention the word '*liberté*,' the President Dupin rang the bell, called out 'Stop, *à propos de liberté*,' . . . jumped down from his seat, sprang into the tribune, pushed out the deputy, and made a long speech himself.

The weather being fine, we made excursions in the neighbourhood. At Sèvres I saw two pieces of china; on one of them was a gnu, on the other a zebra. Somerville had told me that soon after his return from his African expedition, he had given the original drawings to M. Brongniart°, then director of the manufactory.

Baron Louis° invited me to spend a day with him and his niece, Mademoiselle de Rigny, at his country house, not far from Paris. I went with Madame de Laplace, and we set out early, to be in time for breakfast. The road lay through the Forest of Vincennes. The Baron's park, which was close to the village of Petit-Brie, was very large, and richly wooded;

there were gardens, hot-houses, and all the luxuries of an English nobleman's residence. The house was handsome, with a magnificent library; I remarked on the table the last numbers of the *Edinburgh* and *Quarterly Reviews*. Both the Baron and his niece were simple and kind. I was greatly taken with both; the Baron had all the quiet elegance of the old school, and his niece had great learning and the manners of a woman of fashion. She lived in perfect retirement, having suffered much in the time of the Revolution. They had both eventful lives; for Baron Louis, who had been in orders, and Talleyrand° officiated at the Champ de Mars⁷⁰ when Louis the Sixteenth took the oath to maintain the constitution. Field-Marshal Macdonald°, Duc de Tarante, and his son-in-law, the Duc de Massa°; Admiral de Rigny°, Minister of Marine; M. Barthe°, Garde des Sceaux; and the Bouvards°, father and son, formed the party. After spending a most delightful and interesting day, we drove to Paris in bright moonlight.

Our friends in Paris and at La Grange had been so kind to us that we were very sad when we went to express our gratitude and take leave of them. We only stayed two days at La Grange, and when we returned to Paris, Somerville went home and my son joined us, when we made a rapid tour in Switzerland, the only remarkable event of which was a singular atmospheric phenomenon we saw on the top of the Grimsel.⁷¹ On the clouds of vapour below us we saw our shadows projected, of giant proportions, and each person saw his own shadow surrounded by a bright circle of prismatic colours. It is not uncommon in mountain regions.

[General Lafayette and all his family were extremely kind to my mother. He was her constant visitor, and we twice visited him at his country house, La Grange. He wished to persuade my mother to go there for some days, after our return from Switzerland, which we did not accomplish. The General wrote the following letter to my father:—]

FROM LAFAYETTE TO DR SOMERVILLE

La Grange, *31st October, 1833*

My dear Sir,

I waited to answer your kind letter, for the arrival of Mr. Coke's° precious gift, which nobody could higher value, on every account, than the grateful farmer on whom it has been bestowed. The heifers and bull are beautiful; they have reached La Grange in the best order, and shall be tenderly attended to . . . It has been a great disappointment not to see Mrs. Somerville and the young ladies before their departure. Had we not depended on their kind visit, we should have gone to take leave of them. They have had the goodness to regret the impossibility to come before their departure. Be so kind as to receive the affectionate friendship and good wishes of a family who are happy in the ties of mutual attachment that bind us to you and them . . . Public interest is now fixed upon the Peninsula, and while dynasties are at civil war, and despotic or *juste milieu*[72] cabinets seem to agree in the fear of a genuine development of popular institutions, the matter for the friends of freedom is to know how far the great cause of Europe shall be forwarded by these royal squabbles.

We shall remain at La Grange until the opening of the session, hoping that, notwithstanding your and the ladies' absence, your attention will not be quite withdrawn from our interior affairs – the sympathy shall be reciprocal.

With all my heart, I am

Your affectionate friend,

Lafayette

THIRTEEN

*Return to England – Letter from Hallam – Treatise on the
Form and Rotation of the Earth and Planets – Second Edition
of 'Connexion of the Physical Sciences' – Letters from Maria
Edgeworth, Miss Berry, Lord Brougham, Mrs Marcet,
Admiral Smyth – Double Stars – Eclipse of Double Stars –
Letter from Admiral Smyth – Sir William Herschel – Nebulæ –
Letter from Lord Rosse – Letter from Sir John Herschel –
Sir James South's Observatory – Mr John Murray – Miss
Berry – Lord Dudley – Mr Bowditch and other Distinguished
Americans – Mrs Browning Washington – Letter from the
Rev. Dr Tuckerman – Sir William Fairfax Attacked by
Highwaymen*

AS soon as we returned to Chelsea, the *Connexion of the
Physical Sciences* was published. It was dedicated to Queen
Adelaide, who thanked me for it at a drawing-room. Some
time after Somerville and I went to Scotland; we had
travelled all night in the mail coach, and when it became
light, a gentleman who was in the carriage said to Somerville, 'Is not the lady opposite to me Mrs Somerville, whose
bust I saw at Chantrey's?' The gentleman was Mr Sopwith°
of Newcastle-on-Tyne, a civil and mining engineer. He was
distinguished for scientific knowledge, and had been in
London to give information to a parliamentary committee.
He travelled faster than we did, and when we arrived at
Newcastle he was waiting to take us to his house, where we
were hospitably received by Mrs Sopwith. His conversation
was highly interesting, and to him I was indebted for much
information on mining generally, and on the mineral

wealth of Great Britain, while writing on physical geography. Many years after he and Mrs Sopwith came and saw me at Naples, which gave me much pleasure. He was unlike any other traveller I ever met with, so profound and original were his observations on all he saw.

On coming home I found that I had made an error in the first edition of the *Physical Sciences*, in giving 365 days 6 hours as the length of the civil year of the ancient Egyptians. My friend Mr Hallam°, the historian, wrote to me, proving from history and epochs of the chronology of the ancient Egyptians, that their civil year was only 365 days. I was grateful to that great and amiable man for copies of all his works while he was alive, and I am obliged to his daughter for an excellent likeness of him, now that he is no more.

FROM HENRY HALLAM, ESQ., TO MRS SOMERVILLE

WIMPOLE STREET, *March 12th, 1835*

MY DEAR MADAM,

As you will probably soon be called upon for another edition of your excellent work on the *Connexion of the Physical Sciences* I think you will excuse the liberty I take in mentioning to you one passage which seems to have escaped your attention in so arduous a labour. It is in page 104, where you have this sentence:—

'The Egyptians estimated the year at 365d. 6h., by which they lost one year in every 14,601, their Sothiac period. They determined the length of their year by the heliacal rising of Sirius, 2782 years before the Christian era, which is the earliest epoch of Egyptian chronology.'

The Egyptian civil year was of 365 days only, as we find in Herodotus, and I apprehend there is no dispute about it. The Sothiac period, or that cycle in which the heliacal rising of Sirius passed the whole civil year, and took place again on the same day, was of 1461 years, not 14,601. If they had adopted a year of 365d. 6h., this period would have been more than three times 14,601; the excess of the sidereal year above that being only 9′ 9″; which will not amount to a day in less than about 125 years.

I do not see how the heliacal rising of Sirius in any one year could help them to determine its length. By comparing two successive years they could of course have got at a sidereal year; but this is what they did not do; hence the irregularity which produced the canicular cycle. The commencement of that cycle is placed by ancient chronologers in 1322 A.C. It seems not correct to call 2782 A.C. 'the earliest epoch of Egyptian chronology,' for we have none of their chronology nearly so old, and in fact no chronology, properly so called, has yet been made out by our Egyptian researches. It is indeed certain that, if the reckoning by heliacal risings of Sirius did not begin in 1322, we must go nearly 1460 years back for its origin; since it must have been adopted when that event preceded only for a short time the annual inundation of the Nile. But, according to some, the year 1322 A.C. fell during the reign of Sesostris, to whom Herodotus ascribes several regulations connected with the rising of the Nile. Certainly, 2782 A.C. is a more remote era than we are hitherto warranted to assume for any astronomical observation.

> Believe me, dear Mrs. Somerville,
>> Very truly yours,
>>> HENRY HALLAM

I refer you to Montucla,[73] if you have any doubt about the Egyptian year being of 365 days without bissextile of any kind.

I had sent a copy of the *Mechanism of the Heavens* to M. Poisson soon after it was published, and I had received a letter from him dated 30th May 1832, advising me to complete the work by writing a volume on the form and rotation of the Earth and planets. Being again strongly advised to do so while in Paris, I now began the work, and, in consequence, I was led into a correspondence with Mr Ivory, who had written on the subject, and also with Mr Francis Baily, on the density and compression of the earth. My work was extensive, for it comprised the analytical attraction of spheroids, the form and rotation of the earth, the tides of the ocean and atmosphere, and small undulations.

When this was finished, I had nothing to do, and as I preferred analysis to all other subjects, I wrote a work of 246 pages on curves and surfaces of the second and higher orders. While writing this, *con amore*, a new edition of the *Physical Sciences* was much needed, so I put on high pressure and worked at both. Had these two manuscripts been published at that time, they might have been of use; I do not remember why they were laid aside, and forgotten till I found them years afterwards among my papers. Long after the time I am writing about, while at Naples, I amused myself by repairing the time-worn parts of these manuscripts, and was surprised to find that in my eighty-ninth year I still retained facility in the 'Calculus.'

The second edition of the *Physical Sciences* was dedicated to my dear friend, Sir John Herschel. It went through nine editions, and has been translated into German and Italian. The book went through various editions in the United States, to the honour, but not to the profit, of the author. However, the publisher obligingly sent me a copy. I must say that profit was never an object with me: I wrote because it was impossible for me to be idle.

I had the honour of presenting a copy of my book to the Duchess of Kent° at a private audience. The Duchess and Princess Victoria were alone, and received me very graciously, and conversed for half an hour with me. As I mentioned before, I saw the young Princess crowned:

youthful, almost childlike as she was, she went through the imposing ceremony with all the dignity of a Queen.

[A few letters from some of my mother's friends, written at this period, may prove of interest. They are chiefly written to thank her for copies of the Preliminary Dissertation or of the *Physical Sciences*. One from Lord Brougham concerns my mother's estimate of the scientific merit of Dr Young, for whom she had the sincerest admiration, and considered him one of the first philosophers and discoursers of the age.]

FROM MISS EDGEWORTH TO MRS SOMERVILLE

EDGWORTHTOWN, May *31st, 1832*

MY DEAR MRS SOMERVILLE,

There is one satisfaction at least in giving knowledge to the ignorant, to those who know their ignorance at least, that they are grateful and humble. You should have my grateful and humble thanks long ago for the favour – the honour – you did me by sending me that Preliminary Dissertation, in which there is so much knowledge, but that I really wished to read it over and over again at some intervals of time, and to have the pleasure of seeing my sister Harriet read it, before I should write to you. She has come to us, and has just been enjoying it, as I knew she would. For my part, I was long in the state of the boa constrictor after a full meal – and I am but just recovering the powers of motion. My mind was so distended by the magnitude, the immensity, of what you put into it! I am afraid that if you had been aware how ignorant I was you would not have sent me this dissertation, because you would have felt that you were throwing away much that I could not understand, and that could be better bestowed on scientific friends capable of judging of what they admire. I can only assure you that you have given me a great deal of pleasure; that you have enlarged my conception of the sublimity of the universe, beyond any ideas I had ever before been enabled to form.

The great simplicity of your manner of writing, I may say of your *mind*, which appears in your writing, particularly suits the scientific sublime – which would be destroyed by what is commonly called fine writing. You trust sufficiently to the natural interest of your subject, to the importance of the facts, the beauty of the whole, and the adaptation of the means to the ends, in every part of the immense whole. This reliance upon your reader's feeling along with you, was to me very gratifying. The ornaments of eloquence dressing out a sublime subject are just so many proofs either of bad taste in the orator, or of distrust and contempt of the taste of those whom he is trying thus to captivate.

I suppose nobody yet has completely *mastered* the tides, therefore I may well content myself with my inability to comprehend what relates to them. But instead of plaguing you with an endless enumeration of my difficulties, I had better tell you some of the passages which gave me, ignoramus as I am, peculiar pleasure . . . I am afraid I shall transcribe your whole book if I go on to tell you all that has struck me, and you would not thank me for that – you, who have so little vanity, and so much to do better with your time than to read *my* ignorant admiration. But pray let me mention to you a few of the passages that amused my imagination particularly, viz., 1st, the inhabitant of Pallas *going round* his world – or who might go – in five or six hours in one of our steam carriages; 2nd, the moderate-sized man who would weigh two tons at the surface of the sun – and who would weigh only a few pounds at the surface of the four new planets, and would be so light as to find it impossible to stand from the excess of muscular force! I think a very entertaining dream might be made of a man's visit to the sun and planets – these ideas are all like dreamy feelings when one is a little feverish. I forgot to mention (page 58) a passage on the propagation of sound. It is a beautiful sentence, as well as a sublime idea, 'so that at a very small height above the surface of the earth, the noise of the tempest ceases and the thunder is heard no more in those boundless regions, where the heavenly bodies accomplish their periods in eternal and sublime silence.'

Excuse me in my trade of sentence-monger, and believe me, dear Mrs. Somerville, truly your obliged and truly your affectionate friend,

MARIA EDGEWORTH

I have persuaded your dear curly-headed friend, Harriet, to add her own observations; she sends her love to you; and I know you love her, otherwise I would not press her to write her own *say.*

FROM MISS JOANNA BAILLIE TO MRS SOMERVILLE.

HAMPSTEAD, *February 1st, 1832*

MY DEAR MRS SOMERVILLE,

I am now, thank God! recovered from a very heavy disease, but still very weak. I will not, however, delay any longer my grateful acknowledgments for your very flattering gift of your Preliminary Dissertation. Indeed, I feel myself greatly honoured by receiving such a mark of regard from one who has done more to remove the light estimation in which the capacity of women is too often held, than all that has been accomplished by the whole sisterhood of poetical damsels and novel-writing authors. I could say much more on this subject were I to follow my own feelings; but I am still so weak that writing is a trouble to me, and I have nearly done all that I am able.

God bless and prosper you!

Yours gratefully and truly,

J. BAILLIE

FROM MISS BERRY TO MRS SOMERVILLE

BELLEVUE, *18th September, 1834*

MY DEAR MRS SOMERVILLE,

I have just finished reading your book, which has entertained me extremely, and at the same time, I hope, improved my moral character in the Christian virtue of humility. These must appear to you such *odd* results – so little like those produced on the great majority of your readers, that you must allow me to explain them to you. Humbled, I must be, by finding my own intellect unequal to following, beyond a first step, the explanations by which you seek to make easy to comprehension the marvellous phenomena of the universe – humbled, by feeling the intellectual difference between you and me, placing you as much above me in the scale of reasoning beings, as I am above my dog. Still I rejoice with humility at feeling myself, in that order of understandings which, although utterly incapable of following the chain of your reasonings, calculations, and inductions – utterly deprived of the powers necessary *sic itur ad astra*[74] – am yet informed, enlightened, and entertained with the series of sublime truths to which you conduct me.

In some foggy morning of November, I shall drive out to you at Chelsea and surprise you with my ignorance of science, by asking you to explain to me some things which you will *wonder any one* can have so long existed without knowing. In the mean time, I wish you could read in any combination of the stars the probability of our often having such a season as this, of uninterrupted summer since April last, and when last week it was sobering into autumn, has now returned to enter summer again. The thermometer was at 83° in the shade yesterday, and to-day promises to be as much. We are delighted with our two months' residence at this place, which we shall see with regret draw towards a close the end of this month. October we mean to spend at Paris, before we return to the *nebulosities* of London. During my residence in Paris, before we came here, I never had the good luck to meet with your friend M. Arago; had I not been reading your book, I should have begged you to give me a letter for him. But as it is, and as my stay at Paris will now be so short, I shall content myself with looking up at a respectful distance to all your great fixed stars of science, excepting always yourself, dear Mrs. Somerville. No 'disturbing influence' will, I hope, ever throw me out of the orbit of *your* intimacy and friendship, whose value, believe me, is most duly and accurately calculated by your ignorant but very affectionate friend,

M. BERRY

FROM LORD BROUGHAM TO MRS SOMERVILLE

1834

MY DEAR MRS SOMERVILLE,

Many thanks for the sheets, which I have read with equal pleasure and instruction as those I formerly had from you. One or two things I could have troubled you with, but they are of little moment. I shall note them. The only one that is at all material relates to the way you mention Dr. Young – not that I object to the word 'illustrious,' or as applied to him. But as you don't give it to one considerably more so, it looks either as if you overrated him, or underrated Davy, or (which I suppose to be the truth) as if you felt Young had not had his due share of honour, and desired to make it up to his memory. Observe I give him a very high place – but Davy's discoveries are both of more unquestioned originality and more undoubtedly true – perhaps I should say, more brought to a close. The alkalis and the principle of the safety lamp are concluded and fixed, the undulation is in progress, and somewhat uncertain as to how and where it may end. You will please to observe that I reckon both those capital discoveries of Davy the fruit of inquiry, and not at all of chance – for, as to the lamp, it is plain; and as to the metals, if you look at the inquiries that immediately preceded, you will see he was thereby led to the alkalis. Indeed, I well remember saying, when I read them, 'He will analyse lime and barytes.' I am quite ready to admit his extreme folly in some things, but that is nothing to the present purpose.

Yours,

H. B.

(*Henry Brougham*)

FROM MRS MARCET TO MRS SOMERVILLE

GENEVA, *6th April, 1834*

DEAR MRS SOMERVILLE,

I am desired by Professor Prevost to inform you that you were elected an honorary member of the Société de Physique et d'Historie Naturelle de Genève on the 3rd April, and that a diploma will be forwarded to you by the earliest opportunity. After all the honours you have received, this little feather is hardly worthy of waving in your plume, but I am glad that Geneva should know how to appreciate your merit. You receive great honours, my dear friend, but that which you confer on our sex is still greater, for with talents and acquirements of masculine magnitude you unite the most sensitive and retiring modesty of the female sex; indeed, I know not any woman, perhaps I might say, any human being, who would support so much applause without feeling the weakness of vanity. Forgive me for allowing my pen to run away with this undisguised praise, it looks so much like compliment, but I assure you it comes straight from the heart, and you *must* know that it is fully deserved . . . I know not whether you have heard of the death of Professor de la Rive° (the father); it was an unexpected blow, which has fallen heavily on all his family. It is indeed a great loss to Geneva, both as a man of science and a most excellent citizen.

M. Rossi has left us to occupy the chair of political economy of the late M. Say°, at Paris; his absence is sadly felt, and it is in vain to look around for any one capable of replacing him . . .

Yours affectionately,

J. MARCET

FROM ADMIRAL W. H. SMYTH° TO MRS SOMERVILLE

CRESCENT, BEDFORD, *October 3rd, 1835*

MY DEAR MADAM,

As an opportunity offers of sending a note to town, I beg to mention that I have somewhat impatiently waited for some appearance of settled weather, in order to press your coming here to inspect Halley's comet, before it should have become visible to the unassisted eye. That unerring monitor, however, the barometer, held forth no hope, and the ceaseless traveller is already an object of conspicuous distinction without artificial aid, except, perhaps, to most eyes an opera-glass, magnifying three or four times, will be found a pleasant addition. It is now gliding along with wonderful celerity, and the nucleus is very bright. It is accompanied with a great luminosity, and the nucleus has changed its position therein; that is, on the 29th August, the nucleus was like a minute star near the centre of the nebulous envelope; on the 2nd September it appeared in the *n. f.* quarter, and latterly it has been in the *s. f.*

How remarkable that the month of August this year should rattle Halley's name throughout the globe, in identity with an astonishing scientific triumph, and that in the selfsame month the letters of Flamsteed° should have appeared! How I wish some one would give us a life of Newton, with all the interesting documents that exist of his labours! Till such appears, Flamsteed's statements, though bearing strong internal evidence of truth, are *ex-parte*, and it is evident his anxiety made him prone to impute motives which he could not prove. The book is painfully interesting, but except in all that relates to the personal character of Flamsteed, I could almost have wished the documents had been destroyed. People of judgment well know that men without faults are monsters, but vulgar minds delight in seeing the standard of human excellence lowered.

Dear Madam,

Yours faithfully,

W. H. SMYTH

We were deprived of the society of Sir John and Lady Herschel for four years, because Sir John took his telescope and other instruments to the Cape of Good Hope, where he went, accompanied by his family, for the purpose of observing the celestial phenomena of the southern hemisphere. There are more than 6000 double stars in the northern hemisphere, in a large proportion of which the angle of position and distance between the two stars have been measured, and Sir John determined, in the same manner, 1081 in the southern hemisphere, and I believe many additions have been made to them since that time. In many of these one star revolves rapidly round the other. The elliptical orbits and periodical times of sixteen or seventeen of these stellar systems have been determined. In Gamma Virginis the two stars are nearly of the same magnitude, and were so far apart in the middle of the last century that they were considered to be quite independent of each other. Since then they have been gradually approaching one another, till, in March, 1836, I had a letter from Admiral Smyth, informing me that he had seen one of the stars eclipse the other, from his observatory at Bedford.

FROM ADMIRAL SMYTH TO MRS SOMERVILLE

CRESCENT, BEDFORD, *March 26th, 1836*

MY DEAR MADAM,

Knowing the great interest you take in sidereal astronomy,[75] of which so little is yet known, I trust it will not be an intrusion to tell you of a new, extraordinary, and very unexpected fact, in the complete occultation of one 'fixed' star by another, under circumstances which admit of no possible doubt or equivocation.

You are aware that I have been measuring the position and distance of the two stars γ^1 and γ^2 Virginis, which are both nearly of similar magnitudes, and also, that they have approximated to each other very rapidly. They were very close last year, and I expected to find they had crossed each other at this apparition, but to my surprise I find they have become a fair round disc, which my highest powers will not elongate – in fact, *a single star!* I shall watch with no little interest for the reappearance of the second γ.

My dear madam,

Your truly obliged servant,

W. H. SMYTH

This eclipse was also seen by Sir John Herschel at the Cape of Good Hope, as well as by many astronomers in Europe provided with instruments of great optical power. In 1782 Sir William Herschel saw one of the stars of Zeta Herculis eclipse the other.

In the *Connexion of the Physical Sciences* I have given an abridged account of Sir John Herschel's most remarkable discoveries in the southern hemisphere; but I may mention here that he determined the position and made accurate drawings of all the nebulæ that were distinctly visible in his

20 ft telescope. The work he published will be a standard for ascertaining the changes that may take place in these mysterious objects for ages to come. Sir William Herschel had determined the places of 2500 nebulæ in the northern hemisphere; they were examined by his son, and drawings made of some of the most remarkable, but when these nebulæ were viewed through Lord Rosse's° telescope, they presented a very different appearance, showing that the apparent form of the nebulæ depends upon the space-penetrating power of the telescope, a circumstance of vital importance in observing the changes which time may produce on these wonderful objects.

[Long afterwards Lord Rosse wrote in reply to some questions which my mother had addressed to him on this subject:—]

FROM THE EARL OF ROSSE TO
MRS SOMERVILLE

CASTLE, PARSONSTOWN, *June 12th, 1844*

DEAR MRS SOMERVILLE,

I have very reluctantly postponed so long replying to your inquiries respecting the telescope, but there were some points upon which I was anxious to be enabled to speak more precisely. The instrument we are now using is 3 feet aperture, and 27 feet focus, and in the greater proportion of the nebulæ which have been observed with it some new details have been brought out. Perhaps the most interesting general result is that, as far as we have gone, increasing optical power has enlarged the list of clusters, by diminishing that of the nebulæ properly so-called. Such has always been the case since the nebulæ have been observed with telescopes, and although it would be unsafe to draw the inference, it is impossible not to feel some expectation that with sufficient optical power the nebulæ would all be reduced into clusters. Perhaps the two of the most remarkable of the resolved nebulæ are Fig. 26 and Fig. 55. In several of the planetary nebulæ we have discovered a star or bright point in the centre, and a filamentous edge, which is just the appearance which a cluster with a highly condensed centre would present in a small instrument. For instance, Figs. 47 and 32. We have also found that many of the nebulæ have not a symmetrical form, as they appear to have in inferior instruments; for instance, Fig. 81 is a cluster with long resolvable filaments from its southern extremity, and Fig. 85 is an oblong cluster with a bright centre. Fig. 45 is an annular nebula, like Herschel's drawing of the annular nebula in Lyra. I have sent drawings of a few of these objects to the Royal Society, they were forwarded a few days ago. We have upon the whole as yet observed but little with the telescope of 3 feet aperture. You recollect Herschel said that it was a good observing year, in which there were 100 hours fit for observing, and of the average of our hours I have not employed above 30. We have been for the last two years engaged in constructing a telescope of 6 feet aperture and 52 feet focus, and it would have been impossible to have bestowed the necessary attention upon it had we made a business of observing. That instrument is nearly finished, and I hope it will effect something for astronomy. The unequal refraction of the atmosphere will limit its powers, but how far remains to be ascertained . . . Lady Rosse joins me in very kind remembrances and believe me to be,

Dear Mrs Somerville,

Yours very truly and ever,

ROSSE

[Sir John Herschel wrote to my father from the Cape:—]

FROM SIR JOHN HERSCHEL TO MR SOMERVILLE

FELDHAUSEN, NEAR WYNBERG, C.G.H., *July 17th, 1830*[76]

MY DEAR SOMERVILLE,

Since our arrival here, I have, I know in many instances, maintained or established the character of a bad correspondent; and really it is not an inconvenient character to have established. Only, in your case, I should be very sorry to appear in that, or any other negligent or naughty light; but you, I know, will allow for the circumstances which have occasioned my silence. Meanwhile, I am not sorry that the execution of an intention I had more than once formed should have been deferred, till we read in the papers of the well-judged and highly creditable notice (creditable I mean to the government *pro tempore*) which His Majesty has been pleased to take of Mrs. Somerville's elaborate works. Although the Royal notice is not quite so swift as the lightning in the selection of its objects, it agrees with it in this, that it is attracted by the loftiest; and though what she has performed may seem so natural and easy to herself, that she may blush to find it fame; all the rest of the world will agree with me in rejoicing that merit of that kind is felt and recognised at length in the high places of the earth. This, and the honourable mention of Airy by men of both parties in the House of Commons about the same time, are things that seem to mark the progress of the age we live in; and I give Peel credit for his tact in perceiving this mode of making a favourable impression on the public mind.

We are all going on very comfortably, and continue to like the Cape as a place of (temporary) residence as much or more than at first. The climate is so very delicious . . . The stars are most propitious, and, astronomically speaking, I can now declare the climate to be most excellent. Night after night, for weeks and months, with hardly an interruption, of *perfect* astronomical weather, discs of stars reduced almost to points, and tranquilly gliding across the field of your telescope. It is really a treat such as occurs once or perhaps twice a year in England – hardly more. I had almost forgotten that by a recent vote of the Astronomical Society I can now claim Mrs. Somerville as a *colleague*. Pray make my compliments to her in that capacity, and tell her that I hope to meet her there at some future session . . .

Yours very faithfully,

H. W. HERSCHEL

To WILLIAM SOMERVILLE, ESQ.

———————

Spectrum analysis has shown that there is a vast quantity of self-luminous gaseous matter in space, incapable of being reduced into stars, however powerful the telescope through which it is observed. Hence the old opinion once more prevails, that this is the matter of which the sun and stellar systems have been formed, and that other stellar systems are being formed by slow, continuous condensation. The principal constituents of this matter are, the terrestrial gases, hydrogen, and nitrogen. The yellow stars, like the sun, contain terrestrial matter. The nebulous and stellar constituents were chiefly discovered by Dr Huggins°.

Somerville and I were always made welcome by Sir James South, and at Camden Hill I learnt the method of observing, and sometimes made observations myself on the double stars and binary systems, which, worthless as they were, enabled me to describe better what others had done. One forenoon Somerville and I went to pay a visit to Lady South. Sir James, who was present, said, 'Come to the observatory, and measure the distance of Mercury from the sun; for they are in close approximation, and I wish to see what kind of observation you will make.' It was erroneous, as might have been expected; but when I took the mean of several observations, it differed but little from that which

Sir James South had made; and here I learnt practically the importance of taking the mean of approximate quantities.

Dr Wollaston, Dr Young, and the Katers died before I became an author; Lord Brougham was one of the last of my scientific contemporaries, all the rest were younger than myself, and with this younger set, as with their predecessors, we had most agreeable and constant intercourse. Although we lived so much in scientific society we had all along been on the most friendly and intimate terms with the literary society of the day, such as Hallam, Milman°, Moore, Malthus°, &c., &c. The highly intellectual conversation of these was enlivened by the brilliant wit of my early friend, Sydney Smith, who was loved and admired by every one. His daughter married our friend Sir Henry Holland°, the distinguished physician, well known for his eminent literary and scientific acquirements as well as for his refined taste. [*1D, 184 verso:* His son inherited his wit and humour. Like other young men he was fond of sport and horses; his father said to him one day, 'Be on your good behaviour today and don't talk of sport for we are to have the Bishop of so and so and a clerical party.' At dinner he did as his father wished but during a moment's pause in the conversation after, he turned to the Bishop and said, 'My Lord can you tell me how long Nebuchadnezzar was in getting into condition, after being out to grass.']

No house in London was more hospitable and agreeable than that of the late Mr John Murray, in Albemarle Street. His dinner parties were brilliant, with all the poets and literary characters of the day, and Mr Murray himself was gentlemanly, full of information, and kept up the conversation with spirit. He generously published the *Mechanism of the Heavens* at his own risk, which, from its analytical character, could only be read by mathematicians.

Besides those I have mentioned we had a numerous

acquaintance who were neither learned nor scientific; and at concerts at some of their houses I enjoyed much hearing the great artists of the day, such as Pasta, Malibran, Grisi, Rubini°, &c., &c. We knew Lucien Bonaparte, who gave me a copy of his poems, which were a failure.

I had become acquainted with Madame de Montalembert, who was an Englishwoman, and was mother of the celebrated Comte°; she was very eccentric, and at that time was an Ultra-Protestant. One day she came to ask me to go and drive in the Park with her, and afterwards dine at her house, saying, 'We shall all be in high dresses.' So I accepted, and on entering the drawing-room, found a bishop and several clergymen, Lady Olivia Sparrow°, and some other ladies, all in high black satin dresses and white lace caps, precisely the dress I wore, and I thought it a curious coincidence. The party was lively enough, and agreeable, but the conversation was in a style I had never heard before – in fact, it affected the phraseology of the Bible. We all went after dinner to a sort of meeting at Exeter Hall, I quite forget for what purpose, but our party was on a kind of raised platform.[77] I mentioned this to a friend afterwards, and the curious circumstance of our all being dressed alike. 'Do you not know,' she said, 'that dress is assumed as a distinctive mark of the Evangelical party! So you were a wolf in sheep's clothing.'

[*1D, 140–1:* Somerville and I once met with religious zeal under a much less agreeable form at the villa of a wealthy Hamburg merchant near London. The lady was English, liked and lived much in gay society and entertained a great deal. The grounds were beautiful, the house was luxuriously furnished, there were newspapers, reviews, and new novels as well as other books in abundance. It was a pleasant house to spend a few days in; they were kind good people and made every one happy around them. I do not remember why we had not gone to see them for some months, but when we did go, we were surprised at the

change; the lady had been converted, she had given up
society, and the house once so cheerful had now become
sad. On Sunday every book and newspaper was removed,
the library door locked, and tracts scattered about the
tables. The dinner was cold, steel knives and forks and
delft replaced silver and porcelain, and nothing was cleaned
or ever removed until Monday morning. Somerville and I
were much bored, I learnt the lesson never to go from home
without taking a book with me, but he had the wit to send a
note to an acquaintance in the neighbourhood requesting
a loan of the last newspapers. While reading one the
master of the house came in and Somerville offered him
a paper saying it is full of Queen Caroline's trial and very
interesting. 'O, no, no,' he said, 'it is a sin to read it
today,' Somerville said, 'Perhaps you would listen, if I
read aloud.' 'O yes dat makes de difference.' Soon after
this these amiable people lost their fortune and were reduced to comparative indigence, a change which they bore
with exemplary resignation and fortitude especially the
lady.]

I had been acquainted with the Miss Berrys at Raith,
when visiting their cousins, Mr and Mrs Ferguson. Mary,
the eldest, was a handsome, accomplished woman, who
from her youth had lived in the most distinguished society,
both at home and abroad. She published a *Comparative
View of Social Life in France and England*, which was well
received by the public. She was a Latin scholar, spoke and
wrote French fluently, yet with all these advantages, the
consciousness that she might have done something better,
had female education been less frivolous, gave her a characteristic melancholy which lasted through life. She did not
talk much herself, but she had the tact to lead conversation.
She and her sister received every evening a select society in
their small house in Curzon Street. Besides any distinguished foreigners who happened to be in London, among
their habitual guests were my friend, Lady Charlotte

Lindsay°, always witty and agreeable, the brilliant and beautiful Sheridans°, Lady Theresa Lister°, afterwards Lady Theresa Lewis, who edited Miss Berry's *Memoirs*, Lord Lansdowne°, and many others. Lady Davy came occasionally, and the Miss Fanshawes, who were highly accomplished, and good artists, besides Miss Catherine Fanshawe° wrote clever *vers de société*, such as a charade on the letter H, and, if I am not mistaken, 'The Butterfly's Ball,' &c. I visited these ladies, but their manners were so cold and formal that, though I admired their talents, I never became intimate with them. On the contrary, like everyone else, I loved Mary Berry, she was so warm-hearted and kind. When London began to fill, and the season was at its height, the Miss Berrys used to retire to a pretty villa at Twickenham, where they received their friends to luncheon, and strawberries and cream, and very delightful these visits were in fine spring weather. I recollect once, after dining there, to have been fortunate enough to give a place in my carriage to Lord Macaulay, and those who remember his charming and brilliant conversation will understand how short the drive to London appeared.

We sometimes went to see Miss Lydia White°, who received every evening; she was clever, witty, and very free in her conversation. On one occasion the party consisted, besides ourselves, of the Misses Berry, Lady Davy; the three poets, Rogers, William Spencer, and Campbell; Sir James Mackintosh, and Lord Dudley°. Rogers, who was a bitter satirist and hated Lord Dudley, had written the following epigram:—

Ward has no heart, 'tis said; but I deny it.
He has a heart, and gets his speeches by it.

I had never heard of this epigram, and on coming away Lord Dudley said, 'You are going home to sleep and I to work.' I answered, 'Oh! you are going to prepare your speech for to-morrow.' My appropriate remark raised an universal laugh.

Mr Bowditch°, of Boston, U.S., who died in 1838, left among other works a *Commentary on Laplace's Mécanique Céleste* in four volumes. While busily occupied in bringing out an edition of the *Physical Sciences*, I received a letter from his son, Mr H. Bowditch, requesting me to write an elaborate review of that work, which would be published in Boston along with the biography of his father, written by Mr Young, who sent me a copy of it. Though highly sensible of the honour, I declined to undertake so formidable a work, fearing that I should not do justice to the memory of so great a man.

I have always been in communication with some of the most distinguished men of the United States. Washington Irving° frequently came to see me when he was in London; he was as agreeable in conversation as he was distinguished as an author. No one could be more amiable than Admiral Wilkes°, of the U. S. navy: he had all the frankness of a sailor. We saw a good deal of him when he was in London, and I had a long letter from him, giving me an account of his fleet, his plan for circumnavigation, &c., &c. I never had the good fortune to become personally acquainted with Captain Maury°, of the U. S. navy, author of that fascinating book, the *Physical Geography of the Sea*, but I am indebted to him for a copy of that work, and of his valuable charts. Mr Dana°, who is an honour to his country, sent me copies of his works, to which I have had occasion frequently to refer as acknowledged authority on many branches of natural history. I should be ungrateful if I did not acknowledge the kindness I received from the Silliman° family, who informed me of any scientific discovery in the United States, and sent me a copy of their Journal when it contained anything which might interest me. I was elected an honorary member of the Geographical and Statistical Society of New York, U. S. on the 15th May, 1857, and on the 15th October, 1869, I was elected a member of the American Philosophical Society at Philadelphia, for Promoting Useful Knowledge. I shall ever be most grateful for these honours.

While living in Florence, many years after, an American friend invited me to an evening party to meet an American authoress who wished particularly to make my acquaintance. I accordingly went there on the evening in question, and my friends, after receiving me with their accustomed cordiality, presented me to the lady, and placed me beside her to give me an opportunity of conversing with her. I addressed her several times, and made various attempts to enter into conversation, but only received very dry answers in reply. At last she fairly turned her back upon me, and became engrossed with a lady who sat on her other side, upon which I got up and left her and never saw her again. A very different person in every respect was present that evening, as much distinguished by her high mental qualities and poetical genius as by her modesty and simplicity. I allude to our greatest British poetess, Mrs Browning°, who at that time resided in Florence, except when the delicacy of her health obliged her to go to Rome. I think there is no other instance of husband and wife both poets, and both distinguished in their different lines. I can imagine no happier or more fascinating life than theirs; two kindred spirits united in the highest and noblest aspirations. Unfortunately her life was a short one; in the full bloom of her intellect her frail health gave way, and she died leaving a noble record of genius to future ages, and a sweet memory to those who were her contemporaries. The Florentines, who, like all Italians, greatly appreciate genius, whether native or foreign, have placed a commemorative tablet on Casa Guidi, the house Mrs Browning inhabited.

I was extremely delighted last spring in being honoured by a visit from Longfellow°, that most genial poet. It is not always the case that the general appearance of a distinguished person answers to one's ideal of what he ought to be – in this respect Longfellow far surpasses expectation. I was as much charmed with his winning manner and conversation as by his calm, grand features and the expression of his intellectual countenance.

The Barons Fairfax, as I mentioned already, had long been members of the Republic of the United States, and Washington's mother belonged to this family. During the War of Independence, while my father, then Lieutenant Fairfax, was on board a man-of-war on the American station, he received a letter from General Washington claiming him as a relation, and inviting him to pay him a visit, saying, he did not think that war should interfere with the courtesies of private life. Party spirit ran so high at that time that my father was reprimanded for being in correspondence with the enemy. I mentioned to my friend, the Rev. Dr Tuckerman°, of the United States, how much I regretted that so precious a letter had been lost, and he most kindly on going home sent me an autograph letter of General Washington.

FROM THE REV. JOSEPH TUCKERMAN TO MRS SOMERVILLE

BOSTON, *August 28th, 1834*

MY DEAR MADAM,

I have very great pleasure in sending to you an autograph letter of your and our glorious Washington. I obtained it from Mr. Sparks°, who had the gratification of seeing you when he was in England, and who told me when I applied to him for it, that there is no one in the world to whom he would be so glad to give it. It is beyond comparison the best and almost the only remaining one at his disposal among the 'Washington' papers.

I am again in my family and in the field of my ministry.

But very dear to me are my associations with scenes and friends in England; and most glad should I be if I could renew that intercourse with yourself, and with the intellect and virtue around you, to which I have been indebted for great happiness, and which, I hope, has done something to qualify me for a more efficient service. Will you please to present my very sincere respects to your husband, and to recall me to the kind remembrance of your children. With the highest respect and regard, allow me to call myself,

Your friend,
JOSEPH TUCKERMAN

I think it must have been on returning from the American station, or may be later in the career of my father's life, that a circumstance occurred which distressed him exceedingly. Highway robberies were common on all the roads in the vicinity of London, but no violence was offered. My father was travelling alone over Blackheath when the postilion was ordered to stop, a pistol presented at my father, and his purse demanded. My father at once recognised the voice as that of a shipmate, and exclaimed, 'Good God! I know that voice! can it be young—? I am dreadfully shocked; I have a hundred pounds which shall be yours – come into the carriage, and let me take you to London, where you will be safe.' . . . 'No, no,' the young man said, 'I have associates whom I cannot leave – it is too late.' . . . It was too late; he was arrested eventually and suffered. Years afterwards when by some accident my father mentioned this event, he was deeply affected, and never would tell the name of the young man who had been his mess-mate.

[*1D, 191:* Railways have put a stop to highway robberies but now groups of young men and even boys rob with acts of violence in the streets of London. The progress of morality is slow compared with that of intellectual activity.]

FOURTEEN

Rome, Naples, and Como – Baden – Winter at Florence –
Siena – Letter from Lord Brougham – Mr Mountstuart
Elphinstone – Life at Rome – Campagna Cattle

[*1D, 192–3:* We were always on the best of terms with the
governor and officers of the establishment at Chelsea
Hospital, but we disliked the place and with good reason
for we never were well, and at last Somerville was taken
dangerously ill with fever and ague. It was the second
attack; no time was to be lost, so he was removed to
London to be away from the dead air of Chelsea. He
recovered slowly and as soon as he was able to travel he
gave up his appointments and determined to spend the
winter at Rome. Our departure was so sudden, that everything was left in confusion. I sent my cabinet of shells to my
niece, and I left to the care of my son and daughter-in-law
our books, the cabinet of minerals, a valuable collection of
original letters and several manuscripts.

One of these manuscripts is on the attraction of spheroids, the form and rotation of the Earth, the tides of the
oceans and atmosphere, small undulations, etc. It must
have been written soon after the publication of the *Mechanism of the Heavens* for the idea was suggested by M. Poisson
in a letter I received from him dated Paris 30 May 1832. At
this time I had a correspondence with Mr James Ivory on
the form of the Earth and planets, and with Mr Francis
Baily on the compression and density of the earth. Another
of these manuscripts is on the structure of the roots of
equations of the higher orders in which the figures of the

curved lines and surfaces are carefully drawn. I had entirely forgotten that I had written these manuscripts till they were brought to me at Spezia forty years afterwards together with fragments of an analytical investigation of the lunar theory, the rest having been lost in the lapse of time. Now that my hand shakes like an aspen leaf, I wonder at the beauty of my writing and diagrams, and still more why these manuscripts were written at all. I suppose they were thought to be of no use at the time; I am sure they are of none now.]

[My mother was already meditating writing a book upon physical geography, and had begun to collect materials for it, when my father's long and dangerous illness obliged her to lay it aside for a time. My father was ordered to a warmer climate for the winter, and as soon as he was able to travel we proceeded to Rome. We were hardly settled when my mother, with her usual energy, set to work diligently, and began this book, which was not published for some time later, as it required much thought and research. She never allowed anything to interfere with her morning's work; after that was over she was delighted to join in any plan which had been formed for the afternoon's amusement, and enjoyed herself thoroughly, whether in visiting antiquities and galleries, excursions in the neighbourhood, or else going with a friend to paint on the Campagna.[78] My mother was extremely fond of Rome, and often said no place had ever suited her so well. Independently of the picturesque beauty of the place, which, to such a lover of nature, was sufficient in itself, there was a very pleasant society during many seasons we spent there. The visitors were far less numerous than they are now, but on that very account there was more sociability and intimacy, and scarcely an evening passed without our meeting. The artists residing at Rome, too, were a most delightful addition to society. Some of them became our very dear friends. My mother remarks:—]

We took lodgings at Rome, and as soon as we were settled I resumed my work and wrote every morning till two o'clock, then went to some gallery, walked on the Pincio,[79] dined at six, and in the evening either went out or received visits at home – the pleasantest way of seeing friends, as it does not interfere with one's occupations.

We once joined a party that was arranged to see the statues in the Vatican by torchlight, at which Lord Macaulay astonished us by his correct knowledge and learning as we passed through the gallery of inscriptions. To me this evening was memorable; on this occasion I first met with John Gibson°, the sculptor, who afterwards became a dear and valued friend. He must have been a pupil of Canova's or Thorwaldsen's when Somerville and I were first at Rome. Now his fame was as great as that of either of his predecessors.

[In spring we went to Naples for a few weeks, and returned to Rome by the San Germano road, now so familiar to travellers, but then hardly ever frequented, as it was extremely unsafe on account of the brigands. We met with no adventures, although we often reached our night quarters long after sunset, for my mother sketched a great deal on the road. We travelled by *vetturino*[80] and continued this delightful journey to Como. My mother was a perfect travelling companion, always cheerful and contented and interested in all she saw. I leave her to tell of our pleasant residence at Bellaggio in her own words:—]

We remained only a short time at Florence, and then went for a month to Bellaggio, on the Lake of Como, at that time the most lonely village imaginable. We had neither letters, newspapers, nor any books, except the Bible, yet we liked it exceedingly. I did nothing but paint in the mornings, and Somerville sat by me. My daughters wandered about, and in the evening we went in a boat on the lake. Sometimes we made longer excursions. One day we went early to Menaggio, at the upper end of the lake. The day had been beautiful, but while at dinner we were startled by a loud peal of thunder. The boatmen desired us to embark without delay, as a storm was rising behind the mountains; it soon blew a gale, and the lake was a sheet of foam; we took shelter for a while at some place on the coast and set out again, thinking the storm had blown over, but it was soon worse than ever. We were in no small danger for two hours. The boatmen, terrified, threw themselves on their knees in prayer to the Madonna. Somerville seized the helm and lowered the sail and ordered them to rise, saying, the Madonna would help them if they helped themselves, and at last they returned to their duty. For a long time we remained perfectly silent, when one of our daughters said, 'I have been thinking what a paragraph it will be in the newspapers, "Drowned, during a sudden squall on the lake of Como, an English family named Somerville, father, mother and two daughters." ' The silence thus broken made us laugh, though our situation was serious enough, for when we landed the shore was crowded with people who had fully expected to see the boat go down. Twice after this we were overtaken by these squalls, which are very dangerous. I shall never forget the magnificence of the lighting and the grandeur of the thunder, which was echoed by the mountains during the storms on the Lake of Como.

We saw the fishermen spear the fish by torchlight, as they did on the Tweed. The fish were plenty and the water so clear that they were seen at a great depth. There are very large red-fleshed trout in the lake, and a small very delicious fish called *agoni*,[81] caught in multitudes by fine silk nets, to which bells are attached on floats, that keep up a constant tinkling to let the fishermen know where to find their nets when floated away by the wind.

[We now crossed the Alps, by the St Gothard, to Basle and Baden Baden, where we passed the summer, intending to return to England in autumn, but as soon as the rains began my father had so serious a return of his illness that my mother was much alarmed. When he was well enough to travel, we once more crossed the Alps, and reached Florence, where we remained for the winter. My mother resumed her work there.]

Through the kindness of the Grand Duke°, I was allowed to have books at home from his private library in the Pitti Palace, a favour only granted to the four Directors. This gave me courage to collect materials for my long neglected *Physical Geography*, still in embryo. As I took an interest in every branch of science I became acquainted with Professor Amici°, whose microscopes were unrivalled at that time, and as he had made many remarkable microscopic discoveries in natural history, he took us to the Museum to see them magnified and modelled in wax. I had the honour of being elected a member of the Academy of Natural Science at Florence.

There were many agreeable people at Florence that winter and a good deal of gaiety. The Marchese Antinori° presented Somerville and me to the Grand Duke, who had expressed a wish to know me. He received us very graciously, and conversed with us for more than an hour on general subjects. He afterwards wrote me a polite letter, accompanied by a work on the drainage of the Maremma,[82] and gave directions about our being invited to a scientific meeting which was to be held at Pisa. We were presented to the Grand Duchess, who was very civil. [*1D, 194:* As in duty bound we went to an evening reception where I was bored to death. The company was drawn up in two rows and the royal cortège walked between them talking to whom they would.

In passing the Grand Duke stood still before me, said not a word, and after a time asked me some questions in French which I answered, then he looked down exactly like an old buffalo, stood still for a minute and then walked away. Having ended this ceremony the Imperial and Royal party sat down to play whist, but were evidently as much bored as we were, for the instant the clock struck eleven they left the card table in the middle of a hand and went away.] We spent the summer at Siena, and had a cheerful airy apartment with a fine view of the hills of Santa Fiora, and with very pretty arabesques in fresco on the walls of all the rooms, some so very artistic that I made sketches of them. In these old cities many of the palaces and houses are decorated with that artistic taste which formerly prevailed to such an extent in Italy, and which has now yielded, here as elsewhere, to common-place modern furniture.

[While we were at Siena, my mother received the following letter from Lord Brougham, who was a frequent correspondent of hers, but whose letters are generally too exclusively mathematical for the general reader. My mother had described the curious horse-races which are held at Siena every three years, and other mediæval customs still prevalent.]

FROM LORD BROUGHAM TO MRS SOMERVILLE

COLE HILL, KENT, *Sept. 28th, 1840*

MY DEAR MRS SOMERVILLE,

I am much obliged to you for your kind letter which let me know of your movements. I had not heard of them since I saw the Fergusons . . . We have been here since parliament rose, as I am not yet at all equal to going to Brougham. My health is now quite restored; but I shall not soon – nor in all probability ever – recover the losses I have been afflicted with. I passed the greater part of last winter in Provence, expecting some relief from change of scene and from the fine climate; but I came back fully worse than when I went. In fact, I did wrong in struggling at first, which I did to be able to meet parliament in January last. If I had yielded at once, I would have been better. I hope and trust they sent you a book I published two years ago; I mean the *Dissertations* of which one is on the 'Principia,' and designed to try how far it may be taught to persons having but a very moderate stock of mathematics; also, if possible, to keep alive the *true taste* (as I reckon it) in mathematics, which modern analysis has a little broken in upon. Assuming you to have got the book, I must mention that there are some intolerable errors of the press left, such as . . . Excuse my troubling you with these errata, and impute it to my wish that you should not suppose me to have written the nonsense which these pages seem to prove. By the way, it is a curious proof of university prejudice, that though the Cambridge men admit my analysis of the 'Principia' to be unexceptionable, and to be well calculated for teaching the work, yet, *not being by a Cambridge man*, it cannot be used! They are far more liberal at Paris, where they only are waiting for my analysis of the second book; but I put off finishing it, as I do still more my account of the 'Mécanique Céleste.' The latter I have almost abandoned in despair after nearly finishing it; I find so much that cannot be explained elementarily, or anything near it. So that my account to be complete would be nearly as hard reading as yours, and not 1000th part as good . . . I greatly envy you Siena; I never was there above a day, and always desired to stay longer. The language is, as you say, a real charm; but I was not aware of the preservation in which you describe the older manners to be. I fear I shall not be able to visit Provence, as I should have wished this winter . . . but my plans are not quite fixed. The judicial business in Parliament and the Privy Council will also make my going abroad after January difficult. I don't write you any news, nor is there any but what you see in the papers. The Tory restoration approaches very steadily, tho' not very rapidly; and I only hope that the Whigs, having contrived to destroy the Liberal party in the country[83] – I fear past all hope of recovery – may not have a war abroad also to mourn for . . .

Believe me,

Yours ever,

H. Brougham

On going to Rome I required a good many books for continuing my work on *Physical Geography*, and had got *Transactions of the Geographical Society* and other works sent from London. The Hon. Mountstuart Elphinstone° who was then at Rome, was an old acquaintance of ours. He was one of the most amiable men I ever met with, and quite won my heart one day at table when they were talking of the number of singing-birds that were eaten in Italy – nightingales, goldfinches, and robins – he called out, 'What! robins! our household birds! I would as soon eat a child!' He was so kind as to write to the Directors of the East India Company requesting that I might have the use of the library and papers that were in the India House. This was readily granted me; and I had a letter in consequence from Mr Wilson°, the Orientalist, giving me a list of the works they had on the geography of Eastern Asia and the most recent travels in the Himalayas, Tibet, and China, with much useful information from himself. I was indebted to Sir Henry Pottinger°, then at Rome, for information relating to Sind, for he had been for some years British Envoy at Beluchistan. Thus provided, I went on with my work. We lived several winters in an apartment on the second floor of Palazzo Lepri, Via dei Condotti, where we passed many happy days. When we first lived in Via Condotti, the waste-pipes to carry off the rain-water from the roofs projected far into the street, and when there was a violent thunderstorm, one might have thought a waterspout had broken over Rome, the water poured in such cascades from the houses on each side of the street. On one occasion the rain continued in torrents for thirty-six hours, and the Tiber came down in heavy flood, inundating the Ghetto and all the low parts of the city; the water was six feet deep in the Pantheon.[84] The people were driven out of their houses in the middle of the night and took refuge in the churches, and boats plied in the streets supplying the inhabitants with food, which they hauled up in baskets let down from the windows. The Campagna for miles was under water; it covered the Ponte Molle so that the courier could not pass; and seen from the Pincio it looked like an extensive lake. Much anxiety was felt for the people who lived in the farm houses now surrounded with water. Boats were sent to rescue them, and few lives were lost; but many animals perished. The flood did not subside till after three days, when it left everything covered with yellow mud; the loss of property was very great, and there was much misery for a long time.

Our house was in a very central position, and when not engaged I gladly received anyone who liked to come to us in the evening, and we had a most agreeable society, foreign and English, for we were not looked upon as strangers, and the English society was much better during the years we spent in Rome than it was afterwards.

I had an annual visit of an hour from the astronomer Padre De Vico°, and Padre Pianciani°, Professor of Chemistry in the Collegio Romano. I was invited to see the Observatory; but as I had seen those of Greenwich and Paris, I did not think it worth while accepting the invitation, especially as it required an order from the Pope. I could easily have obtained leave, for we were presented to Gregory XVI by the President of the Scotch Catholic College. The Pope received me with marked distinction; notwithstanding I was disgusted to see the President prostrate on the floor, kissing the Pope's foot as if he had been divine. I think it was about this time that I was elected an honorary associate of the Accademia Tiberiana.

I had very great delight in the Campagna of Rome; the fine range of Apennines bounding the plain, over which the fleeting shadows of the passing clouds fell, ever changing and always beautiful, whether viewed in the early morning, or in the glory of the setting sun, I was never tired of admiring; and whenever I drove out, preferred a country drive to the more fashionable Villa Borghese. One day Somerville and I and our daughters went to drive towards the Tavolata, on the road to Albano. We got out of the carriage, and went into a field, tempted by the wild flowers. On one side of this field ran the aqueduct, on the other a deep and wide ditch full of water. I had gone towards the aqueduct, leaving the others in the field. All at once we heard a loud shouting, when an enormous drove of the beautiful Campagna grey cattle with their wide-spreading horns came rushing wildly between us with their heads down and their tails erect, driven by men with long spears mounted on little spirited horses at full gallop. It was so sudden and so rapid, that only after it was over did we perceive the danger we had run. As there was no possible escape, there was nothing for it but standing still, which Somerville and my girls had presence of mind to do, and the drove dividing, rushed like a whirlwind to the right and left of them. The danger was not so much of being gored as of being run over by the excited and terrified animals, and round the walls of Rome places of refuge are provided for those who may be passing when the cattle are driven. Near where this occurred there is a house with the inscription *Casa Dei Spiriti*; but I do not think the Italians believe in either ghosts or witches; their chief superstition seems to be the *Jettatura*, or evil eye, which they have inherited from the early Romans, and, I believe, Etruscans. They consider it a bad omen to meet a monk or priest on first going out in the morning. My daughters were engaged to ride with a large party, and the meet was at our house. A Roman, who happened to go out first, saw a friar, and rushed in again laughing, and waited till he was out of sight. Soon after they set off, this gentleman was thrown from his horse and ducked in a pool; so the *Jettatura* was fulfilled. But my daughters thought his bad seat on horseback enough to account for his fall without the Evil Eye.

FIFTEEN

Albano – Popular Singing – Letters from Mrs Somerville –
Gibson – Perugia – Comet of 1843 – Summer at Venice –
Letters from Mrs Somerville and Miss Joanna Baillie –
Elected Associate of the College of Resurgenti and R. I.
Academy of Science at Arezzo

IN spring we went to Albano, and lived in a villa, high up on
the hill in a beautiful situation not far from the lake. The
view was most extensive, commanding the whole of the
Campagna as far as Terracina, &c. In this wide expanse we
could see the thunderclouds forming and rising gradually
over the sky before the storm, and I used to watch the
vapour condensing into a cloud as it rose into the cool air. I
never witnessed anything so violent as the storms we had
about the equinox, when the weather broke up. Our house
being high above the plain became enveloped in vapour till,
at 3 p.m., we could scarcely see the olives which grew below
our windows, and crash followed crash with no interval
between the lightning and the thunder, so that we felt sure
many places must have been struck; and we were not
mistaken – trees, houses, and even cattle had been struck
close to us. Somerville went to Florence to attend a
scientific meeting, and wrote to us that the lightning there
had stripped the gold leaf off the conductors on the powder
magazine; a proof of their utility.

The sunsets were glorious, and I, fascinated by the
gorgeous colouring, attempted to paint what Turner alone
could have done justice to. I made studies, too, which were
signal failures, of the noble ilex trees bordering the lake of

Albano. Thus I wasted a great deal of time, I can hardly say in vain, from the pleasure I had in the lovely scenery. Somerville sat often by me with his book, while I painted from nature, or amused himself examining the geological structure of the country. Our life was a solitary one, except for the occasional visit from some friends who were at Frascati; but we never found it dull; besides, we made many expeditions on mules or donkeys to places in the neighbourhood. I was very much delighted with the flora on the Campagna and the Alban hills, which in spring and early summer are a perfect garden of flowers. Many plants we cultivate in England here grow wild in profusion, such as cyclamens, gum-cistus,[85] both white and purple, many rare and beautiful orchideæ, the large flowering Spanish broom, perfuming the air all around, the tall, white-blossomed Mediterranean heath, and the myrtle. These and many others my girls used to bring in from their early morning walks. The flowers only lasted till the end of June, when the heat began, and the whole country became brown and parched; but scarcely had the autumnal rains commenced, when, like magic, the whole country broke out once more into verdure, and myriads of cyclamens covered the ground. Nightingales abounded in the woods, singing both by night and by day; and one bright moonlight night my daughters, who slept with their window open, were startled from their sleep by the hooting of one of those beautiful birds, the great-eared owl – 'le grand duc' of Buffon[86] – which had settled on the railing of their balcony. We constantly came across snakes, generally harmless ones; but there were a good many vipers, and once, when Somerville and my daughters, with Mr Cromek°, the artist, had gone from Genzano to Nettuno for a couple of days, a small asp which was crawling among the bent-grass on the sea-shore, darted at one of the girls, who had irritated it by touching it with her parasol. By the natives they are much dreaded, both on this coast and in the pine forest of

Ravenna, where the cattle are said to be occasionally poisoned by their bite.

We had been acquainted with the Rev. Dr, afterwards Cardinal Wiseman° at Rome. He was head of a college of young men educating for the Catholic Church, who had their *villeggiatura*[87] at Monte Porzio. We spent a day with him there, and visited Tusculum; another day we went to Lariccia, where there is a palace and park belonging to the Chigi° family in a most picturesque but dilapidated state. We went also to Genzano, Rocca del Papa, and occasionally to visit friends at Frascati. There was a stone threshing-floor behind our house. During the vintage we had it nicely swept and lighted with torches, and the grape gatherers came and danced till long after midnight, to the great amusement of my daughters, who joined in the dance, which was the Saltarello, a variety of the Tarantella. They danced to the beating of tambourines. Italy is the country of music, especially of melody, and the popular airs, especially the Neapolitan, are extremely beautiful and melodious; yet it is a fact, that the singing of the peasantry, particularly in the Roman and Neapolitan provinces, is most disagreeable and discordant. It is not melody at all, but a kind of wild chant, meandering through minor tones, without rhythm of any sort or apparent rule, and my daughters say it is very difficult to note down; yet there is some kind of method and similarity in it as one hears it shouted out at the loudest pitch of the voice, the last note dwelt upon and drawn out to an immeasurable length. The words are frequently improvised by the singers, who answer one another from a distance, as they work in the fields. I have been told, this style of chanting – singing it can hardly be called – has been handed down from the most ancient times, and it is said, in the southern provinces, to have descended from the early Greek colonists. The ancient Greeks are supposed to have chanted their poetry to music, as do the Italian *improvisatori* at the present day. In Tuscany, the words of the songs are often extremely poetical and graceful. Frequently, these verses, called *stornelli* and *rispetti*, are composed by the peasants themselves, women as well as men;[88] the language is the purest and most classical Italian, such as is spoken at the present day in the provinces of Siena, Pistoia, &c., very much less corrupted by foreign idioms or adaptations than what is spoken, even by cultivated persons, in Florence itself. The picturesque costumes so universal when I first came to Italy, in 1817, had fallen very much into disuse when, at a much later period, we resided in Rome, and now they are rarely seen.

We hired a handsome peasant girl from Albano as housemaid, who was much admired by our English friends in her scarlet cloth bodice, trimmed with gold lace, and the silver *spadone* or bodkin, fastening her plaits of dark hair; but she very soon exchanged her picturesque costume for a bonnet, etc., in which she looked clumsy and commonplace.

[The following are extracts from letters written from Albano by my mother:—]

FROM MRS SOMERVILLE TO HER SON
W. GREIG, ESQ.

ALBANO, *16th June, 1841*

I was thankful to hear, my dearest Woronzow, from your last letter that Agnes is recovering so well . . . We are very much pleased with our residence at Albano; the house, with its high sounding name of 'Villa,' is more like a farmhouse, with brick floors and no carpets, and a few chairs and tables, but the situation is divine. We are near the top of the hill, about half-a-mile above Albano, and have the most magnificent view in every direction, and such a variety of delightful walks, that we take a new one every evening. For painting it is perfect; every step is a picture. At present we have no one near, and lead the life of hermits; but our friends have loaded us with books, and with drawing, painting, music, and writing, we never have a moment idle. Almost every one has left Rome; but the English have all gone elsewhere, as they are not so easily pleased with a house as we are. The only gay thing we have done was a donkey ride yesterday to the top of Monte Cavo, and back by the lake of Nemi . . .

FROM MRS SOMERVILLE TO
WORONZOW GREIG, ESQ.

ALBANO, *29th August, 1841*

I dare say you think it very long since you have heard from me, my dearest Woronzow, but the truth is, I have been writing so hard, that after I had finished my day's work, I was fit for nothing but idleness. The reason of my hurry is, that the scientific meeting takes place at Florence on the 15th of September, and as I think it probable that some of our English philosophers will come to it, I hope to have a safe opportunity of sending home some MS. which it has cost me hard work to get ready, as I have undertaken a book more fit for the combination of a Society than for a single hand to accomplish. Lord Brougham was most kind when at Rome, and took so great an interest in it, that he has undertaken to read it over, and give me his opinion and criticism, which will be very valuable, as I know no one who is a better judge of these matters. He will send it to Mr. Murray, and you had better consult with him about it, whether he thinks it will succeed or not. Both William and Martha like what I have done; but I am very nervous about it, and wish you would read it if you have time . . . We have been extremely quiet all the summer; we have no neighbours, so that we amuse ourselves with our occupations. I get up between six and seven, breakfast at eight, and write till three, when we dine; after dinner, I write again till near six, when we go out and take a long walk; come home to tea at nine, and go to bed at eleven: the same thing day after day, so you cannot expect a very amusing letter . . . I have another commission I wish you would do for me; it is to inquire what discoveries Captain Ross has made at the South Pole. I saw a very interesting account in *Galignani* of what they have done, but cannot trust to a newspaper account so as to quote it.

A new edition of my *Physical Sciences* was required, so the *Physical Geography* was laid aside for the present. On returning to Rome, we resumed our usual life, and continued to receive our friends in the evening without ceremony. There was generally a merry party round the tea table in a corner of the room. I cannot omit mentioning one of the most charming and intellectual of our friends, Don Michelangelo Gaetani°, Duke of Sermoneta, whose brilliant and witty conversation is unrivalled, and for whom I have had a very sincere friendship for many years. I found him lately as charming as ever, notwithstanding the cruel loss of his sight. The last time I ever dined out was at his house at Rome, when I was on my way to Naples in 1867.

John Gibson, the sculptor, the most guileless and amiable of men, was now a dear friend. His style was the purest Grecian, and had some of his works been found among the ruins, multitudes would have come to Rome to admire them. He was now in the height of his fame; yet he was so kind and encouraging to young people that he allowed my girls to go and draw in his studio, and one of my daughters, with a friend, modelled there for some time. His drawings for bas-reliefs were most beautiful. He drew very slowly, but a line once drawn was never changed. He ignored India-rubber or bread-crumbs, so perfect was his knowledge of anatomy, and so decided the character and expression he meant to give.

We had charades one evening in a small theatre in our house, which went off very well. There was much beauty at Rome at that time; no one who was there can have forgotten the beautiful and brilliant Sheridans. I recollect Lady Dufferin at the Easter ceremonies at St Peter's, in her widow's cap, with a large black crape veil thrown over it, creating quite a sensation. With her exquisite features, oval face, and somewhat fantastical head-dress, anything more lovely could not be conceived; and the Roman people crowded round her in undisguised admiration of *la bella monaca Inglese*. Her charm of manner and her brilliant conversation will never be forgotten by those who knew her. To my mind, Mrs Norton was the most beautiful of the three sisters. Hers is a grand countenance, such as artists love to study. Gibson, whom I asked, after his return from England, which he had revisited after twenty-seven years' absence, what he thought of Englishwomen, replied, he had seen many handsome women, but no such sculptural beauty as Mrs Norton's. I might add the Marchioness of Waterford, whose bust at Macdonald's I took at first for an ideal head, till I recognised the likeness.

Lady Davy used to live a great deal at Rome, and took an active part in society. She talked a great deal, and talked well when she spoke English, but like many of us had more pretension with regard to the things she could not do well than to those she really could. She was a Latin scholar, and as far as reading and knowing the literature of modern languages went she was very accomplished, but unfortunately, she fancied she spoke them perfectly, and was never happier than when she had people of different nations dining with her, each of whom she addressed in his own language. Many amusing mistakes of hers in speaking Italian were current in both Roman and English circles, [*2D, 172:* such as her sending to Spillman the pastry cook for *un grosso gatto*, her ordering her cook to make a dish of Costollette *alla Sorella* – her telling a servant she was engaging that one of his duties would be to *puline i lampi*, rather an appalling task, and many more which I forget. This reminds me of a Florentine Lady who is no less memorable for her blunders but in French. She said *J'ai froid car j'ai laissé ma peau à l'antechambre* meaning her fur cape – and not long ago having left her card with *Venus en personne* written in pencil upon, goes by the name now of 'Venus en personne' although if she ever was handsome it was many years ago as she is a grandmother.

When Sir Frederick Adam° was governor of the Ionian Islands he married a Greek lady of great beauty; though no longer young when I knew her at Rome, her eyes were still splendid. I was told that one day her husband said, 'My lady, are you going to the – Embassy you know it is the evening when the ambassadress receives,' 'P'raps I go, p'raps I stay at home, I don't like that woman, – she false, – she false as hell, – she all gumboil.' During the irresistible burst of laughter that followed, Lady Adam's eyes flashed fire. 'Why laugh? Why laugh? there is no need for laughing;' at last Sir Frederick called out, 'You mean humbug.' 'Well, why laugh, humbug, gumboil, all one and the same thing' – she was very angry. Yet she was a good-natured person though fiery, for she laughed heartily afterwards, saying, 'I fool – I great fool to be angry for nothing.' I have no doubt I made a great many mistakes myself. (*written on the verso at the bottom of the page:* Mrs Browning told us this of Lady Adam but I *won't* have her name in my book.]⁸⁹

[*1D, 196–7:* The English society was better than it has been since and the Carnival was very different from what it afterwards became. In the Corso the carriages were handsomer, the ladies better dressed, a flower or bonbon was gently thrown in passing.[90] The masques in the street were noisy and merry but never rude; they were occasionally witty, clever and sometimes even improvised. Latterly the Corso became a perfect bear garden, some trash was thrown with violence instead of flowers, and in place of the bonbons showers of lime were thrown from the street and even from the windows into the carriages which endangered the eyes so much that those who ventured into this rude play wore wire visors. I am grieved to say this change was chiefly owing to my countrymen. The Roman families had large supper parties the last evening of the Carnival preparatory to the fast of forty days,] [*2D, 179:* but in the month of March the English introduced hunting, racing and steeple chases to the astonishment of the Romans. Horses and hounds were brought from England; at the races gentlemen rode their own horses. The Romans got up races too but the horses were ridden by grooms. There was even a race by the *contadini* [peasants] on their wild ponies; they were decked out with various coloured ribbons streaming behind their high crowned hats, more than a dozen of them tearing along was a very pretty sight. All this was making Rome too like an English watering place. The men met at midnight, supped, smoked, and played at cards till morning. The Italians did not join them but they subscribed liberally for the hounds and races.]

A few months were very pleasantly spent one summer at Perugia, where there is so much that is interesting to be seen. The neighbouring country is very beautiful, and the city being on the top of a hill is very cool during the hot weather. We had an apartment in the Casa Oddi-Baglioni – a name well known in Italian history – and I recollect spending some very pleasant days with the Conte Oddi-Baglioni, at a villa called Colle del Cardinale, some ten or twelve miles from the town. The house was large and handsomely decorated, with a profusion of the finest Chinese vases. On our toilet tables were placed perfumes, scented soap, and very elaborately embroidered night-dresses were laid out for use. I remember especially admiring the basins, jugs, &c., which were all of the finest japan enamel. There was a subterranean apartment where we dined, which was delightfully cool and pleasant, and at a large and profusely served dinner-table, while we and the guests with the owner of the house dined at the upper end, at the lower end and below the salt there were the superintendent of the Count's farms, a house decorator and others of that rank. It is not the only instance we met with of this very ancient custom. The first time Somerville and I came to Italy, years before this, while dining at a very noble house, the wet-nurse took her place, as a matter of course, at the foot of the dinner-table.

On the morning after our arrival and at a very early hour there was a very fine eclipse of the sun, though not total at Perugia or the neighbourhood; the chill and unnatural gloom were very striking.

Perugia is one of the places in which the ancient athletic game of *pallone* is played with spirit. It is so graceful when well played that I wonder our active young men have not adopted it. A large leather ball filled with condensed air is struck and returned again by the opponent with the whole force of their right arms, covered to the elbow with a spiked wooden case. The promptness and activity required to keep up the ball is very great, and the impetus with which it strikes is such, that the boxes for spectators in the amphitheatres dedicated to this game are protected by strong netting. It is a very complicated game, and, I am told, somewhat resembles tennis.

On leaving Perugia we went for a few days to Assisi, spent a day at Chiusi, and then returned to Rome, which we found in a great state of excitement on account of three steamers which had just arrived from England to ply on the Tiber.

The Pope and Cardinals made a solemn procession to bless them. No doubt they would have thought our method of dashing a bottle of wine on a vessel on naming her highly profane.

We constantly made expeditions to the country, to Tivoli, Veii, Ostia, &c., and my daughters rode on the Campagna. One day they rode to Albano, and on returning after dark they told me they had seen a most curious cloud which never altered its position; it was a very long narrow stripe reaching from the horizon till nearly over head – it was the tail of the magnificent comet of 1843.[91]

We met with a great temptation in an invitation from Lady Stratford Canning°, to go and visit them at Buyuk-déré, near Constantinople, but *res arcta* prevented us from accepting what would have been so desirable in every respect. At this time I sat to our good friend Mr Macdonald for my bust, which was much liked.[92]

One early summer we went to Loreto and Ancona, where we embarked for Trieste; the weather seemed fine when we set off, but a storm came on, with thunder and lightning, very high sea and several waterspouts. The vessel rolled and pitched, and we were carried far out of our course to the Dalmatian coast. I was obliged to remain a couple of days at Trieste to rest, and was very glad when we arrived at Venice. The summer passed most delightfully at Venice, and we had ample time to see everything without hurry. I wrote very little this summer, for the scenery was so beautiful that I painted all day; my daughters drew in the Belle Arti, and Somerville had plenty of books to amuse him, besides sight-seeing, which occupied much of our time. In the Armenian convent we met with Joseph Warten, an excellent mathematician and astronomer; he was pastor at Neusatz, near Peterwardein in Hungary, and he was making a tour through Europe. He asked me to give him a copy of the *Mechanism of the Heavens*, and afterwards wrote in Latin to Somerville and sent me some errors of the press he had met with in my book, but they were of no use, as I never published a second edition. We returned to Rome by Ravenna, where we stayed a couple of days, then travelled slowly along the Adriatic Coast. From thence we went by Gubbio and Perugia to Orvieto, one of the most interesting towns in Italy, and one seldom visited at that time; now the railway will bring it into the regular track of travellers.

[A few extracts from letters, written and received during this summer by my mother, may not be without interest. Also parts of two from my mother's old and valued friend Miss Joanna Baillie. The second letter was written several years later, and is nearly the last she ever wrote to my mother.]

FROM MRS SOMERVILLE TO WORONZOW GREIG, ESQ.

VENICE, *21st July, 1843*

I most sincerely rejoice to hear that Agnes and you have gone to the Rhine, as I am confident a little change of air and scene will be of the greatest service to you both . . . We are quite enchanted with Venice; no one can form an idea of its infinite loveliness who has not seen it in summer and in moonlight. I often doubt my senses, and almost fear it may be a dream. We are lodged to perfection, the weather has been charming, no oppressive heat, though the thermometer ranges from $75°$ to $80°$, accompanied by a good deal of scirocco; there are neither flies nor fleas, and as yet the mosquitoes have not molested us. We owe much of our comfort to the house we are in, for there are scarcely any furnished lodgings, and the hotels are bad and dear, besides situation is everything at this season, when the smaller canals become offensive at low water, for,

though there is little tide in the Mediterranean, there are four
feet at new and full moon here, which is a great blessing. We
have now seen everything, and have become acquainted with
everybody, and met with kindness and attention beyond all
description. Many of the great ducal families still exist, and live
handsomely in their splendid palaces; indeed, the decay of
Venice, so much talked of, is quite a mistake; certainly it is very
different from what it was in its palmy days, but there is a good
deal of activity and trade. The abolition of the law of primo-
geniture has injured the noble families more than anything
else. We rise early, and are busy indoors all morning, except
the girls, who go to the Academy of the Belle Arti, and paint
from ten till three. We dine at four, and embark in our gondola
at six or seven, and row about on the glassy sea till nine, when
we go to the Piazza of San Marco, listen to a very fine military
band, and sit gossiping till eleven or twelve, and then row
home by the Grand Canal, or make a visit in one of the various
houses that are open to us. One of the most remarkable of
these is that of the Countess Mocenigo's°, who has in one of
her drawing-rooms the portraits of six doges of the Mocenigo
name. I was presented by her to the Duc de Bordeaux°, the
other evening, a fat good-natured looking person. I was presented also to the Archduke – I forget what – son of the
Archduke Charles°, and admiral of the fleet here; a nice youth,
but not clever. We meet him everywhere, and Somerville
dined with him a few days ago. The only strangers of note
are the Prince of Thurn and Taxis°, and Marshal Marmont°.
The Venetian ladies are very ladylike and agreeable, and speak
beautifully. We have received uncommon kindness from Mr
Rawdon Brown°; he has made us acquainted with everybody,
as he is quite at home here, having been settled in Venice for
several years, and has got a most beautiful house fitted up, in
rococo style, with great taste;[93] he is an adept at Venetian
history. He supplies us with books, which are a great comfort
. . . The other evening we were surprised by a perfect fleet of
gondolas stopping under our windows, from one of which we

had the most beautiful serenade; the moonlight was like day, and the effect was admirable. There was a *festa* the other night in a church on the water's edge; the shore was illuminated and hundreds of gondolas were darting along like swallows, the gondoliers rowing as if they had been mad, till the water was as much agitated as if there had been a gale of wind: nothing could be more animated. You will perceive from what I have said that the evening, till a late hour, is the time for amusement, in consequence of which I follow the Italian custom of sleeping after dinner, and am much the better for it. This place agrees particularly well with all of us, and is well suited for old people, who require air without fatigue . . .

Most affectionately,
MARY SOMERVILLE

FROM MRS SOMERVILLE TO WORONZOW GREIG, ESQ.

VENICE, *27th August, 1843*

MY DEAR WORONZOW,

Your excellent letter, giving an account of your agreeable expedition up the Rhine, did not arrive till nearly a month after it was written . . . I regret exceedingly you could not stay longer, and still more that you could not come on and pay us a visit, and enjoy the charm of summer in Venice, so totally unlike every other place in every respect. I wished for you last night particularly. As we were leaving the Piazza San Marco, about eleven, a boat came up, burning blue lights, with a piano, violins, flutes, and about twenty men on board, who sang choruses in the most delightful manner, and sometimes solos. They were followed by an immense number of gondolas, and we joined the *cortège*, and all went under the Bridge of Sighs, where the effect was beautiful beyond description. We then all turned and entered the Grand Canal, which was entirely filled with gondolas from one side to the other, jammed together, so that we moved *en masse*, and stopped every now and then to burn blue or red Bengal lights before the principal palaces, singing going on all the while. We saw numbers of our Venetian friends in their gondolas, enjoying the scene as much as we did, to whom it was almost new. I never saw people who enjoyed life more, and they have much the advantage of us in their delicious climate and aquatic amusements, so much more picturesque than what can be done on land. However, we have had no less than three dances lately. The Grand Duke of Modena,[94] with his son and daughter-in-law, were here, and to them a *fête* was given by the Countess de Thurn. The palace was brilliant with lights; it is on the grand canal, and immediately under the balcony was a boat from which fireworks were let off, and then a couple of boats succeeded them, in which choruses were sung. The view from the balcony is one of the finest in Venice, and the night was charming, and there I was while the dancing went on . . . I never saw Somerville so well; this place suits us to the life, constant air and no fatigue; I never once have had a headache . . . Now, my dear W., tell me your tale; my tale is done.

Yours affectionately,

MARY SOMERVILLE

FROM MRS SOMERVILLE TO
WORONZOW GREIG, ESQ.

ROME, PALAZZO LEPRI, VIA DEI CONDOTTI,
27th October, 1843

MY DEAREST WORONZOW,
    . . . We had a beautiful journey to Rome, with fine weather and no annoyance, notwithstanding the disturbed state of the

country. At Padua we only remained long enough to see the churches, and it was impossible to pass within a few miles of Arquà without paying a visit to the house of Petrarch. At Ferrara we had a letter to the Cardinal Legate, who was very civil. His palace is the ancient abode of the house of Este[95] . . .

We had a long visit from him in the evening, and found him most agreeable; he regretted that there was no opera, as he would have been happy to offer us his box. Fourteen of those unfortunate men who have been making an attempt to raise an insurrection were arrested the day before; and the night before we slept at Lugo, the Carabineers had searched the inn during the night, entering the rooms where the people were sleeping. We should have been more than surprised to have been wakened by armed men at midnight. In travelling through Italy the *reliques* and history of the early Christians and of the Middle Ages have a greater attraction for me than those of either the Romans or Etruscans, interesting though these latter be, and in this journey my taste was amply gratified, especially at Ravenna, where the church of San Vitale and the Basilica of St. Apollinare in Classis, both built early in the 6th century, are the most magnificent specimens imaginable. Here also is the tomb of Theodore,[96] a most wonderful building; the remains of his palace and numberless other objects of interest, too tedious to mention. Every church is full of them, and most valuable MSS. abound in the libraries. I like the history of the Middle Ages, because one feels that there is something in common between them and us; their names still exist in their descendants, who often inhabit the very palaces they dwelt in, and their very portraits, by the great masters, still hang in their halls; whereas we know nothing about the Greeks and Romans except their public deeds – their private life is a blank to us. Our journey through the Apennines was most beautiful, passing for days under the shade of magnificent oak forests or valleys rich in wine, oil, grain, and silk. We deviated from the main road for a short distance to Gubbio, to see the celebrated Eugubian tables,[97] which are as sharp as if they had been engraved yesterday, but in a lost language. We stopped to rest at Perugia, but all our friends were at their country seats, which we regretted. The country round Perugia is unrivalled for richness and beauty, but it rained the morning we resumed our journey. It signified the less as we had been previously at Città della Pieve and Chiusi; so we proceeded to Orvieto in fine weather, still through oak forests. Orvieto is situated on the top of an escarped hill, very like the hill forts of India, and apparently as inaccessible; yet, by dint of number-less turns and windings, we did get up, but only in time for bed. Next morning we saw the sun rise on the most glorious cathedral. After all we had seen we were completely taken by surprise, and were filled with the highest admiration at the extreme beauty and fine taste of this remarkable building . . .

Your affectionate mother,

MARY SOMERVILLE

FROM MISS JOANNA BAILLIE TO MRS SOMERVILLE

HAMPSTEAD, *December 27th, 1843*

MY DEAR MRS SOMERVILLE,

Besides being proud of receiving a letter from you, I was much pleased to know that I am, though at such a distance, sometimes in your thoughts. I was much pleased, too, with what you have said of the health and other gratifications you enjoy in Italy. I should gladly have thanked you at the time, had I known how to address my letter; and after receiving your proper direction from our friend Miss Montgomery, I have been prevented from using it by various things . . . But though so long silent I have not been ungrateful, and thank you with all my heart. The account you give of Venice is very interest-ing. There is something affecting in still seeing the descendants of the former Doges holding a diminished state in their remaining palaces with so much courtesy. I am sure you have found yourself a guest in their saloons, hung with paintings of their ancestors, with very mixed feelings. However, Venice to the eye, as you describe it, is Venice still; and with its lights at night gleaming upon the waters makes a very vivid picture to my fancy. You no doubt have fixed it on canvas, and can carry it about with you for the delight of your friends who may never see the original.

In return to your kind inquires after us, I have, all things considered, a very good account to give. Ladies of four score and upwards cannot expect to be robust, and need not be gay. We sit by the fire-side with our books (except when those plaguy notes are to be written) and receive the visits of our friendly neighbours very contentedly, and, I ought to say, and trust I may say, very thankfully . . . This morning brought one in whom I feel sure that you and your daughters take some interest, Maria Edgeworth. She has been dangerously ill, but is now nearly recovered, and is come from Ireland to pass the winter months with her sisters in London; weak in body, but the mind as clear and the spirits as buoyant as ever. You will be glad to hear that she even has it in her thoughts to write a new work, and has the plan of it nearly arranged. There will be nothing new in the story itself, but the purpose and treating of it will be new, which is, perhaps, a better thing. In our retired way of living, we know little of what goes on in the literary world . . . I was, however, in town for a few hours the other day, and called upon a lady of rank who has *fashionable* learned folks coming about her, and she informed me that there are new ideas regarding philosophy entertained in the world, and that Sir John Herschel was now considered as a slight, second-rate man, or person. Who are the first-rate she did not say, and, I suppose, you will not be much mortified to hear that your name was not mentioned at all. So much for our learning. My sister was much disappointed the other day when, in expectation of a ghost story from Mr. Dickens, she only got a grotesque moral allegory; now, as she delights in a ghost and hates an allegory, this was very provoking.

Believe me,
My dear Mrs. Somerville,
Yours with admiration and esteem,
J. BAILLIE

FROM MISS JOANNA BAILLIE TO MRS SOMERVILLE

HAMPSTEAD, *January 9th, 1851*

MY DEAR FRIEND,

My dear Mary Somerville, whom I am proud to call my friend, and that she so calls me. I could say much on this point, but I dare not. I received your letter from Mr. Greig last night, and thank you very gratefully. If my head were less confused I should do it better, but the pride I have in thinking of you as philosopher and a woman cannot be exceeded. I shall read your letter many times over. My sister and myself at so great an age are waiting to be called away in mercy by an Almighty Father, and we part with our earthly friends as those whom we shall meet again. My great monster book is now published, and your copy I shall send to your son who will peep into it, and then forward it to yourself. I beg to be kindly and respectfully remembered to your husband; I offer my best wishes to your daughters . . .

Yours, my dear Friend,
Very faithfully,
JOANNA BAILLIE

My sister begs of you and all your family to accept her best wishes.

FROM SIR JOHN HERSCHEL TO
MRS SOMERVILLE

18th March, 1844

MY DEAR MRS SOMERVILLE,

To have received a letter from you so long ago, and not yet to have thanked you for it, is what I could hardly have believed myself – if the rapid lapse of time in the uniform retirement in which we live were not pressed upon me in a variety of ways which convince me that as a man grows older, his sand, as the grains get low in the glass, slips through more glibly, and steals away with accelerated speed. I wish I could either send you a copy of my Cape observations, or tell you they are published or even in the press. Far from it – I do not expect to 'go to press' before another year has elapsed, for though I have got my catalogues of Southern nebulæ and Double stars reduced and arranged, yet there is a great deal of other matter still to be worked through, and I have every description of reduction entirely to execute myself. These are very tedious, and I am a very slow computer, and have been continually taken off the subject by other matter, forced upon me by 'pressure from without.' What I am now engaged on is the monograph of the *principal* Southern nebulæ, the object of which is to put on record every ascertainable particular of their actual appearance and the stars visible in them, so as to satisfy future observers whether *new stars* have appeared, or changes taken place in the nebulosity. To what an extent this work may go you may judge from the fact that the catalogue of visible stars actually mapped down in their places within the space of less than a square degree in the nebula about η Argus which I have just completed comprises between 1300 and 1400 stars. This is indeed a stupendous object. It is a vastly extensive branching and looped nebula, in the centre of the densest part of which is η Argus, itself a most remarkable star, seeing that from the fourth magnitude which it had in Ptolemy's time, it has risen (by *sudden starts*, and not gradually) to such a degree of brilliancy as *now* actually to surpass Canopus, and to be second only to Sirius. One of these *leaps* I myself witnessed when in the interval of ceasing to observe it in one year, and resuming its observation in two or three months after in the next, it had sprung over the heads of *all the stars of the first* magnitude, from Fomalhaut and Regulus (the two least of them) to α Centauri, which it then just equalled, and which is the brightest of all but Canopus and Sirius! It has since made a fresh jump – and who can say it will be the last?

One of the most beautiful objects in the southern hemisphere is a pretty large, perfectly round, and very well-defined planetary nebula, of a fine, full *independent* blue colour – the only object I have ever seen in the heavens fairly entitled to be called *independently* blue, *i.e.*, not by contrast. Another superb and most striking object is Lacaille's 30 Doradus, a nebula of great size in the larger nubicula, of which it is impossible to give a better idea than to compare it to a 'true lover's knot,' or assemblage of nearly circular nebulous loops uniting in a centre, in or near which is an exactly circular round dark hole. Neither this nor the nebula about η Argus have any, the slightest, resemblance to the representations given of them by Dunlop . . . As you are so kind as to offer to obtain information on any points interesting to me at Rome, here is one on which I earnestly desire to obtain the means of forming a correct opinion, *i.e.*, the *real* powers and merits of De Vico's great refractor at the Collegio Romano. De Vico's accounts of it appear to me to have not a little of the extra-marvellous in them. Saturn's *two* close satellites regularly observed – eight stars in the trapezium of Orion! α Aquilæ (as Schumacher inquiringly writes to me) divided into three! the supernumerary divisions of Saturn's ring well seen, &c., &c. And all by a Cauchoix refractor of eight inches? I fear me that these wonders are not for *female eyes*, the good monks are too well aware of the penetrating qualities of such optics to allow them entry within the seven fold walls of their Collegio. Has Somerville ever looked through it? On his report I know I could quite rely. As for Lord Rosse's great reflector, I can only tell you what I hear, having never seen it, or even his three feet one. The great one is not yet completed. Of the other, those who *have* looked through it speak in raptures. I met not long since an officer who, at Halifax in Nova Scotia, saw *the comet* at noon close to the sun, and very conspicuous the day after the perihelion passage.

Your account of the pictures and other *deliciæ* of Venice makes our mouths water; but it is of no use, so we can only congratulate those who are in the full enjoyment of such things.

Ever yours most truly,

J. HERSCHEL

On returning to Rome I was elected Associate of the College of Risurgenti, and in the following April I became an honorary member of the Imperial and Royal Academy of Science, Literature and Art at Arezzo. I finished an edition of the *Physical Sciences*, at which I had been working, and in spring Somerville hired a small house belonging to the Duca Sforza Cesarini, at Genzano, close to and with a beautiful view of the Lake of Nemi; but as I had not seen my son for some time, I now availed myself of the opportunity of travelling with our friend Sir Frederick Adam to England. We crossed the Channel at Ostend, and at the mouth of the Thames lay the old *Venerable*, in which my father was flag-captain at the battle of Camperdown. I had a joyful meeting with my son and his wife, and we went to see many things that were new to me. One of our first expeditions was to the British Museum. I had already seen the Elgin Marbles, and the antiquities collected at Babylon by Mr Rich, when he was Consul at Baghdad, but now the Museum had been enriched by the marbles from Halicarnassus, and by the marvellous remains excavated by Mr

Layard from the ruins of Nineveh, the very site of which had been for ages unknown.[98]

I frequently went to Turner's studio, and was always welcomed.[99] No one could imagine that so much poetical feeling existed in so rough an exterior. The water-colour exhibitions were very good; my countrymen still maintained their superiority in that style of art, and the drawings of some English ladies were scarcely inferior to those of first-rate artists, especially those of my friend, Miss Blake, of Danesbury.

While in England I made several visits; the first was to my dear friends Sir John and Lady Herschel, at Collingwood, who received me with the warmest affection. I cannot express the pleasure it gave me to feel myself at home in a family where not only the highest branches of science were freely discussed, but where the accomplishments and graces of life were cultivated. I was highly gratified and proud of being godmother to Rosa, the daughter of Sir John and Lady Herschel. Among other places near Collingwood I was taken to see an excellent observatory formed by Mr Dawes°, a gentleman of independent fortune; and here I must remark, to the honour of my countrymen, that at the time I am writing, there are twenty-six private observatories in Great Britain and Ireland, furnished with first-rate instruments, with which some of the most important astronomical discoveries have been made.

[I received the following letter from my mother while we were at Genzano. It is one of several which record in her natural and unaffected words my mother's profound admiration for Sir John Herschel.]

MRS SOMERVILLE TO MISS SOMERVILLE

SYDENHAM, *1st September, 1844*
Sunday Night

MY DEAR MARTHA,

. . . We go to the Herschels' to-morrow, and there I shall finish this letter, as it is impossible to get it in time for Tuesday's post, but I have so much to do now that you must not expect a letter every post, and I had no time to begin this before, and I am too tired to sit up later to-night . . .

COLLINGWOOD, *Monday*

This appears to be a remarkably beautiful place, with abundance of fine timber . . . W. brought your dear nice letter; it makes me long to be with you, and, please God, I shall be so before long, as I set off this day fortnight.

Wednesday

Yesterday I had a great deal of scientific talk with Sir John, and a long walk in the grounds which are extensive, and very pretty. Then the Airys arrived, and we had a large party at dinner . . . I think, now, as I always have done, that Sir John is by much the highest and finest character I have ever met with; the most gentlemanly and polished mind, combined with the most exalted morality, and the utmost of human attainment. His view of everything is philosophic, and at the same time highly poetical, in short, he combines every quality that is admirable and excellent with the most charming modesty, and Lady Herschel is quite worthy of such a husband, which is the greatest praise I can give her. Their kindness and affection for me has been unbounded Lady H. told me she heard such praises of you two that she is anxious to know you, and she hopes you will always look upon her and her family as friends. The christening went off as well as possible. Mr. Airy was godfather, and Mrs. Airy and I god- mothers, but I had the naming of the child – Matilda Rose, after Lady Herschel's sister. I assure you I was quite adroit in taking the baby from the nurse and giving her to the clergy- man. Sir John took Mrs. Airy and me a drive to see a very fine picturesque castle a few miles off . . . I have got loads of things for experiments on light from Sir John with a variety of papers, and you may believe that I have profited not a little by his conversation, and have a thousand projects for study and writing, so I think painting will be at a standstill, only that I have promised to paint something for Lady Herschel. Sir John computes four or five hours every day, and yet his Cape observations will not be finished for two years. I have seen everything he is or has been doing.

Your affectionate mother,
MARY SOMERVILLE

[My mother continues her recollections of this journey.]

My next visit was to Lord and Lady Charles Percy°, at Guy's Cliff, in Warwickshire, a pretty picturesque place of historical and romantic memory. The society was pleasant, and I was taken to Kenilworth and Warwick Castle, on the banks of the Avon, a noble place, still bearing marks of the Wars of the Roses. I never saw such magnificent oak-trees as those on the Leigh estate, near Guy's Cliff.

I then visited my maiden namesake, Mrs Fairfax, of Gilling Castle, Yorkshire. She was a highly cultivated person, had been much abroad, and was a warm-hearted friend. I was much interested in the principal room, for a deep frieze surrounds the wall, on which are painted the coats of arms of all the families with whom the Fairfaxes have intermarried, ascending to very great antiquity; besides, every pane of glass in a very large bay window in the same room is stained with one of these coats of arms. Every morning after breakfast a prodigious flock of pea-fowl came from the woods around to be fed.

I now went to the vicinity of Kelso to visit my brother and sister-in-law, General and Mrs Elliot, who lived on the banks of the Tweed. We went to Jedburgh, the place of my birth. After many years I still thought the valley of the Jed very beautiful: I fear the pretty stream has been invaded by manufactories; there is a perpetual war between civilisation and the beauty of nature. I went to see the spot from whence I once took a sketch of Jedburgh Abbey and the manse in which I was born, which does not exist, I believe, now. When I was a very young girl I made a painting from this sketch. Our next excursion was to a lonely village called Yetholm, in the hills, some miles from Kelso, belonging to the gipsies. The 'king' and the other men were absent, but the women were civil, and some of them very pretty. Our principal object in going there was to see a stone in the wall of a small and very ancient church at Linton, nearly in ruins, on which is carved in relief the wyvern[100] and wheel, the crest of the Somervilles.

From Kelso I went to Edinburgh to spend a few days with Lord Jeffrey° and his family. No one who had seen his gentle kindness in domestic life, and the warmth of his attachment to his friends, could have supposed he possessed that power of ridicule and severity which made him the terror of authors. His total ignorance of science may perhaps excuse him for having admitted into the *Review* Brougham's intemperate article on the undulatory theory of light, a discovery which has immortalised the name of Dr Young. I found Edinburgh, the city of my early recollections, picturesque and beautiful as ever, but enormously increased both to the north and to the south. Queen Street, which in my youth was open to the north and commanded a view of the Forth and the mountains

beyond, was now in the middle of the new town. All those
I had formerly known were gone – a new generation had
sprung up living in all the luxury of modern times. On
returning to London I spent a pleasant time with my son
and his wife, who invited all those to meet me whom they
thought I should like to see.

[*1D, 214:* I was now preparing to return to the rest of my
family, when a widow lady, whom I had long known, was
going to Rome with her daughter and offered me a seat in
her carriage on paying my share of the expenses. I heartily
repented having accepted her offer for I never witnessed
such meanness. At breakfast when the waiter went out of
the room, she would wrap a fowl and the left bread and
butter in paper and put it in her bag to save the expense of
dinner, and the squabbling with postboys at each stage
brought a crowd around us and made me quite ashamed. I
was thankful when this disagreeable journey was at an end,
which was no doubt very ungrateful in me who had the
benefit of her economy and who most needed it, for the
lady in question left a hundred thousand pounds at her
death. *This story is also in the second draft but Martha must
have thought it best not to publish it.*]

[My mother returned to Rome in autumn in company with an
old friend and her daughter.]

————————————

The winter passed without any marked event, but always
agreeably; new people came, making a pleasant variety in the
society, which, though still refined, was beginning to be very
mixed, as was amusingly seen at Torlonia's balls and tableaux, where many of the guests formed a singular contrast
with the beautiful Princess, who was of the historical family
of the Colonnas. I was often ashamed of my countrymen,
who, all the while speaking of the Italians with contempt,

tried to force themselves into their houses. Prince Borghese refused the same person an invitation to a ball five times.[101] I was particularly scrupulous about invitations, and never asked for one in my life; nor did I ever seek to make acquaintance with the view of being invited to their houses.

[*1D, 217–8:* A lady asked me to receive a friend of hers from the United States who wished to make my acquaintance. He was accordingly announced next day and to my surprise entered followed by six or eight American friends all of whom were presented to me. When he had conversed with me for a few minutes, one of his companions said, 'You have talked with Mrs Somerville long enough, now I want to talk with her,' so down he sat, by and by another came and said, 'Give me your place for it is my turn to have a talk with Mrs Somerville.' So after each had had his *talk* they went away. The gravity with which this was carried on made it the more comical, I did not dare to look at Somerville or my girls all the time for fear I should laugh outright. That evening I told Mrs Butler, well-known as Fanny Kemble°, that a party of her American friends who were no doubt *doing Rome* had come to have a *talk* with Mrs Somerville, 'O yes,' she said, 'they came directly from you to me and acted the same comedy.']

[The following letters give a sketch of life during the summer months at Rome:—]

―――――――――

MRS SOMERVILLE TO W. GREIG, ESQ.

ROME, *3rd August, 1845*

MY DEAR WORONZOW,

    . . . I am glad you are so much pleased with my bust, and that it is so little injured after having been at the bottom of the sea. You will find Macdonald a very agreeable and original person. As to spending the summer in Rome, you may make yourself quite easy, for the heat is very bearable, the thermometer varying between 75° and 80° in our rooms during the day, which are kept in darkness, and at night it always becomes cooler. Thank God, we are all quite well, and Somerville particularly so; he goes out during the day to amuse himself, and the girls paint in the Borghese gallery. As for myself I have always plenty to do till half past three, when we dine, and after dinner I sleep for an hour or more, and when the sun is set we go out to wander a little, for a long walk is too fatiguing at this season. We have very little society, the only variety we have had was a very pretty supper party given by Signore Rossi, the French minister to the Prince and Princess de Broglie, son and daughter-in-law of the duke. The young lady is extremely beautiful, and as I knew the late Duchesse de Broglie (Madame de Staël's daughter) we soon got acquainted. They are newly married, and have come to spend part of the summer in Rome, so you see people are not so much alarmed as the English . . . We went yesterday evening to see the Piazza Navona full of water; it is flooded every Saturday and Sunday at this season; there is music, and the whole population of Rome is collected round it, carts and carriages splashing through it in all directions. I think it must be about three feet deep. It was there the ancient Romans had their naval games; and the custom of filling it with water in summer has lasted ever since. The fountain is one of the most beautiful in Rome, which is saying a great deal; indeed the immense gush of the purest water from innumerable fountains in every street and every villa is one of the peculiarities of Rome. I fear from what I have heard of those in Trafalgar Square that the quantity of water will be very miserable.

The papers (I mean *The Times*), are full of abuse of Mr Sedgwick and Dr Buckland, but their adversaries write such nonsense that it matters little. I do not think I have anything to add to my new edition. If you hear of anything of moment let me know. Perhaps something may have transpired at the British Association . . .

Your affectionate mother,

MARY SOMERVILLE

MRS SOMERVILLE TO W. GREIG, ESQ.

ROME, *May 28th, 1845*

MY DEAR WORONZOW,

I don't know why I have so long delayed writing to you. I rather think it is because we have been living so quiet a life, one day so precisely similar to the preceding, that there has been nothing worth writing about. This is our first really summer-like day, and splendid it is; but we are sitting in a kind of twilight. The only means of keeping the rooms cool is by keeping the house dark and shutting out the external air, and then in the evening we have a delightful walk; the country is splendid, the Campagna one sheet of deep verdure and flowers of every kind in abundance. We generally have six or seven large nosegays in the room; we have only to go to some of the neighbouring villas and gather them. Most of the English are gone; people make a great mistake in not remaining during the hot weather, this is the time for enjoyment. We are busy all the morning, and in the afternoon we take our book or drawing materials and sit on the grass in some of the lovely villas for hours; then we come home to tea, and are glad to see anyone who will come in for an hour or two. We have had a son of Mr. Babbage here. He is employed in making the railway that is to go from Genoa to Milan, and he was travelling with eight other Englishmen who came to make arrangements for covering Italy with a network of these iron roads, connecting all the great cities and also the two seas from Venice to Milan and Genoa and from Ancona by Rome to Civita Vecchia. However the Pope is opposed to the latter part, but they say the cardinals and people wish it so much that he will at last consent . . . Many thanks for the *Vestiges, &c.* I think it a powerful production, and was highly pleased with it, but I can easily see that it will offend in some quarters; however it should be remembered that there has been as much opposition to the true system of astronomy and to geological facts as there can be to this. At all events free and open discussion of all natural and moral phenomena must lead to truth at last. Is Babbage the author? I rather think he would not be so careful in concealing his name . . . [probably *Vestiges of the Natural History of Creation* by Robert Chambers].

[My mother made some curious experiments upon the effect of the solar spectrum on juices of plants and other substances, of which she sent an account to Sir John Herschel, who answered telling her that he had communicated her account of her experiments to the Royal Society.]

SIR JOHN HERSCHEL TO MRS SOMERVILLE

COLLINGWOOD, *November 21st, 1845*

MY DEAR MRS SOMERVILLE,

I cannot express to you the pleasure I experienced from the receipt of your letter and the perusal of the elegant experiments it relates, which appear to me of the highest interest and show (what I always suspected), that there is a world of wonders awaiting disclosure in the solar spectrum, and that influences widely differing from either light, heat or colour are transmitted to us from our central luminary, which are mainly instrumental in evolving and maturing the splendid hues of the vegetable creation and elaborating the juices to which they owe their beauty and their vitality. I think it certain that heat goes for something in evaporating your liquids and thereby causing some of your phenomena; but there is a difference of *quality* as well as of *quantity* of heat brought into view which renders it susceptible of analysis by the coloured juices so that in certain parts of the spectrum it is retained and fixed, in others reflected according as the nature of the tint favours the one or the other. Pray go on with these delightful experiments. I wish you could save yourself the fatigue of watching and directing your sunbeam by a clock work. If I were at your elbow I could rig you out a heliotrope quite sufficient with the aid of any common wooden clock . . . Now I am going to take a liberty (but not till after duly consulting Mr Greig with whose approbation I act, and you are not to gainsay our proceedings) and that is to communicate your results in the form of 'an extract of a letter' to myself – to the Royal Society. You may be very sure that I would not do this if I thought that the experiments were not intrinsically quite deserving to be recorded in the pages of the Phil. Trans, and if I were not sure that they will lead to a vast field of curious and beautiful research; and as you have already once contributed to the Society, (on a subject connected with the spectrum and the sunbeam) this will, I trust, not appear in your eyes in a formidable or a repulsive light, and it will be a great matter of congratulation to us all to know that these subjects continue to engage your attention, and that you can turn your residence in that sunny clime to such admirable account. So do not call upon me to retract (for before you get this the papers will be in the secretary's hands).

I am here nearly as much out of the full stream of scientific matters as you at Rome. We had a full and very satisfactory meeting at Cambridge of the British Association, with a full attendance of continental magnetists and meteorologists, and within these few days I have learned that our Government meant to grant all our requests and continue the magnetic and meteorological observations. Humboldt has sent me his Cosmos (Vol.I.), which is good, all but the first 60 pages, which are occupied in telling his readers what his book is *not* to be. Dr. Whewell has just published *another* book on the Principles of Morals, and also *another* on education, in which he cries up the geometrical processes in preference to analysis . . .

Yours very faithfully,

J. HERSCHEL

The Prince and Princesse de Broglie came to Rome in 1845, and Signore Pellegrino Rossi, at this time French Minister at the Vatican, gave them a supper party, to which we were invited. We had met with him long before at Geneva, where he had taken refuge after the insurrection of 1821. He was greatly esteemed there and admired for his eloquence in the lectures he gave in the university. It was a curious circumstance, that he, who was a Roman subject, and was exiled, and, if I am not mistaken, condemned to death, should return to Rome as French Minister. He had a remarkably fine countenance, resembling some ancient Roman bust. M. Thiers° had brought in a law in the French Chambers to check the audacity of the Jesuits, and Rossi was sent to negotiate with the Pope. We had seen much of him at Rome, and were horrified, in 1848, to hear that he had been assassinated on the steps of the Cancelleria, at Rome, where the Legislative Assembly met, and whither he was proceeding to attend its first meeting. No one offered to assist him, nor to arrest the murderers except Dr Pantaleone°, a much esteemed Roman physician, and member of the Chamber, who did what he could to save him, but in vain; he was a great loss to the Liberal cause.

Towards the end of summer we spent a month most agreeably at Subiaco, receiving much civility from the Benedictine monks of the Sacro Speco, and visiting all the neighbouring towns, each one perched on some hill-top, and one more romantically picturesque than the other.

It was in this part of the country that Claude Lorrain and Poussin studied and painted.[102] I never saw more beautiful country, or one which afforded so many exquisite subjects for a landscape painter. We went all over the country on mules – to some of the towns, such as Cervara, up steep flights of steps cut in the rock. The people, too, were extremely picturesque, and the women still wore their costumes, which probably now they have laid aside for tweeds and Manchester cottons.

I often during my winters in Rome went to paint from nature in the Campagna, either with Somerville or with Lady Susan Percy°, who drew very prettily. Once we set out a little later than usual, when, driving through the Piazza of the Bocca della Verità,[103] we both called out, 'Did you see that? How horrible!' It was the guillotine; an execution had just taken place, and had we been a quarter of an hour earlier we should have passed at the fatal moment. Under Gregory XVI everything was conducted in the most profound secrecy; arrests were made almost at our very door, of which we knew nothing; Mazzini° was busily at work on one side, the Jesuitical party actively intriguing, according to their wont, on the other; and in the mean time society went on gaily at the surface, ignorant of and indifferent to the course of events. We were preparing to leave Rome when Gregory died. We put off our journey to see his funeral, and the Conclave, which terminated, in the course of scarcely two days, in the election of Pius IX°. We also saw the new Pope's coronation, and witnessed the beginning of that popularity which lasted so short a time. Much was expected from him, and in the beginning of his reign the moderate liberals fondly hoped that Italy would unite in one great federation, with Pius IX at the head of it; entirely forgetting how incompatible a theocracy or government by priests ever must be with all progress and with liberal institutions. Their hopes were soon blighted, and after all the well-known events of 1848 and 1849, a reaction

set in all over Italy, except in gallant little Piedmont, where
the constitution was maintained, thanks to Victor Emma-
nuel°, and especially to that great genius, Camillo Cavour°,
and in spite of the disastrous reverses at Novara. Once
more in 1859 Piedmont went to war with Austria, this time
with success, and with the not disinterested help of France.
One province after another joined her, and Italy, freed from
all the little petty princes, and last, not least, from the
Bourbons, has become that one great kingdom which was
the dream of some of her greatest men in times of old.

We went to Bologna for a short time, and there the
enthusiasm for the new Pope was absolutely intolerable.
'Viva Pio Nono!' was shouted night and day. There was no
repose; bands of music went about the streets, playing airs
composed for the occasion, and in the theatres it was even
worse, for the acting was interrupted, and the orchestra
called upon to play the national tunes in vogue, and repeat
them again and again, amid the deafening shouts and
applause of the excited audience. We found the Bolognese
very sociable, and it was by far the most musical society I
ever was in. Rossini° was living in Bologna, and received in
the evening, and there was always music, amateur and
professional, at his house. Frequently there was part-sing-
ing or choruses, and after the music was over the evening
ended with a dance. We frequently saw Rossini some years
later, when we resided at Florence. He was clever and
amusing in conversation, but satirical. He was very bitter
against the modern style of opera-singing, and considered
the singers of the present day, with some exceptions, as
wanting in study and finish. He objected to much of the
modern music, as dwelling too constantly on the highest
notes of the voice, whereby it is very soon deteriorated, and
the singer forced to scream; besides which, he considered
the orchestral accompaniments too loud. I, who recollected
Pasta, Malibran, Grisi, Rubini, and others of that epoch,
could not help agreeing with him when I compared them to

the singers I heard at the Pergola and elsewhere. The theatre, too, was good at Bologna, and we frequently went to it.

One evening we were sitting on the balcony of the hotel, when we saw a man stab another in the back of the neck, and then run away. The victim staggered along for a minute, and then fell down in a pool of blood. He had been a spy of the police under Gregory XVI, and one of the principal agents of his cruel government. He was so obnoxious to the people that his assassin has never been discovered.

From Bologna we went for a few weeks to Recoaro, where I drank the waters, after which we travelled to England by the St Gothard Pass.

SIXTEEN

*Publishes 'Physical Geography' – Letter from Humboldt –
Christmas at Collingwood – Letter from Mrs Somerville –
Faraday – Letter from Faraday – Keith Johnstone's Maps –
Winter at Munich – Salzburg – Lake of Garda – Miniscalchi –
Poem by Caterina Brenzoni – Letter from Brenzoni – Letter
from Mrs Somerville – Eloge by Miniscalchi – Winter at
Turin – Baron Plana – Camillo Cavour – Colline near
Turin – Genoa – Teresa Doria – Florence – Miss F. P. Cobbe –
Vivisection – Excursions in the Neighbourhood – Cholera –
Misericordia – Pio Nono in Tuscany – Comet – Tuscan
Revolution – War in Lombardy – Entry of Victor Emmanuel
into Florence – Letters from Mrs Somerville – My Father's
Death – Letter from Miss Cobbe*

WE spent the autumn in visiting my relations on the banks
of the Tweed. I was much out of health at the time. As
winter came on I got better, and was preparing to print my
Physical Geography when *Kosmos* appeared. I at once determined to put my manuscript in the fire when Somerville
said, 'Do not be rash – consult some of our friends –
Herschel for instance.' So I sent the MS. to Sir John
Herschel, who advised me by all means to publish it. It
was very favourably reviewed by Sir Henry Holland in the
Quarterly, which tended much to its success. I afterwards
sent a copy of a later edition to Baron Humboldt, who
wrote me a very kind letter in return.

BARON HUMBOLDT TO MRS SOMERVILLE

A SANS SOUCI, *ce 12 Juillet, 1849*

MADAME,

C'est un devoir bien doux à remplir, Madame, que de vous offrir l'hommage renouvellé de mon dévouement et de ma respectueuse admiration. Ces sentimens datent de bien loin chez l'homme antidiluvien auquel vous avez daigné adresser des lignes si aimables et la nouvelle édition de ce bel ouvrage qui m'a charmé et *instruit* dès qu'il avait paru pour la première fois. A cette grande supériorité que vous possedez et qui a si noblement illustré votre nom, dans les hautes régions de l'analyse mathématique, vous joignez, Madame, une variété de connaissances dans toutes les parties de la physique et de l'histoire naturelle descriptive. Après votre 'Mechanism of the Heavens,' le philosophique ouvrage 'Connexion of the Physical Sciences' avait été l'objet de ma constante admiration. Je l'ai lu en entier et puis relu dans la septième édition qui a paru en 1846 dans les tems où nous étions plus calme, où l'orage politique ne grondait que de loin. L'auteur de l'imprudent 'Cosmos' devoit saluer plus que tout autre la 'Géographie Physique' de Mary Somerville. J'ai su me la procurer dès les premières semaines par les soins de notre ami commun le Chev. Bunsen. Je ne connais dans aucune langue un ouvrage de Géographie physique que l'on pourrait comparer au votre. Je l'ai de nouveau étudié dans la dernière édition que je dois à votre gracieuse bienveillance. Le sentiment de précision que vos habitudes de 'Géomètre' vous ont si profondement imprimé, pénètre tous vos travaux, Madame. Aucun fait, aucune des grandes vues de la nature vous échappent. Vous avez profité et des livres et des conversations des voyageurs dans cette malheureuse Italie où passe la grande route de l'Orient et de l'Inde. J'ai été surpris de la justice de vos aperçus sur la Géographie des plantes et des animaux. Vous

dominez dans ces régions comme en astronomie, en mé-
téorologie, en magnetisme. Que n'ajoutez-vous pas la sphère
céleste, l'uranologie, votre patrimoine, à la sphère terrestre?
C'est vous seule qui pourriez donner à votre belle litérature
un ouvrage cosmologique original, un ouvrage écrit avec
cette lucidité et ce goût que distingue tout ce qui est emané
de votre plume. On a, je le sais, beaucoup de bienveillance
pour mon Cosmos dans votre patrie; mais il en est des *formes*
de composition littéraires, comme de la variété des races et
de la différence primitive des langues. Un ouvrage traduit
manque de vie; ce que plait sur les bords du Rhin doit
paraître bizarre sur les bords de la Tamise et de la Seine.
Mon ouvrage est une production essentiellement allemande,
et ce caractère même, j'en suis sûr, loin de m'en plaindre lui
donne le goût du terroir. Je jouis d'une bonne fortune à
laquelle (à cause de mon long séjour en France, de mes
prédilections personnelles, de mes hérésies politiques) le
Léopard ne m'avait pas trop accoutumé. Je demande à
l'illustre auteur du volume sur la Mécanique Céleste d'avoir
le courage d'aggrandir sa Géographie Physique. Je suis sûr
que le grand homme que nous aimons le plus, vous et moi,
Sir John Herschel, serait de mon opinion. Le MONDE, je me
sers du titre que Descartes voulait donner à un livre dont
nous n'avons que de pauvres fragmens; le *Monde* doit être
écrit pour les Anglais par un auteur de race pure. Il n'y a pas
de sève, pas de vitalité dans les traductions les mieux faites.
Ma santé s'est conservé miraculeusement à l'âge de quatre-
vingts ans, de mon ardeur pour le travail nocturne au milieu
des agitations d'une position que je n'ai pas besoin de vous
depeindre puisque l'excellente Mademoiselle de — vous l'a
fait connaître. J'ai bouleversé, changé mes deux volumes des
'Ansichten.' Il n'en est resté que 1/4. C'est comme un
nouvel ouvrage que j'aurai bientôt le bonheur de vous
adresser si M. Cotta pense pouvoir hasarder une publication
dans ces tems où la force physique croit guérir un mal moral
et *vacciner* le contentement à l'Allemagne unitaire!! Le

troisième volume de mon Cosmos avance, mais la sérénité manque aux âmes moins crédules.

Agréez, je vous supplie, l'hommage de mon affectueuse et respectueuse reconnaissance,

ALEXANDRE DE HUMBOLDT

Somerville and I spent the Christmas at Collingwood with our friends the Herschels. The party consisted of Mr Airy, Astronomer Royal, and Mr Adams°, who had taken high honours at Cambridge. This young man and M. Leverrier°, the celebrated French astronomer, had separately calculated the orbit of Neptune and announced it so nearly at the same time, that each country claims the honour of the discovery. Mr Adams told Somerville that the following sentence in the sixth edition of the *Connexion of the Physical Sciences*, published in the year 1842, put it into his head to calculate the orbit of Neptune. 'If after the lapse of years the tables formed from a combination of numerous observations should be still inadequate to represent the motions of Uranus, the discrepancies may reveal the existence, nay, even the mass and orbit of a body placed for ever beyond the sphere of vision.' That prediction was fulfilled in 1846, by the discovery of Neptune revolving at the distance of 3,000,000,000 of miles from the sun. The mass of Neptune, the size and position of his orbit in space, and his periodic time, were determined from his disturbing action on Uranus before the planet itself had been seen.

We left Collingwood as ever with regret.

[The following is an extract from a letter written by my mother during this visit:—]

FROM MRS SOMERVILLE TO W. GREIG, ESQ.

COLLINGWOOD, *1st January, 1848*

. . . You can more easily conceive than I can describe the great kindness and affection which we have received from both Sir John and Lady Herschel; I feel a pride and pleasure beyond what I can express in having such friends. Collingwood is a house by itself in the world, there certainly is nothing like it for all that is great and good. The charm of the conversation is only equalled by its variety – every subject Sir John touches turns to doubly refined gold; profound, brilliant, amiable, and highly poetical, I could never end admiring and praising him. Then the children are so nice and he so kind and amusing to them, making them quite his friends and companions.

Yours, my dearest Woronzow,

Most affectionately,

M. SOMERVILLE

We had formed such a friendship with Mr Faraday that while we lived abroad he sent me a copy of everything he published, and on returning to England we renewed our friendship with that illustrious philosopher, and attended his lectures at the Royal Institution. He had already magnetised a ray of polarised light, but was still lecturing on the magnetic and diamagnetic properties of matter. At the last lecture we attended he showed the diamagnetism of flame, which had been proved by a foreign philosopher. Mr Faraday never would accept of any honour; he lived in a circle of friends to whom he was deeply attached. A touching and beautiful memoir was published of him by his friend and successor, Professor Tyndall°, an experimental philosopher of the very highest genius.

[The following letter was the last my mother received from Faraday:—]

FROM PROFESSOR FARADAY TO
MRS SOMERVILLE

ROYAL INSTITUTION, *17th January, 1859*

MY DEAR MRS. SOMERVILLE,

So you have remembered me again, and I have the delight of receiving from you a new copy of that work which has so often instructed me; and I may well say, cheered me in my simple homely course through life in this house. It was most kind to think of me; but ah! how sweet it is to believe that I have your *approval* in matters where kindness would be nothing, where judgment alone must rule. I almost doubt myself when I think I have your approbation, to some degree at least, in what I may have thought or said about gravitation, the forces of nature, their conservation, &c. As it is, I *cannot* go back from these thoughts; on the contrary, I feel encouraged to go on by way of experiment, but am not so able as I was formerly; for when I try to hold the necessary group of thoughts in mind at one time, with the judgment suspended on almost all of them, then my head becomes giddy, and I am obliged to lay all aside for a while. I am trying for *time* in magnetic action, and do not despair of reaching it, even though it may be only that of light. *Nous verrons.*

I have been putting into one volume various papers of mine on experimental branches in chemistry and physics. The index and title-page has gone to the printer, and I expect soon to receive copies from him. I shall ask Mr. Murray to help me in sending one to you which I hope you will honour by acceptance. There is nothing new in it, except a few additional pages about '*regelation*,'[104] and also 'gravity.' It is useful to get one's scattered papers together with an index, and society seems to like the collection sufficiently to pay the expenses . . . Pray

remember me most kindly to all with whom I may take that
privilege, and believe me to be most truly,

Your admirer and
faithful servant,
M. FARADAY

[My mother wrote of this letter:—]

FLORENCE, *8th February, 1859*

. . . I have had the most charming and gratifying letter from
Faraday; I cannot tell you how I value such a mark of
approbation and friendship from the greatest experimental
philosopher and discoverer next to Newton.

We returned to the continent in autumn, so I could not
superintend the publication of my *Physical Geography*, but
Mr Pentland kindly undertook to carry it through the press.
Though I never was personally acquainted with Mr Keith
Johnston°, of Edinburgh, that eminent geographer gave me
copies of both the first and second editions of his splendid
Atlas of Physical Geography, which were of the greatest use to
me. Besides, he published some time afterwards a small
School Atlas of Ancient, Modern, and Physical Geography,
intended to accompany my work; obligations which I gratefully acknowledge. No one has attempted to copy my *Connexion of the Physical Sciences*, the subjects are too difficult;
but soon after the publication of the *Physical Geography* a
number of cheap books appeared, just keeping within the
letter of the law, on which account it has only gone through
five editions. However a sixth is now required.

The moment was unfavourable for going into Italy, as war
was raging between Charles Albert° and the Austrians, so

we resolved to remain at Munich, and wait the course of
events. We got a very pretty little apartment, well furnished
with stoves, and opposite the house of the Marchese Fabio
Pallavicini, formerly Sardinian minister at Munich. We
spent most of our evenings very pleasantly at their house.
We attended the concerts at the Odeon of classical music:
the execution was perfect, but the music was so refined and
profound that it passed my comprehension, and I thought
it tedious. The hours at Munich were so early that the opera
ended almost at the time it began in London.

In the spring we went to Salzburg, where we remained all
summer. We had an apartment in a dilapidated old château, about an hour's walk from the town, called Leopold's
Krone. The picturesque situation of the town reminded me
of the Castle and Old Town of Edinburgh. The view from
our windows was alpine, and the trees bordering the roads
were such as I have rarely seen out of England. We made
many excursions to Berchtesgaden, where King Louis° and
his court were then living, and went to the upper end of the
Königsee. I have repeatedly been at sea in very stormy
weather without the smallest idea of fear; but the black,
deep water of this lake, under the shadow of the precipitous
mountains, made a disagreeable impression on me. I
thought if I were to be drowned I should prefer the blue
sea to that cold, black pool. The flora was lovely, and on
returning from our expeditions in the evening, the damp,
mossy banks were luminous with glowworms: I never saw
so many, either before or since. We never fail to make
acquaintances wherever we go, and our friends at Munich
had given us letters to various people who were passing the
summer there, many of whom had evening receptions once
a week. At the Countess Irene Arco's beautiful Gothic
château of Anif,[105] which rises out of a small pellucid lake,
and is reached by a bridge, we spent many pleasant eve
nings, as well as at Countess Bellegarde's, and at Aigen,
which belonged to the Cardinal Schwartzenberg°. We

never saw him, but went to visit his niece, with whom we were intimate.

The war being over, we went by Innsbrück and the Brenner to Colà, on the Lago di Garda, within five miles of Peschiera, where we spent a month with Count and Countess Erizzo Miniscalchi° who had been our intimate friends for many years. The devastation of the country was frightful. Peschiera and its fortifications were in ruins; the villages around had been burnt down, and the wretched inhabitants were beginning to repair their roofless houses. Our friends themselves had but recently returned to Colà, which, from its commanding situation, was always the head-quarters of whatever army was in possession of the country around. On this account, the family had to fly more than once at the approach of the enemy. In 1848 the Countess had fled to Milan, and was confined at the very time the Austrians under Radetzky° were besieging the town, which was defended by Charles Albert. Fearing what might occur when the city was surrendered, the lady, together with her new-born infant and the rest of her family, escaped the next day with considerable difficulty, and travelled to Genoa.

Although not acquainted with quite so many languages as Mezzofanti, Count Miniscalchi is a remarkable linguist, especially with regard to Arabic and other oriental tongues. He has availed himself of his talent, and published several works, the most interesting of which is a translation of the Gospel of St John from Syro-Chaldaic (the language probably spoken by our Saviour) into Latin. The manuscript, from which this translation is made, is preserved in the Vatican.

[While we were at Colà my mother received a visit from a very distinguished and gifted lady, the Countess Bon-Brenzoni°. As an instance of the feelings entertained by an Italian woman towards my mother, I insert a letter written by the Countess some time afterwards, and also an extract from her poems:—]

FROM THE COUNTESS BON-BRENZONI TO MRS SOMERVILLE

VERONA, *28 Maggio, 1853*

ILLUSTRE SIGNORA,

Fui molto contenta udendo che finalmente le sia giunto l' involto contenente le copie stampate del Carme, ch' ebbi l' onore di poterle offerire, mentre io era in gran pensiero non forse fossero insorte difficoltà, o ritardi, in causa della posta. Ma, ben più che per questo la sua graziosissima lettera mi fù di vera consolazione, per l' accoglienza tutta benevola e generosa ch' Ella fece a' miei versi. La ringrazio delle parole piene di bontà ch' Ella mi scrive, e di aversi preso la gentil cura di farlo in italiano; così potess' io ricambiarla scrivendo a Lei in inglese! Pur mi conforta la certezza che il linguaggio delle anime sia uno solo; mentre io non so s' io debba chiamar presunzione, o ispirazione questa, che mi fa credere, che esista fra la sua e la mia una qualche intelligenza, e quantunque i suoi meriti e la sua bontà me ne spieghino in gran parte il mistero, pure trovo essere cosa non comune questo pensiero, che al mio cuore parla di Lei incessantemente, da quel giorno ch' io l' ho veduta per la prima e l' unica volta!

Ah se è vero che fra i sentimenti di compiacenza ch' Ella provò per gli elogi ottenuti de' suoi lavori, abbia saputo trovar luogo fra i più cari quello che le destò nell' animo l' espressione viva e sincera della mia ammirazione e del mio umile affetto, io raggiunsi un punto a cui certo non avea osato aspirare!

Il trovarmi con Lei a Colà, od altrove che fosse, è uno de' miei più cari desideri, e son lieta delle sue parole che me ne danno qualche speranza.

Voglia presentare i miei distinti doveri all' eccelente suo Sig^{re} marito ed alle amabili figlie; e mentre io le prego da Dio le più desiderabili benedizioni, Ella si ricordi di me siccome di una persona, che sebbene lontana fisicamente, le è sempre vicina coll' animo, nei sentimenti della più affetuosa venerazione.

Incoraggiata dalla sua bontà, mi onoro segnarmi

amica affezionatissima

CATERINA BON-BRENZONI

The 'Carme' spoken of in the above letter form a long poem on modern astronomy, entitled *I Cieli* (published by Vallardi, Milan; 1853). The opening lines contain the following address to Mrs Somerville, – doubtless a genuine description of the author's feelings on first meeting the simple-mannered lady whose intellectual greatness she had long learned to appreciate:—

> Donna, quel giorno ch' io ti vidi in prima,
> Dimmi, hai Tu scôrto sul mio volto i segni
> Dell' anima commossa? – Hai Tu veduto
> Come trepida innanzi io ti venia,
> E come reverenza e maraviglia
> Tenean sospesa sull' indocil labbro
> La parola mal certa – Ah! dimmi, hai scôrto
> Come fur vinte dall' affetto allora
> Che t'udii favellar soave e piana,
> Coll' angelica voce e l' umiltade,
> Che a' suoi più cari sapïenza insegna?—
> Questa, io dicea tra me, questa è Colei,
> Di che le mille volte udito ho il nome
> Venerato suonar tra i più famosi?
> Questa è Colei che negli eterei spazj
> Segue il cammin degli astri, e ne misura
> Peso, moto, distanza, orbita e luce?

_____

[Another record of our visit to Colà is in a letter of my mother to my brother:—]

MRS SOMERVILLE TO W. GREIG, ESQ.

TURIN, *4th Dec., 1849*

MY DEAREST WORONZOW,

We arrived here all well the day before yesterday, after a fair but bitterly cold journey, bright sunshine and keen frost, and to-day we have a fall of snow . . . It was a great disappointment not finding letters here, and I fear many have been lost on both sides, though we took care not to touch on political events, as all letters are opened by the Austrian police in Lombardy. We spent five weeks with our friends the Miniscalchis very agreeably, and received every mark of kindness and hospitality. They only live at Verona during the winter, and we found them in their country house at Colà situated on a height overlooking the Lago di Garda, with the snowy Alps on the opposite side of the lake. The view from their grounds is so fine that I was tempted to paint once more. They took us to see all the places in the neighbourhood; often a sad sight, from having been the seat of war and siege. The villages are burnt and the churches in ruin. But the people are repairing the mischief as fast as possible, and the fields are already well cultivated. The Count is a man of great learning and is occupied in the comparison of languages, especially the Eastern; he knows twenty-four and speaks Arabic as fluently as Italian. He is in the habit of speaking both Arabic and Chaldee every day, as there is a most learned Chaldean priest living with them, whose conversation gave me great pleasure and much information. The Count has moreover a black servant who speaks these languages, having been bought by the Count during his long residence in the East, and is now treated like one of the family. I obtained much information which will be useful in my next edition of the Physical Geography . . .

Your affectionate mother,

MARY SOMERVILLE

[After my mother's death, our old friend Count Miniscalchi made a beautiful and touching 'éloge' on her at a meeting of the Royal Italian Geographical Society, to a numerous audience assembled in the great hall of the Collegio Romano at Rome.

My mother was an honorary member of this Society, besides which the first gold medal granted by them was voted by acclamation to her. Her Recollections continue as follows:—]

———————

From Colà we went to Turin, where I became personally acquainted with Baron Plana°, Director of the Observatory. He had married a niece of the illustrious mathematician Lagrange, who proved the stability of the solar system. Plana, himself, was a very great analyst; his volume on the Lunar Perturbations is a work of enormous labour. He gave me a copy of it and of all his works; for I continued to have friendly intercourse with him as long as he lived. As soon as he heard of our arrival, he came to take us out to drive. I never shall forget the beauty of the Alps, and the broad valley of the Po and Dora, deeply covered with snow, and sparkling in bright sunshine. Another day the Baron took us to a church, from the cupola of which a very long pendulum was swinging, that we might see the rotation of the Earth visibly proved by its action on the pendulum, according to M. Foucault's° experiment. He devoted his time to get us established, and we found a handsome apartment in Casa Cavour, and became acquainted with both the brothers to whom it belonged. Count Camillo Cavour, then Minister of the Interior, was the only great statesman Italy ever produced in modern times. His premature death is deplorably felt at the present day. He was a real genius, and the most masterly act of his administration was that of sending an army to act in concert with the French and English in the Crimean War. By it he at once gave Italy the rank of an independent European power, which was the first step towards Italian unity. He was delightful and cheerful in society, and extremely beloved by his family and friends. [*1D, 229:* Camillo Cavour and Garibaldi° are the only men of genius whose names will live in the history of the revolution. The latter is certainly the most extraordinary considering his origin and want of education. By his disinterested devotion and amiable character he wields a power over the people formidable to his enemies, but unfortunate for Italy.]

In spring we hired a villa on the Colline above Turin. The house was in a garden, with a terrace, whence the ground sank rapidly to the plain; low hills, clothed with chestnut forests, abounding in lilies of the valley, surrounded us behind. The summer had been stormy, and one evening we walked on the terrace to look at the lightning, which was very fine, illuminating the chain of Alps. By and by it ceased, and the darkness was intense; but we continued to walk, when, to our surprise, a pale bluish light rose in the Val di Susa, which gradually spread along the summit of the Alps, and the tops of the hills behind our house; then a column of the same pale blue light, actually within our reach, came curling up from the slope close to the terrace, exactly as if wet weeds had been burning. In about ten minutes the whole vanished; but in less than a quarter of an hour the phenomena were repeated exactly as described, and were followed by a dark night and torrents of rain. It was a very unusual instance of what is known as electric glow; that is, electricity without tension.

On our road to Genoa, we went to see some kind Piedmontese friends, who have a château in the Monferrat, not many miles from Asti, where we left the railroad. We had not gone many miles when the carriage we had hired was upset, and, although nobody had broken bones, I got so severe a blow on my forehead that I was confined to bed for nearly a month, and my face was black and blue for a much longer time. Nothing could equal the unwearied kindness of our friends during my illness.

When I was able to travel, we went to Genoa for the winter, and lived on the second floor of a large house on the Acqua Sola, and overlooking the sea. Here first began our friendship with the Marchesa Teresa Doria°, whose maiden name was Durazzo; in her youth one of the handsomest women in Genoa, a lady distinguished for her generous character and cultivated mind, and who fearlessly avowed her opinions at a time when it was a kind of disgrace to be called a Liberal. Her youngest son, Giacomo, has devoted his life to the study of natural history, and his mother used all her influence to encourage and help him in a pursuit so unusual amongst people of rank in this country. Later, he travelled in Persia for two years, to make collections, and since then resided for a long time in Borneo, and is now arranging a museum in his native city. The Marchesa has always been a warm and devoted friend to me and mine.

It was here that we got our dear old parrot Lory, who is still alive and merry.

[*1D, 234:* We had a cook at Genoa who spent the evenings in reading and had leave to read any French books we possessed. One day while Somerville was walking in the garden the cook came to thank him, he had been reading the Bible and said, 'C'est une drôle d'histoire celle d'Adam et d'Eve qui étoient punis selon leur crime; mais le serpent doit condamné de rampler sur le ventre toute sa vie. Pouvez-vous me dire Monsieur si avant cela il avait de pattes?']¹⁰⁶

Our next move was to Florence, where we already knew many people. We had a lease of a house in Via del Mandorlo, which had a small garden and a balcony, where we often sat and received in the warm summer evenings.

My daughters had adorned it and the garden with rare creepers, shrubs, and flowers.

We had a visit from our friend Gibson, as he passed through Florence on his way to Switzerland. He told us the history of his early life, as given in his biography, and much that is not mentioned there. He was devotedly attached to the Queen, and spoke of her in his simple manner as a charming lady.

Miss Hosmer° was travelling with Gibson, an American young lady, who was his pupil, and of whose works he was very proud. He looked upon her as if she had been his daughter, and she took care of him; for he was careless and forgetful when travelling. I have the sincerest pleasure in expressing my admiration for Miss Hosmer, who has proved by her works that our sex possesses both genius and originality in the highest branches of art.

It was at Florence that I first met my dear friend and constant correspondent, Frances Power Cobbe°. She is the cleverest and most agreeable woman I ever met with, and one of the best. There is a distant connection between us, as one of her ancestors married a niece of Lord Fairfax, the Parliamentary general, many of whose letters are in the possession of her family. A German professor of physiology at Florence roused public indignation by his barbarous vivisections, and there was a canvass for a Memorial against this cruel practice. Miss Cobbe took a leading part in this movement, and I heartily joined, and wrote to all my acquaintances, requesting their votes; among others, to a certain Marchese, who had published something on agriculture. He refused his vote, saying, 'Perhaps I was not aware that the present state of science was one of induction.' Then he went on explaining to me what 'induction' meant, &c., &c., which amused me not a little. It made my family very indignant, as they thought it eminently presumptuous, addressed to me by a man who, though a good patriot and agriculturist, knew nothing whatever about science, past or present. A good deal of political party spirit was brought into play in this instance, as is too often the case here. It is not complimentary to the state of civilisation in Italy, that in Russia and Poland, both of them very far behind her in many respects, there should exist societies for the prevention of cruelty to animals, to which all the most distinguished people have given their names.

[I rejoice to say that this stain on Italian civilisation is now wiped away. My mother just lived to hail the formation of the Società Protettrice degli Animali. – ED.]

In summer we sometimes made excursions to avoid the heat of Florence. One year we went to Vallombrosa[107] and the convents of La Vernia, and Camaldoli, which are now suppressed. We travelled on mules or ponies, as the mountain paths are impracticable to carriages. I was disappointed in Vallombrosa itself, but the road to it is beautiful. La Vernia is highly picturesque, there we remained two days, which I spent in drawing. The trees round the convent formed a striking contrast to the arid cliffs we had passed on the road. The monks were naturally delighted to see strangers. They belonged to the order of St Francis, and each in his turn wandered over the country begging and living on the industry of others. We did not pay for our food and lodging, but left much more than an equivalent in the poor-box. Somerville slept in the convent, and we ladies were lodged in the so-called *Foresteria* outside; but even Somerville was not admitted into the *clausura* at Camaldoli, for the monks make a vow of perpetual silence and solitude. Each had his little separate hut and garden, and some distance above the convent, on the slopes of the Apennines, they had an establishment called the *Eremo*, for those who sought for even greater solitude. The people told us that in winter, when deep snow covers the whole place, wolves are often seen prowling about. Not far from the Eremo there is a place from whence both the Mediterranean and the Adriatic can be seen.

We occasionally went for sea-bathing to Viareggio, which is built on a flat sandy beach. The loose sand is drifted by the wind into low hillocks, and bound together by coarse grass thickly coated with silex. Among this and other plants a lovely white amaryllis, the *Pancratium maratimum*,[108] with a sweet and powerful perfume, springs up. We often tried to get the bulb, but it lay too deep under the sand. One evening we had gone a long way in search of these flowers, and sat down to rest, though it was beginning to be dark. We had not sat many minutes when we were surrounded by a number of what we supposed to be bats trying to get at the flowers we had gathered, but at length we discovered that they were enormous moths, which followed us home, and actually flew into the room to soar over the flowers and suck the honey with their long proboscides. They were beautiful creatures with large red eyes on their wings.

Our life at Florence went on pretty much as usual when all at once cholera broke out of the most virulent kind. Multitudes fled from Florence; often in vain, for it prevailed all through Tuscany to a great extent. The terrified people were kneeling to the Madonna and making processions, after which it was remarked that the number of cases was invariably increased. The Misericordia went about in their fearful costume, indefatigable in carrying the sick to the hospitals. The devotion of that society was beyond all praise; the young and the old, the artisan and the nobleman, went night and day in detachments carrying aid to the sufferers, not in Florence only, but to Fiesole and the villages round. We never were afraid, but we consulted Professor Zanetti°, our medical adviser, whether we should leave the town, which we were unwilling to do, as we thought we should be far from medical assistance, and he said, 'By no means; live as usual, drive out as you have always done, and make not the smallest change.' We followed his advice, and drove out every afternoon till near dark, and then passed the rest of the evening with those friends who, like ourselves, had remained in town. None of us took the disease except one of our servants, who recovered from instant help being given.

The Marquis of Normanby° was British minister at that time, and Lady Normanby and he were always kind and hospitable to us. At her house we became acquainted with Signora Barbieri-Nini°, the celebrated opera singer, who had retired from the stage, and lived with her husband, a Sienese gentleman, in a villa not far from Villa Normanby. She gave a musical party, to which she invited us. The music, which was entirely artistic, was excellent, the entertainment very handsome, and it was altogether very enjoyable. As we were driving home afterwards, late at night, going down the hill, our carriage ran against one of the dead carts which was carrying those who had died that day to the burying-ground at Trespiano. It was horribly ghastly – one could distinguish the forms of the limbs under the canvas thrown over the heap of dead. The burial of the poor and rich in Italy is in singular contrast; the poor are thrown into the grave without a coffin, the rich are placed in coffins, and in full dress, which, especially in the case of youth and infancy, leaves a pleasant impression. An intimate friend of ours lost an infant, and asked me to go and see it laid out. The coffin, lined with white silk, was on a table, covered with a white cloth, strewed with flowers, and with a row of wax lights on either side. The baby was clothed in a white satin frock, leaving the neck and arms bare; a rose-bud was in each hand, and a wreath of rose-buds surrounded the head, which rested on a pillow. Nothing could be prettier; it was like a sleeping angel.

Pio Nono had lost his popularity before he came to visit the Grand Duke of Tuscany. The people received him respectfully, but without enthusiasm; nevertheless, Florence was illuminated in his honour. The Duomo, Campanile, and the old tower in the Piazza dei Signori were very fine, but the Lung' Arno was beautiful beyond description; the river was full, and reflected the whole with dazzling splendour.

I made the acquaintance of Signore Donati°, afterwards celebrated for the discovery of one of the most brilliant comets of this century, whose course and changes I watched with the greatest interest. On one occasion I was accompanied by my valued friend Sir Henry Holland, who had come to Florence during one of his annual journeys. I had much pleasure in seeing him again.

Political parties ran very high in Florence; we sympathised with the Liberals, living on intimate terms with the chief of them. As soon as the probability of war between Piedmont and Austria became known, many young men of every rank, some even of the highest families, hastened to join as volunteers. The most sanguine long hoped that the Grand Duke might remember that he was an Italian prince rather than an Austrian archduke, and would send his troops to join the Italian cause; but his dynasty was doomed, and he blindly chose the losing side. At last the Austrians crossed the Mincio, and the war fairly broke out, France coming to the assistance of Piedmont. The enthusiasm of the Tuscans could then no longer be restrained, and on the 27th April 1859, crowds of people assembled on the Piazza dell' Indipendenza, and raised the tri-coloured flag. The government, who, the day before, had warning of what was impending, had sent sealed orders to the forts of Belvedere and del Basso, which, when opened on the eventful morning, were found to contain orders for the bombardment of the town. This the officers refused to do, after which the troops joined the popular cause. When this order became generally known, as it soon did, it proved the last blow to the dynasty, although the most eminent and respected Liberals used their best efforts during the whole

of the 27th to restore harmony between the Grand Duke
and the people. They advised his immediate abdication in
favour of his son, the Archduke Ferdinand, the proclama-
tion of the Constitution, and of course insisted on the
immediate alliance with Piedmont as their principal condition. It was already too late! All was of no avail, and in the
evening, whilst we were as usual at the Cascine, the whole
Imperial family, accompanied by the Austrian minister,
and escorted by several of the Corps Diplomatique, drove
round the walls from Palazzo Pitti to Porta San Gallo
unmolested amid a silent crowd, and crossing the frontier
on the Bologna road, bade farewell for ever to Tuscany.
The obnoxious ministers were also permitted to retire
unnoticed to their country houses.

Thus ended this bloodless revolution; there was no
disorder of any kind, which was due to the young men
belonging to the principal families of Florence, such as
Corsini, Incontri, Farinola, and others, using their influence with the people to calm and direct them. Indeed, so
quiet was everything that my daughters walked about the
streets, as did most ladies, to see what was going on; the
only visible signs of the revolution throughout the whole
day were bands of young men with tri-coloured flags and
cockades shouting national songs at the top of their voices.
As I have said already, we took our usual drive to the
Cascine after dinner, and went to the theatre in the evening; the streets were perfectly quiet, and next morning the
people were at work as usual. Sir James Scarlett° was our
minister, and had a reception the evening after these events,
where we heard many predictions of evil which never were
fulfilled. The least of these was the occupation of Florence
by a victorious Austrian army. The Tuscan archdukes
precluded all chance of a restoration by joining the Austrian
army, and being present at the Battle of Solferino.[109] At
Florence a provisional government was formed with Bettino Ricasoli° at its head; a parliament assembled three times

in the Sala dei Cinquecento, in the Palazzo Vecchio, and
voted with unanimity the expulsion of the House of Lorraine, and the annexation of Tuscany to the kingdom of
Italy. In the meantime the French and Italian arms were
victorious in Lombardy. As, however, it is not my intention
to give an historical account of the revolution of 1859, but
merely to jot down such circumstances as came under my
own immediate notice, I shall not enter into any particulars
regarding the well-known campaign which ended in the
cession of Milan and Lombardy to Italy.

We were keenly interested in the alliance between the
Emperor Napoleon and the King of Italy, in hopes the
Quadrilateral would be taken, and Venice added to the
Italian States. We had a map of Northern Italy spread on a
table, and from day to day we marked the positions of the
different headquarters with coloured-headed pins. I can
hardly describe our indignation when all at once peace was
signed at Villafranca, and Napoleon received Nice and
Savoy in recompense for his aid, which were given up to
him without regard to the will of the people. When the
peace was announced in Tuscany it caused great consternation and disgust; the people were in the greatest excitement, fearing that those rulers so obnoxious to them might
by this treaty be again forced upon them; and it required
the firm hand of Ricasoli to calm the people, and induce the
King to accept the annexation which had been voted without one dissentient voice.

Baron Ricasoli had naturally many enemies amongst the
Codini, or retrograde party. Hand-grenades were thrown
against the door of his house, as also at those of other
ministers, but without doing harm. One evening my daughters were dressing to go to a ball that was to take place at the
Palazzo delle Crocelle, close to us, in a street parallel to
ours, when we were startled by a loud explosion. An
attempt had been made to throw a shell into the ball-room,
which had happily failed. The streets were immediately

lined with soldiers, and the ball, which was given by the Ministers, as far as I recollect, took place.

When the war broke out, a large body of French troops, commanded by Prince Jerôme Napoleon, came to Florence, and were bivouacked in the Cascine. The people in the streets welcomed them as deliverers from the Austrians, whose occupation of Tuscany, when first we came to reside in Florence, was such a bitter mortification to them, and one of the causes of the unpopularity of the Grand Duke, whom they never forgave for calling in the Austrian troops after 1848. The French camp was a very pretty sight; some of the soldiers playing at games, some mending their clothes, or else cooking. They were not very particular as to what they ate, for one of my daughters saw a soldier skin a rat and put it into his soup-kettle.

We were invited by the Marchesa Lajatico, with whom we were very intimate, to go and see the entry of Victor Emmanuel into Florence from the balcony of the Casa Corsini in the Piazza del Prato, where she resides. The King was received with acclamation: never was anything like the enthusiasm. Flowers were showered down from every window, and the streets were decorated with a taste peculiar to the Italians.

[I think the following extracts from letters written by my mother during the year 1859 and the following, ever memorable in Italian history, may not be unwelcome to the reader. My mother took the keenest interest in all that occurred. Owing to the liberal opinions she had held from her youth, and to which she was ever constant, all her sympathies were with the Italian cause, and she rejoiced at every step which tended to unite all Italy in one kingdom. She lived to see this great revolution accomplished by the entry of Victor Emmanuel into Rome as King of Italy; a consummation believed by most politicians to be a wild dream of poets and hot-headed patriots, but now realised and accepted as a matter of course. My mother had always firm faith in this result, and it was with inexpressible pleasure she watched its completion. Our intimacy with the leading politicians both in Tuscany and Piedmont naturally added to our interest. Ricasoli, Menabrea°, Peruzzi°, Minghetti°, &c., we knew intimately, as well as Camillo Cavour, the greatest statesman Italy ever produced. No one who did not witness it can imagine the grief and consternation his death occasioned, and of which my mother writes in a letter dated June 19th, 1861.

FROM MRS SOMERVILLE TO W. GREIG, ESQ.

FLORENCE, *May 5th, 1859*

MY DEAREST W.,

Your letter of the 28th would have made me laugh heartily were we not annoyed that you should have suffered such uneasiness on our account; the panic in England is ridiculous and most unfounded. The whole affair has been conducted with perfect unanimity and tranquillity, so that there has been no one to fight with. The Austrians are concentrated in Lombardy, and not in Tuscany, nor is there any one thing to disturb the perfect peace and quietness which prevail over the whole country; not a soul thinks of leaving Florence. You do the greatest injustice to the Tuscans. From first to last not a person has been insulted, not a cry raised against anyone; even the obnoxious ministers were allowed to go to their country houses without a word of insult, and troops were sent with the Grand Duke to escort him and his family to the frontier. Martha and Mary went all through the town the morning of the revolution, which was exactly like a common festa, and we found the tranquillity as great when we drove through the streets in the afternoon. The same quiet still prevails, the people are at their usual employments, the theatres and private receptions go on as usual, and the provisional government is excellent. Everyone knew of the revolution long before it took place and the quietness with which it was to be conducted. I am grieved at the tone of English politics, and trust, for the honour of the country and humanity, that we do not intend to make war upon France and Sardinia. It would be a disgrace and everlasting stigma to make a crusade against the oppressed, being ourselves free. The people here have behaved splendidly, and we rejoice that we have been here to witness such noble conduct. No nation ever made such progress as the Tuscans have done since the year 48. Not a word of republicanism, it has never been named. All they want is a constitutional government, and this they are quietly settling . . .

FROM MRS SOMERVILLE TO W. GREIG, ESQ.

FLORENCE, *29th May, 1859*

. . . Everything is perfectly quiet here; the Tuscans are giving money liberally for carrying on the war. We have bought quantities of old linen, and your sisters and I spend the day in making lint and bandages for the wounded soldiers; great quantities have already been sent to Piedmont. Hitherto the war has been favourable to the allied army. God grant that England may not enter into the contest till the Austrians are driven out of Italy! After that point has been gained, our honour would be safe. To take part with the oppressors and maintain despotism in Italy would be infamous. Tuscany is to be occupied by a large body of troops under the command of Prince Napoleon. A great many are already encamped on the meadows at the Cascine – fine, spirited, merry young men; many of them have the Victoria medal. They are a thorough protection against any attack by the Austrians, of which, however, there is little chance, as they have enough to do in Lombardy. There is to be a great affair this morning at nine o'clock; an altar is raised in the middle of the camp, and the tricolour (Italian) flag is to be blessed amidst salvoes of cannon. Your friend, Bettino Ricasoli, is thought by far the most able and statesmanlike person in Tuscany; he is highly respected. Martha and I dined with Mr. Scarlett, and met . . . who said if the Grand Duke had not been the most foolish and obstinately weak man in the world, he might still have been on the throne of Tuscany; but that now he has made that impossible by going to Vienna and allowing his two sons to enter the Austrian army . . . We have had a visit from Dr. Falkner°, his two nieces and brother. They had been spending the winter in Sicily, where he discovered rude implements formed by man mixed with the bones of prehistoric animals in a cave, so hermetically shut up that not a doubt is left of a race of men having lived at a period far anterior to that assigned as the origin of mankind. Similar discoveries have recently been made elsewhere. Dr. Falkner had travelled much in the Himalayas, and lived two years on the great plain of Tibet; the account he gave me of it was most interesting. His brother had spent fifteen years in Australia, so the conversation delighted me; I learnt so much that was new. I am glad to hear that the Queen has been so kind to my friend Faraday; it seems she has given him an apartment at Hampton Court nicely fitted up. She went to see it herself, and having consulted scientific men as to the instruments that were necessary for his pursuits, she had a laboratory fitted up with them, and made him a present of the whole. That is doing things handsomely, and no one since Newton has deserved it so much.

FROM MRS SOMERVILLE TO W. GREIG, ESQ.

FLORENCE, *5th June, 1859*

. . . All is perfectly quiet; a large body of French troops are now in Tuscany, and many more are expected probably to make a diversion on this side of the Austrian army through Modena; but nothing is known; the most profound secrecy is maintained as to all military movements. Success has hitherto attended the allied army, and the greatest bravery has been shown. The enthusiasm among the men engaged is excessive, the King of Sardinia himself the bravest of the brave, but exposes himself so much that the people are making petitions to him to be mòre careful. The Zouaves[110] called out in the midst of the battle, 'Le roi est un Zouave!' Prince Napoleon keeps very quiet, and avoids shewing himself as much as possible. The French troops are very fine indeed – young, gay, extremely civil and well bred. The secrecy is quite curious; even the colonels of the regiments do not know where they may be sent till the order comes: so all is conjecture . . . The young King of Naples seems to follow the footsteps of his father; I hope in God that we may not protect and defend him. How anxious we are to know what the House of Commons will do! Let us hope they will take the liberal side; but the conservative party seems to be increasing.

———————

FROM MRS SOMERVILLE TO W. GREIG, ESQ.

FLORENCE, *22nd August, 1859*

. . . Public affairs go on admirably. A few weeks ago the elections took place of the members of the Tuscan parliament with a calm and tranquillity of which you have no idea. Every proprietor who pays 15 pauls of taxes (75 pence) has a vote.

There are 180 members, consisting of the most ancient nobility, the richest proprietors, the most distinguished physi-
cians and lawyers, and the most respectable merchants. They
hold their meetings in the magnificent hall of the Palazzo
Vecchio – the Sala Dei Cinquecento. The first two or three
days were employed in choosing a president, &c., &c.; then a
day was named to determine the fate of the house of Lorraine.
I could not go, but Martha went with a Tuscan friend. There
was no speaking; the vote was by ballot, and each member
separately went up to a table before the president, and silently
put his ball into a large vase. Two members poured the balls
into a tray, and on examination, said, 'No division is necessary;
they are *all* black,' – which was followed by long and loud
cheering. They have been equally unanimous in the Legations
in Parma and Modena; and the wish of the people is to form
one kingdom of these four states under an Italian prince,
excluding all Austrians for ever. The union is perfect, and
the determination quiet but deep and unalterable. If the
Archduke is forced upon them, it must be by armed force,
which the French emperor will not likely permit, after the
Archduke was fool enough to fight against him at Solferino. All
the four states have unanimously voted union with Piedmont;
but they do not expect it to be granted. The destinies of
Europe are now dependent on the two emperors . . .

FROM MRS SOMERVILLE TO W. GREIG, ESQ.

FLORENCE, *23rd April, 1860*

You would have had this letter sooner, my dearest Woronzow,
if I had not been prevented from writing to you yesterday
evening . . . The weather has been atrocious; deluges of rain
night and day, and so cold that I have been obliged to lay in a
second supply of wood. The only good day, and the only one I

have been out, was that on which the king arrived. It fortunately was fine, and the sight was magnificent; quite worthy of so great an historical event. No carriages were allowed after the guns fired announcing that the king had left Leghorn; so we should have been ill off, had it not been for the kindness of our friend the Marchesa Lajatico, who invited us to her balcony, which is now very large, as they have built an addition to their house for the eldest son and his pretty wife. We were there some hours before the king arrived; but as all the Florentine society was there, and many of our friends from Turin and Genoa, we found it very agreeable. The house is in the Prato, very near the gate the king was to enter. On each side of it stages were raised like steps in an amphitheatre, which were densely crowded, every window decorated with gaily-coloured hangings and the Italian flag; the streets were lined with 'guardie civiche,' and bands of music played from time to time. The people shouted 'Evviva!' every time a gun was fired. In the midst of this joy there appeared what resembled a funeral procession – about a hundred emigrants following the Venetian, Roman, and Neapolitan colours, all hung with black crape; they were warmly applauded, and many people shed tears. They went to the railway station just without the gate to meet the King, and when they hailed him as '*Re d' Italia!*' he was much affected. At last he appeared riding a fine English horse, Prince Carignan° on one hand and Baron Ricasoli on his left, followed by a numerous '*troupe dorée*' of generals and of his suite in gay uniforms and well mounted. The King rides well; so the effect was extremely brilliant. Then followed several carriages; in the first were Count Cavour, Buoncompagni, and the Marchese Bartolommei. You cannot form the slightest idea of the excitement; it was a burst of enthusiasm, and the reception of Cavour was as warm. We threw a perfect shower of flowers over him, which the Marchesa had provided for the occasion; and her youngest son Cino, a nice lad, went himself to present his bouquet to the King, who seemed quite pleased with the boy. I felt so much for Madame de Lajatico herself . . . I said to her how kind I thought it in her to open her house; she burst into tears, and said, though she was in deep affliction, she could not be so selfish as not offer her friends the best position in Florence for seeing what to many of them was the most important event in their lives, as it was to her even in her grief. The true Italian taste appeared to perfection in every street through which the procession passed to the Duomo, and thence to the Palazzo Pitti. Those who saw it declare nothing could surpass the splendour of the cathedral when illuminated; but that we could not see, nor did we see the procession again; it was impossible to penetrate the crowd. They say there are 40,000 strangers in Florence . . . I was much too tired to go out again to see the illuminations and the fireworks on the Ponte Carraja; your sisters saw it all, so I leave them to tell you all about it. The King and Prince are terribly early; they and Ricasoli are on horseback by *five* in the morning; the King dines at twelve, and never touches food afterwards, though he has a dinner party of 60 or 80 every day at six . . . Now, my dearest Woronzow, I must end, for I do not wish to miss another post. I am really wonderfully well for my age.

Your devoted mother,
MARY SOMERVILLE

FROM MRS SOMERVILLE TO W. GREIG, ESQ.

FLORENCE, *19th June, 1861*

. . . Italy has been thrown into the deepest affliction by the death of Cavour. In my long life I never knew any event whatever which caused so universal and deep sorrow. There is not a village or town throughout the whole peninsula which has not had a funeral service, and the very poorest people, who had hardly clothes on their backs, had black crape tied round their arm or neck. It was a state of consternation, and no wonder! Every one felt that the greatest and best man of this century has been taken away before he had completely emancipated his country. All the progress is due to him, and to him alone; the revolution has called forth men of much talent, yet the whole are immeasurably his inferior in every respect – even your friend, Ricasoli, who is most able, and the best successor that can be found, is, compared with Cavour, as Tuscany to Europe. Happily the sad loss did not occur sooner. Now things are so far advanced that they cannot go back, and I trust that Ricasoli, who is not wanting in firmness and moral courage, will complete what has been so happily begun. I am sorry to say he is not in very good health, but I trust he will not fall into the hands of the physician who attended Cavour, and who mistook his disease, reduced him by loss of blood, and then finding out his real illness, tried to strengthen him when too late. There was a most excellent article in the 'Times' on the two statesmen.

[My mother's recollections continue thus:—]

_____

One night the moon shone so bright that we sent the carriage away, and walked home from a reception at the Marchesa Ginori's°. In crossing the Piazza San Marco, an acquaintance, who accompanied us, took us to the Maglio, which is close by, to hear an echo. I like an echo; yet there is something so unearthly in the aërial voice, that it never fails to raise a superstitious chill in me, such as I have felt more than once as I read 'Ossian' while travelling among our Highland hills in my early youth.[III] In one of the grand passes of the Oberland, when we were in Switzerland, we were enveloped in a mist, through which peaks were dimly seen. We stopped to hear an echo; the response came clear and distinct from a great distance, and I felt as if the Spirit of the Mountain had spoken. The impression depends on accessory circumstances; for the roar of a railway train passing over a viaduct has no such effect.

I lost my husband in Florence on the 26th June, 1860 . . . From the preceding narrative may be seen the sympathy, affection, and confidence, which always existed between us . . .

[After what has already been said of the happiness my mother enjoyed during the long years of their married life, it may be imagined what grief was hers at my father's death after only three days' illness. My mother's dear friend and correspondent, Miss F. P. Cobbe, wrote to her as follows on this occasion:—]

'I have just learned from a letter from Captain Fairfax to my brother the great affliction which has befallen you. I cannot express to you how it has grieved me to think that such a sorrow should have fallen on you, and that the dear, kind old man, whose welcome so often touched and gratified me, should have passed away so soon after I had seen you both, as I often thought, the most beautiful instance of united old age. His love and pride in you, breaking out as it did at every instant when you happened to be absent, gives me the measure of what his loss must be to your warm heart.'

[The following letter from my mother, dated April, 1861, addressed to her sister-in-law, was written after reading my grandfather's *Life and Times*, the publication of which my father did not live to see.—]

FROM MRS SOMERVILLE TO MRS ELLIOT, OF ROSEBANK, ROXBURGHSHIRE

FLORENCE, *28th April, 1861*

MY DEAR JANET,

I received the precious volume [The Rev. T. Somerville's *Life and Times*] you have so kindly sent to me some days ago, but I have delayed thanking you for it till now because we all wished to read it first. We are highly pleased, and have been deeply interested in it. The whole tone of the book is characteristic of your dear father; the benevolence, warm-heartedness, and Christian charity which appeared in the whole course of his life and ministry. That which has struck us all most forcibly is the liberality of his sentiments, both religious and political, at a time when narrow views and bigotry made it even dangerous to avow them, and it required no small courage to do so. He was far in advance of the age in which he lived; his political opinions are those of the present day, his religious opinions still before it. There are many parts of the book which will please the general reader from the graphic description of the manners and customs of the time, as well as the narrative of his inter-course with many of the eminent men of his day. Your most dear father's affectionate remembrance of me touches me deeply. I have but one regret, dear Jenny, and that is that our dear William did not not live to see the accomplishment of what was his dying wish; but God's will be done . . . We are all much as usual; I am wonderfully well, and able to write, which I do for a time every day. I do not think I feel any difference in capacity, but I become soon tired, and then I read the newspapers, some amusing book, or work . . . Everything is flourishing in Italy, and the people happy and contented, except those who were employed and dependent on the former sovereigns, but they are few in comparison; and now there is a fine army of 200,000 men to defend the country, even if Austria should make an attack, but that is not likely at present. Rome is still the difficulty, but the Pope must and soon will lose his temporal power, for the people are determined it shall be so . . .

I am, dear sister,

Most affectionately yours,

MARY SOMERVILLE

To MRS ELLIOT, of Rosebank, Roxburghshire.

SEVENTEEN

Spezia – Genoa – Begins Molecular and Microscopic Science –
Turin – Spezia – British Fleet – Letters from Mrs Somerville –
Garibaldi – Severe Illness – Florence – My Brother's Death –
Naples – Eruption of Vesuvius – J. S. Mill – Change in Public
Opinion on Women's Education – Eighty-Ninth Year –
Describes her Own Character – Thoughts on a Future Life –
Progress in Knowledge of Geography – Victoria Medal –
Medal from Royal Italian Geographical Society – Letter
from Menabrea – Rome, Capital of Italy – Aurora Borealis

SOON after my dear husband's death, we went to Spezia, as
my health required change, and for some time we made it
our headquarters, spending one winter at Florence, another at Genoa, where my son and his wife came to meet
us, and where I had very great delight in the beautiful
singing of our old friend Clara Novello°, now Countess
Gigliucci, who used to come to my house, and sing Handel
to me. It was a real pleasure, and her voice was as pure and
silvery as when I first heard her, years before. Another
winter we spent at Turin. On returning to Spezia in the
summer of 1861, the beautiful comet visible that year
appeared for the first time the very evening we arrived.
On the following, and during many evenings while it was
visible, we used to row in a small boat a little way from
shore, in order to see it to greater advantage. Nothing could
be more poetical than the clear starlit heavens with this
beautiful comet reflected, nay, almost repeated, in the calm
glassy water of the gulf. The perfect silence and stillness of
the scene was very impressive.

I was now unoccupied, and felt the necessity of having something to do, desultory reading being insufficient to interest me; and as I had always considered the section on chemistry the weakest part of the connection of the *Physical Sciences*, I resolved to write it anew. My daughters strongly opposed this, saying, 'Why not write a new book?' They were right; it would have been lost time; so I followed their advice, though it was a formidable undertaking at my age, considering that the general character of science had greatly changed. By the improved state of the microscope, an invisible creation in the air, the earth, and the water, had been brought within the limits of human vision; the microscopic structure of plants and animals had been minutely studied, and by synthesis many substances had been formed of the elementary atoms similar to those produced by nature. Dr Tyndall's experiments had proved the inconceivable minuteness of the atoms of matter; M. Gassiot° and Professor Plücker° had published their experiments on the stratification of the electric light; and that series of discoveries by scientific men abroad, but chiefly by our own philosophers at home, which had been in progress for a course of years, prepared the way for Bunsen and Kirchhoff's marvellous consummation.

Such was the field opened to me; but instead of being discouraged by its magnitude, I seemed to have resumed the perseverance and energy of my youth, and began to write with courage, though I did not think I should live to finish even the sketch I had made, and which I intended to publish under the name of *Molecular and Microscopic Science*, and assumed as my motto, 'Deus magnus in magnis, maximus in minimis,' from Saint Augustine.[112]

My manuscript notes on science were now of the greatest use; and we went for the winter to Turin (1861–62), where I could get books from the public libraries, and much information on subjects of natural history from Professor De

Filippi°, who has recently died, much regretted, while on a scientific mission to Japan and China, as well as from other sources. I subscribed to various periodicals on chemical and other branches of science; the transactions of several of our societies were sent to me, and I began to write. I was now an old woman, very deaf and with shaking hands; but I could still see to thread the finest needle, and read the finest print, but I got sooner tired when writing than I used to do. I wrote regularly every morning from eight till twelve or one o'clock before rising. I was not alone, for I had a mountain sparrow, a great pet, which sat, and indeed is sitting on my arm as I write these lines.

The Marchese Doria has a large property at Spezia, and my dear friend Teresa Doria generally spent the evening with us, when she and I chatted and played Bézique together. Her sons also came frequently, and some of the officers of the Italian navy. One who became our very good friend is Captain William Acton°, now Admiral, and for two years Minister of Marine; he is very handsome, and, what is better, a most agreeable, accomplished gentleman, who has interested himself in many branches of natural history, besides being a good linguist. In summer the British squadron, commanded by Admiral Smart°, came for five weeks to Spezia. My nephew, Henry Fairfax°, was commander on board the ironclad *Resistance*. Notwithstanding my age, I was so curious to see an ironclad that I went all over the *Resistance*, even to the engine-room and screw-alley. I also went to luncheon on board the flagship *Victoria*, a three-decker, which put me in mind of olden times.

[The following extracts are from letters of my mother's, written in 1863 and 1865:—]

FROM MRS SOMERVILLE TO W. GREIG, ESQ.

SPEZIA, *12th May, 1863*

How happy your last letter has made me, my dearest Woronzow, to hear that you are making real progress, and that you begin to feel better from the Bath waters . . . Of your general health I had the very best account this morning from your friend Colonel Gordon. I was most agreeably surprised and gratified by a very kind and interesting letter from him, enclosing his photograph, and giving me an account of his great works at Portsmouth with reference to the defence by iron as well as stone . . .

I wish I could show you the baskets full of flowers which Martha and Mary bring to me from the mountains. They are wonderfully beautiful; it is one of my greatest amusements putting them in water. I quite regret when they cannot go for them. The orchises and the gladioles are the chief flowers now, but such a variety and such colours! You see we have our quiet pleasures. I often think of more than '60 years ago,' when I used to scramble over the Bin at Burntisland after our tods-tails and leddies-fingers, but I fear there is hardly a wild spot existing now in the lowlands of Scotland . . .

God bless you, my dearest Woronzow.

FROM MRS SOMERVILLE TO W. GREIG, ESQ.

SPEZIA, *27th Sept., 1865*

MY DEAREST WORONZOW,

I fear Agnes and you must have thought your old mother had gone mad when you read M.'s letter. In my sober senses, however, though sufficiently excited to give me strength for the time, I went over every part of the *Resistance*,[113] and examined everything in detail except the *stokehole!* I was not even hoisted on board, but mounted the companion-ladder bravely. It was a glorious sight, the perfection of structure in every part astonished me. A ship like that is the triumph of human talent and of British talent, for all confess our superiority in this respect to every other nation, and I am happy to see that no jealousy has arisen from the meeting of the French and English fleets. I was proud that our 'young admiral' had the command of so fine a vessel . . . I also spent a most agreeable day on board the *Victoria*, three-decker, and saw every part of the three decks, which are very different from what they were in my father's time; everything on a much larger scale, more elegant and convenient. But the greatest change is in the men; I never saw a finer set, so gentlemanly-looking and well-behaved; almost all can read and write, and they have an excellent library and reading-room in all the ships. No sooner was the fleet gone than the Italian Society of Natural History held their annual meeting here, Capellini° being president in the absence (in Borneo) of Giacomo Doria. There were altogether seventy members, Italian, French, and German. I was chosen an Associate by acclamation, and had to write a few lines of thanks. The weather was beautiful and the whole party dined every day on the terrace below our windows, which was very amusing to Miss Campbell and your sisters, who distinctly heard the speeches. I was invited to dinner and the wife of the celebrated Professor Vogt° was asked to meet me; I declined dining, as it lasted so long that I should have been too tired, but I went down to the dessert. Capellini came for me, and all rose as I came in, and every attention was shown me, my health was drank, &c., &c. It lasted four days, and we had many evening visits, and I received a quantity of papers on all subjects. I am working very hard (for me at least), but I cannot hurry, nor do I see the need for it. I write so slowly on account of the shaking of my hand that although my head is clear I make little but steady progress . . .

Your affectionate mother,

MARY SOMERVILLE

After the battle of Aspromonte,[114] Garibaldi arrived a prisoner on board a man-of-war, and was placed at Varignano under surveillance. His wound had not been properly dressed, and he was in a state of great suffering. Many surgeons came from all parts of Italy, and one even from England, to attend him, but the eminent Professor Nélaton° saved him from amputation, with which he was threatened, by extracting the bullet from his ankle. I never saw Garibaldi during his three months' residence at Varignano and Spezia; I had no previous acquaintance with him; consequently, as I could be of no use to him, I did not consider myself entitled to intrude upon him merely to gratify my own curiosity, although no one admired his noble and disinterested character more than I did. Not so, many of my countrymen, and countrywomen too, as well as ladies of other nations, who worried the poor man out of his life, and made themselves eminently ridiculous. One lady went so far as to collect the hairs from his comb, – others showered tracts upon him.

I had hitherto been very healthy; but in the beginning of winter I was seized with a severe illness which, though not immediately dangerous, lasted so long, that it was doubtful whether I should have stamina to recover. It was a painful and fatiguing time to my daughters. They were quite worn out with nursing me; our maid was ill, and our man-servant, Luigi Lucchesi, watched me with such devotion that he sat up twenty-four nights with me. He has been with us eighteen years, and now that I am old and feeble, he attends me with unceasing kindness. It is but justice to say that we never were so faithfully or well served as by Italians; and none are more ingenious in turning their hands to anything, and in never objecting to do this or that, as not what they were hired for, – a great quality for people who, like ourselves, keep few servants.

After a time they identify themselves with the family they serve, as my faithful Luigi has done with all his heart. I am sincerely attached to him.

In the spring, when I had recovered, my son and his wife came to Spezia, and we all went to Florence, where we had the pleasure of seeing many old friends. We returned to Spezia, and my son and his wife left us to go back to England, intending to meet us again somewhere the following spring. I little thought we never should meet again . . . My son sent his sisters a beautiful little cutter, built by Mr Forrest in London, which has been a great resource to them. I always insist on their taking a good sailor with them, although I am not in the least nervous for their safety. Indeed, small as the *Frolic* is – and she is only about twenty-eight feet from stem to stern – she has weathered some stiff gales gallantly, as, for instance, when our friend, Mr Montagu Brown°, British consul at Genoa, sailed her from Genoa to Spezia in very bad weather; and in a very dangerous squall my daughters were caught in, coming from Amalfi to Sorrento. The *Frolic* had only just arrived at Spezia, when we heard of the sudden death of my dear son, Oct., 1865.

[This event, which took from my mother's last years one of her chief delights, she bore with her usual calm courage, looking forward confidently to a reunion at no distant date with one who had been the most dutiful of sons and beloved of friends. She never permitted herself, in writing her *Recollections*, to refer to her feelings under these great sorrows.]

———————

Some time after this, my widowed daughter-in-law spent a few months with us. On her return to London, I sent the manuscript of the *Molecular and Microscopic Science* with her for publication. In writing this book I made a great mistake, and repent it. Mathematics are the natural bent of my mind. If I had devoted myself exclusively to that study, I might probably have written something useful, as a new era had begun in that science. Although I got Chales on the Higher Geometry,[115] it could be but a secondary object while I was engaged in writing a popular book. Subsequently, it became a source of deep interest and occupation to me.

Spezia is very much spoilt by the works in progress for the arsenal, though nothing can change the beauty of the gulf as seen from our windows, especially the group of the Carrara mountains, with fine peaks and ranges of hills, becoming more and more verdant down to the water's edge. The effect of the setting sun on this group is varied and brilliant beyond belief. Even I, in spite of my shaking hand, resumed the brush, and painted a view of the ruined Castle of Ostia, at the mouth of the Tiber, from a sketch of my own, for my dear friend Teresa Doria.

We now came to live at Naples; and on leaving Spezia, I spent a fortnight with Count and Countess Usedom° at the Villa Capponi, near Florence, where, though unable to visit, I had the pleasure of seeing my Florentine friends again.

We spent two days in Rome, and dined with our friends the Duca and Duchesa di Sermoneta. We were grieved at his blindness, but found him as agreeable as ever.

Through our friend, Admiral Acton, I became acquainted with Professor Panceri°, Professor of Comparative Anatomy; Signore de Gasparis°, who has discovered nine of the minor planets, and is an excellent mathematician, and some others. To these gentlemen I am indebted for being elected an honorary member of the Accademia Pontoniana.

We were much interested in Vesuvius, which, for several months, was in a state of great activity. At first, there were only volumes of smoke and some small streams of lava, but these were followed by the most magnificent projections of red-hot stones and rocks rising 2000 feet above the top of the mountain. Many fell back again into the crater, but a large portion were thrown in fiery showers down the sides of the cone. At length, these beautiful eruptions of *lapilli* ceased, and the lava flowed more abundantly, though, being intermittent and always issuing from the summit, it was quite harmless; volumes of smoke and vapour rose from the crater, and were carried by the wind to a great distance. In sunshine the contrast was beautiful, between the jet-black smoke and the silvery-white clouds of vapour. At length, the mountain returned to apparent tranquillity, though the violent detonations occasionally heard gave warning that the calm might not last long. At last, one evening, in November, 1868, when one of my daughters and I were observing the mountain through a very good telescope, lent us by a friend, we distinctly saw a new crater burst out at the foot of the cone in the Atrio del Cavallo, and bursts of red-hot *lapilli* and red smoke pouring forth in volumes. Early next morning we saw a great stream of lava pouring down to the north of the Observatory, and a column of black smoke issuing from the new craters, because there were two, and assuming the well-known appearance of a pine-tree. The trees on the northern edge of the lava were already on fire. The stream of lava very soon reached the plain, where it overwhelmed fields, vineyards, and houses. It was more than a mile in width and thirty feet deep. My daughters went up the mountain the evening after the new craters were formed; as for me, I could not risk the fatigue of such an excursion, but I saw it admirably from our own windows. During this year the volcanic forces in the interior of the earth were in unusual activity, for a series of earthquakes shook the west coast of South America for more than 2500 miles, by which many thousands of the inhabitants perished, and many more were rendered homeless. Slight shocks were felt in many parts of Europe, and even in England. Vesuvius was our safety-valve. The pressure must have been very great which opened two new craters in the Atrio del Cavallo and forced out such a mass of matter. There is no evidence that water had been concerned in the late eruption of Vesuvius; but during the whole of the preceding autumn, the fall of rain had been unusually great and continuous. There were frequent thunder-storms; and, on one occasion, the quantity of rain that fell was so great, as to cause a land-slip in Pizzifal-cone, by which several houses were overwhelmed; and, on another occasion, the torrent of rain was so violent, that the Riviera di Chiaja was covered, to the depth of half a metre, with mud, and stones brought down by the water from the heights above. This enormous quantity of water pouring on the slopes of Vesuvius, and percolating through the crust of the Earth into the fiery caverns, where volcanic forces are generated, being resolved into steam, and possibly aided by the expansion of volcanic gases, may have been a partial agent in propelling the formidable stream of lava which has caused such destruction. We observed, that when lava abounded, the projection of rocks and *lapilli* either ceased altogether, or became of small amount. The whole eruption ended in a shower of impalpable ashes, which hid the mountain for many days, and which were carried to a great distance by the wind. Sometimes the ashes were pure white, giving the mountain the appearance of being covered with snow. Vapour continued to rise from Vesuvius in beautiful silvery clouds, which ceased and left the edge of the crater white with sublimations. I owe to Vesuvius the great pleasure of making the acquaintance of Mr Phillips°, Professor of Geology in the University of Oxford; and, afterwards, that of Sir John Lubbock°, and Professor Tyndall, who had come to Naples on purpose to see the eruption. Unfortunately, Sir John Lubbock and Professor Tyndall were so limited for time, that they could only spend one evening with us; but I enjoyed a delightful evening, and had much scientific conversation.

Notwithstanding the progress meteorology has made since it became a subject of exact observation, yet no explanation has been given of the almost unprecedented high summer temperature of 1868 in Great Britain, and even in the Arctic regions. In England, the grass and heather were dried up, and extensive areas were set on fire by sparks from railway locomotives, the conflagrations spreading so rapidly, that they could only be arrested by cutting trenches to intercept their course. The whalers found open water to a higher latitude than usual; but, although the British Government did not avail themselves of this opportunity for further Arctic discovery, Sweden, Germany, France, and especially the United States, have taken up the subject with great energy. Eight expeditions sailed for the North Polar region between the years 1868 and 1870; several for the express purpose of reaching the Polar Sea, which, I have no doubt, will be attained, now that steam has given such power to penetrate the fields of floating ice. It would be more than a dashing exploit to make a cruise on that unknown sea; it would be a discovery of vast scientific importance with regard to geography, magnetism, temperature, the general circulation of the atmosphere and oceans, as well as to natural history. I cannot but regret that I shall not live to hear the result of these voyages.

[*2D, 223:* Among some of the Eastern nations women were respected and even now an attempt is in some instances made to improve their condition but it is to the pure and holy doctrine of Christianity that the sex is indebted for deliverance imperfect as it still is from the most debasing thraldom (*in margin* I ardently pray for the spread of Christianity for it is) among Christian nations alone that women are considered to be the companion and joint heir of salvation with man. In most Eastern nations the sex is degraded to the state of animals and in savage life a woman's home is hell. Among the Hindoos after a life of wretchedness with their tyrant husband, women were burnt alive at his death as a sacrifice to his *manes*. This atrocity was put a stop to by my cousin Samuel McPherson° to his infinite honour and to an immortal reward for he never met with a terrestrial one.]

[*2D, 225–6:* It is a deplorable fact that even among the better class of society both in the United States and Great Britain there should be men and women who believe in spirit rapping, a superstition that one would scarcely expect to meet with in African savages. But there are strange inconsistencies in the British character for while Christian sects were showing their intolerance of one another with regard to education, a Mahommedan emperor was received with acclamation in the streets of London, an inconsistency however in the right direction, that of tolerance.]

The British laws are adverse to women; and we are deeply indebted to Mr Stuart Mill° for daring to show their iniquity and injustice. The law in the United States is in some respects even worse, insulting the sex, by granting suffrage to the newly-emancipated slaves, and refusing it to the most highly-educated women of the Republic.

[For the noble character and transcendent intellect of Mr J. S. Mill my mother had the greatest admiration. She had some correspondence with him on the subject of the petition to Parliament for the extension of the suffrage to women, which she signed; and she also wrote to thank him warmly for his book on the *Subjection of Women*. In Mr Mill's reply to the latter he says:—]

FROM JOHN STUART MILL, ESQ.,
TO MRS SOMERVILLE

BLACKHEATH PARK, *July 12th, 1869*

DEAR MADAM,

Such a letter as yours is a sufficient reward for the trouble of writing the little book. I could have desired no better proof that it was adapted to its purpose than such an encouraging opinion from you. I thank you heartily for taking the trouble to express, in such kind terms, your approbation of the book, – the approbation of one who has rendered such inestimable service to the cause of women by affording in her own person so high an example of their intellectual capabilities, and, finally, by giving to the protest in the great Petition of last year the weight and importance derived from the signature which headed it.

I am,
Dear Madam,
Most sincerely and respectfully yours,
J. S. MILL

Age has not abated my zeal for the emancipation of my sex from the unreasonable prejudice too prevalent in Great Britain against a literary and scientific education for women. The French are more civilised in this respect, for they have taken the lead, and have given the first example in modern times of encouragement to the high intellectual culture of the sex. Madame Emma Chenu, who had received the degree of Master of Arts from the Academy of Sciences in Paris, has more recently received the diploma of Licentiate in Mathematical Sciences from the same illustrious Society, after a successful examination in algebra, trigonometry, analytical geometry, the differential and integral calculi, and astronomy. A Russian lady has also taken a degree; and a lady of my acquaintance has received a gold medal from the same Institution.

I joined in a petition to the Senate of London University, praying that degrees might be granted to women; but it was rejected. I have also frequently signed petitions to Parliament for the Female Suffrage, and have the honour now to be a member of the General Committee for Woman Suffrage in London.

[*1D, 223 (in margin 'omitted' in pencil):* Among the many distinguished Americans whom I have had the good fortune to know was Paulina W. Davis°. When at Naples she came to see me with her daughter and niece. She has a gentle pleasing manner, a soft voice that must have been very pretty in her youth. For twenty years she had taken a decided part in the struggle for women's freedom in the U.S. and had practised as a physician. Though a few women have been successful practitioners in London the Faculty need not be alarmed for there are not many women that medical practice would suit, but I think one department ought to be entirely allotted to the sex. Children have been brought into the world by women time immemorial and women have occasionally died and so they do now when men officiate though aided by chloroform, the most blessed discovery that ever has been granted to mortal.]

[My mother, in alluding to the great changes in public opinion which she had lived to see, used to remark that a commonly well-informed woman of the present day would have been looked upon as a prodigy of learning in her youth, and that even till quite lately many considered that if women were to receive the solid education men enjoy, they would forfeit much of their feminine grace and become unfit to perform their domestic duties. My mother herself was one of the brightest examples of the fallacy of this old-world theory, for no one was more thoroughly and gracefully feminine than she was, both in manner and appearance; and, as I have already mentioned, no amount of scientific labour ever induced her to neglect her home duties. She took the liveliest interest in all that has been done of late years to extend high class education to women, both classical and scientific, and hailed the establishment of the Ladies' College at Girton as a great step in the true direction, and one which could not fail to obtain most important results. Her scientific library, as already stated, has been presented to this College as the best fulfilment of her wishes.][116]

I have lately entered my 89th year, grateful to God for the innumerable blessings He has bestowed on me and my children; at peace with all on earth, and I trust that I may be at peace with my Maker when my last hour comes, which cannot now be far distant.

Although I have been tried by many severe afflictions, my life upon the whole has been happy. In my youth I had to contend with prejudice and illiberality; yet I was of a quiet temper, and easy to live with, and I never interfered with or pried into other people's affairs. However, if irritated by what I considered unjust criticism or interference with myself, or any one I loved, I could resent it fiercely. I was not good at argument; I was apt to lose my temper; but I never bore ill will to any one, or forgot the manners of a gentlewoman, however angry I may have been at the time. But I must say that no one ever met with such kindness as I have done. I never had an enemy. I have never been of a melancholy disposition; though depressed sometimes by circumstances, I always rallied again; and although I seldom laugh, I can laugh heartily at wit or on fit occasion. The short time I have to live naturally occupies my thoughts. In the blessed hope of meeting again with my beloved children, and those who were and are dear to me on Earth, I think of death with composure and perfect confidence in the mercy of God.

Yet to me, who am afraid to sleep alone on a stormy night, or even to sleep comfortably any night unless some one is near, it is a fearful thought, that my spirit must enter that new state of existence quite alone. We are told of the infinite glories of that state, and I believe in them, though it is incomprehensible to us; but as I do comprehend, in some degree at least, the exquisite loveliness of the visible world, I confess I shall be sorry to leave it. I shall regret the sky, the sea, with all the changes of their beautiful colouring; the earth, with its verdure and flowers; but far more shall I grieve to leave animals who have followed our steps affectionately for years, without knowing for certainty their ultimate fate, though I firmly believe that the living principle is never extinguished. Since the atoms of matter are indestructible, as far as we know, it is difficult to believe that the spark which gives to their union life, memory, affection, intelligence, and fidelity, is evanescent. Every atom in the human frame, as well as in that of animals, undergoes a periodical change by continual waste and renovation; the abode is changed, not its inhabitant. If animals have no future, the existence of many is most wretched; multitudes are starved, cruelly beaten, and loaded during life; many die under a barbarous vivisection. I cannot believe that any creature was created for uncompensated misery; it would be contrary to the attributes of God's mercy and justice. I am sincerely happy to find that I am not the only believer in the immortality of the lower animals.

When I was taught geography by the village schoolmaster at Burntisland, it seemed to me that half the world was *terra incognita*, and now that a new edition of my *Physical Geography* is required, it will be a work of great labour to bring it up to the present time. The discoveries in South Africa alone would fill a volume. Japan and China have been opened to Europeans since my last edition. The great continent of Australia was an entirely unknown country, except part of the coast. Now telegrams have been sent and answers received in the course of a few hours, from our countrymen throughout that mighty empire, and even from New Zealand, round half the globe. The inhabitants of the United States are our offspring; so whatever may happen to Great Britain in the course of events, it still will have the honour of colonising, and consequently civilising, half the world.

In all recent geographical discoveries, our Royal Geographical Society has borne the most important part, and none of its members have done more than my highly-gifted friend the President, Sir Roderick Murchison, geologist of Russia, and founder and author of the colossal *Silurian System*. To the affection of this friend, sanctioned by the unanimous approval of the council of that illustrious Society, I owe the honour of being awarded the Victoria Medal for my *Physical Geography*. An honour so unexpected, and so far beyond my merit, surprised and affected me more deeply than I can find words to express.

In the events of my life it may be seen how much I have been honoured by the scientific societies and universities of Italy, many of whom have elected me an honorary member or associate; but the greatest honour I have received in Italy has been the gift of the first gold medal hitherto awarded by the Geographical Society at Florence, and which was coined on purpose, with my name on the reverse. I received it the other day, accompanied by the following letter from General Menabrea, President of the Council, himself a distinguished mathematician and philosopher:—

FROM GENERAL MENABREA TO
MRS SOMERVILLE

FLORENCE, *30 Juin, 1869*

MADAME,

J'ai pris connaissance avec le plus grand intérêt de la belle édition de votre dernier ouvrage sur la Géographie Physique, et je désire vous donner un témoignage d'haute estime pour vos travaux. Je vous prie donc, Madame, d'accepter une médaille d'or à l'effigie du Roi Victor Emmanuel, mon auguste souverain. C'est un souvenir de mon pays dans lequel vous comptez, comme chez toutes les nations où la science est honoré, de nombreux amis et admirateurs. Veuillez croire, Madame, que je ne cesserai d'être l'un et l'autre en même temps que je suis,

Votre très dévoué Serviteur,

MENABREA

At a general assembly of the Italian Geographical Society, at Florence, on the 14th March, 1870, I was elected by acclamation an Honorary Associate of that distinguished society. I am indebted to the President, the Commendatore Negri, for having proposed my name, and for a very kind letter, informing me of the honour conferred upon me.

I have still (in 1869) the habit of studying in bed from eight in the morning till twelve or one o'clock; but, I am left solitary; for I have lost my little bird who was my constant companion for eight years. It had both memory and intelligence, and such confidence in me as to sleep upon my arm while I was writing. My daughter, to whom it was much attached, coming into my room early, was alarmed at its not flying to meet her, as it generally did, and at last, after a long search, the poor little creature was found drowned in the jug.

On the 4th October, while at dinner, we had a shock of earthquake. The vibrations were nearly north and south; it lasted but a few seconds, and was very slight; but in Calabria, &c., many villages and towns were overthrown, and very many people perished. The shocks were repeated again and again; only one was felt at Naples; but as it occurred in the night, we were unconscious of it. At Naples, it was believed there would be an eruption of Vesuvius; for the smoke was particularly dense and black, and some of the wells were dried up.

I can scarcely believe that Rome, where I have spent so many happy years, is now the capital of united Italy. I heartily rejoice in that glorious termination to the vicissitudes the country has undergone, and only regret that age and infirmity prevent me from going to see Victor Emmanuel triumphantly enter the capital of his kingdom. The Pope's reliance on foreign troops for his safety was an unpardonable insult to his countrymen.

The month of October this year (1870), seems to have been remarkable for displays of the Aurora Borealis. It seriously interfered with the working of the telegraphs, particularly in the north of England and Ireland. On the night of the 24th October, it was seen over the greater part of Europe. At Florence, the common people were greatly alarmed, and at Naples, the peasantry were on their knees to the Madonna to avert the evil. Unfortunately, neither I nor any of my family saw the Aurora; for most of our windows have a southern aspect. The frequent occurrence of the Aurora in 1870 confirms the already known period of maximum intensity and frequency, every ten or twelve years, since the last maximum occurred in 1859.

EIGHTEEN

Eclipse – Visits of Scientific Men – Life at Naples – Darwin's Books – Remarks on Civilisation – Fine Aurora Borealis – Death of Herschel – Summer at Sorrento – Bill for Protection of Animals – Ninety-Second Year – Letter from Professor Sedgwick – Grand Eruption of Vesuvius – Last Summer at Sorrento, Plants Found There – Conclusion

THE summer of 1870 was unusually cool; but the winter has been extremely gloomy, with torrents of rain, and occasionally such thick fogs, that I could see neither to read nor to write. We had no storms during the hot weather; but on the afternoon of the 21st December, there was one of the finest thunderstorms I ever saw; the lightning was intensely vivid, and took the strangest forms, darting in all directions through the air before it struck, and sometimes darting from the ground or the sea to the clouds. It ended in a deluge of rain, which lasted all night, and made us augur ill for the solar eclipse next day; and, sure enough, when I awoke next morning, the sky was darkened by clouds and rain. Fortunately, it cleared up just as the eclipse began; we were all prepared for observing it, and we followed its progress through the opening in the clouds till at last there was only a very slender crescent of the sun's disc left; its convexity was turned upwards, and its horns were nearly horizontal. It was then hidden by a dense mass of clouds; but after a time they opened, and I saw the edge of the moon leave the limb of the sun. The appearance of the landscape was very lurid, but by no means very dark. The common people and children had a very good view of the eclipse, reflected by the pools of water in the streets.

Many of the astronomers who had been in Sicily observing the eclipse came to see me as they passed through Naples. One of their principal objects was to ascertain the nature of the corona, or bright white rays which surround the dark lunar disc at the time of the greatest obscurity. The spectroscope showed that it was decidedly auroral, but as the aurora was seen on the dark disc of the moon it must have been due to the Earth's atmosphere. Part of the corona was polarised, and consequently must have been material; the question is, Can it be the ethereal medium? A question of immense importance, since the whole theory of light and colours and the resistance of Encke's comet[117] depends upon that hypothesis. The question is still in abeyance, but I have no doubt that it will be decided in the affirmative, and that even the cause of gravitation will be known eventually.

At this time I had the pleasure of a visit from Mr Peirce°, Professor of Mathematics and Astronomy in the Harvard University, U.S., and Superintendent of the U.S. Coast Survey, who had come to Europe to observe the eclipse. On returning to America he kindly sent me a beautiful lithographed copy of a very profound memoir in linear and associative algebra. Although in writing my popular books I had somewhat neglected the higher algebra, I have read a great part of the work; but as I met with some difficulties I wrote to Mr Spottiswoode°, asking his advice as to the books that would be of use, and he sent me Serret's *Cours d'Algèbre Supérieure*, Salmon's *Higher Algebra*, and Tait on *Quaternions*; so now I got exactly what I wanted, and I am very busy for a few hours every morning; delighted to have an occupation so entirely to my mind. I thank God that my intellect is still unimpaired. I am grateful to Professor Peirce for giving me an opportunity of exercising it so agreeably. During the rest of the day I have recourse to

Shakespeare, Dante, and more modern light reading, besides the newspapers, which always interested me much. I
have resumed my habit of working, and can count the
threads of a fine canvas without spectacles. I receive every
one who comes to see me, and often have the pleasure of a
visit from old friends very unexpectedly. In the evening I
read a novel, but my tragic days are over; I prefer a cheerful
conversational novel to the sentimental ones. I have recently been reading Walter Scott's novels again, and enjoyed the broad Scotch in them. I play a few games at
Bézique with one of my daughters, for honour and glory,
and so our evenings pass pleasantly enough.

It is our habit to be separately occupied during the
morning, and spend the rest of the day together. We are
fond of birds and have several, all very tame. Our tame
nightingales sing very beautifully, but, strange to say, not at
night. We have also some solitary sparrows, which are, in
fact, a variety of the thrush (*Turdus cyaneus*), and some
birds which we rescued from destruction in spring, when
caught and ill-used by the boys in the streets; besides, we
have our dogs; all of which afford me amusement and
interest.

[*Mary Somerville also has this to say about Darwin's* Origin
of Species, *1859: 1D, 256–7:* Mr Darwin [has already]
published a book on the *Origin of Species by Natural Selection*
which was much discussed in general society, and produced a great sensation in the scientific world. His theory is
that in the organic creation, animal and vegetable, an
accidental variety sometimes occurs which either from
greater strength, fertility, or some other favourable circumstance becomes superior to its kindred, prevails over them,
possibly extirpates them and establishes itself as a species.
Moreover he conceives that a casual variety may occur in
the latter, which has to struggle for life and mastery like its
predecessor. Thus according to Mr Darwin's theory, the

organic world, animal and vegetable, has been transformed by an insensible and continuous metamorphosis of species during innumerable ages to its present state. He maintains his theory with so much talent that it is daily prevailing. Yet it is imperfect, for he does not explain the origin of the varieties of first organic forms, the primordial types or varieties whence by a slow evolution he conceives the species of all terrestrial beings to have arisen, yet that is the important question which Mr Darwin himself confesses he has not solved. Palaeontologists have demonstrated that the Earth has been inhabited by a multitude of organic beings which through innumerable ages have been rising higher and higher in structure and intelligence from a monad to man. Although we know not the means employed by a foreseeing will to introduce one form of life after another into the world, there cannot be a doubt that it is governed by an eternal fixed law established by the Deity when he created the first living organism.]

Mr Murray has kindly sent me a copy of Darwin's° recent work on the *Descent of Man*. Mr Darwin maintains his theory with great talent and with profound research. His knowledge of the characters and habits of animals of all kinds is very great, and his kindly feelings charming. It is chiefly by the feathered race that he has established his law of selection relative to sex. The males of many birds are among the most beautiful objects in nature; but that the beauty of nature is altogether irrelative to man's admiration or appreciation, is strikingly proved by the admirable sculpture on Diatoms and Foraminifera; beings whose very existence was unknown prior to the invention of the microscope. The Duke of Argyll° has illustrated this in the *Reign of Law*, by the variety, graceful forms and beautiful colouring of the humming birds in forests which man has never entered.

In Mr Darwin's book it is amusing to see how conscious the male birds are of their beauty; they have reason to be so, but we scorn the vanity of the savage who decks himself in their spoils. Many women without remorse allow the life of a pretty bird to be extinguished in order that they may deck themselves with its corpse. In fact, humming birds and other foreign birds have become an article of commerce. Our kingfishers and many of our other birds are on the eve of extinction on account of a cruel fashion.

I have just received from Frances Power Cobbe an essay, in which she controverts Darwin's theory, so far as the origin of the moral sense is concerned. It is written with all the energy of her vigorous intellect as a moral philosopher, yet with a kindly tribute to Mr Darwin's genius. I repeat no one admires Frances Cobbe more than I do. I have ever found her a brilliant, charming companion, and a warm, affectionate friend. She is one of the few with whom I keep up a correspondence.

To Mr Murray I am indebted for a copy of Tylor's° *Researches on the Early History of Mankind, and the Development of Civilization* – a very remarkable work for extent of research, original views, and happy illustrations. The gradual progress of the pre-historic races of mankind has laid a foundation from which Mr Tylor proves that after the lapse of ages the barbarous races now existing are decidedly in a state of progress towards civilisation. Yet one cannot conceive human beings in a more degraded state than some of them are still; their women are treated worse than their dogs. Sad to say, no savages are more gross than the lowest ranks in England, or treat their wives with more cruelty.

In the course of my life Paris has been twice occupied by foreign troops, and still oftener has it been in a state of anarchy. I regret to see that Laplace's house at Arcœuil has been broken into, and his manuscripts thrown into the river, from which some one has fortunately rescued that of the *Mécanique Céleste*, which is in his own handwriting. It is greatly to the honour of French men of science that during the siege they met as usual in the hall of the Institute, and read their papers as in the time of peace. The celebrated astronomer Janssen even escaped in a balloon, that he might arrive in time to observe the eclipse of the 22nd November, 1870.

We had a most brilliant display of the Aurora on the evening of Sunday, the 4th February, 1871, which lasted several hours. The whole sky from east to west was of the most brilliant flickering white light, from which streamers of red darted up to the zenith. There was also a lunar rainbow. The common people were greatly alarmed, for there had been a prediction that the world was coming to an end, and they thought the bright part of the Aurora was a piece of the moon that had already tumbled down! This Aurora was seen in Turkey and in Egypt.

I am deeply grieved and shaken by the death of Sir John Herschel, who, though ten years younger than I am, has gone before me. In him I have lost a dear and affectionate friend, whose advice was invaluable, and his society a charm. None but those who have lived in his home can imagine the brightness and happiness of his domestic life. He never presumed upon that superiority of intellect or the great discoveries which made him one of the most illustrious men of the age; but conversed cheerfully and even playfully on any subject, though ever ready to give information on any of the various branches of science to which he so largely contributed, and which to him were a source of constant happiness. Few of my early friends now remain – I am nearly left alone.

We went to pass the summer and autumn at Sorrento, where we led a very quiet but happy life. The villa we lived in was at a short distance from and above the town, quite buried in groves of oranges and lemons, beyond which lay the sea, generally calm and blue, sometimes stormy; to our left the islands of Ischia and Procida, the Capo Miseno, with Baia, Pozzuoli, and Posilipo; exactly opposite to us, Naples, then Vesuvius, and all the little towns on that coast, and lastly, to our right, this wonderful panorama was bounded by the fine cliffs of the Monte Santangelo. It was beautiful always, but most beautiful when the sun, setting behind Ischia, sent a perfect glory over the rippling sea, and tinged the Monte Santangelo and the cliffs which bound the Piano di Sorrento literally with purple and gold. I spent the whole day on a charming terrace sheltered from the sun, and there we dined and passed the evening watching the lights of Naples reflected in the water and the revolving lights of the different lighthouses. I often drove to Massa till after sunset, for from that road I could see the island of Capri, and I scarcely know a more lovely drive. Besides the books we took with us we had newspapers, reviews, and other periodicals, so that we were never dull. On one occasion my daughters and I made an expedition up the hills to the Deserto, from whence one can see the Gulf of Salerno and the fine mountains of Calabria. My daughters rode and I was carried in a *portantina*.[118] It was fine, clear, autumnal weather, and I enjoyed my expedition immensely, nor was I fatigued.

In November we returned to Naples, where I resumed my usual life. I had received a copy of Hamilton's° *Lectures on Quaternions* from the Rev. Whitewell Elwin. I am not acquainted with that gentleman, and am the more grateful to him. I have now a valuable library of scientific books and transactions of scientific societies, the greater part gifts from the authors.

Foreigners were so much shocked at the atrocious cruelty to animals in Italy, that an attempt was made about eight years ago to induce the Italian Parliament to pass a law for their protection, but it failed. As Italy is the only civilised country in Europe in which animals are not protected by law, another attempt is now being made; I have willingly given my name, and I received a kind letter from the Marchioness of Ely, from Rome, to whom I had spoken upon the subject at Naples, telling me that the Princess Margaret, Crown Princess of Italy, had been induced to head the petition. Unless the educated classes take up the cause one cannot hope for much change for a long time. Our friend, Mr Robert Hay, who resided at Rome for many years, had an old horse of which he was very fond, and on leaving Rome asked a Roman prince, who had very large possessions in the Campagna, if he would allow his old horse to end his days on his grassy meadows. 'Certainly,' replied the prince, 'but how can you care what becomes of an animal when he is no longer of use?' We English cannot boast of humanity, however, as long as our sportsmen find pleasure in shooting down tame pigeons as they fly terrified out of a cage.

I am now in my 92nd year (1872), still able to drive out for several hours; I am extremely deaf, and my memory of ordinary events, and especially of the names of people, is failing, but not for mathematical and scientific subjects. I am still able to read books on the higher algebra for four or five hours in the morning, and even to solve the problems. Sometimes I find them difficult, but my old obstinacy remains, for if I do not succeed to-day, I attack them again on the morrow. I also enjoy reading about all the new discoveries and theories in the scientific world, and on all branches of science.

Sir Roderick Murchison has passed away, honoured by all, and of undying fame; and my amiable friend, almost my contemporary, Professor Sedgwick, has been obliged to resign his chair of Geology at Cambridge, from age, which he had filled with honour during a long life.

[The following letter from her valued friend Professor Sedg-wick, in 1869, is the last my mother received from him:—]

FROM PROFESSOR SEDGWICK TO
MRS SOMERVILLE

CAMBRIDGE, *April 21st, 1869*

MY DEAR MRS SOMERVILLE,

I heard, when I was in London, that you were still in good bodily health, and in full fruition of your great intellectual strength, while breathing the sweet air of Naples. I had been a close prisoner to my college rooms through the past winter and spring; but I broke from my prison-house at the beginning of this month, that I might consult my oculist, and meet my niece on her way to Italy . . . My niece has for many years (ever since 1840) been my loving companion during my annual turn of residence as canon of Norwich; and she is, and from her childhood has, been to me as a dear daughter. I know you will forgive me for my anxiety to hear from a living witness that you are well and happy in the closing days of your honoured life; and for my longing desire that my beloved daughter (for such I ever regard her) should speak to you face to face, and see (for however short an interview) the Mrs. Somerville, of whom I have so often talked with her in terms of honest admiration and deep regard. The time for the Italian tour is, alas! far too short. But it will be a great gain to each of the party to be allowed, even for a short time, to gaze upon the earthly paradise that is round about you, and to cast one look over its natural wonders and historic monuments . . . Since you were here, my dear and honoured guest, Cambridge is greatly changed. I am left here like a vessel on its beam ends, to mark the distance to which the current has been drifting during a good many bygone years. I have outlived nearly all my early friends. Whewell, Master of Trinity, was the last of the old stock who was living here. Herschel has not been here for several years. Babbage was here for a day or two during the year before last. The Astronomer-Royal belongs to a more recent generation. For many years long attacks of suppressed gout have made my life very unproductive. I yesterday dined in Hall. It was the first time I was able to meet my brother Fellows since last Christmas day. A long attack of bronchitis, followed by a distressing inflammation of my eyes, had made me a close prisoner for nearly four months. But, thank God, I am again beginning to be cheery, and with many infirmities (the inevitable results of old age, for I have entered on my 85th year) I am still strong in general health, and capable of enjoying, I think as much as ever, the society of those whom I love, be they young or old. May God preserve and bless you; and whensoever it may be His will to call you away to Himself, may your mind be without a cloud and your heart full of joyful Christian hope!

I remain,

My dear Friend,

Faithfully and gratefully yours,

ADAM SEDGWICK

After all the violence and bloodshed of the preceding year, the Thanksgiving of Queen Victoria and the British nation for the recovery of the Prince of Wales will form a striking event in European history. For it was not the congregation in St Paul's alone, it was the spontaneous gratitude of all ranks and all faiths throughout the three kingdoms that were offered up to God that morning; the people sympathised with their Queen, and no sovereign more deserves sympathy.

Vesuvius has exhibited a considerable activity during the winter and early spring, and frequent streams of lava flowed from the crater, and especially from the small cone to the north, a little way below the principal crater. But these

streams were small and intermittent, and no great outbreak
was expected. On the 24th April a stream of lava induced us
to drive in the evening to Santa Lucia. The next night,
Thursday, 25th April, my daughter Martha, who had been
to the theatre, wakened me that I might see Vesuvius in
splendid eruption. This was at about 1 o'clock on Friday
morning. Early in the morning I was disturbed by what I
thought loud thunder, and when my maid came at 7 a.m. I
remarked that there was a thunderstorm, but she said, 'No,
no: it is the mountain roaring.' It must have been very loud
for me to hear, considering my deafness, and the distance
Vesuvius is from Naples, yet it was nothing compared to
the noise later in the day, and for many days after. My
daughter, who had gone to Santa Lucia to see the eruption
better, soon came to fetch me with our friend Mr James
Swinton, and we passed the whole day at windows in an
hotel at Santa Lucia, immediately opposite the mountain.
Vesuvius was now in the fiercest eruption, such as has not
occurred in the memory of this generation, lava overflow-
ing the principal crater and running in all directions. The
fiery glow of lava is not very visible by daylight; smoke and
steam is sent off which rises white as snow, or rather as
frosted silver, and the mouth of the great crater was white
with the lava pouring over it. New craters had burst out the
preceding night, at the very time I was admiring the beauty
of the eruption, little dreaming that, of many people who
had gone up that night to the Atrio del Cavallo to see the
lava (as my daughters had done repeatedly and especially
during the great eruption of 1868),[119] some forty or fifty had
been on the very spot where the new crater burst out, and
perished, scorched to death by the fiery vapours which
eddied from the fearful chasm. Some were rescued who
had been less near to the chasm, but of these none eventually recovered.

Behind the cone rose an immense column of dense black
smoke to more than four times the height of the mountain,

and spread out at the summit horizontally, like a pine tree, above the silvery stream which poured forth in volumes. There were constant bursts of fiery projectiles, shooting to an immense height into the black column of smoke, and tinging it with a lurid red colour. The fearful roaring and thundering never ceased for one moment, and the house shook with the concussion of the air. One stream of lava flowed towards Torre del Greco, but luckily stopped before it reached the cultivated fields; others, and the most dangerous ones, since some of them came from the new craters, poured down the Atrio del Cavallo, and dividing before reaching the Observatory flowed to the right and to the left – the stream which flowed to the north very soon reached the plain, and before night came on had partially destroyed the small town of Massa di Somma. One of the peculiarities of this eruption was the great fluidity of the lava; another was the never-ceasing thundering of the mountain. During that day we observed several violent explosions in the great stream of lava: we thought from the enormous volumes of black smoke emitted on these occasions that new craters had burst out – some below the level of the Observatory; but that can hardly have been the case. My daughters at night drove to Portici, and went up to the top of a house, where the noise seems to have been appalling; but they told me they did not gain anything by going to Portici, nor did they see the eruption better than I did who remained at Santa Lucia, for you get too much below the mountain on going near. On Sunday, 28th, I was surprised at the extreme darkness, and on looking out of the window saw men walking with umbrellas; Vesuvius was emitting such an enormous quantity of ashes, or rather fine black sand, that neither land, sea, nor sky was visible; the fall was a little less dense during the day, but at night it was worse than ever. Strangers seemed to be more alarmed at this than at the eruption, and certainly the constant loud roaring of Vesuvius was appalling enough amidst the darkness and gloom of the falling ashes. The railroad was crowded with both natives and foreigners, escaping; on the other hand, crowds came from Rome to see the eruption. We were not at all afraid, for we considered that the danger was past when so great an eruption had acted as a kind of safety-valve to the pent-up vapours. But a silly report got about that an earthquake was to take place, and many persons passed the night in driving or walking about the town, avoiding narrow streets. The mountain was quite veiled for some days by vapour and ashes, but I could see the black smoke and silvery mass above it. While looking at this, a magnificent column, black as jet, darted with inconceivable violence and velocity to an immense height; it gave a grand idea of the power that was still in action in the fiery caverns below.

Immense injury has been done by this eruption, and much more would have been done had not the lava flowed to a great extent over that of 1868. Still the streams ran through Massa di Somma, San Sebastiano, and other villages scattered about the country, overwhelming fields, woods, vineyards, and houses. The ashes, too, have not only destroyed this year's crops, but killed both vines and fruit trees, so that altogether it has been most disastrous. Vesuvius was involved in vapour and ashes till far on in May, and one afternoon at sunset, when all below was in shade, and only a few silvery threads of steam were visible, a column of the most beautiful crimson colour rose from the crater, and floated in the air. Many of the small craters still smoked, one quite at the base of the cone, which is a good deal changed – it is lower, the small northern cone has disappeared, and part of the walls of the crater have fallen in, and there is a fissure in them through which smoke or vapour is occasionally emitted.

On the 1st June we returned to Sorrento, this time to a pretty and cheerful apartment close to the sea, where I led very much the same pleasant life as the year before – busy in the morning with my own studies, and passing the rest of the day on the terrace with my daughters. [*2D, 234:* It is our habit to be separately occupied during the morning, to meet at dinner and spend the evening together. My daughter Mary draws very cleverly in water-colours and has a remarkably good eye for colour and my eldest daughter Martha has carved a frame in walnut wood for my portrait with great success. It is about six feet high and on the top there is a winged figure playing on the lute. On the flat sides of the frame there are six beautiful heads, in high relief, four are female heads, the other two are young fauns, at the bottom of the frame there is a shield with the Fairfax arms. In the spaces between there are arabesques . . . The whole is of the natural pale brown colour of the wood.] My daughters brought me beautiful wild flowers from their excursions over the country. Many of the flowers they brought were new to me, and it is a curious fact that some plants which did not grow in this part of the country a few years ago are now quite common. Amongst others, the *Trachelium cæruleum*,[120] a pretty wall-plant, native of Calabria, and formerly unknown here, now clothes many an old wall near Naples, and at Sorrento. The ferns are extremely beautiful here. Besides those common to England, the *Pteris cretica* grows luxuriantly in the damp ravines, as well as that most beautiful of European ferns, the *Woodwardia radicans*, whose fronds are often more than six feet long. The inhabitants of Sorrento are very superior to the Neapolitans, both in looks and character; they are cleanly, honest, less cruel to animals, and have pleasant manners – neither too familiar nor cringeing. As the road between Sorrento and Castellamare was impassable, owing to the fall of immense masses of rock from the cliffs above it, we crossed over in the steamer with our servants and our pet birds, for I now have a beautiful long-tailed parroquet called Smeraldo, who is my constant companion and is very familiar. And here I must mention how much I was pleased to hear that Mr Herbert°, M.P., has brought in a bill to protect land birds, which has been passed in Parliament; but I am grieved to find that 'The lark which at Heaven's gate sings' is thought unworthy of man's protection. Among the numerous plans for the education of the young, let us hope that mercy may be taught as a part of religion.

Though far advanced in years, I take as lively an interest as ever in passing events. I regret that I shall not live to know the result of the expedition to determine the currents of the ocean, the distance of the earth from the sun determined by the transits of Venus, and the source of the most renowned of rivers, the discovery of which will immortalise the name of Dr Livingstone°. But I regret most of all that I shall not see the suppression of the most atrocious system of slavery that ever disgraced humanity – that made known to the world by Dr Livingstone and by Mr Stanley, and which Sir Bartle Frere° has gone to suppress by order of the British Government.

The Blue Peter has been long flying at my foremast, and now that I am in my ninety-second year I must soon expect the signal for sailing. It is a solemn voyage, but it does not disturb my tranquillity. Deeply sensible of my utter unworthiness, and profoundly grateful for the innumerable blessings I have received, I trust in the infinite mercy of my Almighty Creator. I have every reason to be thankful that my intellect is still unimpaired, and, although my strength is weakness, my daughters support my tottering steps, and, by incessant care and help, make the infirmities of age so light to me that I am perfectly happy.

I have very little more to add to these last words of my Mother's *Recollections*. The preceding pages will have given the reader some idea – albeit perhaps a very imperfect one – of her character and opinions. Only regarding her feelings on the most sacred of themes, is it needful for me to say a few words. My mother was profoundly and sincerely religious; hers was not a religion of mere forms and doctrines, but a solemn deep-rooted faith which influenced every thought, and regulated every action of her life. Great love and reverence towards God was the foundation of this pure faith, which accompanied her from youth to extreme old age, indeed to her last moments, which gave her strength to endure many sorrows, and was the mainspring of that extreme humility which was so remarkable a feature of her character.

At a very early age she dared to think for herself, fearlessly shaking off those doctrines of her early creed which seemed to her incompatible with the unutterable goodness and greatness of God; and through life she adhered to her simple faith, holding quietly and resolutely to the ultimate truths of religion, regardless alike of the censure of bigots or the smiles of sceptics. The theories of modern science she welcomed as quite in accordance with her religious opinions. She rejected the notion of occasional interference by the Creator with His work, and believed that from the first and invariably He has acted according to a system of harmonious laws, some of which we are beginning faintly to recognise, others of which will be discovered in course of time, while many must remain a mystery to man while he inhabits this world. It was in her early life that the controversy raged respecting the incompatibility of the Mosaic account of Creation, the Deluge, &c., with the revelations of geology. My mother very soon accepted the modern theories, seeing in them nothing in any way hostile to true religious belief. It is singular to recall that her candid avowal of views now so common, caused her to be publicly censured by name from the pulpit of York Cathedral.[121] She foresaw the great modifications in opinion which further discoveries will inevitably produce; but she foresaw them without doubt or fear. Her constant prayer was for light and truth, and its full accomplishment she looked for confidently in the life beyond the grave. My mother never discussed religious subjects in general society; she considered them far too solemn to be talked of lightly; but with those near and dear to her, and with very intimate friends, whose opinion agreed with her own, she spoke freely and willingly. Her mind was constantly occupied with thoughts on religion; and in her last years especially she reflected much on that future world which she expected soon to enter, and lifted her heart still more frequently to that good Father whom she had loved so fervently all her life, and in whose merciful care she fearlessly trusted in her last hour.

My mother's old age was a thoroughly happy one. She often said that not even in the joyous spring of life had she been more truly happy. Serene and cheerful, full of life and activity, as far as her physical strength permitted, she had none of the infirmities of age, except difficulty in hearing, which prevented her from joining in general conversation. She had always been near-sighted, but could read small print with the greatest ease without glasses, even by lamp-light. To the last her intellect remained perfectly unclouded; her affection for those she loved, and her sympathy for all living beings, as fervent as ever; nor did her ardent desire for and belief in the ultimate religious and moral improvement of mankind diminish. She always retained her habit of study, and that pursuit, in which she had attained such excellence and which was always the most congenial to her, – mathematics – delighted and amused her to the end. Her last occupations, continued to the actual day of her death, were the revision and completion of a treatise, which she had written years before, on the 'Theory of Differences' (with diagrams exquisitely drawn), and the study of a book on Quaternions. Though too religious to fear death, she dreaded outliving her intellectual powers, and it was with intense delight that she pursued her intricate calculations after her ninetieth and ninety-first years, and repeatedly told me how she rejoiced to find that she had the same readiness and facility in comprehending and developing these extremely difficult formulæ which she possessed when young. Often, also, she said how grateful she was to the Almighty Father who had allowed her to retain her faculties unimpaired to so great an age. God was indeed loving and merciful to her; not only did He spare her this calamity, but also the weary trial of long-continued illness. In health of body and vigour of mind, having lived far beyond the usual span of human life, He called her to Himself. For her Death lost all its terrors. Her pure spirit passed away so gently that those around her scarcely perceived when she left them. It was the beautiful and painless close of a noble and a happy life.

My mother died in sleep on the morning of the 29th Nov., 1872. Her remains rest in the English Campo Santo of Naples.

Brief Biographies

Abrantès, Laure Junot (née Permon), Duchesse d'Abrantès (1788–1838) memoirist. Napoleon arranged her marriage in 1800 to his aide-de-camp, Andoche Junot. The marriage was unhappy and the Duchess had various lovers including Metternich, the Austrian ambassador. Angered by her infidelities and her continuing relationships with émigrés, Napoleon ordered her to leave Paris in 1813 after the death of her husband; after the fall of the Empire she was obliged to stay in exile in Rome. Many years later, she eventually returned to Paris, where she wrote entertaining, but often incorrect and malicious memoirs.

Acton, Guglielmo (William) (1825–96) Admiral in the Italian navy. He was first director general of the arsenal of La Spezia. In 1870–71 he was minister of marine and in 1879 promoted to Vice-Admiral.

Adam, Sir Frederick (1781–1853) Scottish soldier. In 1804 he was a lieutenant-colonel in the Coldstream Guards and in 1805, at the age of 24, had command of the 21st Regiment. He fought in Spain in the Napoleonic Wars, becoming major-general in 1814 and distinguishing himself at Waterloo. He was a full general by 1846.

Adams, John Couch (1819–92) astronomer. He became professor at Cambridge University in 1858. In 1845 he predicted to within 2° the position of the still undiscovered planet Neptune. This was confirmed the following year by the independent prediction of Leverrier (*q.v.*). Adams also worked on lunar parallax (apparent displacement in the position of an object caused by actual change in position of the point of observation), the earth's magnetism and Leonid meteors (meteors which appear to emanate from the constellation Leo).

Adelaide of Saxe-Meiningen (1792–1849) consort of William IV of England. Before William married her in 1818, he had ten illegitimate children by the Irish actress Dorothea Jordan, but Adelaide's two daughters died in infancy, and so William was succeeded by his niece, Victoria. Adelaide was unpopular because of her supposed interference in politics during the agitation for parliamentary reform.

Airy, Sir George Biddell (1801–92) Astronomer Royal from 1835–81. In 1826 he estimated the Earth's density from gravity measurements in mines. By showing that the motions of the Earth and Venus are not in a simple ratio, he uncovered existing errors in planetary theory. The story (Frances Power Cobbe, *Life, as Told by Herself* (1894) that he refused to support the commemoration of Mary Somerville in Westminster Abbey because he had not read her works seems odd in view of his acquaintance with her.

Albany, Countess of (1752–1823) Charles Edward Stuart, the Young Pretender, died in 1788 at the age of 68 but the Countess had already left him in 1780. She spent the following years in an informal union with Alfieri (*q.v.*) until his death in 1803. Clearly, Mary Somerville must have heard that the Countess of Albany was supposed to have been married to Alfieri.

Albrizzi. A Venetian family of printers and editors.

Alembert, Jean le Rond, Duc d' (1717–83) French mathematician, philosopher and man of letters, who studied vibrating strings to produce the general solution to the wave equation. D'Alembert's principle is a theorem in mechanics which is essentially a form of Newton's second law of motion.

Alfieri, Vittorio, Conte (1749–1803) Italian poet and dramatist. He gave up his military career to travel in Europe during the years 1767–72. His first play, *Cleopatra* (1775), was a success and this induced him to devote himself to his writing. Nineteen of his 28 plays focus on romantic heroes fighting oppression. He also wrote poetry and published an autobiography, *La Vita*, in 1804.

Amélie, Queen (1782–1866) wife of Louis-Philippe of France. Louis-Philippe married Marie-Amélie, daughter of King Ferdinand IV of Naples. Known as 'King of the French' instead of the previous title of 'King of France', Louis-Philippe reigned from 1830–48, when, during the political unrest of 1848, he abdicated and went to live in Surrey.

Amici, Giovanni Battista (1786–1863) Italian astronomer, microscopist and optical-instrument maker. He invented the achromatic lens which eliminated distortion resulting from different colours passing through the lens. In botany, he discovered details of orchid pollination and seed development; in astronomy, he studied double stars and the moons of Jupiter. He also designed mirrors for reflecting telescopes.

Ampère, André Marie (1775–1836) French physicist, professor at Bourg and Paris. He became and remains a household name after his work on the physics and mathematics of electricity and electromagnetism. The distinction between current and voltage was introduced by him. He demonstrated that wires that carry current exert force on each other, and the unit of electric current is named after him. He also explained magnetism in terms of electric currents.

Antinori, Vincenzio, Marchese (1792–1865) scientist. He worked and wrote within the Italian scientific tradition. He studied Galileo and corresponded with Plana (*q.v.*).

Antonelli, Giacomo (1806–76) cardinal and secretary of state to Pius IX (*q.v.*). Pius IX made him a cardinal in 1847, although he was not an ordained priest. In 1848 he was premier of the Papal States; he stayed with the Pope and fled with him to Gaeta after the assassination of Rossi (*q.v.*). He returned with the Pope to Rome in 1850 and remained his secretary of state until his death. It is said that the impurity of his life and his manner of accumulating wealth made the Pope rather glad to be rid of him notwithstanding his loyalty.

Arago, (Dominique) François (Jean) (1786–1853) French astronomer and physicist, Professor of Physics at the École Polytechnique in Paris. His important work covered astronomy, electricity, magnetism, meteorology and optics. He was an advocate of the wave theory of light.

Argyll, George Douglas Campbell, 8th Duke of Argyll (1823–1900). The Duke was an amateur of science and President of the Royal Society of Edinburgh in 1861. He exerted a considerable influence on scientific progress, but he remained committed to the cataclysmal school of geology, never coming round to the newer evolutional school. He published on religion and politics as well as science.

Babbage, Charles (1792–1871) mathematician and inventor. In an attempt to produce more accurate mathematical tables, Babbage conceived the idea of a calculating machine, a kind of computer which could store information. He never completed the project but his idea is recognised as the forerunner of the modern computer. Babbage was a difficult man and his outspoken criticism of the Royal Society made him enemies. Yet he was in many ways right about the conservatism of British science in the first part of the 19th century and its refusal to look beyond Newtonian physics and mathematics.

Baillie, Joanna (1762–1851) Scottish dramatist and poet. She was one of the three children of Dorothea Hunter and James Baillie, minister of Bothwell, Lanarkshire and later Professor of Divinity at Glasgow University. She and her elder sister, Agnes, were educated at a boarding school in Glasgow. Her mother's brothers were the celebrated surgeons, anatomists and collectors, William and John Hunter. When in 1783 her brother, Matthew, who had been educated at Glasgow and Balliol College, inherited William's School of Anatomy in Great Windmill Street in London, his mother and sisters moved to London to keep house for him. When Matthew married in 1791 the three women eventually settled in Hampstead.

Joanna Baillie became the pre-eminent female dramatist of her day and, although her plays had very limited stage success, it was significantly greater than that enjoyed by any of the now more celebrated male romantic poets. The first volume of her *Series of Plays: In Which It Is Attempted to Delineate the Stronger Passions of the Mind* appeared in 1798; two subsequent volumes were published as well as a number of other plays, one of which, *The Family Legend*, enjoyed some success in Edinburgh;

her early verses and some later productions were collected as *Fugitive Verses* in 1840. Joanna Baillie had a long publishing life, seeing the first edition of her collected works through the press before she died in 1851, aged 88.

Baily, Francis (1774–1844) English amateur astronomer. Baily's bead, the broken line of sunlight that shines through the valleys of the moon close to total eclipse, are named after him. He also revised the then-current catalogues of the stars and calculated accurate values for the density and ellipticity of the earth.

Bannister, John (1760–1836). The only Bannister I can find whose dates fit is John Bannister, who was principally, however, a comic actor. He worked mainly at Drury Lane, with some appearances at the Haymarket and in Glasgow and Edinburgh. Interestingly, given what Mary Somerville says about the moral character of 'our principal actors', it was said of Bannister on his death 'The stage can point to few men of more solid virtue and unblemished character.'

Barbauld, Anna Laetitia (1743–1825) poet, writer of prose and scholar. Anna Laetitia Aikin, Mrs Barbauld, with her husband, a dissenting clergyman, ran a school for boys at Palgrave, Sussex. The school closed in 1785 and the Barbaulds eventually settled in 1802 in Stoke Newington. The mental health of Mrs Barbauld's husband deteriorated until be became violent towards her and had to be put under restraint. He escaped from his keeper and was found drowned in 1808. In 1812 Mrs Barbauld published a poem, 'Eighteen Hundred and Eleven', which lamented the decline of moral, political and artistic life in Britain. The poem was reviewed so harshly by J. W. Croker in the *Quarterly Review* in June 1812 that it put an end to her public career as a writer.

Although Mrs Barbauld had a classical education, she said that she saw no point in producing *femmes savantes*, rather than good wives or agreeable companions.

Barbieri-Nini, Marianna (1820–87) Florentine diva. She studied with Pasta (*q.v.*) and made her operatic debut in Milan in Donizetti's *Belisario*. She is said to have been so ugly in face and upper body that the audience made it clear they thought so and she was advised to wear a mask. When she played more bloodthirsty roles, like Donizetti's Lucrezia Borgia and Verdi's Lady Macbeth, her appearance seemed to suit better. She retired early in 1856 but she had already sung all over Italy, and in Barcelona, Madrid and Paris.

Barclay, Misses The Misses Barclay, who looked after Mary Somerville during her illness in Switzerland, were the daughters of Robert Barclay of Bury Hill. In 1814 the fourth Barclay daughter married the Cornish philosopher and inventor, Robert Were Fox, of Falmouth (1789–1877; FRS, 1848) (EP, p. 27). The Barclays were also members of the Clapham Sect (see p. 404, n.57).

Barthe, Félix (1795–1863) lawyer and politician. The Garde des Sceaux is the French Minister of Justice, roughly equivalent to the Lord Chancellor in Britain. During his first period in the office in the ministry of the Duc de Broglie, he reformed the penal code.

Bartolommei, Ferdinando, Marchese (1821–69) Italian statesman, one of the founders of the journal *La Nazione* (1859), and senator in 1862.

Beaufort, Sir Francis (1774–1857) Admiral. In 1805 he devised the Beaufort Scale, a scale of wind speed, based on observable indicators such as smoke, tree movement and damage incurred.

Becker, Karl Ferdinand (1775–1849) educationalist and linguist. Becker had five sons and three daughters.

Becquerel, Antoine César (1788–1878). Originally in the army, Becquerel left it to work with Ampère (*q.v.*) in his study of electricity, thus becoming one of the founders of electrochemistry. His grandson, **(Antoine) Henri** (1852–1908), physicist, became professor at the Conservatoire des Arts et Métiers in Paris and shared the Nobel Prize in 1903 with Pierre and Marie Curie.

Bell, Sir Charles (1774–1842) anatomist. Educated in Edinburgh, Bell published widely on anatomy and surgery. He was a Royal Society medallist in 1829 and Professor of Surgery in Edinburgh University in 1836. He discovered the distinct function of the nerves.

Berry, Marie-Caroline de Bourbon-Sicile, Duchesse de (1798–1870) wife of Charles, Duc de Berry (1778–1820), son of Charles X (*q.v.*). After the death of Charles X, she conspired to obtain the throne for her son, Henri, Comte de Chambord (1820–83). In 1832 she instituted an unsuccessful revolt in the Vendée.

Berry, Mary (1763–1852). Celebrated for her beauty, wit and most of the other reputedly female virtues, she lived a single and singularly happy life with her sister Agnes, who was born a year after her, for nearly 88 years. She and her sister had a famous friendship with Horace Walpole, the landscape gardener, poet and, with *The Castle of Otranto*, inventor of Gothic fiction. They lived in a house owned by Walpole, known as Little Strawberry Hill after the parent house owned by Walpole; Walpole bequeathed the house to them. When Miss Berry received Joanna Baillie's first volume of the *Plays on the Passions*, she apparently sat up all night in a ball dress to read it. From the first she believed the plays to have been written by a woman, because the female characters were rational before beautiful.

Billington, Elizabeth Weichsel, Mrs (1765 or 1768–1818) a celebrated singer, actress and composer.

Biot, Jean-Baptiste (1774–1862) physicist, Professor of Mathematics at the University of Beauvais. He helped to formulate laws concerning magnetic fields. With Gay-Lussac (*q.v.*), he made the first balloon flight for scientific purposes. He also worked with Arago (*q.v.*) on the refractive purposes of gases and received the Rumford Medal in 1840.

Blair, Hugh (1718–1800) minister of Athelstaneford in East Lothian, where he was succeeded by Home (*q.v.*). He was Professor of Rhetoric and Belles-Lettres at Edinburgh, and his lectures on rhetoric made him famous. He also published his sermons in five volumes (1777–1801). He was one of the defenders of the authenticity of the Ossian poems (see p.411, n.111).

Bonaparte or **Buonaparte, Lucien** (1778–1846) brother of the Emperor Napoleon. Under the Directory he was president of the Council of Five Hundred, and subsequently became a critic of Napoleon's policies. The brothers were reconciled on the eve of Waterloo. After Napoleon's defeat, Lucien lived in exile in Italy.

Bon-Brenzoni, Caterina, Contessa (1813–1856) The Countess's poems were collected and published in 1857, preceded by a biography by Dr Angola Messadaglia.

Bordeaux, Henri-(Charles-Ferdinand-Marie-Dieu-donné), Comte de Chambord, Duc de Bordeaux

(1820–83). He received as a birth present the Château of Chambord. A relic of the old régime in France, he travelled widely in Austria and Italy. In 1843 he went to England, visited Scotland, and finally settled in Belgravia Square, London.

Boswell Claude Irvine, Lord Balmuto (1742–1824) nephew of James Boswell, Johnson's biographer. He was educated at Edinburgh University, became a member of the Faculty of Advocates in 1766 and was Lord of Session (1799–1822).

Bouvard, Alexis (1767–1843; FRS 1826) astronomer and Director of the Paris Observatory. He discovered eight comets and wrote *Tables astronomiques* of Jupiter and Saturn (1808) and Uranus (1821). His hypothesis of an unknown celestial body was confirmed by John Couch Adams's discovery of Neptune.

Bouvard, Jean-Louis-Eloi (1768–1834) French general. Bouvard took part in the Peninsular campaign.

Bowditch, Nathaniel (1773–1838) self-educated American mathematician and astronomer. He translated and updated the first four volumes of Laplace's *Mécanique Céleste* as *Celestial Mechanics*, 1829–39. He refused professorships at several American universities. From 1829 until his death he was President of the American Academy of Arts and Sciences.

Bradley, James (1693–1762) astronomer and divine; Astronomer Royal (1742). He announced his discovery of 'aberration of light' in a paper read to the Royal Society in 1729 and, in a paper in 1748, published his discovery of the nutation of the Earth's axis. He was also Copley medallist.

Brand or **Brande, William Thomas** (1788–1866; FRS 1809) chemist. He succeeded Sir Humphry Davy (*q.v.*) as Professor of Chemistry at the Royal Institution (1813). He was one of the secretaries of the Royal Society (1816–26) and chief officer of coinage at the Department of the Mint (1854).

Brewster, Sir David (1781–1868; FRS 1815) Scottish physicist. He studied the polarisation of light, double refractions in crystals and relations between crystalline forms and optical properties, giving his name to Brewster's Law. He invented the kaleidoscope. In 1831 he helped to found the British Association for the Advancement of Science. He was principal of St Andrews and Edinburgh Universities, Edinburgh (1860). He was Copley medallist in 1815 and Rumford medallist in 1818.

Broglie, 3rd Duc de (1785–1879) politician and diplomat. He was Prime Minister from 1835–36. Always antipathetic to Napoleon III, he spent the last 20 years of his life in literary and philosophical pursuits.

Brongniart, Alexandre (1770–1847; FRS 1825). Originally intended for medicine, Brongniart was also interested in zoology, botany and chemistry. He travelled to England where he learned the art of enamelling. On his return to France in 1800, he became director of the Sèvres factory, a post he held until his death. He was also chief engineer for mines in 1818 and professor of mineralogy at the Museum of Natural History in 1822.

Brougham, Henry Peter, Baron Brougham and Vaux (1778–1868). He was educated at Edinburgh High School and Edinburgh University and finally became Lord Chancellor; he was a celebrated orator and advocate of Queen Caroline. He published widely on social, political and literary matters. In addition to his literary activities, he effected improvements in the Court of Chancery and assisted in the founding of London University (1828). With Jeffrey and Sydney Smith, he founded *The Edinburgh Review* in 1802.

Brown, Montagu Yeats- (1834–1912) member of the Diplomatic Service. The son of a former consul at Genoa, Yeats-Brown was himself consul at Genoa in 1858. In 1893 he was consul in Boston.

Brown, Rawdon Lubbock (1803–83) student of history. He lived in Venice 1833–83, working in the archives there, particularly on the reports sent by Venetian ambassadors from London. He wrote historical works in both English and Italian.

Brown, Robert (1773–1858) traveller and botanist. Brown was born in Montrose. In 1801 he embarked from Portsmouth under the command of Flinders (*q.v.*) and explored the vegetable world of new Holland and Van Diemen's Land. He wrote 'General Remarks, Geographical and Systematical on the Botany of Terra Australis' appended to the *Narrative of Captain Flinders's Voyage* (1814). He also wrote botanical appendices to *Voyages and Travels of the Most Celebrated Navigators and Travellers*. Humboldt (*q.v.*) dedicated *Synopsis Plantarum Orbis Novi* to him. He was librarian of the Linnean Society.

Browning, Elizabeth Barrett (1806–61) poet. She married the poet Robert Browning in 1846. After their marriage the Brownings lived mostly in Italy. Her poem, *Casa Guidi Windows* (1851) from the name of the house in Florence in which they had an apartment, recorded political events in Italy coloured by Elizabeth Barrett Browning's enthusiasm for the cause of Italian liberty.

Buchan, see **Erskine**.

Buckland, William (1784–1856) geologist. He was educated at Corpus Christi College and became a Fellow there (1808–25). He was President of the Geological Society in 1824 and 1840. He wrote a number of geological papers and in his 'Bridgewater Treatise' upheld the Mosaic account of the Flood. He became Dean of Winchester in 1845.

Buller, Charles (1806–48) Liberal politician, taught by Thomas Carlyle from 1822–25. He was MP for West Looe, Cornwall. Buller generally had a reputation for decency and progressive ideas. Why he should have attacked Mary Somerville is rather obscure. He also spoke against her Civil List pension but it is easier to understand this as a point of principle about pensions. Carlyle was rather dismissive of Mary Somerville in one of his letters to his brother John: 'We have seen Mrs Somerville (an unblameable, unpraising *canny* Scotch lady, of intellect enough to study Euclid, and not more than enough)' 30 April 1835 (*The Carlyle Correspondence*, vol. 8, 1981).

Bunbury/Napier/Fox families. Elizabeth, daughter of Henry Fox, Charles James Fox's younger brother, married Sir Henry Bunbury. Her younger sister, Caroline, married William Napier (1785–1860). George Napier was the second husband of Sarah Lennox (1745–1826). Richard Napier (1787–1868) married Louisa Staples. Later, after Sarah's death, her daughter Emily married Sir Henry Bunbury as his second wife: Sir Henry was the son of Sarah's first husband who divorced her for adultery. Lady Sarah Napier was said to be the last surviving great-granddaughter of Charles II; she had five sons and three daughters. The complicated affairs of these families make up the fascinating story of Stella Tillyard's *Aristocrats* (London: Chatto & Windus, 1994).

Bunsen, Robert Wilhelm (1811–99) German chemist. He did not actually invent the Bunsen burner, which bears his name, but was responsible for its popular use. He worked with Gustav Kirchhoff (*q.v.*) to develop the technique of spectroscopy, which they used to discover the elements caesium and rubidium in 1861.

Buoncompagni or **Boncompagni di Mombello, Carlo** (1804–80) Italian statesman. Cavour (*q.v.*) contributed much to his political formation.

Byron, Ada see **Lovelace**.

Byron, George Gordon, 6th Baron (1788–1824) poet. Byron wrote the first five cantos of *Don Juan* between 1818 and 1820. In 1819 he had already begun his relationship with Teresa, Countess Guiccioli, with whom he was probably living when Mary Somerville saw him in Venice.

Byron, Lady Noel (Annabella (Anne Isabella) Milbanke). She married Lord Byron in 1815 but left him the following year. Annabella was a bluestocking, called by Byron 'Princess of Parallelograms'. For Ada Byron see **Lovelace**.

Campbell, Thomas (1777–1844) poet. He was the son of a Glasgow merchant and was educated at Glasgow University. 'The Pleasures of Hope' (1799), and 'Gertrude of Wyoming' (1809), in Spenserian stanzas, both became very popular. He is remembered also for such stirring battle songs as 'Ye Mariners of England'.

Canning, Stratford, 1st Viscount Stratford de Redcliffe (1786–1880) diplomat. He was styled the 'Great Elchi', ambassador *par excellence*. He was ambassador at Constantinople (1842–44) and again in 1848–58.

Canova, Antonio (1757–1822) Italian neoclassical sculptor. He worked at first in Venice and then in Rome from 1781. He travelled to Vienna and Paris and was employed by Napoleon. His marble of Napoleon's sister, Pauline Borghese, as 'Venus Victrix' (1805–07) in the Borghese Gallery in Rome remains one of his best known images.

Capellini, Giovanni (1833–1922) geologist. He published *Geologia dei colli di Val d'Elsa* when he was 25 and became Professor of Geology at Bologna when only 28.

Carignani. Neapolitan noble family.

Catalani, Madame Valabrèque (1780–1849) soprano. She made her debut at the Fenice Theatre in Venice in 1795. She sang in Florence in 1799 and Milan 1801; in the same year she married Paul Valabrèque, a French attaché in Lisbon. She had a commanding stage presence and range. She retired in 1828 to her country home near Florence.

Cavour, Camillo Benso di, Count (1810–61) Italian statesman, generally held to be the architect of Unification. A liberal from an early age, he was one of the founders of the organ *Il Risorgimento* in 1847. Under Victor Emmanuel II of Sardinia-Piedmont, he formed a government in 1852. With the object of ejecting the Austrians from Italy, Cavour formed an alliance with Britain and France during the Crimean War. He resigned when France came to terms with Austria but became Prime Minister again in 1860. He negotiated the union of Sardinia-Piedmont with Parma, Modena, Tuscany and the Romagna. By 1861 he had achieved the establishment of a united Italy.

Champollion, Jean-François (1790–1832) French Egyptologist who, without proper recognition, built on Young's intuitions about hieroglyphs. His *Lettre à M. Dacier* (1822) identified and assigned phonetic values to about 40 symbols. These results were expanded in his *Précis du système hieroglyphique* (1824).

Chantrey, Sir Francis Leggatt (1781–1841). The son of a carpenter, he was originally apprenticed to a wood carver but went to London about 1802 and studied at the Royal Academy Schools. He was a Royal Academician from 1811 and became a fellow of the Royal Society in 1818. As an amateur of science, Chantrey was an appropriate person to do the bust of Mary Somerville which is in the Royal College of Surgeons (EP, pp. 89–90). He is perhaps best known for his equestrian statue of George IV in Trafalgar Square but he did many of the famous of the age, including Scott twice. He became very rich and left £150,000, the bulk of his fortune, to the Royal Academy to buy high-quality art.

Chapone, Hester (née Mulso) (1727–1801). A friend of the novelist Samuel Richardson, author of *Clarissa*, she published poems and stories (1750–53), as well as essays (1773–77). She also had a hand in the periodical *The Rambler*. Her *Letters on the Improvement of the Mind, Addressed to a Young Lady* was published in 1774. This is presumably the work Mary Somerville has in mind.

Charles, Archduke (1771–1847) Austrian archduke and field marshal. He was an army reformer and theoretician, who modernised the Austrian army and thus did much to enable French defeats during the Napoleonic period.

Charles X (1757–1836) King of France (1824–30). Charles lived abroad after the Revolution, but returned to become leader of the ultraroyalist party at the restoration of the Bourbons. His own reactionary rule led to his overthrow in 1830, when he returned to England.

Charles Albert (1798–1849) King of Sardinia-Piedmont (1831–49). During the Risorgimento (the movement for Italian Unification), he introduced reforms and reluctantly granted representative government to Sardinia in 1848. He joined the revolt of the city of Milan against Austrian government but abdicated after his defeat at Custoza (1848) and Novara (1849).

Chigi. This old Sienese family rose from 13th-century banking to princely rank in papal Rome and the Holy Roman Empire in the 17th century.

Choiseul, Étienne François, Duc de (1719–85) an extremely powerful French minister. As foreign minister, he negotiated good terms for France in the Treaty of Paris, which closed the Seven Years' War. By the later part of the century, his position had been undermined and he was exiled in 1770.

Clarke (more usually **Clark**), **William** (1788–1869) anatomist. He was a professor at Cambridge from 1817 to 1866. He was a friend of Byron.

Clerk, William, of Eldin (1771–1847) brother of John Clerk, Lord Eldin (1757–1832). It was said by his friends that only William's diffidence prevented him from being as great a success as his brother, the judge.

Cobbe, Frances Power (1822–1904) philanthropic and religious writer. She published *The Theory of Intuitive Morals* (1855–57), *Darwinism in Morals* (1872), *The Duties of Women* (1881) and an autobiography (1904). She was associated with Mary Carpenter in her educational advances, including the ragged schools, and concerned herself also with relief of destitution and philanthropy in the workhouses. She campaigned for suffrage for women and for the admission of women to degrees; she was joint secretary of the National Anti-Vivisection Society, a cause that was particularly close to Mary Somerville's heart.

Coke, Thomas William, Earl Leicester of Holkham (1752–1842) agriculturist. Coke introduced new farming systems. On his own estate he replaced cattle with sheep and introduced new crops. The note in the original edition merely points out that Mr Coke later became Earl of Leicester.

Colbert, Auguste-Napoléon-Joseph, Marquis de Chabanais (1805–83). Colbert's father was killed during the Peninsular campaign in 1809; the English Colonel Napier paid tribute to his bravery. Colbert himself began as a soldier but left the army and married the niece (not the granddaughter, as Mary Somerville has it) of Laplace.

Condé a French princely family, a branch of the Bourbon royal house.

Cooper, James Fenimore (1789–1851) American novelist, best known for *The Last of the Mohicans* (1826). His *England, with Sketches of Society in the Metropolis*, a highly critical account of English society, appeared in 1837. Despite Mary Somerville's slightly equivocal account of him, their families became quite intimate. Cooper had a copy of his *Rural Hours* sent to Mary Somerville and, in a letter to Samuel Rogers (*q.v.*) in 1832, he asks to be remembered to the Somervilles (*Letters and Journals*, ed. James Franklin Beard, Cambridge, Mass.: Belknap P., 1968, vol. 2, p. 181). Mary Somerville wrote Harriet Martineau (*q.v.*) a letter of introduction to him when Martineau toured America.

Corri, Natale (1765–1822) Mary Somerville's mentor must have been Natale, the brother of the more famous Domenico, who took over his brother's music-publishing establishment when Domenico moved to London in 1790. Natale was involved in concert promotion as well as other musical activities and, although he was declared bankrupt, he remained in Edinburgh until 1821, when he left for the continent with his daughters, Frances and Rosalie.

Craig, Sir James Henry (1748–1812) general. Craig took the Cape Colony in 1795 and was governor there (1795–97). He was governor of Canada from 1807–11 and was made a general in 1812. William Somerville named his illegitimate child after him (EP, p.7).

Cromek, Robert Hartley (1770–1812) engraver and publisher. He studied under Bartolozzi. Cromek published an edition of Robert Blair's *Grave* with etchings after Blake. He compiled *Reliques of Burns* (1808) and *Select Scottish Songs* (1810).

Cuvier, Georges, Baron (1769–1832) French zoologist, who founded the sciences of comparative anatomy and palaeontology. By extending his study of animal skeletons to fossils, he was able to construct entire skeletons from the incomplete ones in existence. His system of classification, although subsequently superseded, was an advance on Linnaeus.

Dana, James Dwight (1813–95) geologist, zoologist and teacher, member of the Royal Society. He was assistant in chemistry to Silliman (*q.v.*). He became Professor of Natural History at Yale in 1855. He was a devout believer and it took him 15 years to accept a version of Darwin.

Daniell, Samuel (1775–1811) artist. He served with William Somerville for years at the Cape; they both returned to Britain in 1803. He was the draughtsman on a mission to explore Bechuanaland in 1801. He died in Ceylon and his *Sketches Representing the Native Tribes, Animals, and Scenery of Southern Africa, from Drawings made by the Late Samuel Daniell, Engraved by William Daniell*, were published posthumously in 1820.

Darwin, Charles Robert (1809–82) naturalist, widely known for his theory of natural selection, first published in *The Origin of Species* (1859). Since his views conflicted with the biblical account of creation, they aroused fierce controversy at the time and later. The modern, modified version of his theories is known as neo-Darwinism. Mary Somerville was already an old lady when Darwin's theory reached her and she never wrote extensively about it nor wholly embraced it but, typically, she did not reject it either.

David d'Angers, Pierre-Jean (1789–1856) French sculptor. Although he worked with Canova in Rome, David d'Angers rebelled against the prevailing neoclassical style of early-19th-century French sculpture in the interest of a greater degree of realism. He visited England in 1827. David was always radical in politics and in 1831 presented a bust of Goethe to the poet.

Davis, Paulina Kellogg Wright (1813–76) American abolitionist, suffragist and educator. Her first husband died in 1845, leaving her sufficiently wealthy and free to pursue studies in medicine. In 1849 she married Thomas Davis and adopted two daughters. She lectured on anatomy with particular reference to the female body and began a literary magazine called *The Una* from Spenser's pure heroine in *The Faerie Queene*. She spent the latter part of her life in Providence, where it was said she was too serious for society women and too radical for the college community.

Davy, Lady (née **Kerr**, formerly **Mrs Jane Apreece**) (1780–1855). When her first husband, Sir Shuckburgh Ashby Apreece, died in 1807, she became the wife of the scientist, Sir Humphry Davy (*q.v.*). Lady Davy was well known in society in her own right and was also a close friend and correspondent of Joanna Baillie. She was commended by Madame de Staël, who did not commend many women.

Davy, Sir Humphry (1778–1829). He invented the miners' safety lamp in 1815 and discovered the use of nitrous oxide as an anaesthetic. For this he was invited to join the Royal Institution. By passing electricity through molten metallic compounds, he discovered potassium in 1807 and, in 1808, sodium, calcium, barium, magnesium and strontium. He encouraged Michael Faraday (*q.v.*), employing him as his assistant at the Royal Institution, and Faraday eventually took over from him there.

Dawes, William Rutter (1799–1868; FRS 1865) astronomer. He had charge of the observatory at South Villa, Regents Park (1839–44), and was gold medallist of the Astronomical Society in 1855. He established the non-atmospheric character of the redness of Mars.

De Candolle, Augustin Pyrane (1778–1841) Swiss botanist. After Darwin, De Candolle's scientific structural criteria for determining natural relations among plant genera provided the empirical foundation for a modern evolutionary history of plants. His most important work was his *Théorie élémentaire de la botanique* (1813). He held the Natural History chair at the University of Geneva (1817–41) and was first director of the botanical gardens there.

De Filippi, Filippo (1814–67) Italian zoologist. Born in Milan, he studied medicine at Pavia. He went to Turin in 1848 and organised the natural history collections of the university museum. In 1862 he went on a diplomatic mission and a round-the-world voyage on the frigate *Magenta* in 1865. He never returned to Italy and died in Hong Kong.

De la Rive, Auguste Arthur (1801–73) Swiss physicist. He held the Natural Philosophy chair at the Academy of Geneva from 1823. He was one of the founders of the electrochemical theory of batteries and shared Faraday's view that voltaic electricity was caused by chemical action.

De la Rive, Gaspard (1770–1824) one of the Genevese *savants* that the Somervilles met through their connection with the Marcets (EP, pp. 26, 29).

De Morgan, Augustus (1806–71) mathematician and logician. He was important in the development of modern algebra and symbolic logic. His *Elements of Algebra Preliminary to the Differential Calculus* was published in 1837. He was the first President of the Mathematical Society, 1865.

De Vico, Padre Francesco (1805–48) cleric and scientist. De Vico became a Jesuit in 1823 and director of the astronomical observatory at the Collegio Romano in Rome in 1838. He was a member of various European scientific academies.

Donati, Giovanni Battista (1826–73) astronomer. He was the first to observe the spectrum of a comet (Comet 1864 II). This observation indicated that comet tails contain luminous gas. From 1854–64 he observed six comets and that of 2 June 1858 bears his name. He was Professor of Astronomy and director of the observatory at Florence.

Doria, Teresa, Marchesa. The Dorias were a leading family in the political, military and economic life of Genoa from the 12th century.

Duchênois, Catherine Josephine Rufuin (dite **Rafin**), **Mademoiselle** (1777 1835) French actress. She made her début at Versailles in 1802 and then joined the Comédie Française. She was much loved by audiences and between 1804 and 1829 played at least 36 roles, including Andromaque, Marie Stuart and Clytemnestra.

Dudley, John William Ward, 1st Earl of Dudley of Castle Dudley, Staffordshire (1781–1833) politician. He was foreign secretary, 1827–28. Rogers (*q.v.*) hated Ward after he attacked his 'Columbus' in a review in the *Quarterly* (vol. ix, 207).

Duncan, Adam, Viscount Duncan (1731–1804) Admiral. He was Commander-in-Chief in the North Sea (1795–1801). In 1797, after the victory at Camperdown, he was created Baron Duncan of Lundie and Viscount Duncan of Camperdown. Mary Somerville is tart about him, thinking that he overshadowed her father, but Duncan, a Scotsman, was an extremely impressive figure both morally and physically: he was six foot four and built in proportion.

Dupin, (François Pierre) Charles (1784–1873) French mathematician and politician. President of the Chamber of Deputies (1824). He was interested also in the useful arts and came to Britain in 1836 for the sixth meeting of the British Association (EP, 119, 180). He was made a grand officer of the Légion d'honneur in 1840.

Edgeworth, Maria (1767–1849) Irish novelist, educationist, and writer of moral tales for children. She is best known for her novels, *Castle Rackrent* (1800) and *Belinda* (1801). Maria Edgeworth knew Scott well and knew and corresponded with Joanna Baillie (*q.v.*). She was one of the children of Richard Lovell Edgeworth (1744–1817), also an educationist, who wrote the Rousseau-esque *Practical Education* with Maria. She refers, in her letter to Mary Somerville (p. 165), to her sister Harriet. Her *Letters in England* are a useful source of information about Mary Somerville.

Edwards, Henri Milne- (1800–1885). Born in Bruges of English parents, Milne-Edwards became a doctor of medicine in Paris in 1823 and at first did medical work. He was elected in 1838 to the Académie des Sciences as Cuvier's successor. He published widely in zoology and natural history.

Elgin, Thomas Bruce, 7th Earl of Elgin (1766–1841). He gave his name to the famous and still-disputed Elgin Marbles. He arranged for the transportation of the Parthenon frieze, etc. to England in 1803–12 at a time when the Turks were apparently using them for target practice. He sold these marbles to the nation in 1816. He was married first to Mary Hamilton Nisbet (1778–1855) and, after divorcing her in 1808, to Elizabeth Oswald of Dunnikier. Mary Nisbet married her lover Robert Ferguson (see *Fergusons of Raith*) and the couple remained good friends of Mary Somerville.

Elliot, Gilbert, 2nd Earl of Minto (1785–1859) politician and diplomat. He was educated at Edinburgh University. He was ambassador to Berlin (1822–4) but, from Mary Somerville's point of view, his most important act was to persuade the King of Naples to grant Sicily a separate parliament.

Elphinstone, Mountstuart (1779–1859) Governor of Bombay. He declined Governor-Generalship of India on his retirement. He wrote a *History of India* (1841) and *The Rise of British Power in the East* (published 1887).

Erskine, David Stuart, 11th Earl of Buchan (1742–1829). The Erskines gave Mary Somerville one of her American connections: in 1792, the Earl presented Washington with a snuffbox made from a tree that supposedly sheltered Wallace. He also founded an annual festival to commemorate the poet James Thomson.

Erskine, Thomas, 1st Baron Erskine (1750–1823) Erskine's defence of the radicals in the infamous Treason Trials of 1794 made him famous. He was an MP from 1783–84 and 1790–1806, and Lord Chancellor in 1806–07. He also successfully defended the leader of the Gordon Riots in 1781 and he got Hadfield, who attempted to assassinate George III, acquitted on the grounds of insanity.

Fairfax, Admiral Sir Henry (1837–1900). Mary Somerville's nephew became an Admiral in 1897.

Fairfax, Margaret Charters, Lady Fairfax (1741–1832). Mary Somerville's mother was the daughter of Samuel Fairfax, Solicitor of Customs for Scotland. Mary was the fifth of her seven children, four of whom, Samuel, Mary, Margaret and Henry, survived infancy. The house in Burntisland where she brought up her children is still standing.

Fairfax, Vice-Admiral Sir William George (1739–1813) father of Mary Somerville with his second wife, Margaret Charters. The original edition of *Personal Recollections* has the following note: 'Sir William Fairfax was the son of Joseph Fairfax, Esq. of Bagshot, in the county of Surrey, who died in 1783, aged 77, having served in the army previous to 1745. It is understood that his family was descended from the Fairfaxes of Walton in Yorkshire, the main branch of which were created Viscounts Fairfax of Emly, in the peerage of Ireland (now extinct), and a younger branch Barons Fairfax of Cameron, in the peerage of Scotland. Of the last-named was the great Lord Fairfax, Commander-in-Chief of the armies of the parliament (1645–50), whose title is now held by the 11th Lord Fairfax, a resident in the United States of America.' He was a prisoner in France 1778–82; fought in the successful sea battle of Camperdown in 1797 and was made Vice-Admiral of the Red in 1810.

Falkner or **Falconer, Hugh** (1808–65) palaeontologist and botanist. Falconer was educated at Aberdeen University and Edinburgh, where he graduated MD in 1829. While working for the East India Company, he discovered fossil mammals in the Sivalik Hills. He was Vice-President of the Royal Society. Latterly he travelled in South Europe for his health and made discoveries during this period too.

Fanshawe, Catherine Maria (1765–1834) minor poet. Her charade/riddle on the letter 'h', which was sometimes attributed to Byron, ran ''Twas in heaven pronounced, and 'twas muttered in hell.' 'The Butterfly's Ball' was actually by William Roscoe. She gave several pieces to Joanna Baillie for her *Collection* (1823), which was designed to provide a charitable contribution to the poet Struthers.

Faraday, Michael (1791–1867) chemist and physicist. He was born into a poor London family and apprenticed to a bookbinder where he found books on science that stimulated his interest, notably one by Jane Marcet (*q.v.*). He met Humphry Davy after attending lectures at the Royal Institution and became his apprentice, later in 1833 succeeding him there as Professor of Chemistry. Lady Davy may not have made life wholly easy for him in the earlier stages of his relationship with her husband and she is rumoured to have treated him like a menial (DNB). He worked on the liquefaction of gases and discovered benzene. But his enduring contribution to science was in the field of electricity and electrochemistry, in which he discovered the process of electrolysis and the laws that control it. He discovered the connection between electricity and magnetism and first showed that electromagnetic induction was possible. Using induction, he produced the first electrical generator in 1831, and the first transformer. Faraday, a deeply religious man, who belonged to the extreme Sandemanian sect, had a breakdown in 1839, but continued to do useful work after this point. Mary Somerville's praise of him as the greatest experimental philosopher and discoverer since Newton is not hyperbolic.

Ferguson, Sir Adam (1770–1854). He was the son of Professor Adam Ferguson (1723–1816), Professor of

Philosophy at the University of Edinburgh; he was one of Scott's closest friends. Having served with distinction in the Peninsular campaign against Napoleon, he was appointed Keeper of the Regalia of Scotland in 1818 and was knighted during the visit of George IV in 1822.

Fergusons of Raith. Robert Ferguson (1771–1840; FRS 1805) was a radical MP for Kirkcaldy. Mary Somerville knew the Fergusons from her early life in Burntisland and had become friendly with Mary Nisbet (1778–1855), Robert's wife after her divorce from Thomas Bruce, Lord Elgin (EP, p. 160).

Finlayson, George (1790–1823) traveller who, as naturalist, accompanied the expedition of 1821 to Siam and Cochin China. His journal was edited by Sir Stamford Raffles in 1826.

Fiorelli, Giuseppe (1823–96) Neapolitan archaeologist. His systematic excavation at Pompeii helped to preserve much of the ancient city as nearly intact as possible. In this way, he made an important contribution to modern archaeological methods. His initial work was completed in 1848. Fiorelli was Director of the National Museum in Naples from 1863.

Flamsteed, John (1646–1719) was appointed the first Astronomer Royal in 1675 and was permitted by Charles II to establish a national observatory at Greenwich. He catalogued and gave the position of more than 3000 stars. The references in Admiral Smyth's letter to Mary Somerville (p. 169) seem to confirm Flamsteed's reputation as a quarrelsome man, who argued with both Newton and Halley when they requested access to his astronomical observations.

Flinders, Matthew (1771–1814) British navigator and hydrographer. He joined the navy in 1789, the year of the French Revolution, sailed in the Pacific with the notorious Captain Bligh and saw active service in the wars with France. He explored the Bass Strait and was commissioned to survey the coasts of Australia and Tasmania. The Flinders range of mountains in E. South Australia is named after him.

Foscolo, Niccolò Ugo (1778–1827) a great Italian patriot. His early tragedy, *Tieste* (1797) and his poem *A Bonaparte liberator* reflect his anti-Austrian sentiments, although his trust in Napoleon was somewhat misplaced. He served in the Napoleonic armies but settled in Britain in 1816. He made only a precarious living there by his pen and by teaching Italian. His remains were removed to Florence in 1871.

Foucault, Jean Bernard Léon (1819–68) French physicist, after whom Foucault's pendulum, which demonstrates the rotation of the earth, is named. He also worked on light, showing that its speed decreases in water, and he invented the gyroscope. His pendulum was first demonstrated in Paris in 1851.

Franklin, Sir John (1786–1847) explorer. While in the Royal Navy, he fought at Trafalgar (1805) and was subsequently governor of Tasmania, then Van Diemen's Land. His ill-fated expedition with two ships to discover the Northwest Passage never returned. Various expeditions to find him were unsuccessful until 1859, when the skeletons of the crew and their records were found on King William Island. The 'deplorable fate' that Mary Somerville alludes to is that they became ice-locked and must have died of scurvy or starvation.

Fraunhofer, Joseph von (1787–1826) German physicist, whose work improved the quality of lenses and prisms and the design of optical instruments. This equipment enabled him to detect numerous dark lines in the sun's spectrum (1814), which are now known as Fraunhofer lines. Eight of the lines are still known by the letters he gave them.

Frere, Sir (Henry) Bartle Edward, 1st Baronet (commonly called **Sir Bartle Frere**) (1815–84) statesman. He was Governor of Bombay (1862–67). Mary Somerville remarks the occasion on which he was sent to Zanzibar to negotiate the suppression of the slave trade in 1872. He was subsequently governor of the Cape and first high commissioner of South Africa (1877).

Fry, Elizabeth (née **Gurney**) (1780–1845) Quaker prison reformer, who first visited Newgate in 1813, aiming to improve the conditions under which women prisoners lived. She worked also for improvement of conditions on convict ships to Australia and with vagrants in London and Brighton. Later she travelled in Europe visiting prisons, hospitals and mental asylums.

Gaetani, Don Michelangelo, Duke of Sermoneta. The Gaetani are the oldest of the Roman princely families. There are two lines: the Princes of Teano and Dukes of Sermoneta, and the Princes of Piedmont and Dukes of Laurenzana.

Gaimard, Joseph-Paul (1793–1858) naval surgeon. In the course of his voyages, he collected zoological and botanical specimens. He also published several accounts of his voyages.

Garibaldi, Giuseppe (1807–82). The hero of the Italian Unification Movement was an enormously popular figure in Britain, which he visited in April 1864. It was said that the crowds that gathered to welcome him constituted the largest spontaneous gathering of all time in London. He spent ten years in exile in South America, fighting in various liberation movements there, and returned to Italy in 1848 to fight the Austrians. After the flight of Pope Pius IX, he played a heroic part in the unsuccessful defence of Rome against the French. Exiled again, he returned to assist Cavour (*q.v.*) and Victor Emmanuel II (*q.v.*) in the Unification Movement. In 1860 he set out from Genoa on the celebrated Expedition of a Thousand, which achieved the conquest of Sicily and Naples; after this, he continued to serve Victor Emmanuel II.

Gasparis, Annibale de (1819–92) Neapolitan Professor of Astronomy and senator. He was head of the observatory at Capodimonte.

Gassiot, John Peter (1797–1877) business man and physicist. Gassiot was born in London in 1797 of French parentage He became an FRS in 1840. He worked on electricity in its relations with light, heat and chemical compounds and his work had important practical applications, for example in the development of batteries.

Gay-Lussac, Joseph Louis (1778–1850) French chemist and physicist. In 1808 he discovered the element boron, a non-metallic solid normally found as green-brown powder or crystals. Gay-Lussac's law states that gases combine in a simple ratio by volume. He also discovered Charles's law, on the proportionality of the volume of a gas at constant pressure to its absolute temperature, independently of Charles.

George III (1738–1820). He was, as Mary Somerville suggests, very popular with the middle classes. Indeed, the majority of his subjects approved the decency of his life and his determination, which his enemies called obstinacy.

Gibson, John (1790–1866) neoclassical sculptor. Originally a monumental mason in Liverpool and protégé of the banker William Roscoe, Gibson went to London in 1817 and studied with Flaxman. Flaxman sent him to Rome with an introduction to Canova (*q.v.*), whose pupil he became. He was later taught by Thorwaldsen (*q.v.*). He lived mostly in Italy, with occasional visits to England. He experimented with polychromy: his *Tinted Venus* is in the Walker Gallery, Liverpool. He opposed the use of modern clothing in statues and this limited his commissions but he, nevertheless, made a substantial fortune, which, like Chantrey (*q.v.*), he left to the Royal Academy. He is said to have exclaimed, 'I thank God for every morning I open my eyes in Rome.'

Ginori an old and notable Tuscan family.

Glaisher, James (1809–1903) British astronomer and meteorologist. Glaisher made a series of balloon ascents in the 1860s, reaching the unprecedented height of 9 km. He also used balloons in a weather-station network.

Glover, John (1767–1849) landscape painter. He became President of the Water-Colour Society in 1815. He exhibited at Paris, and sketched in Switzerland and Italy. After his important exhibition of watercolours and oils in Old Bond Street in 1821, he was one of the founders of the Society of British Artists, with whom he exhibited (1824–30). In 1831 he emigrated to Australia, dying in Tasmania in 1849.

Grand Duke, see **Tuscany**.

Grant, Anne (Mrs Grant of Laggan) (1755–1838) didactic writer. Anne Macvicar Grant wrote sometimes penetratingly about small communities in both Albany in America, where she spent her late childhood and early adolescence, and the Scottish Highlands, where her husband was the minister in Laggan. She seldom, however, forgot her didactic intent and always disapproved of more forthright feminists. Her Tory politics, too, were not calculated to please Mary Somerville. Yet her *Letters from the Mountains* (1806), her *Memoirs of an American Lady* (1808) and her *Essays on the Superstitions of the Highlanders of Scotland* (1811) are still of interest to a modern reader.

Granville, Lord. James Fenimore Cooper describes Lord Granville as a 'large well-looking man' who 'wanted the perfect command of movement and manner that so much distinguish his brethren in diplomacy'. He came to the conclusion, however, that Granville was a 'straightforward, good fellow' (*Gleanings in Europe*, 'France' Albany: SUNY Press (1983), p. 86).

Gregory, James (1753–1821) Scottish physician. He was born in Aberdeen but went to Edinburgh and graduated in medicine from Edinburgh University in 1774. He became head of the medical school on the death of Cullen in 1790 and, for the last ten years of his life, was head of the profession in Scotland.

Gregory XVI, Bartolommeo Alberto Cappellari (1765–1846) Pope from 1830 to 1846. Made cardinal in 1825, he was unexpectedly chosen to succeed Pius VIII. Reactionary in every way he even objected to railways and illuminating gas. Spies and prisons characterised his term of office.

Greig, Sir Alexis Samuilovich (1775–1845) Admiral in the Russian service. Son of Sir Samuel Greig (*q.v.*) and brother-in-law of Mary Somerville, he was enrolled at birth as a midshipman in the Russian navy. He distinguished himself in the Russo-Turkish War (1828–29), receiving the rank of full Admiral in its course. He devoted himself after the war to the organisation of the Russian navy: the formation and development of the Black Sea fleet is owed to him.

Greig, Sir Samuel Carlowitz (1735–88) Russian Admiral. Samuel Greig was born in Inverkeithing, son of Charles Greig, shipmaster, and his wife Jean Charters. At 23 he moved from the merchant service to the navy and subsequently served in the Seven Years' War (1756–63). In 1764 he responded to a request from Catherine the Great of Russia for British officers to help build up the Russian navy. Greig was hugely successful in the Russian navy; he seems to have been a most able navigator and administrator. Greig visited Scotland again in October 1777, when he was given the freedom of the City of Edinburgh. He was given an elaborate State funeral when buried at Tallinn. He left two sons: Alexis (*q.v.*) and Samuel, Mary Somerville's first husband.

Greig, Woronzow (1805–65; FRS 1833) Mary Somerville's son by her first marriage. He was a barrister and became Clerk of the Peace for Surrey. He married Agnes Graham in 1837. Agnes's brother James looked after Mary Somerville's affairs following Woronzow's death. Woronzow had some amateur scientific interests. See John H. Appleby, 'Woronzow Greig and His Scientific Interests', *Notes and Records of the Royal Society*, 53:1 (1999), 95–106.

Grisi, Giulia (1811–69) Italian soprano with a brilliant dramatic voice. Bellini wrote Juliet for her in his *Montagues and Capulets* in 1830. Bellini wrote *I Puritani* for Grisi, Lablache (*q.v.*), Rubini (*q.v.*) and Tamburini in 1835 and Donizetti wrote *Don Pasquale* for the same voices in 1839.

Gurney, Hudson (1775–1864; FRS 1818). Gurney was a man of substance who was also an amateur of science and the arts. In 1831 he published a *Memoir of the Life of Thomas Young, MD, FRS* (*q.v.*) (EP, 233). He was also an antiquary and a writer of verse and vice-president of the Society of Antiquaries (1822–46).

Hall, Sir James, 4th Baronet (1761–1832) geologist and chemist. Hall was a friend of Playfair (*q.v.*). He used laboratory experiments to refute Wernerian views. He was president of the Royal Society of Edinburgh and published an *Essay on Gothic Architecture* (1813).

Hallam Henry (1777–1859) historian, educated at Eton and Christ Church, Oxford. His first published work was *A View of the State of Europe during the Middle Ages* (1818): it had been in preparation for ten years. He was best known for his *Constitutional History of England* (1827) which discusses the relationship between the royal prerogative and the British principles of law.

Hamilton, Elizabeth (1756–1816) novelist and didactic writer. Although born in Belfast, Elizabeth Hamilton was brought up in Scotland by an aunt and learned early to identify herself closely with Scotland and Scottish affairs and manners. Throughout her writing life she showed an unusual interest in Scots, which she used in her poems and, although only for lower-class characters, in her last satirical and didactic novel, *The Cottagers of Glenburnie*

(1808). Among her other novels, *Memoirs of Modern Philosophers* (1800) attacks feminist pretensions in blue-stocking Bridgetina Botherim, who is supposed to be based on the feminist, Mary Hays. Other works include the rather dully humourless *Letters on Education*. Eliza Hamilton maintained a friendship with Mary Somerville's close friend Joanna Baillie (*q.v.*).

Hamilton, Sir William Rowan (1805–65) Irish mathematician. Hamilton was a child prodigy and was appointed Professor of Astronomy at Trinity College, Dublin. His most important work was on quaternions but he also contributed to the mathematics of light rays and helped to establish the wave theory of light.

Hardy, Thomas (1752–1832) bootmaker and radical politician. In 1792 Hardy founded the London Corresponding Society, to promote parliamentary reform. He was tried, along with Horne Tooke (*q.v.*) and John Thelwall (*q.v.*), in the Treason Trials of 1794.

Haüy, René-Just, Abbé (1743–1822) French mineralogist, one of the founders of the science of crystallography. He originally studied theology but later, in 1802, became Professor of Mineralogy at the Museum of Natural History in Paris; in 1809 he took up a similar post at the Sorbonne. He is also known for studies of pyro-electricity and piezo-electricity in crystals.

Herbert, Auberon Edward William Molyneux (1838–1906) political philosopher and politician, Herbert was altogether a remarkable man. He was present in America during the Civil War and he was at Sedan during the Franco-Prussian War (1870–71). He was Liberal MP for Nottingham (1872–74), during which period he declared himself a republican, causing great consternation. His

Wild Birds' Protection Act was passed in 1872. Always a radical, he spoke at a mass meeting in Leamington in 1872, when Warwickshire's Agricultural Labourers' Union was formed. In later life he became an agnostic and a vegetarian, at which point he gave up the sports he had previously enjoyed.

Herschel, Caroline Lucretia (1750–1848) astronomer, sister of Sir William Herschel and aunt of Sir John Herschel. In 1788 the Royal Astronomical Society published her revision of the *Index to Flamsteed's Observations of the Fixed Stars*, which included a catalogue of 561 previously omitted stars.

Herschel, Sir John (1792–1871; FRS 1813) astronomer, son of Sir William Herschel and nephew of Caroline Herschel. Sir John was a close correspondent and friend of Mary Somerville throughout his life. Much of their correspondence is in the library of the Royal Society. Sir John used his father's telescope to continue the mapping of binary stars and nebulae. The observatory in Cape Town was set up in 1834. He also used photography for astronomical purposes and his advances in this field include the first use of sodium thiosulphate (hypo) as a fixer and the development of sensitised photographic paper.

Herschel, Sir William (1738–1822; FRS 1871) British astronomer, who worked with his sister Caroline (*q.v.*). They became expert in grinding lenses, which enabled them to build the largest telescopes then known. Herschel discovered the planet Uranus in 1781, binary stars, two new satellites of Saturn and, in 1800, infra-red rays from the sun. He was a Copley medallist.

Hobhouse, Sir John Cam, Baron Broughton de Gyfford (1786–1869) politician and friend of Byron. He wrote the notes to the Fourth Canto of *Childe Harold*, which Byron dedicated to him. He was Byron's executor and advised the destruction of his memoirs (1824).

Holland, Sir Henry, 1st Baronet (1788–1873; FRS 1816) physician. Holland graduated from Edinburgh in 1811, having visited Iceland the year before. He became medical attendant to Caroline, Princess of Wales (1814) and gave evidence in her favour (1820). He later became physician-in-ordinary to Prince Albert in 1840 and Queen Victoria in 1852.

Home, John (1722–1808) minister of Athelstaneford, was later secretary to Lord Bute and tutor to the Prince of Wales. His first tragedy, *Agis*, was rejected by Garrick but *Douglas* was successfully performed in Edinburgh in 1756 and at Covent Garden in 1757. In spite of the scandal of the involvement of a minister in the theatre, *Douglas* was frequently revived.

Hope, James (later **Hope Scott**) (*d*.1873). He married Scott's granddaughter, Charlotte. Only their first child, Mary Monica, survived. In 1874 she married the Honourable Joseph Constable Maxwell who also assumed the name Scott. Their eldest son, Sir Walter Maxwell Scott died 3 April 1954.

Hosmer, Harriet Goodhue (1830–1908) American sculptor. She was a friend of Fanny Kemble (*q.v.*) from her schooldays. In 1852 she went to Rome to study with John Gibson. One of her most famous productions was her *Puck*, which she thought would be commercial and it was indeed widely reproduced. She began to receive public commissions throughout Europe. When her *Zenobia* was purchased for Dublin, she sued the *Art Journal* and *Queen* for their suggestions that it had been the work of Gibson: they retracted. Her Roman circle included the Brownings (*q.v.*). She died in England of influenza. On her death it was remarked, 'She has not creative power, but has acquired no small degree of executive skill and force', a remark oddly like Mary Somerville's estimate of her own abilities (p. 145).

Huggins, Sir William (1824–1910) British astronomer, knighted for his services to science in 1897. It was his application of spectroscopy to astronomy that enabled him to discover that the stars consist of the same elements as those found on Earth. He also discovered the red shift in the lines of a star's spectrum, which was used in 1929 by Edward Hubble as the basis of the theory that the universe is expanding.

Humboldt, Alexander von (1769–1859) scientist and explorer. He travelled in Central and South America and in central Asia, collecting material of great importance for life sciences. In his monumental work *Kosmos* (five vols) (1845–62), he laid out his view of the entire universe. Active until the end, he died while still writing the fifth volume of *Kosmos*.

Hume, David (1711–76) philosopher and historian born in Edinburgh. In 1739 he published his *Treatise of Human Nature* and in 1748 his *Enquiry Concerning Human Understanding*. His *History of England* (1754–62) was written while he was librarian of the Advocates' Library in Edinburgh and was enormously influential, a bestseller of its time.

Irving, Washington (1783–1859) American writer. Born in New York, the son of an Englishman, he wrote a humorous history of New York (1809). He was attached to the American legation in Spain (1826), secretary of legation in London (1829) and minister in Spain (1842).

He wrote in a number of different genres and his greatest work is probably his *Life of George Washington* (1855–59). But he is now chiefly remembered for his tales in *The Sketch-Book*, which include 'Rip van Winkle' and 'The Legend of Sleepy Hollow'. He was the first American writer to be truly internationally celebrated.

Ivory, Sir James (1765–1842; FRS 1815) mathematician, who pursued French analytical methods and worked on refraction. He was Professor of Mathematics at the Royal Military College at Marlow (1805–19); he was awarded two gold medals, the Copley (1814) and the Royal (1826). He also received a pension and a knighthood. But his correspondence with Mary Somerville reveals that he was distressed by the persistent denigration of his work as impractical (EP, pp.113–14).

Jameson, Robert (1774–1854; FRS 1826) mineralogist and follower of Werner (*q.v.*). He studied at Edinburgh University and became Professor of Natural History there (1804–05). In 1813, William Somerville joined Jameson's Wernerian Society, founded in 1808. With Brewster (*q.v.*), Jameson established the *Edinburgh Philosophical Journal* (1819). He published *Mineralogy of the Scottish Isles* in 1800 (EP, 13–14, 16).

Jeffrey, Francis, Lord (1773–1850). He was educated at Edinburgh and Glasgow Universities and became a judge and an MP. His political sympathies were Whig and with Sydney Smith and Henry Brougham he founded the *Edinburgh Review* in 1802, being editor until 1829. As a critic, Jeffrey approved of Byron, Scott and Keats but is known as the scourge of Wordsworth and the Lake Poets – his review of Wordsworth's 'The Excursion' famously begins 'This will never do.' He was also severe, although less so, on Joanna Baillie.

Johnston, (Alexander) Keith (1804–71) geographer. Johnston was educated in Edinburgh and gained the Victoria medal of the Royal Geographical Society. His *Dictionary of Geography* was published in 1850. He also travelled in Palestine.

Kater, Captain Henry and **Mrs (Mary Frances Reeves)** (1777–1835; FRS 1814). Kater was a man of science who was originally an army officer. Kater prepared standard measures for the Russian government and made mainly pendulum and telescopic experiments. He was Copley medallist in 1817. Mrs Kater assisted her husband with his calculations. Wollaston (*q.v.*) and Thomas Young (*q.v.*) befriended Kater when he moved to London and made sure that he took an active part in the management of the Royal Society (EP, 35, 41).

Kean, Edmund (c.1787–1833) actor. Kean made his name as Shylock in the 1814 *Merchant of Venice*; other famous Shakespearean roles were Richard III, Macbeth, and Iago in *Othello*, all of which suited his large passionate style. He also played Barabas in Marlowe's *Jew of Malta*, as well as numerous other tragic roles, including the title role in Joanna Baillie's *De Monfort*.

Kemble, Charles (1775–1854) actor, younger brother of Sarah Siddons (*q.v.*) and John Kemble (*q.v.*). He was a leading actor for twenty-five years, most successful in comedy and romance. His main success in tragedy was as Romeo.

Kemble, Frances Ann (Fanny) (1809–93) actress and memoirist. Fanny Kemble was the daughter of the actor Charles Kemble (1775–1854), who managed Covent Garden Theatre from 1822. Her successful début at Covent Garden in 1829 was made to save her father from bankruptcy She toured several times in the USA, where she married Pierce Mease Butler, a Philadelphia plantation owner. The marriage was difficult in any case but became impossible when Fanny Kemble became fully aware of her husband's involvement in slavery and in some of its worst aspects. Her *Journal of a Residence on a Georgian Plantation* appeared in 1863. She obtained a divorce in 1849 and in 1853 paid a second visit to Italy. She published a volume of *Poems* (1844), and *Records of Later Life* in 1822. In Italy she was intimate with Mary Somerville and her daughters.

Kemble, John Philip (1757–1823) actor, elder brother of Charles Kemble and Mrs Siddons. He played a number of Shakespearean roles – Romeo, Iago, Prospero, etc. – with huge success. John Kemble played De Monfort and Mrs Siddons played his sister, Jane de Monfort in the first performance of Joanna Baillie's *De Monfort* at Drury Lane on 29 April 1800. It had a total of eight performances in this run.

Kent, Victoria of Saxe-Coburg-Gotha, Duchess of Kent (1786–1861) mother of Queen Victoria who, in 1837, succeeded to her uncle, William IV, whose two legitimate daughters died in infancy.

Kirchhoff, Gustav Robert (1824–87) German physicist, appointed professor at Heidelberg University, where he worked with Bunsen (*q.v.*) to invent the technique of spectroscopy. Working alone, investigating the solar spectrum, he discovered several elements in the sun. He also worked on thermal radiation and on networks of electrical wires, laying down Kirchoff's laws.

Kosloffsky (Koslofski), Petr Borisovich, Prince (1783–1840). Wrote an elementary book on conic sections for 'the little Imperial Majesty of Russia', later Tsar Alexander II. Koslofski's private life was somewhat scandalous but Mary Somerville, here faithful to her refusal of private lives, does not mention it (EP, 113). He also published *Lettres au Duc de Broglie sur les prisonniers de Vincennes*, 1830.

Lablache, Luigi (1794–1858) Italian bass of French and Irish descent. He sang all over Europe and when in England (1836–37), acted as singing master to Princess Victoria. Schubert dedicated his three Italian songs to him.

Lacroix, Sylvestre François (1765–1843) French mathematician. Lacroix was, above all, a great teacher, and his many *Traités élémentaires* formed generations of mathematicians. Notable are his two volumes of 1797–98, *Traité du calcul différential et du calcul intégral*.

Lafayette, General Marie Joseph Gilbert Motier, Marquis de (1757–1834) French general and politician. His early military career was principally spent fighting against the British during the American War of Independence. He was prominent in the early stages of the French Revolution: in 1789 as representative of the States General he presented the Declaration of the Rights of Man and became commander of the new National Guard after the storming of the Bastille. By 1792, however, he was threatened by the rising power of Robespierre and gave himself up to Austria. Lafayette never deserted the liberal cause and, in 1830, he was prominent again in the July revolution which overthrew Charles X (*q.v.*).

Lagrange, Joseph Louis, Comte de (1736–1813) mathematician and astronomer. Although of French parentage, Lagrange was born in Italy. His *Mécanique analytique* was published in 1788: it develops mechanics algebraically and solves problems by the application of general equations. He worked with Laplace on planetary perturbations. He also headed the commission that produced the metric system of units in 1795.

Lansdowne, Sir Henry Petty-Fitzmaurice, 3rd Marquis of Lansdowne (1780–1863) politician. He supported the abolition of the slave trade and other liberal measures. A moderate Whig, he held various offices in the course of his political life.

Laplace, Pierre Simon, Marquis de (1749–1827) French mathematician and astronomer. His first paper to appear in print was on the integral calculus. He worked with Lagrange (*q.v.*) on the small gravitational forces that planets exert on each other. The effects of this were called perturbations. The pair deduced that perturbations cause small oscillations in the planets' motions but no permanent movement and in this way they demonstrated the stability of the solar system. Laplace published the results, without due recognition of Lagrange, as the five-volume *Mécanique céleste* (1799–1825), translated by Mary Somerville as *Mechanism of the Heavens* and published in 1831. Laplace is credited with the witticism that only two women ever understood his work: Mary Greig and Mary Somerville. This later was elaborated to three by the addition of Mary Fairfax.

Larrey, Dominique-Jean, Baron (1766–1842) French military surgeon in the service of Napoleon. Larrey introduced field hospitals, ambulance services and first-aid practices to the battlefield. After the fall of Napoleon his medical reputation saved him from disgrace. In 1812, he gave the first description of trench foot. The first draft of the autobiography has a comment that he 'had the reputation of having poisoned at his master's command the sick and wounded soldiers before the flight from St Jean d'Acre' [1D, 89]. His record seems to speak against this possibility and it was no doubt one of the wise omissions from the printed text.

Lavoisier, Antoine Laurent (1743–94) French chemist. Born into an aristocratic family, he also secured a fortune by investments in a private company that collected government taxes. He used his wealth to build a laboratory, where he discovered (1778) that air is a mixture of two gases and he called the gases oxygen and nitrogen. He went on to discover the role of oxygen in combustion and the law of conservation of mass. He devised the modern method of naming compounds. During the French Revolution, Lavoisier was tried and condemned to the guillotine for his role in the tax-collecting company.

Leslie, Sir John (1766–1832) mathematician and natural philosopher. He was educated at St Andrews and Edinburgh Universities, becoming Professor of Mathematics at Edinburgh in 1805, and of Natural Philosophy in 1819. He was knighted in 1832.

Leverrier, Urbain Jean Joseph (1811–77) French astronomer. Independently of John Couch Adams (*q.v.*), he predicted the existence of Neptune after investigating anomalies in the orbit of Uranus. The planet was first observed by the German astronomer Johann Galle in 1846, using Leverrier's information.

Lindsay, Lady Charlotte (*d.*1849) daughter of the 2nd Earl of Guildford and widow of Lieutenant-Colonel, the

Honorable John Lindsay. Lady Charlotte was a lady-in-waiting to Queen Caroline (see 'Biographical Index', *Maria Edgeworth, Letters from England*, ed. Colvin, 1971).

Lister, Lady Theresa (afterwards **Lewis**) (1803–65) editor of Mary Berry's memoirs as *Extracts of the Journals and Correspondence of Miss Berry* (1865). Her other productions include *The Semi-Detached House*, by the Hon. Emily Eden, edited by Lady Theresa Lewis, and the dramatisation of the stories 'Beauty and the Beast' and 'Cinderella' for juvenile performers in 1844.

Liston, John (1776?–1846) actor. He played comic parts at the Haymarket Theatre (1805), Covent Garden (1808–22), and Drury Lane (1823). He retired in 1837. His parts include Polonius, Sir Andrew Aguecheek and Bottom.

Livingstone, David (1813–73) Scottish missionary and explorer in Africa. Livingstone was self-educated and embarked for the Cape of Good Hope in 1840. He found Lake Ngami in 1849 and the Zambesi in 1851, publishing *Missionary Travels in Africa* in 1857 and *The Zambesi and Its Tributaries* in 1865. On an expedition to find the source of the Nile he was believed to have been lost. Sir Henry Morton Stanley (1841–1904) was sent by Gordon Bennett, owner of the *New York Herald*, to find David Livingstone. He found him at Ujiji and published an account of his travels in *How I Found Livingstone*. Livingstone died in Ilala and was buried in Westminster Abbey. Livingstone's horror of the slave trade was such that he refused to travel under the protection of the Arab traders.

Lockhart, John Gibson (1794–1854). *The Quarterly Review*, founded in 1809 as a Tory rival to *The Edinburgh Review*, was promoted by Scott and his son-in-law, John

Gibson Lockhart. Lockhart was editor from 1825 to 1853. He was also celebrated as a novelist and critic but is perhaps best remembered for his controversial biography (1837–38) of his father-in-law, Scott.

Longfellow, Henry Wadsworth (1807–82) American poet. He was born in Maine and, in 1836, became Professor of Modern Languages at Harvard. He travelled widely in Europe before taking up his professorship. He was an enormously popular poet with his narrative poems and is still well known as the author of 'The Song of Hiawatha' (1855).

Louis, Joseph-Dominique, Baron (1755–1837) French statesman. He fled to England on the arrest of the fleeing Louis XVI at Varennes. At the Restoration he returned to various financial positions under succeeding régimes. He is supposed to have said, 'Give me good politics and I will give you good finances' (*Faites-moi de la bonne politique et je vous ferai de bonnes finances*).

Louis I, King of Bavaria (1786–1868). Louis had strong artistic tendencies: he was a patron of art and beautified his capital, Munich. His fascination for the Spanish dancer, Lola Montez, and political troubles in the country led him to abdicate in 1848 in favour of his son.

Lovelace, Ada Augusta Byron King, Lady Lovelace (1815–52) the daughter of Byron and his wife Annabella Milbanke. Annabella left Byron when Ada was only a month old. Her mother, who had herself taken lessons in mathematics, encouraged Ada Byron's mathematical bent. Lady Byron became acquainted with the Somervilles in the early 1830s and Ada became friendly with the Somerville daughters. The families remained friendly and Mary Somerville helped to direct Ada's studies.

Ada's husband William Lovelace had been at Cambridge with Woronzow Greig and this strengthened the friendship between the families. After the Somervilles left Britain, Ada Lovelace was advised by De Morgan (*q.v.*) and Charles Babbage (*q.v.*). De Morgan said that Ada had more mathematical genius than Mary Somerville but unfortunately she lacked her application (EP, 150). She helped Babbage with his calculating machine. She translated a paper by General Menabrea (*q.v.*). She died in great pain from uterine cancer with disturbing, but never quite proved, stories of gambling debts hanging over her.

Lowry, Joseph Wilson (1762–1824) engraver, whose wife instructed Mary Somerville in mineralogy. He studied in the Royal Academy schools. He was best known as an engraver of architecture and mechanism and devised special instruments for the work. He was first to use diamond points for ruling in steel.

Lubbock, Sir John William (1803–65; FRS 1829) mathematician, who was at Trinity with Woronzow Greig. Treasurer of the Royal Society from 1830–35 and 1838–45. He and Mary Somerville shared an involvement with Laplace. While Mary Somerville was engaged in *The Mechanism of the Heavens* Lubbock had begun to apply Laplace's probability theory to annuities, lunar theory and study of the tides. Mary Somerville and Lubbock read each other's work (EP, 65, 108–9).

Lyell, Sir Charles (1797–1875) traveller and geologist. His works include *The Principles of Geology* (1830–3), *The Elements of Geology* (1838) and, following the publication of Darwin's *Origin of Species*, *The Antiquity of Man* (1863). Lyell was Professor of Geology at King's College, London (1831–33), and President of the Geological

Society (1835–36 and 1849–50). He lectured in the US in 1841 and 1852. Lyell is mainly responsible for the view that the Earth was formed by slow continual processes and is much older than had been believed. He married Miss Mary Horner, daughter of Leonard Horner, who was a member of the Geological Society. Mary Horner Lyell was a devoted and capable wife. She travelled with her husband and assisted him in his researches, particularly by acting as his scribe when his sight became very bad. They were both also lovers of literature and had many literary friendships.

Macaulay, Thomas Babbington, 1st Baron (1800–59) historian, politician, man of letters. Macaulay is best known for his *History of England* in five volumes (1849–61), the last volume published posthumously, edited by his sister Lady Trevelyan. He was liberal MP for Calne in 1830 and for Leeds in 1831, and a member of the Supreme Council of India (1834–38).

Macdonald, Jacques-Etienne-Joseph-Alexandre, Duc de Tarante (1765–1840) Marshall of France (1765–1840). Originally of a Scottish family, he came to France with the Stuarts. He was a great soldier and tried with some success to maintain his independence of political régimes.

Macdonald, Lawrence (1799–1878) Scottish sculptor. He was born in Perthshire and moved to Edinburgh to work as an ornamental sculptor. In 1822 he went to Rome, where, the following year, he was one of the founders of the British Academy of the Arts in Rome. He returned to work in Edinburgh from 1827, returning to Rome in 1832. He was a member of the Scottish Academy and his busts include Scott, Fanny Kemble (*q.v.*) and J. G. Lockhart (*q.v.*). His studio was said to be filled with the 'peerage done into marble, a plaster gallery of rank and fashion'.

Mackintosh, Sir James (1765–1832; FRS 1813) (EP, 45) philosopher and statesman. Educated in Aberdeen and studied medicine in Edinburgh. He went to London in 1788. He published *Vindicae gallicae* in 1791, in answer to Burke's *Reflections on the Revolution in France* (1790). He was judge in the Vice-Admiralty Court in Bombay from 1806–11 and Commissioner of the Board of Control in 1830.

Maclane, Miss Clephane (possibly **Anna Jane Maclean Clephane**) second daughter of Mrs Maclean Clephane of Torloisk. Scott assisted the family in business matters: *The Journal of Sir Walter Scott*, ed. W. E. K. Anderson (Edinburgh: Canongate, 1998), p. 99.

Macpherson, Samuel Charters (1806–60) political agent in India. Macpherson was educated at Edinburgh University and Trinity College, Cambridge. In India he was the governor-general's agent for the suppression of human sacrifice and female infanticide among the Khonds in Orissa. Orissa is still a most undeveloped part of the country. He died in India.

Macready, William Charles (1793–1873) actor-manager, distinguished as a tragedian and famous for his Lear, Hamlet and Macbeth. He tried to be more faithful to Shakespeare's text than was customary at the time. Edmund Kean was his principal rival.

Majendie or **Magendie, François** (1783–1855) French physiologist, who worked on the nervous system. He experimented on nutritional requirements and the effects of drugs on the body. It may be seen from these concerns, and from the fact that he was a vivisectionist and experimenter on animals, why Mary Somerville disliked and disapproved of him.

Malibran, Mme Maria Felicita Garcia (1808–36) celebrated soprano, born in Paris. She sang throughout Europe, but principally in Paris and London. The poet Alfred de Musset wrote 'Stances à la Malibran' in tribute to her.

Malthus, Thomas Robert (1766–1834). He became curate of Albury in Surrey after a brilliant career at Cambridge. In 1798 he published *An Essay on the Principle of Population*, partly as a reply to Godwin's radical *Political Justice* of 1793, in which he argued that since population would soon increase beyond the possibility of subsistence, poverty, disease, starvation and disaster were necessary checks. In 1803, recognising what was offensive in such a position, he argued that the regulation of human greed and sexuality might provide the necessary checks. Liberal thinkers, like Godwin, Cobbett and Hazlitt, attacked Malthus's work but it remained influential throughout the 19th century.

Marcello, Benedetto (1686–1739) Italian composer of operas, oratorios, etc.

Marcet, Alexander John Gaspard (1770–1822; FRS 1815) physician and chemist. A Swiss, he fled from Geneva in 1794 to Edinburgh, where he studied medicine, graduating in 1799. He married Jane Haldimand, became a naturalised British citizen and, by 1803, was physician and chemical lecturer at Guy's Hospital. He was an able experimentalist, one of the founders of the Medical and Chirurgical Society (1805), and became a

Fellow of the Royal Society in 1815. He and Wollaston (*q.v.*) were good friends (EP, 12).

Marcet, Jane Haldimand (1769–1858) popularising science writer. Jane Haldimand was the daughter of a Swiss banker and his English wife. After her marriage to Alexander Marcet (*q.v.*) in 1799, her husband persuaded her to try her hand at a simple book on chemistry written in a way that would make it accessible to the young women who attended Sir Humphry Davy's lectures at the Royal Institution. Her textbook, *Conversations on Chemistry*, published anonymously in 1806, gained a wider readership than this and was the book that awakened Michael Faraday's (*q.v.*) interest in the subject. Jane Marcet followed this success with a series of 'Conversations' on various subjects. She did not pretend to professional scientific knowledge but was well regarded in intellectual circles because she was an intelligent woman and a good hostess. She became a good friend of Mary Somerville (EP, 12–13).

Marmont, (Auguste-Frédéric-Louis-) Viesse de, Duc de Raguse (1774–1852) Marshal of France. He wrote self-aggrandising memoirs, described as a monument to pride.

Mars, Mademoiselle (Anne-Françoise-Hippolyte) (1779–1847) French actress, who appeared from childhood, at her best in Molière's comedies. Her last appearance in 1841 was as Elmire in Molière's *Tartuffe*.

Martineau, Harriet (1802–76) novelist, essayist and educationalist. She began to go deaf in her teens and so, despite a good Unitarian education, she could not teach. When she was still in her early 20s, her father died, and her fiancé, a Unitarian minister, went mad. She wrote in order to look after the rest of her family and came to make more by her pen than any previous woman writer. When she toured America she was outspoken against slavery and for women's rights.

Maskelyne, Nevil (1732–1811; FRS 1758) astronomer. He was educated at Trinity College, Cambridge. In 1761 he was sent by the Royal Society to observe the transit of Venus at St Helena; although he was unsuccessful in this, he made other useful observations. He became Astronomer Royal in 1765 and was Copley medallist in 1775.

Massa, Nicolas-François-Sylvestre Régnier, Comte de Gronan (afterwards **duc de Massa**) (1783–1851) minor statesman. He attached himself to the Bourbons in 1815 but never played a major role.

Maury, Matthew Fontaine (1806–73) US naval captain. For his pioneering work in oceanography, he was given the appellation 'the Pathfinder of the Seas'.

Mazzini, Giuseppe (1805–72) leader of the Risorgimento, the movement for Italian Unification. For much of his life, he lived in exile in England, France and Switzerland. He planned a rising in Piedmont and an invasion of Savoy in the 1830s but both were unsuccessful. Mazzini returned to Italy for the 1848 revolutions in Piedmont, Milan, Tuscany and Rome. Mazzini was a republican and so, although Italy became a unified kingdom in 1861, his ideal republic never was achieved.

Melbourne, William Lamb, 2nd Viscount (1779–1848) Whig Prime Minister in 1834 and 1835–41. He was an influence on the young Queen Victoria. His private life had been somewhat scandalous: in 1805 he had married Lady Caroline Ponsonby, who had an affair with Byron

(1812–13). After he and his disturbed wife formally separated, he was named in two divorce suits, one of which
also involved the Sheridan sister (*q.v.*) Caroline Norton.

Menabrea, Luigi Federico, Conte (1809–96) general,
politician and scientist. Devoted throughout his life to
physics and mathematics, he was Professor of Mechanics
at the military academy, Turin, and ambassador in
London (1876–82) and Paris (1882–92).

Mezzofanti, Giuseppe Caspar (1774–1849). Italian cardinal and linguist. He was ordained in 1774 and in the
same year became Professor of Hebrew and Oriental
Languages at the University of Bologna. He had the
peculiar talent of speaking 50 to 60 languages from
the most widely separated families but was not otherwise
an intellectual.

Mill, John Stuart (1806–73) a great thinker in a number of
different areas. Following in the tradition of Adam Smith
and Malthus (*q.v.*), he published *Principles of Political
Economy* (1848). Working within the Lockean empirical
tradition, Mill published *Utilitarianism*, for which he is
popularly famous, in 1859. Mill tried to combine a con-
cern for the individual with the principles of early soci-
alism. His importance for Mary Somerville was as an
advocate of women's rights. His *The Subjection of Women*
(1869) famously stated that if women lived in another
country from men they would have a 'literature of their
own'. He too wrote an *Autobiography*, which appeared in
1873, the same year as Mary Somerville's *Recollections*.

Miller, Hugh (1802–56) a stonemason to trade. Hugh
Miller was one of the great 19th-century geologists. He
published *The Old Red Sandstone* (1847), *Footprints of the
Creator* (1847), and an autobiography, *My Schools and*

Schoolmasters (1854). Miller committed suicide, some believe because he could not reconcile his religious beliefs with his geological knowledge, others simply cite depression brought on by overwork. *The Testimony of the Rocks* was published in 1857.

Milman, Henry Hart (1791–1868). He was educated at Eton and Oxford. He took orders but subsequently became Professor of Poetry at Oxford (1821–31) and then Dean of St Paul's in 1849. He wrote plays, one of which, *Fazio*, was reasonably successful on the stage, but his enduring work is his historical writing, including *The History of the Jews* (1830) and *The History of Latin Christianity* (1854–55).

Minghetti, Marco (1818–86) Italian statesman. Minghetti joined the Piedmont-Sardinian army in 1848 to fight the Austrians. In 1859 Cavour appointed him secretary-general of the Piedmontese foreign office. He finally became Prime Minister of a united Italy in 1863 and again in 1873, when his period of office was characterised by balanced budgets but somewhat arbitrary treatment of the Opposition.

Miniscalchi, Count Erizzo (1810–1875) geographer and philologist.

Minto, Earl of see Elliot.

Mitford, Mary Russell (1787–1855). *Our Village* sketches of rural life, was begun in *The Lady's Magazine* (1819) and published separately in 1824–32. She also published a novel, plays and, in 1852, *Recollections of a Literary Life*.

Mocenigi one of the most renowned patrician families of the Venetian Republic, producing military leaders, churchmen, scholars, diplomats and statesmen, including seven doges.

Montalembert, Charles-(Forbes-René), Comte de (1810–70) orator, politician and historian. Born in London during the exile of his father, he became a leader in the struggle against absolutism in Church and State in France. He began his career with the journal *L'Avenir*, helped found a Roman Catholic school in 1831, opposing the state monopoly. The school was closed by the police but, at the same time, his insistence that the Catholic Church should embrace civil and religious liberty brought him into conflict with Rome. His motto was 'a free Church in a free State'.

Moore, Thomas (1779–1852) Irish poet born in Dublin. Moore was a grocer's son. He was educated at Trinity College, Dublin and entered at the Middle Temple. Moore was appointed Admiralty registrar in Bermuda in 1803; he left a deputy in charge and returned to London. When his deputy decamped with the official funds, Moore was declared bankrupt and lived in Europe until his debts were discharged in 1822. He became, in a sense, the national poet of Ireland, or at least its national lyricist. His range of writing was considerable: poetry, fiction, biography, but he still probably remains most famous as the burner of his friend Byron's *Memoirs*. It is likely that Moore felt that he had no choice, given the representations of Lady Byron (*q.v.*) and the advice of Hobhouse (*q.v.*).

More, Hannah (1745–1833) didactic writer. More was educated at her sisters' boarding school in Bristol where she learned Italian, Spanish and Latin. She went to London in 1774 and became a member of various intellectual circles, joining Elizabeth Montagu as one of the 'Blue Stocking' circle. Her didactic writing covered several genres, from plays to tracts, and she was a brilliant letter writer.

Murchison, Sir Roderick Impey, 1st Baronet (1792–1871; FRS 1826). Originally an army officer, Murchison retired from the army to pass his time in travel and study. He ultimately became a celebrated geologist, notably attempting to unravel the complicated structure of the Scottish Highlands.

Murray, John (1778–1843) publisher, the second John Murray of the celebrated house. He started the *Quarterly Review* in 1809. He published Byron and Jane Austen among many others. He was succeeded by his son John Murray (1808–92), who published the works of Milman (*q.v.*) and Darwin (*q.v.*), as well as Mary Somerville's later works.

Naldi, Giuseppe (1770–1820) Italian bass singer, who made his début in Milan in 1789 and subsequently played in a number of Italian cities. His first appearance in London was in 1806 and he went on to play twelve seasons there: he was Figaro in the first performance of *The Barber of Seville* in 1818. The tragic accident which killed him actually occurred at the house of his friend, the tenor Manuel Garcia.

Napoleon III (1808–73) nephew of Napoleon. Louis Napoleon was Emperor of the French from 1852–73. After the defeat of the Second Empire in the Franco-Prussian War (1870–71), he and his wife, the Empress Eugénie, went into exile in England.

Nasmyth, Alexander (1758–1840) painter of portraits and landscapes. Born in Edinburgh, the son of an architect, Nasmyth studied in London under Allan Ramsay, and also worked in Italy. On returning to Edinburgh he turned to portrait painting, producing perhaps the most famous image of Burns, with whom he became friendly. He was always interested in science and designed the bow-and-string bridge used at Charing Cross and Birmingham Stations.

Nélaton, Auguste (1807–73) surgeon, celebrated for his skill. He attended Garibaldi (*q.v.*) after he was wounded at Aspromonte.

Newton, Sir Isaac (1642–1727) the great philosopher and mathematician. The first book of his *Philosophiae Naturalis Principia Mathematica*, which contained his laws of motion and expounded his idea of universal gravitation, was exhibited at the Royal Society in 1686 and the whole published in 1687. Newton was knighted in 1705. He became, like Mary Somerville's friend, Sir John Herschel, Master of the Mint in 1699. He is buried in Westminster Abbey.

Nightingale, Florence (1820–1910) celebrated hospital reformer, best known as 'The Lady with the Lamp', the name given to her by her patients in the hospital in Scutari during the Crimean War (1853–56). After the war, she agitated for and got improved living conditions in the army. She organised a subscription, the Nightingale Fund, with which she established the Nightingale School for Nurses at St Thomas's Hospital, London in 1860. In 1907 she was the first woman to be awarded the OM (Order of Merit).

Normanby, Sir Constantine Henry Phipps, 1st Marquis of Normanby and 2nd Earl of Mulgrave (1797–

1863) politician and diplomat. He became MP for Scarborough in 1818 and supported parliamentary reform. He was Governor of Jamaica in 1832–34 and Lord Lieutenant of Ireland in 1835, where he annoyed Protestants by his friendship with Catholic leaders, such as O'Connell. Again, as ambassador in Paris (1846–53) and minister in Florence (1854–58), he tended to involve himself too much in the politics of the foreign states.

Northesk, William Carnegie, 7th Earl of Northesk (1771–1806) Admiral. He was imprisoned by the Nore mutineers (see p. 400 n. 28), fought at Trafalgar (1805) and was Commander-in-Chief at Plymouth (1827–30).

Novello, Clara Anastasia noted lyric singer. In 1843 she married Giovan Battista Gigliucci (1815–93), a statesman and supporter of Cavour.

O'Neill, Miss, Lady Becher a great tragic actress. She was lost to the stage when in 1829 she married William Wrixon Becher, MP for Mallow in 1819. Becher was created Baronet in 1831.

Opie, Amelia (1769–1853) novelist and poet, wife of John Opie, the painter. Her novel *Adeline Mowbray* (1804) was suggested by the story of Mary Wollstonecraft. She became a Quaker under the influence of Hudson Gurney (*q.v.*) and family. She was a friend of Sydney Smith (*q.v.*) and Madame de Staël (*q.v.*).

Oswald, Elizabeth (1790–1860) second wife of Thomas Bruce, Lord Elgin (*q.v.*). Mary Somerville is right that she was a classical scholar and that she would apparently have liked to study mathematics, but wrong about her age. She was ten years younger than Mary Somerville and may have acquired her desire to learn mathematics from the older girl.

Panceri, Paolo (1833–77) doctor and zoologist. He was Professor of Comparative Anatomy at Naples from 1866.

Pantaleone, Diomede (1810–85) doctor and politician. An intimate of Cavour, Pantaleone treated a number of English and American tourists.

Parry, Sir William Edward (1790–1855) navigator and explorer. He made three unsuccessful journeys in search of the Northwest Passage, the sea route along the coast of America which gives access from the Atlantic to the Pacific Ocean. In 1827 he tried to reach the North Pole by sledge from Spitsbergen.

Pasta, Giudetta (Maria Constanza) (née **Negri**) (1797–1865) soprano with remarkable range and expressiveness. She made her début in 1815, sang Desdemona in Rossini's *Otello* in Paris in 1821 and various Rossini roles in London in 1821. In 1850 she retired to a villa on Lake Como to teach.

Peacock, George, Professor, Dean of Ely (1791–1858; FRS 1818) mathematician and Dean of Ely (1839–58). Peacock was a Fellow of Trinity College, Cambridge (1814). With Whewell (*q.v.*) he prescribed Mary Somerville's *Mechanism of the Heavens* for their advanced mathematics students at Cambridge (EP). Together with Herschel (*q.v.*) and Babbage (*q.v.*) he introduced modern analytical methods and differential notation into the mathematical course at Cambridge. In Ely he persuaded the chapter to undertake the complete restoration of the cathedral under Sir Gilbert Scott, the architect of St Pancras Station and Glasgow University.

Peel, Sir Robert (1788–1850) Conservative Prime Minister (1834–35) and (1841–61). Peel is remembered as a moderniser and reformer. The question of Civil List pensions for scientists became something of a political matter with Tories apparently anxious to be as friendly to science and literature as the Whigs had been. A full account is given in EP, chapter 8, pp.151–162.

Peirce, Benjamin (1809–80) US mathematician and astronomer. He was born in Salem, Mass., where he attended Salem Private Grammar School with Henry Ingersoll Bowditch, son of Nathaniel Bowditch (*q.v.*). From there he proceeded to Harvard, becoming Professor of Mathematics and Natural Philosophy there (1833–42). He established Harvard as the most important centre for mathematics and astronomy in the USA. He was elected FRS (foreign member) in 1852.

Pentland, Joseph Barclay (1797–1873) traveller. 'Joseph Barclay Pentland, Consul-General in Bolivia (1836–39) died in London, July, 1873. He first discovered that Illimani and Sorata (not Chimborazo) were the highest mountains in America. (See Humboldt's *Kosmos*)': note in original edition of *Personal Recollections*.

Percy, Charles, Lord son of Lord Algernon Percy, Earl of Beverley and brother of Lady Susan Percy (*q.v.*). He married Anne, heiress of Guy's Cliff or Guycliffe, Warwickshire.

Percy, Lady Susan one of the three daughters of Lord Algernon Percy, Earl of Beverley. She died unmarried in 1847.

Peruzzi a very old Italian family of bankers from medieval times.

Phillips, John (1800–74; FRS 1834) geologist. He was professor at Trinity College, Dublin (1844–53), keeper of the Ashmolean Museum, Oxford (1854–70). He published over 100 papers on scientific subjects, as well as more extended works on geology (EP, 113).

Pianciani, Padre (1784–1862) possibly the Jesuit, man of letters and naturalist.

Pillans, James (1778–1864) rector of the High School of Edinburgh from 1810 to 1820. He went on to be Professor of Humanity at Edinburgh University (1820–63). Byron, in *English Bards and Scotch Reviewers*, has the following verses:

> Smug Sydney too thy bitter page shall seek,
> And classic Hallam, much renowned for Greek;
> Scott may perchance his name and influence lend,
> And paltry Pillans shall traduce his friend.
> (Ll. 512–15)

The lines are more witty than just.

Pius VII, Gregorio Barnaba Chiaramenti (1740–1823) Pope from 1800–23. He tried but failed to preserve papal privileges in the face of Napoleon's demands. He was forced in 1804 to consecrate Napoleon Emperor. In 1809 he was taken prisoner after the French conquest and forced to make concessions to the secular power in the Concordat of Fontainebleau (1813). After the fall of Napoleon, Pius was able to negotiate agreements with a number of the victorious powers and to achieve the restoration of the papal estates.

Pius IX, Giovanni Maria Mastai-Feretti (1792–1878). Elected in 1846, Pius IX was a liberalising pope, allowing freedom of the press and establishing a civic guard. This encouraged the United Italy movement and worried the Austrians. Elizabeth Barrett Browning (*q.v.*) expressed enthusiasm for him in *Casa Guidi Windows*, but Pius IX never became the leader that she hoped for. *Nonno* is the familiar term for grandfather and so his nickname puns on 'ninth' and 'grandpa'.

Plana, Giovanni Antonio Amedeo, Baron (1781–1864; FRS 1827) French mathematician and astronomer. He was taught by Lagrange (*q.v.*) and his early career was much influenced by political events in France and elsewhere in Europe during the Napoleonic Empire. He ended up in a Chair of Astronomy at the University of Turin. His most famous work in astronomy relates to the motion or perturbations of the moon. He did a great deal to improve the international reputation of Italian science. He maintained useful relationships with Charles Babbage (*q.v.*).

Playfair, John (1748–1819; FRS 1807). Son of the minister of Benvie, near Dundee, Playfair was educated at St Andrews University, where he studied divinity. After some time in the Church, during which he met Maskelyne, the Astronomer Royal, he worked as tutor to the sons of Ferguson of Raith, before becoming Professor of Mathematics and Natural Philosophy at Edinburgh University in 1785. He was also a noted geologist. His work, particularly his *Outlines of Natural Philosophy*, two of the projected three volumes of which were completed before his death, influenced Mary Somerville in the writing of her second book, *On the Connexion of the Physical Sciences* (1834). Playfair lived in Burntisland from 1818. Lord Coburn confirms Mary Somerville's estimate of Playfair's charm: 'He was admired by all men, and beloved by all women.'

Plücker Julius (1801–68) German mathematician and physicist. His work suggested the far-reaching principle of duality, which states the equivalence of certain related types of theorems. He worked in Heidelberg, Berlin and Paris. In 1829 he became extraordinary Professor at the University of Bonn, Professor of Mathematics at Bonn in 1836 and of Physics in 1847.

Poinsot, Louis (1777–1859) French mathematician. Although Poinsot had a rather chequered early career, he published a number of works on geometry, mechanics and statistics while he was a schoolteacher of mathematics. These gained him a reputation and by 1816 he was admissions examiner at the École Polytechnique. He did important research in geometry, statics and dynamics, invented geometrical mechanics and worked on number theory. He did much for the status of geometry by creating a Chair of Advanced Geometry at the Sorbonne in 1846. He was involved in both the politics of education and of the State, in which he was moderately liberal in his political opinions.

Poisson, Siméon Denis (1781–1840) French mathematician. He became professor at the École Polytechnique in 1806. He made important contributions to the theory of electricity, magnetism and mechanics and his mathematical discoveries are still of practical use to engineers.

Pond, John (1767–1836; FRS 1802) Astronomer Royal before Airy. He translated Laplace's *Système du Monde* in two volumes in 1809. In 1833 he produced a catalogue of more than 1113 stars and he reformed the National Observatory by procuring modern equipment for it.

Pontécoulant, Philippe Gustave le Doulcet (1795–1874; FRS 1833). He turned from soldiering to mathematics and astronomy. Elizabeth Patterson quotes a letter from Mary Somerville to her husband which describes him as 'agreeable and gentlemanlike' and talking amusingly of military matters (EP, p. 101).

Pottinger, Sir Henry, 1st Baronet (1789–1856) soldier and diplomat. Pottinger served in the Indian Army during the Mahratta War and from 1836–40 was political agent in Sind. Made a Baronet in 1840, he proceeded as envoy to China (1842), as first British Governor of Hong Kong (1843). He was Governor of the Cape Province (1846–47) and Madras (1847). His last place was unsuccessful and he retired in 1854.

Pozzo di Borgo, Count Russian ambassador in Paris. Fenimore Cooper describes him as follows: 'handsome, good size, fine dark eye' (*Gleanings in Europe*, p. 87). He was Corsican by birth and perhaps distantly related to Napoleon Bonaparte. In 1827 he held a ball in Paris at which 1500 people are said to have been present.

Prévost, Pierre (1751–1834; FRS 1806) Genevese *savant*, married to Alexander Marcet's sister. Mary Somerville's recognition by learned societies in Geneva was in part due to his sponsorship of her.

Prony, (Gaspard-François-Clair-Marie) Riche, Baron de (1775–1839) leading member of the French scientific establishment (EP, p. 100). He was an engineer, mathematician and physicist. In 1798 he was appointed Inspector General and Director of L'École des ponts et chaussées and he continued to serve the Restoration régime.

Quetelet, Lambert Adolphe Jacques (1796–1874) Belgian mathematician, astronomer, statistician and sociologist, known for the application of statistics and the theory of probability to social phenomena. He studied under Laplace, and founded and directed the Royal Observatory, Brussels (1828). His concept of *l'homme moyen* or 'average man' and his propensity theory (in which various age groups or social groups are believed to display propensities to kinds of behaviour) were controversial.

Radetzky, Josef, Count of Radetz (1766–1853) Austrian soldier, originally from a Hungarian family. Radetzky was conspicuous for his bravery in the Napoleonic Wars. He tried unsuccessfully to reform the Austrian Army but, in spite of this and his age, he won a remarkable victory against the Piedmontese at Novara in 1849. In the history of the Austrian Army, he was known as *Vater* ('Father') Radetzky and idolised by his soldiers.

Ricasoli, Bettino, Baron (1809–80) Italian statesman and scientist. He studied natural science and physics. Elected Italian deputy in 1861, he succeeded Cavour in the premiership. As premier he admitted Garibaldian volunteers to the regular army, revoked the decree of exile against Mazzini and attempted, but failed in, a reconciliation with the Vatican.

Rigny, Henri Gautheir, Comte de (1782–1835) Admiral and statesman. He fought in the Egyptian campaign during the Napoleonic Wars, but later commanded the fleet at the battle of Navarin in 1827 and was Minister of Marine under Louis-Philippe from 1831, when he effected improvements in the administration of the colonies.

Robertson, John (1712–76) His *The elements of navigation; containing the theory and practice. With all the necessary tables. To which is added, a treatise of marine fortification* had gone into four editions by 1780. He was first master of the Royal Naval Academy at Portsmouth (1755–66).

Rogers, Samuel (1763–1855) poet and man of letters. The son of a banker and relatively wealthy, Rogers was able to pursue his love of literature without money worries. His 'The Pleasures of Memory' (1792) became popular and his verse tales, *Italy* (1822–28) obtained a certain degree of fame.

Ross, Sir James Clark (1800–62) explorer. He accompanied Sir William Parry (*q.v.*) on his Arctic expeditions and also his uncle, Sir John Ross, with the latter discovering the North Magnetic Pole in 1831. Later, 1839–43, he explored the Antarctic, where the Ross Sea is named after him.

Rosse, William Parsons, 3rd Earl of Rosse (1800–67) Irish MP and astronomer. He constructed a large 72-inch reflecting telescope, which he used to study one of the blurred objects first listed by the French astronomer, Messier; this he named the Crab Nebula from its shape. In 1845 he discovered the first spiral galaxy.

Rossi, Count Pelligrino (1787–1848) the Pope's chief minister, he was stabbed to death on 15 November on his arrival at the Roman Senate for the first sitting of the Chamber of Deputies. His assassins, members of the extreme revolutionary faction, escaped. A note in the original edition reads: 'M. Pellegrino Rossi, afterwards Minister of France at Rome, then Prime Minister to Pius the Ninth; murdered in 1848 on the steps of the Chancelleria, at Rome.'

Rossini, Gioacchino Antonio (1792–1868) composer. His father was a trumpeter and his mother an opera singer. He studied in Bologna, writing, before 1829, 36 successful operas, including the ever-popular *The Barber of Seville, Cenerentola* and *William Tell*. In his later life Rossini complained about the decline in vocal art and the need to seek expressive rather than imitative music; he insisted that delight should be the basis and aim of the musical art.

Rubini, Giovanni Battista (1794–1854). The son of a horn player, Rubini sang from the age of eight. His first professional engagement was in Pavia in 1814, after which he worked for ten years in Naples. From 1831–43 he alternated between London and Paris. He was neither good-looking nor a particularly good actor but had beautiful tone.

Rumford, Thompson, Benjamin, Count Rumford (1753–1814). The American-born scientist had a remarkably eventful life. He spied for the British during the War of Independence and so was forced to flee the country in 1776, leaving his wife behind. In England his research into ballistics and the theory of heat was again interrupted when he was suspected of spying for the French. In 1785 he left for Paris and then Bavaria, where he was made a Count of the Holy Roman Empire by the Elector, Karl Theodore: Rumford, now Concord, was the name of his home town. In 1795 he returned to England, where, in 1799, he founded the Royal Institution, one of the first research centres for science.

Russell, John, 1st Earl (1792–1878). Russell had been home secretary under Lord Melbourne's administration (1835–39) and himself became Whig (Liberal) Prime Minister (1846–52 and 1865–66). The increase in Mary Somerville's pension probably had more to do with Melbourne than Russell but he was interested in science and was himself a member of the Royal Society.

Rutherfurds of Edgerton. The family was also known to Scott. See Burke's *Landed Gentry*.

Sabine, General Sir Edward (1788–1883; FRS 1818) scientist and explorer. Sabine was astronomer to Arctic expeditions under Ross (*q.v.*) and Parry (*q.v.*) and Copley medallist in 1821. He worked with Herschel on longitude in 1825 and later on magnetic surveys of the British islands (1834–36 and 1861). His wife Elizabeth Juliana, Lady Sabine, translated Humboldt's (*q.v.*) *Kosmos* (1846) and *Aspects of Nature* (1849).

Say, Jean-Baptiste (1767–1832) French economist. He held that in the law of markets, supply creates its own demand and, until the great Depression of the 1930s, Say's law remained more or less the orthodoxy.

Scarlett, Sir James. According to Fenimore Cooper, who met him in London, Scarlett was a handsome, genteel, well-formed and well-dressed man of fashion. An English politician remarked, however, 'Yes, yes; he is, good-looking and all that, but he is an impudent dog in the House; most of the lawyers are impudent dogs in the House' (*Gleanings in Europe*, 'France', p. 181).

Schlegel, August Wilhelm von (1767–1845) German critic, poet and translator. His criticism, especially *Über dramatische Kunst und Literatur*, 3 vols. (1809–11), and his translation of Shakespeare made a great impression on the early romantic writers.

Schwartzenberg, Friedrich (Johann Josef Cölestin) Cardinal (1809–85) Austrian churchman, archbishop in Salzburg and Prague, and then cardinal.

Scoresby, William (1760–1829) Arctic navigator. He was employed in the Greenland whale fishery (1785–90); made a captain in 1790, he retired in 1823. In 1806 he reached 81° 30″ N and this was for a long time the highest latitude reached by any ship.

Sebright, Sir John Saunders, 7th Baronet (1767–1852) politician, who supported political and agricultural reform. Although Sebright gave up pure science, his animal-breeding activities and his studies of animal behaviour were useful to other scientists, such as Henri Milne Edwards (*q.v.*).

Sedgwick, Adam (1785–1873; FRS 1821) geologist. Fellow of Trinity College, Cambridge, he was president of the Cambridge Philosophical Society. He was Wollaston medallist in 1851 and Copley medallist in 1863. He greatly improved the geological collection of Cambridge University.

Shee, Sir Martin Archer (1769–1850). Mary Somerville gets the name slightly wrong of the portrait painter, President of the Royal Academy (1830–50) and one of the founders of the British Institution. Shee also wrote in a minor way.

Sheridan, Helen Selina, Caroline and **Jane Georgina**. The Sheridans, known as the 'Three Graces', were the granddaughters of Richard Brinsley Sheridan, the playwright and politician. The eldest, Helen Selina (1807–67), became Lady Dufferin, afterwards Countess of Gifford: she wrote songs and a play which was performed at the Haymarket Theatre in 1863; the second sister, Caroline (1808–77), was a writer who wrote for money when she separated from her husband, the Honourable George Norton, who deprived her of her children and tried to attach her earnings. When he died, she married Sir William Stirling Maxwell in 1877; the youngest and, by most accounts, the most beautiful, Jane Georgina, married the 12th Duke of Somerset and was Queen of Beauty at the Eglinton Tournament in 1839.

Siddons, Sarah (née **Kemble**) (1755–1831) the most celebrated actress of her generation. She made her London début at Drury Lane in 1782. She played the part of Jane de Monfort in Joanna Baillie's *De Monfort*. Her son, the actor-manager, Henry Siddons, was responsible for the Edinburgh production of *The Family Legend* in 1810 at the Theatre Royal, Edinburgh.

Silliman, Benjamin (1779–1864) professor at Yale University. He edited the *American Journal of Science and the Arts*, which supported Mary Somerville's work.

Sismondi, J(ean)-C(harles)-L(éonard) Simonde de (1773–1842) Swiss economist (1809–18), who in many ways inspired the Risorgimento. As an economist, he began as a disciple of Adam Smith, but came to believe in regulation to assist the poor.

Smart, Admiral Sir Robert (1796–1874). Smart became a full admiral in 1869, having been knighted in 1865.

Smith, Sir (William) Sidney (1764–1840) Admiral. He was imprisoned for two years in the Temple during the wars with France; he escaped in 1798 and went off to defend Saint Jean d'Acre in May 1799, when he repulsed the French. He is described in the DNB as 'theatrical and fond of self-laudation; but brave and energetic', which accords with Mary Somerville's remarks.

Smith, Rev. Sydney (1771–1845) divine, philosopher and wit, who, in 1802, founded *The Edinburgh Review* with Brougham and Jeffrey. He came to London in 1803 and lectured on Moral Philosophy at the Royal Institution. He held a number of livings and in 1831 was made a canon of St Paul's. He was a famed conversationalist, noted for his wit and humour.

Smith, William (1756–1835) politician. The son of a London merchant, he was a noted abolitionist and emancipator. Always radical, he opposed the war with France. He was a friend of Rogers (*q.v.*) and Wilberforce.

Smyth, Admiral W.H. (1788–1865; FRS 1826). After an active naval career, he retired to Bedford, where he built himself an observatory. His wife acted as his assistant, as well as raising a large family. He took an active part in the Royal Society, the Geological Society and the Astronomical Society (EP, 143–4).

Somerville, Rev. Dr Thomas (1741–1830) Mary Somerville's uncle and father-in-law. A note in the original edition of *Personal Recollections* explains that Martha Charters was his wife and that he was '. . . minister of Jedburgh . . . author of Histories of Queen Anne and of William and Mary, and also of an autobiography.' In his *Memoirs of Sir Walter Scott* (5 vols) (London; Macmillan, 1900), Lockhart says, 'Dr Somerville survived to a great age, preserving his faculties quite entire, and I have spent many pleasant hours under his hospitable roof in company with Sir Walter Scott. We heard him preach an excellent sermon when he was upwards of ninety-two, and at the Judges' dinner afterwards he was among the gayest of the company,' vol. 1, p.220. His autobiography, *My Own Life and Times*, was, according with his own directions, published 30 years after his death.

Somerville, Samuel brother of William Somerville. He died suddenly in London in 1823. See *Gentleman's Magazine*, xciii, Part 1 (1823), 651 (quoted in EP, p.204).

Somerville, William (1771–1860; FRS 1818) Mary Somerville's second husband. He was the eldest son of Thomas Somerville (*q.v.*) and Martha Charters. He entered the army as a surgeon and accompanied the expedition of Sir James Henry Craig (*q.v.*) to the Cape of Good Hope in 1795. In an interval from his African experiences, he took his MD from Aberdeen University in 1800. He travelled widely on government missions into the African interior, one of which is described in an appendix to John Barrow's *Voyage to Cochin China* (1806). He also served with Craig in the Mediterranean and in Canada in 1807. After his marriage to Mary Fairfax Greig, he became, first, head of the army medical department in Edinburgh, and then one of the principal inspectors of the army medical board in London. In 1819 he was appointed Physician to Chelsea Hospital and continued in this post until forced by his health to retire to the continent in 1838. In 1840 he fully resigned his post and the Somervilles made their residence in various places in Italy. Somerville lived long after all, dying at 89.

Sopwith, Sir Thomas (1803–79) civil and mining engineer. He worked on stratigraphical geology and produced a number of valuable technical works.

Sotheby, William (1757–1833; FRS 1794) a minor literary figure, a friend of Scott, Joanna Baillie (*q.v.*) and Wollaston (*q.v.*). In his poem *Lines Suggested by the Third Meeting of the British Association for the Advancement of Science, Held at Cambridge, in June 1833*, he praises Mary Somerville and regrets her absence from the meeting (EP, 117).

South, Sir James (1785–1867; FRS 1821) astronomer. He observed in London with Herschel (*q.v.*) and in Paris with Laplace (*q.v.*). He was one of the founders of the Astronomical Society, of which he was President in 1829 (EP).

Sparks, Jared (1789–1866) historian, editor and clergyman. In the early 1820s he was asked to edit and publish the writings of George Washington and in 1827 Washington's nephew, Bushrod Washington, gave his permission. His *The Life and Writings of George Washington* was published in 12 vols. (1834–37).

Sparrow, Lady Olivia an aristocratic confidante of Wilberforce. Apparently, she regularly spent her holidays on the French Riviera in an effort to convert the Jewish and Catholic populations there: see Ian Bradley, *The Call to Seriousness: The Evangelical Impact on the Victorians* (London: Cape, 1976).

Spencer, William Robert (1769–1834) poet and wit. He was friendly with Sheridan, Sydney Smith (*q.v.*) and other noted literary/political wits. He died in obscure poverty in Paris after a life of extravagance.

Spottiswoode, William (1825–83) mathematician and physicist. He worked on curves and surfaces and the polarisation of light. He was President of the Royal Society (1878–83).

Stabilini, Girolamo (Hieronymo) (1762–1815). Stabilini was invited from Rome to Edinburgh to replace Giuseppe Puppo as leader of the St Cecilia Hall concerts (1783–98). He was very popular in Scotland, partly because he performed and arranged Scots tunes like 'I'll gae nae mair to yon toon'. He was also a noted member of the Masons, Canongate Lodge Kilwinning No. 2, and of the Royal Edinburgh Volunteers.

Staël, Anne Louise Germaine Necker, Madame de (1766–1817) daughter of the financier Jacques Necker, she became famous as a writer and literary hostess. She married but separated from the Baron de Staël-Holstein, Swedish ambassador in Paris. Her salon was a centre of liberal intellectual thought from the eve of the Revolution. She later quarrelled with Napoleon and was forced to live in exile at her château on Lake Geneva. There she was part of the intellectual network of Europe, acquainted with Schiller and Goethe. She returned to Paris after the restoration of the Bourbons in 1814. Although her most important work for France was probably *De l'Allemagne* (1810–13), which introduced German literature and philosophy to France, in Britain she was best known for her novels *Delphine* (1802) and the universally read *Corinne* (1807). Her passionate friendship with Benjamin Constant is in part reflected in his novel *Adolphe* (1816).

Stanley, Arthur Penrhyn (1815–81) Dean of Westminster (1864). Stanley was a tiny and, in many ways, physically insignificant, man but he was, as Mary Somerville says, a liberal intellectual. He published *Lectures on the History of the Jewish Church*, 3 vols. (1863–76).

Stanley, Lady Augusta (1822–76) the daughter of Thomas Bruce, Lord Elgin (*q.v.*) and Mary Hamilton Nisbet, who later married Robert Ferguson of Raith (*q.v.*). Formerly lady-in-waiting to Queen Victoria, she married the Rev. Arthur Penryn Stanley (*q.v.*), Dean of Westminster, when she was 42. Lady Augusta was a considerable woman, ran an intellectual salon and tried to educate the Queen to the wider world. A splendid picture of her and her diminutive husband is in Sydney Checkland, *The Elgins* (1988).

Swinton, James Rannie (1816–88) portrait painter. He was born in Berwickshire and studied in Edinburgh and in London at the schools of the Academy. On the advice of Sir David Wilkie, he visited Spain and Italy. He painted most of the fashionable beauties of the period, including a large group portrait of the Sheridan sisters (*q.v.*). His drawing of Mary Somerville is in the National Portrait Gallery.

Talleyrand-Périgord, Charles Maurice de (1754–1838) French politician and diplomat. He was excommunicated for the part he played in the reform of the church during the Revolution. Talleyrand was a survivor and was foreign minister from 1797 until 1807, when he quarrelled with Napoleon. He served again under Louis XVIII.

Talma, François-Joseph (1763–1826) French actor, who spent some of his early years in England. He made his début at the Comédie Française in 1787. He influenced costume reform in the direction of authenticity. In 1817 he played at Covent Garden in London. He was admired by Mme de Staël (*q.v.*).

Thelwall, John (1764–1834) radical reformer and lecturer on elocution. He supported Horne Tooke (*q.v.*) at Westminster and joined the Society of the Friends of the People. He was arrested in 1794 and sent to the Tower but acquitted after Erskine's (*q.v.*) defence.

Thiers, Louis Adolphe (1797–1877) French statesman and historian and first President of the Third Republic (1870–73). After the fall of Napoleon III, Thiers became President and negotiated peace with Prussia, and his policies facilitated France's economic recovery. His *Histoire de la Révolution française* runs to ten volumes (1823–27).

Thomson, George (1757–1851) son of Robert Thomson, schoolmaster in Dunfermline. Employed as a junior clerk, first in the office of a writer to the signet, and then to the Board of Trustees. He became principal clerk to the Board in 1780. In 1781 he married Katherine Miller, with whom he had six daughters and two sons. He lived in Edinburgh during his working life, retired to London and finally settled in Leith. Thomson was an accomplished violinist and particularly loved playing Haydn and Pleyel quartets.

Thorwaldsen Bertel (1768–1844) Danish sculptor. His highly successful career began in Rome in 1797. He returned to Denmark, to Copenhagen, in 1832. Like Canova, he worked within the tradition of neoclassicism, reworking ancient Greek sculpture, His subjects were generally mythological or religious. Many of his works are in the Thorwaldsen Museum in Copenhagen.

Thurn and Taxis. The Thurn and Taxis family founded its fortune on a courier service in the Italian city-states from about 1290. Franz von Taxis became postmaster to the Holy Roman Emperor Maximilian I from 1489 and Philip of Spain from 1504. By the 19th century, branches of the family operated postal services in Spain, Germany, Austria, Italy, Hungary and the Low Countries. The last postal system was purchased and nationalised by the Prussian government in 1867 but the family fortunes were by this point firmly established. The coiled post-horn symbol remains that of a number of European postal services.

Thury, (Louis-Étienne François) Héricault, Vicomte de (1776–1854) engineer and agriculturalist. He was educated at the Ecole des mines and wrote a number of papers on agriculture, geology and public works. In charge of the inspection of the catacombs of Paris from 1810 to 1830, he made remarkable improvements.

Tooke, (John) Horne (1736–1812) radical politician and philologist. Tried for treason with Thelwall and Hardy in 1794. Tooke was an old-fashioned radical, who appealed to Magna Carta but did not have much time for the new-fangled 'rights of man'. His philological work was called *The Diversions of Purley*.

Trendelenburg, Friedrich Adolf (1802–72). Trendelenburg became Professor of Philosophy at Berlin in 1837.

Tuckerman, Rev. Joseph (1778–1840) American minister, best known for his ministry to the urban poor. He was educated at Harvard College and subsequently studied Theology. He began as an obscure rural parson in Chelsea, Mass. in 1801 but always had cosmopolitan friendships. In 1812 he was the force behind the Boston Society for the Religious and Moral Improvement of Seamen. His religious inclinations were Unitarian. When he assumed an urban ministry in Boston, his health made preaching difficult but he worked hard for the welfare of the people and, by encouraging private relief for poverty, assisted the poor in retaining their self-respect. In 1833–34, he visited England, where he helped to establish urban ministries in London and Liverpool.

Tuscany, Leopold II, Grand Duke of (1797–1870; FRS 1838) a Hapsburg prince of Italian blood. Leopold 'was one of the most enlightened rulers in Italy and a generous patron of science. His library at the Pitti Palace had an excellent collection of scientific books and many current scientific periodicals. In addition to maintaining an observatory and museums, he undertook in 1838 the establishments of a Tuscan scientific society' (EP, 190–191).

Tylor, Sir Edward Burnett (1832–1917) anthropologist. First Professor of Anthropology at Oxford in 1884, he was knighted in 1912. *Primitive Culture* was published in 1871 and *Researches on the Early History of Mankind and the Development of Civilization* in 1865.

Tyndall, John (1820–93; FRS 1852) Irish physicist. In 1869 he discovered the effect of scattering of light by minute particles such as those in dust. He used this effect to explain the blue of the sky; he was also one of the first to show that the air contains microorganisms. He succeeded Faraday (*q.v.*) at the Royal Institution (1867–87), celebrating him in *Faraday as a Discoverer* (1868). He was Rumford medallist in 1869.

Usedom, Guido, Conte von (1805–84) Prussian diplomat. From 1845–54 Usedom was Prussian Minister at the Holy See. He held various posts until he gave up diplomacy in 1869 and took over the direction of the royal Prussian museums.

Veitch, James, Laird of Inchbonny, Roxburghshire (*fl.* 1810–40) (EP, p. 203) see note 42.

Victor Emmanuel II (1820–78) King of Italy (1861–78). He succeeded to the throne of Sardinia-Piedmont in 1849, when his father Charles Albert (*q.v.*) abdicated. He appointed Cavour Prime Minister in 1852, fought against the Austrians at Solferino and Magenta, freed Lombardy from Austrian rule and co-operated with Garibaldi (*q.v.*)

in the campaign that freed Southern Italy. He acquired Venetia in 1866 and Rome in 1870.

Vogt, Professor possibly Karl Vogt, the German philosopher who suggested that the brain secretes thought in the same manner as the liver secretes bile.

Wallace, William (1768–1843) Scottish mathematician. He was largely self-educated; originally, like Faraday (*q.v.*), apprenticed to a bookbinder, he met Playfair (*q.v.*) while working in a bookshop in Edinburgh and attending classes at the university. With Playfair's influence, he became assistant mathematics teacher at Perth Academy. While he worked there, he contributed papers on Mathematics to the Royal Society and wrote for the *Encyclopaedia Britannica*. 'In 1803, again at Playfair's urging he competed in examination for the post of mathematics master at the Royal Military College at Great Marlow and won' (EP, 5). In 1819 he was appointed Professor of Mathematics at Edinburgh University. He invented the pantograph, an instrument for duplicating a geometric shape at a reduced or enlarged scale. He also took an interest in astronomy and was involved in the erection of the Observatory on Calton Hill.

Wellwood, Sir Henry Moncreiff (afterwards **Wellwood, 8th Baronet of Tullibole**) (1750–1827) Scottish divine. He was educated in Glasgow and Edinburgh, became minister of Blackford in 1771 and of St Cuthbert's, Edinburgh in 1775. He was moderator of the General Assembly of the Church of Scotland in 1785 and chaplain to George III in 1793.

Werner, Abraham Gottlob (1750–1817) mineralogist. Werner was educated in Freiburg and Leipzig. He returned to Freiburg College as a teacher and studied rocks in the Harz Mountains. The Somervilles visited his collection of minerals at Freiburg in the Black Forest in 1836 (EP, 181). Despite the fact that much of his theoretical work turned out to be erroneous, he nevertheless made a tremendous contribution to science in demonstrating the chronological succession of rocks.

Whewell, William (1794–1866; FRS 1820). Whewell remained a good friend of Mary Somerville throughout his life and sent his work to her, as well as reading hers. Mary Somerville, however, expresses irritation with him in a private letter to her son quoted by Elizabeth Patterson:

> I am rather angry with him for joining in the hue and cry against mathematicians for irreligion; a vulgar and monkish prejudice. All the philosophers were unbelievers before, and during the French revolution, the time when mathematics were cultivated with the greatest success, the fault is owing to the period, and not to the pursuit, I have no doubt however that it will make the book very popular among the saints (EP, p. 116).

White, Lydia. 'Miss Lydia White was a lady who delighted in giving parties to as many celebrated people as she could collect': R. Ellis Roberts, *Samuel Rogers and his Circle* (London: Methuen, 1910).

Wilkes, Charles (1798–1877) naval officer and explorer, mathematician and scientist. His most important command was with the US Exploring and Surveying Expedition to the Pacific Ocean and South Seas (1838–42). This was the first government sponsorship of scientific endeavour and it was instrumental in the nation's westward expansion. Specimens gathered during it became the foundation collections of the Smithsonian.

Wilson, Andrew (1831–81) traveller and author. He was educated at Edinburgh and Tübingen Universities, and travelled in southern China. He contributed to *Blackwood's* and published on his travels and on Gordon's Chinese campaigns.

Wilson, John (1785–1854). Although he lived for a time in the Lake district, Wilson was educated at Glasgow University and Magdalen College, Oxford. His Professorship of Moral Philosophy at Edinburgh University was a political appointment, based on his Tory principles. He joined the editorial staff of *Blackwood's Magazine* when it was founded in 1817. The magazine which also had J. G. Lockhart (*q.v.*) and James Hogg on its staff, was intended as a rival to *The Edinburgh Review*, and was of a lighter kind than *The Quarterly Review*. In it, Wilson features as 'Christopher North' in the 'Noctes Ambrosianae', a series of imaginary conversations supposed to have been held in Ambrose's Tavern in Edinburgh. Wilson was a prolific essayist who also wrote poetry: 'The Isle of Palms' was published in 1812.

Wiseman, Nicholas Patrick Stephen (1802–65) churchman and philosopher. He became Vice-Rector of the English college in Rome in 1827 and Rector from 1828–40. He published his lectures on *The Connection between Science and Revealed Religion* in 1836. He also had some influence on the development of the Oxford Movement. He became cardinal-archbishop of Westminster in 1850. He is supposed to be the model for Browning's poem 'Bishop Blougram's Apology', although his beliefs were not really those expressed by Blougram.

Wollaston, William Hyde (1766–1828; FRS 1793) physiologist, chemist and physicist. Wollaston was a friend to science in many different ways. He was Copley medallist in 1802 and secretary of the Royal Society from 1804–16. He left money to the Geological Society, which formed the Wollaston Fund and to the Royal Society, forming the Donation Fund.

Woronzow, Catharine, Countess of Pembroke (1783–1856) daughter of the Russian ambassador, Count Simon Woronzow (1744–1832), after whom Woronzow Greig was named.

Young, Charles Mayne (1777–1856) actor. He worked in Liverpool in 1798 and later in Manchester and Edinburgh, and was a friend of Scott. He played both comic and tragic, Shakespearean and other, roles.

Young, Thomas (1773–1829) British physician and physicist. Also something of a polymath, he apparently spoke twelve languages by the age of 20. He studied in Germany and Cambridge, practised medicine in London and became a professor at the Royal Institution (1801–3). He demonstrated the interference of light and from this suggested a wave theory of light in opposition to Newton's corpuscular theory. The ratio of stress to strain is known as Young's modulus, from his work in this area. He was also an Egyptologist and helped to decipher the Rosetta Stone. The Rosetta Stone from Rosetta, near Alexandria, carries a decree of Ptolemy V Epiphanes, who reigned 205–180 BC, in two languages and three scripts: Egyptian hieroglyphic, demotic and Greek. Repetition of Ptolemy's name in different scripts gave Young the clue to deciphering hieroglyphics.

Zanetti, Ferdinando (1802–81) senator and Professor of Medicine.

Translations of Letters

P. 93 FROM M. DE CANDOLLE TO MRS SOMERVILLE

LONDON, *5 June, 1819*

DEAR MADAM,

Now that you have got over the initial difficulties of the study of plants you do me the honour of consulting me about the means of proceeding; knowing your taste and your talent for the most advanced sciences, I am not afraid of advising you to move out of elementary botany and advance to the concerns and studies which constitute a science susceptible of general ideas, useful applications and relationships with other branches of human knowledge. For this it is necessary to study not only the nomenclature and the scaffolding constructed to sustain it, but also the relationships of plants to one another and to the external environment, or in other words, the classification of the natural world and physiology.

For both of these branches of science it is necessary in the first place to familiarise oneself with the structure of plants with respect to the specific characteristics of individual plants. You will find a short précis of these characteristics in the first volume of French flora;[1] you will find a more developed version with plates (illustrations) in Michel's *Elements of Botany*. As for the structure of fruit which is one of the most difficult and most important points (issues), you are about to have available a fine work, translated and extended by one of your clever, young compatriots, Mr

Lindley – that is M. Richard's analysis of fruit.[2] The translation will be worth more than the original. As well as this reading, what especially will teach you about the structure of plants, is analysing them and describing them yourself according to the technical terms; this work would become laborious and useless if done on a large number of plants, and it would be more valuable to do it on a small number of chosen species in very distinct classes. It is possible that a few descriptions done as completely as you can will teach you more than any book.

As soon as you know the constituent parts well, along with this study you should seek to get an idea of the classification of the natural world. I am afraid of appearing presumptuous to you if I urge you to this end to read first my Elementary Theory. After these studies or nearly at the same time in order to take advantage of the season, you would do well to assign to their natural orders all the plants that you have collected. Reading about the characteristics of the families with the plants in your hand and the act of arranging your plants in families will make you familiar in theory and in practice with these natural groupings. I advise you in this study, especially at the beginning, only to give a small amount of attention to the general system which binds the families, but a great deal to knowing the physical features peculiar to each one of them. In this respect you might be interested in reading – first Humboldt's *Tableaux de la nature*; secondly my essay on the properties of plants compared with their external forms; thirdly the remarks on botanical geography inserted by Robert Brown at the end of the voyage of Flinders and the expedition to the Congo.[3]

As for the study of physiology or knowledge about plants as living beings, I urge you to read these works in the following order: Philibert, *Eléments de Botanique et de Physiologie*, 3 vols.; the second part of the elementary principles of the botany of French flora. You will find the anatomical element in the work of Mirbel; the chemical element in T. de Saussure's chemical research on plants; the statical element in the statics of plants by Hales, etc., etc.[4] But I urge you especially to see for yourself plants at all stages, to follow their development, to describe them in detail, in a word to live with them more than with books.

I hope, dear lady,[5] that this advice gets you involved in following the study of plants under this programme from which I believe you will derive much of importance and interest. I shall count myself fortunate if by pointing you in the right direction, I can help to bring about your future success and to initiate you into a study which I have always regarded as one of those which has most to contribute to daily happiness.

Your most devoted servant,

DE CANDOLLE

P. 141 FROM M. BIOT TO MRS SOMERVILLE

DEAR MADAM,

Having been back from Lyons for several days, I have found in Paris the two letters with which you have honoured me, and at the same time I have received a copy of the work that you want to add to the last one. It's a thousand times too good of you, dear lady, to thank me for what gave me so much pleasure. In giving an account of that astonishing treatise, I was fulfilling first of all a task, since the Academy had asked me to read it for them; but you will easily understand that this task was an attractive one for me, if you can remember the lively and profound admiration that I have felt for a long time at the extraordinary union of every talent and grace with strict knowledge that we men have been foolish enough to believe our exclusive preserve. What charmed me then, dear lady, I have not forgotten; and mutual friendship which is dear to me has additionally, at your instigation, strengthened these sentiments. Judge, therefore, dear lady, how happy I am to give an impression of what I understand so well, and what I have observed with such lively interest. The most amusing thing for me in this business, is to see our gravest colleagues, for example, Lacroix and Legendre, who are certainly not frivolous, nor gallant as a rule, nor easy to rouse, scolding me, as they do at each meeting, about what's holding me up in making my report, about why I'm making it so carelessly and with so little grace; in a word, dear lady, it's a complete intellectual conquest. I haven't failed to mention this situation as one of the most precious jewels in your crown. That's the way that I have responded to them; and in your case, dear lady, bearing in mind the way you talk about your work, I have some hope of having presented it as you would wish. But, in paying you this fair and sincere tribute and inserting it into the *Journal des Savants*, I have not taken the precaution of asking that it be placed elsewhere; today when the collection is printed, I regret not having been more farsighted. What's more, dear lady, there is nothing in this piece that everyone who knows you does not think, or even those who have had the good fortune to meet you only once. Your friends will find that I have expressed very feebly the charms of your spirit and your character; charms that they must appreciate more since they enjoy them more often; but you, dear lady, who are indulgent, will forgive me for the feebleness of a portrait which had to be done from memory.

I am honoured to be, with the greatest respect,
dear lady,
Your very humble and obedient servant,
BIOT

p.233 FROM BARON HUMBOLDT
TO MRS SOMERVILLE

SANS SOUCI, *12 July, 1849*

DEAR MADAM,

It is a most pleasant task, dear lady, to offer you once more my devotion and my respectful admiration. These sentiments have been held for a long time by this antediluvian man to whom you have deigned to address such amiable lines and the new edition of that fine work which has charmed me from its first appearance and from which I have learned much. To the great superiority which you possess and which so nobly illuminated your name, in the high regions of mathematical analysis, you join, dear lady, a range of knowledge in all aspects of physics and descriptive natural history. After your *Mechanism of the Heavens*, the philosophic work, *On the Connexion of the Physical Sciences* has been the object of my constant admiration. I read it in its entirety and then reread it in the seventh edition which appeared in 1846 at a time when we were more at peace, when the political storm did not rumble from afar. The imprudent author of the *Kosmos* must salute above all the *Physical Geography* of Mary Somerville. I was able to procure it in its first weeks through the efforts of our mutual friend the Chevalier Bunsen. I do not know in any language a work on physical geography to compare with yours. I studied it again in the latest edition which I owe to your gracious generosity. The feeling for precision which is habitual to you in geometry, has penetrated all your work, dear lady. No fact, none of the broad views of nature escapes you. You have profited from the books and conversation of travellers in unhappy Italy through which passes the main route to the East and to India. I was surprised by the justice of your observations on the geography of plants and animals. You are queen of regions such as astronomy, meteorology, magnetism. You have, indeed, joined the celestial sphere, astronomy, your inheritance, to the earthly sphere. Only you could have given to your fine literature an original work of cosmology, a work written with the lucidity and the taste which distinguish everything that comes from your pen. My *Kosmos* has been welcomed, I know, in your country; but there are different kinds of literary composition, just as there are differences among races and the original difference of languages. A translated work lacks life; what pleases on the banks of the Rhine must seem bizarre on the banks of the Thames and of the Seine. My work is essentially a German production, and this very character, I am sure, far from being something for me to complain about, is what gives it its flavour of the land. I am in possession of a good fortune to which (because of my long stay in France, my personal convictions and my political heresies) the *Léopard* had not too much accustomed me.[6] I am asking the illustrious author of the volume on the *Mechanism of the Heavens* to have the courage to expand her *Physical Geography*. I am certain that that great man, Sir John Herschel, whom we both love most, will be of my opinion. *Le Monde*, I make use of the title that Descartes wished to give to a book of which we have only poor fragments; *Le Monde* has to be written for the English by an author of that race. There is no sap, no vitality in even the best translations. My health has miraculously preserved at the age of eighty, my ardour for nocturnal work in the middle of the agitations of a situation which I do not need to paint for you since the excellent Mademoiselle de — will have made you familiar with it. I have radically altered my two volumes of *Ansichten*[7] There is only a quarter of it left. It is like a new work which I should soon have the pleasure to address to you if M. Cotta [the publisher of *Ansichten*] thinks himself able to risk a publication in these times when physical force believes it can heal a moral ill and *inject* contentment into a united Germany!! The third volume of my *Kosmos* proceeds, but less credulous minds might be less serene.

Yours most affectionately and respectfully,[8]
ALEXANDER VON HUMBOLDT

p.241 FROM THE COUNTESS BON-BRENZONI TO MRS SOMERVILLE

VERONA, *28 May, 1853*

ILLUSTRIOUS LADY,

I was very pleased to hear that the package containing the printed copies of the Carme [Songs] which I had the honour of being able to offer you, had finally reached you, meanwhile I was in great anxiety that perhaps some difficulties had arisen, or that there were postal delays. But, your most gracious letter more than made up for that anxiety, in the wholly kind and generous reception that you have given to my verses. Thank you so much for the kind words you have written to me, and for having courteously taken the care to do so in Italian; I wish that I were able to reciprocate by writing to you in English! yet I comfort myself with the certainty that our hearts speak the same language; for my part I do not know if it is presumption or inspiration that makes me believe that there exists between you and me, a kind of understanding, and although your merits and your goodness for the most part explain the mystery, still I find that it is not common that such an idea has spoken of you incessantly to my heart, from the day that I saw you for the first and only time!

Oh, if it is true that among the feelings of pleasure that you experience from the praises given to your work, you have been able to find a place among those things most precious to you for what the lively and sincere expression of my humble affection awakened in your mind, I have reached a point which I certainly had not dared aspire to.

To be with you at Colà, or anywhere at all, is one of my dearest wishes, and I am happy that your words have given me some hope of this.

Please give my sincere regards to your excellent husband and your lovely daughters; while for my part I ask God to bless you abundantly. Please remember me as one who though far from you in body is always close to you in spirit, with feelings of great affection and respect.

Encouraged by your kindness, I am honoured to sign myself your most affectionate friend,

CATERINA BON-BRENZONI

Lady, that day when I first saw you, tell me, did you discern on my face the signs of my agitated spirit? – Did you see how fearfully I came into your presence and how worship and wonder held my uncertain words hanging on my lip that would not answer to my bidding. – Oh, tell me, did you discern how they [worship and wonder] were overcome by love when I heard you speak gently and quietly, with your angelic voice and your humility, which teaches wisdom to those who are dear to you? – Is this she, I said to myself, is this indeed she, whose honoured name I have a thousand times heard spoken among the most celebrated? Is this the woman who in the ethereal spaces follows the road to the stars, and measures their weight, motion, distance, orbits and light?

P.283 FROM GENERAL MENABREA TO MRS SOMERVILLE

FLORENCE, *30 June, 1869*

DEAR MADAM,

I have got to know the fine edition of your last work on Physical Geography with the greatest interest, and I wish to give you a token of my high esteem for your work. I beg you, therefore, dear lady, to accept a gold medal with the effigy of Victor Emmanuel, my noble sovereign. It is a remembrance of my country in which, as in all nations where science is honoured, you may number many friends and admirers. Please believe, dear lady, that I shall continue to be both one and the other, as well as being,

Your most devoted servant,

MENABREA

1 Jean-Baptiste de Monet, Chevalier de Lamarck (1744–1829), *Flore française* (Paris: 1778). In 1809 Lamarck published his theory of evolution, *Philosophie zoologique* which has generally, but not universally, been rejected in favour of Darwin.

2 John Lindley (1799–1865) *Observations on the Structure of Fruits and Seeds,* trans. from Louis-Claude Richard's *Analyse du fruit* (London: 1819).

3 Flinders and Brown: see 'Brief Biographies'.

4 De Candolle is presumably working from memory: the books are probably J. C. Philibert, *Introduction à l'étude de la botanique,* 3 vols. (Paris; 1799); Brisseau de Mirbel, *Eléments de physiologie végétale et de botanique* (Paris; 1815); Stephen Hales, *Vegetable Staticks: or, an account of some statical experiments on the sapin vegetables* (1727).

5 In all the letters from men to Mary Somerville I have translated 'Madame' as 'dear lady' except in the salutation.

6 Humboldt's fortune was seriously depleted by the costs of his expeditions and he was intermittently in financial straits. He was always magnanimous to poor students of promise: the chemist Justus von Liebig was indebted to him. He also assisted Arago (*q.v.*). Humboldt lived through difficult times in France and, under the illiberal post-1848 régime in Prussia, he was placed under police surveillance, his house was watched and his letters opened. I am afraid, however, that I do not understand the reference to the *Léopard*: it could perhaps be a mistranscription.

7 *Ansichten der Natur* (Aspects of Nature) was Humboldt's favourite work.

8 Literally 'I beg you to accept the homage/tribute of my affectionate and respectful acquaintance.'

Notes

ONE

1   The Test and Corporation Acts stipulated that public-office
     holders must take Holy Communion in the Church of
     England, 1673, and excluded all Roman Catholics from
     Parliament, 1678. In Scotland the Act, 1681, required all
     public-office holders to declare their belief in Protestantism.

2   'Scons', more commonly 'scones', are little breads with
     bicarbonate of soda as a raising agent rather than yeast. They
     may be sweetened or unsweetened, or flavoured with treacle.

3   Penny-weddings: the painter David Allan (1744–96), some-
     times regarded as the founder of Scottish genre painting, has
     a pen-and-watercolour sketch, 'The Penny Wedding', 1795.
     My father remembered going in the early 1930s to what he
     called a 'pay-wedding' in Maybole in Ayrshire.

4   Tolbooth: a Tolbooth is a town prison, originally the cells
     under the Town Hall. The Tolbooth in Edinburgh is now
     marked by a heart-shaped design in the causeway of the High
     Street. Formerly the Parliament and law courts and finally a
     prison, it was built about 1466 and pulled down in 1817: its
     doorway and keys are now at Scott's house at Abbotsford.

5   Edie Ochiltree is a licensed travelling beggar in Scott's *The
     Antiquary* (1816).

6   The first draft has 'horridly' for 'strongly'. Mary Somerville
     also remarks that the battles between 'Gowns and Plebs',
     which her son described when he was at Cambridge, re-
     minded her of these Scottish fights.

7   The 'cutty stool' was the stool of repentance in the church for
     fornication. Sitting there, the guilty party could be arraigned
     from the pulpit. Mary Somerville's mother's problem was
     presumably in explaining the nature of the offence. Usually
     the evidence of fornication was pregnancy.

8   'Scotch and English': in her autobiography, *Curriculum Vitae*,
     Muriel Spark invokes this passage from Mary Somerville to
     illustrate what remained the concerns of her childhood in
     Edinburgh.

TWO

9 Kraken: this mythical sea monster was first described in Pontoppidan's *Natural History of Norway* (1752), translated from the Norwegian in 1755.

10 '*Muckle*' or '*mickle*': 'big' (Scots).

11 A Memoria Technica was a method of aiding memory e.g.: *Memoria Technica, or a New Method of Artificial memory* . . . *applied to* . . . *Chronology, History etc* [By R. Grey] London, 1730.

12 Aurora: this luminous atmospheric phenomenon, ascribed to electricity, radiating from the magnetic poles is usually more visible in northern or southern regions, hence Northern Lights.

13 *Repulse*: actually a 64-gun ship. The *Repulse* was initially involved in the Nore mutiny but was one of the first ships to leave it. The *Venerable*, Fairfax's later command, was a 74-gun ship.

14 *Hop job*: the artist should have carved 'My days are swifter than a weaver's shuttle and are spent without hope', 'Job' (*Job, 7, 6*).

15 A 'bodle' is a small copper coin, twopence Scots, hence something of little value.

16 Allerly: the home of Sir David Brewster (*q.v.*) near Melrose was called 'Allerly': he settled in this half-cottage, half-villa near Gattonside, Roxburghshire in 1824.

17 This is presumably Slitrig Water, a tributary of the River Teviot.

THREE

18 Mary Somerville's note from the original edition: 'Many people evidently think the science of astronomy consists entirely in observing the stars, for I have been frequently asked if I passed my nights looking through a telescope, and I have astonished the enquirers by saying I did not even possess one.'

19 Xenophon and Herodotus: it is perhaps worth remembering here that, although Mary Somerville speaks lightly of her achievement, she could have been no more than 16.

20 A note in the original edition reads: 'Nasmyth told a lady still alive who took lessons from him in her youth, that the cleverest young lady he ever taught was Miss Mary Fairfax.'

21 Pleyel, Clementi, Steibelt, Mozart and Beethoven: all of these composers except Mozart were still living and working at this point and so music 'in vogue' was genuinely up to date.

22   *The Gamester* is a tragedy by Edward Moore (1712–57). Some
     admired passages are attributed to Garrick.

23   The *Elegant Extracts* (1789) were compiled by Vicesimus
     Knox (1752–1821). These were 'useful and entertaining ex-
     tracts' generally for the use of youth. Knox was educated at St
     John's College, Oxford; he also wrote *Essays Moral and
     Literary* (1778).

FOUR

24   In 1825 John Wilson (see 'Brief Biographies') bought a plot of
     ground above Windermere with a picturesque cottage, Eller-
     ay, and a beautiful view. Initially, he extended the cottage but
     finally built a house there. Wilson, eccentric in a number of
     ways, built the house on three sides of a square and only one
     storey high because he disliked stairs. The house looked west
     over the lake and so presumably 'eastern-looking' refers to its
     having been a bungalow which was not a normal western
     construction. Wilson did wear sailor's dress and had quite a
     fleet of boats – seven sailing vessels and a ten-oared Oxford
     barge: see Elsie Swann, *Christopher North (John Wilson)*
     (Edinburgh; Oliver & Boyd, 1934). But this part of the draft
     is difficult to decipher and 'lantern' rather than 'eastern' has
     been suggested to me. But, unless it refers to light shining
     from the cottage/house, I can't make much sense of it as a
     shape. The point of the story is, however, clear: whoever
     owns the house and all the boats must be a strange sort of
     man, but the traveller has no idea that he is speaking to him.

25   All Gothic novels: Clara Reeve, *The Old English Baron (1777)*;
     Ann Radcliffe, *A Romance of the Forest* (1791); *The Mysteries of
     Udolpho* (1794).

26   In the case of this story, Martha may have realised that her
     mother's memory had played her false. Sir Alexander Boswell
     of Affleck (1775–1822) was indeed killed in a duel by James
     Stuart of Dunearne (1775–1849) but not until much later
     than the period Mary Somerville chooses for the event.
     Boswell, the eldest son of Johnson's biographer, had attacked
     the Whig Stuart in the *Glasgow Sentinel* and this occasioned
     the duel in which the inexperienced Stuart killed his man,
     probably by mistake. Stuart was tried and acquitted, but did
     go to America. He had, however, married in 1892 and so,
     presumably, Mary Somerville remembers gossip from an
     earlier period and conflates it with later events.

27   The original edition has the following note: 'The late Justice

Coltman told us, when he and Lady Coltman came to see my father and mother at Siena, that he recollected when he first went the circuit seeing more than twenty people hanged at once at York, chiefly for horse-stealing and such offences.' – Editor.

28 The Texel is an island off the north tip of Holland. Earlier in 1797 had occurred the more notorious mutiny at the Nore, a sandbank anchorage in the Thames estuary; the leader, Richard Parker, was hanged from the yardarm of his ship. The spate of mutinies was certainly a protest against the appalling conditions of the men. As Mary Somerville explains, two ships, the *Venerable* and a frigate, remained loyal, undoubtedly in part due to the courage of Admiral Duncan, a man of great height, girth and presence. After Camperdown, Duncan commended William Fairfax in despatches but Fairfax did not significantly profit financially.

29 The Battle of Camperdown: the village of Camperdown is in the Northwest Netherlands on the North Sea. The British defeated the Dutch here in 1797. Admiral Duncan's flagship, the *Venerable*, with William Fairfax as captain, was subjected to severe fire. The British finally captured eleven ships and suffered 220 killed and 812 wounded; the Dutch suffered 540 killed and 620 wounded. The victory was a remarkable one and there was some feeling in the country that Duncan should immediately have been made an Earl.

30 The Greenwich Royal Hospital was designed by Wren and became the Royal Naval College in 1873. The painting is by Samuel Drummond, RA, who also painted Richard Parker of the Nore mutiny.

FIVE

31 James Ferguson (1710–76), *Astronomy Explained on Sir Isaac Newton's Principles* (1756).

32 'These books and all the other mathematical works belonging to my mother at the time of her death have been presented to the College for Women, at Girton, Cambridge': note from original edition. 'Isoperimetrical' problems are problems concerning figures with the same perimeter. The titles given are approximations of the French (or Latin) titles.

33 See also p. 80. *The Edinburgh Review* and *The Quarterly Review* were rival reviews. The *Edinburgh* was established in October 1802 by Francis Jeffrey, Henry Brougham (*q.v.*) and Sydney Smith (*q.v.*). Francis, Lord Jeffrey (1773–1850),

who was its editor until 1829, was educated at Edinburgh and Glasgow Universities and became a judge and an MP. As a critic, Jeffrey approved of Byron, Scott and Keats but is known as the scourge of Wordsworth and the Lake Poets – his review of Wordsworth's 'The Excursion' famously begins 'This will never do.' He was also severe, although less so, on Mary Somerville's friend, Joanna Baillie. Although early contributors to the *Edinburgh* included Tories like Scott, its sympathies became clearly Whig and in February 1809 the *Quarterly* was set up as a Tory rival. Scott's son-in-law Lockhart (*q.v.*) was an important contributor and its editor from 1825–53. The *Quarterly*'s antipathies were directed rather to Keats and Shelley than the older Romantics.

SIX

34 Caffres: Kaffirs was the former collective name for the Pondo and Xhosa peoples of the East Cape Province of South Africa.

35 Hottentots: the Hottentots, originally a Bushman–Bantu cross, called themselves Khoi-Khoin, 'men of men'.

36 In June 1814, six weeks after what was believed to be the last shot in the Napoleonic Wars had been fired, Alexander I of Russia and his ally, Frederick William II of Prussia, arrived at Boulogne. With them were leading princes, statesmen and generals. These included Field Marshal Prince von Blücher, Prince Metternich, the Chancellor of the Austrian Empire, Prince Hardenberg, the Chancellor of Prussia, the scholar von Humboldt, Count Hetman Platoff of the Don Cossacks and the young royal princes of Prussia. They were hugely popular and rapturously received in London.

37 The detail of the story is not given in the draft and the name of Cervantes's doctor is confused but the substance of the story is to the point. In Part II, chapter 47 of *Don Quixote*, Sancho Panza is persuaded in a hoax that he is Governor of an island called Barataria. A table covered in wonderful food is spread before him, but a doctor, Pedro Recio de Aguero, a native of Tirteafuera, tells him that it is all bad for him and advises him to eat nothing. Sancho doesn't like the advice any more than the King.

38 The taking of Quebec in 1756: General Wolfe's victory over the French led by Mountcalm was remarkable for the scaling of the undefended Heights of Abraham by the British and for the death in the conflict of both commanders.

39   Dominie Abel Sampson is the librarian to Colonel Mannering in Scott's *Guy Mannering* (1815).

40   Burning of the Water: this episode is in *Guy Mannering*,
chapter 26. A *leister* is a trident or spear with three barbed
prongs.

41   The article, 'Astronomy – the comet', appeared in *The
Quarterly Review*, lv (December 1835), 195–223.

42   Thomas Dick in his *The Sidereal Heavens and Other Subjects
Connected with Astronomy* (London: Ward, 1840) confirms
Veitch's claim: 'The most remarkable comet which has
appeared in modern times, since that of 1680, was *the comet
of* 1811. About the beginning of September in that year, about
eight or nine in the evening, as I was taking a random sweep
with my telescope over the north-western quarter of the
heavens, an uncommon object appeared to pass rapidly
across the field of view, which on examination appeared to
be a splendid comet. Not having heard of the appearance of
any such body at that time, I was led to imagine that I had
fortunately got the first peep of this illustrious stranger; but I
afterwards learned from the public prints that it had been
seen a day or two before by Mr Veitch in the neighbourhood
of Kelso, who appears to have been the first that observed it in
this country.'

43   'Parallax' is an apparent change in the position of an object
which is actually a change in the position of the observer of
that object.

SEVEN

44   Watt and Boulton's factory at Soho, Birmingham had been a
tourist attraction for many years. Samuel Smiles, *Lives of
Boulton and Watt* (1865) quotes Matthew Boulton, writing in
1767: 'I had lords and ladies to wait on yesterday, I have
French and Spaniards to-day, and to-morrow I shall have
Germans, Russians and Norwegians' (p.176). In 1772 he is
saying: 'Scarcely a day passes without a visit from some
distinguished personage' (p.180). Elizabeth Patterson thinks
that Mary Somerville must have made this visit with her first
husband since Matthew Boulton died in 1809 (EP, p.43) but
since Boulton's son took over from his father, Mary Somerville's statement probably refers to him.

45   The Mont Cenis Railway Tunnel which crosses the Franco-
Italian frontier was begun in 1857 and finished in 1871. This,
the first great trans-Alpine tunnel reaches a summit level of

1295 m. It had an immediate effect on world communications, speeding up the transmission of mail from the East to northern Europe by several days. It was originally 12.2 km long, was realigned in 1881 and again after WWII: it is now 12.8 km.

46 The Royal Institution, one of the first research centres for science, was founded by Benjamin Thompson, Count Rumford (*q.v.*) in 1799 and was given a royal charter in 1800. Sir Humphry Davy (*q.v.*), Michael Faraday (*q.v.*) and Bragg worked there. Among the famous lectures still given there are the Friday evening discourses for members and the Christmas lectures for children.

47 Count Rumford's (*q.v.*) steam kitchen was an early and unfortunate form of pressure cooker.

48 In spite of its name, Jardin des Plantes in Paris was also the zoological gardens. The museum is the National Museum of Natural History.

49 I cannot find this episode in the St Peter's visit in *Corinne*. When Corinne visits the studio of Canova she sees a 'wonderful statue intended for a tomb. It represented the spirit of grief, leaning against a lion, the symbol of strength' (*Corinne*, World's Classics edition, translated Sylvia Raphael, p.143).

50 Monza is a city of great age in Lombardy. Enclosed in the altar of the 13th–14th-century cathedral is the Iron Crown of Lombard used in the coronation of the Holy Roman Emperors since 1311. It contains a strip of iron said to have been hammered from one of the nails used at the Crucifixion.

51 The picture gallery of the Palazzo di Brera is in Milan.

52 The church of Santa Maria degli Angeli, which lies below the hill town of Assisi was designed in 1569 and finished by 1679. The earthquake which necessitated its rebuilding was, however, in 1832, not earlier as is suggested here. The first draft of the autobiography refers to the church mistakenly as 'St Franceso d'Assisi' [*1D, 195*] but does put the incident at a later stage after the Somervilles had begun to live permanently in Italy: presumably the corrected passage has been misplaced in the published text.

53 Paestum is the Roman name for Posidonia, founded c.600 BC, named after the Greek god, Poseidon. The remains of three Doric temples still stand there. The eruption of Vesuvius in 79 AD engulfed both Herculaneum and Pompeii; the latter was first excavated in 1748.

EIGHT

54 A goniometer is an instrument for measuring angles. In measuring the angles of crystals two kinds are used; the older is the contact or hand goniometer; more accurate is the reflecting goniometer, invented by Wollaston (*q.v.*).

55 The Bridgewater Treatises on the 'power, wisdom and goodness of God as manifested in the creation' were funded by the bequest of the Right Honourable and Reverend Francis Henry, Earl of Bridgewater who in 1829 left £8000 to be held at the disposal of the President of the Royal Society of London. The first, in 1833, was by the Scottish theologian, Thomas Chalmers, who afterwards led the 1843 secession from the Scottish Church, known as the Disruption.

56 *Philosophical Transactions of the Royal Society of London*, cxvi (1826), 132.

57 'The Clapham Sect' included the Thornton family of bankers, Zachary Macaulay, father of the historian (*q.v.*), James Stephen, the great-grandfather of Virginia Woolf's father Leslie Stephen, a number of Quaker families like the Barclays (*q.v.*), over 100 MPs associated with the Evangelical movement, including William Wilberforce. Hannah More, educationalist and moral writer, was also a member of the Clapham Sect. Sir Robert Inglis was a Tory politician and edited works by Henry Thornton. But he opposed parliamentary reform.

NINE

58 The differential calculus, often just called the 'calculus', is a method of calculation which depends on the infinitesimal difference between consecutive values of a constantly varying function.

59 Mary Somerville, like many of her contemporaries and a number of modern critics misspells the title of the play as '*Montfort*'. Indeed so strong is the pressure for the 't' that Joanna Baillie herself once admits it in a letter. The first performance of *De Monfort* was at Drury Lane, 29 April 1800. It had a total of eight performances in this run. John Kemble played De Monfort and Mrs Siddons played his sister, Jane de Monfort. Mary Somerville is wrong in stating that the play was not acted again. It was staged again in a revised version at Drury Lane in November and December 1821 with the famous tragedian, Edmund Kean (1789–1833) as De Monfort. Kean performed the part again in June 1822 in Bath, and

in July at the Theatre Royal, Birmingham. In Scotland the play was performed with Mrs Siddons after the celebrated production of Baillie's *The Family Legend* in 1810 but it was not well received, having no local interest. Scott suggested that, if the play had had as much tartan as *The Family Legend*, it would have gone down better. The play was also staged in America at a number of locations.

60 George IV was crowned in 1821. His estranged Queen, Caroline, died in the same year. After the separation of the couple in 1796, George forbade Caroline to see their child, Charlotte. When he became King in 1820, George attempted to divorce Caroline but popular support for the Queen stopped this, but not her exclusion from the coronation. Victoria was crowned in 1837.

61 The perihelion is the point in the orbit of a body round the sun at which the body is nearest the sun. The earth is at perihelion about 3 January.

TEN

62 In the first and second drafts of the autobiography, Mary Somerville shows that even she was susceptible to the suspicion that too much brainwork might be bad for physical health, when she expresses her worries that she might have pushed her daughter too hard [*1D, 150:* I felt her loss the more acutely because I feared I had strained her young mind too much. My only reason for mentioning this family affliction is to warn mothers against the fatal error I have made].

63 The second draft of the autobiography gives a bit more detail about the financial affair which involved a Scottish lawsuit and a dishonest agent [*2D, 123*]. See also EP, pp. 44–45.

64 James Abercromby, later Baron Dunfermline, was the son of the celebrated soldier Sir Ralph. Sir Ralph was wounded at Alexandria when fighting the French under Menou. He was taken aboard the flagship of the fleet and died at sea. He was buried in Malta. The point of the story is missing: in the draft it is explained that someone replied that it was rather the French who slew him.

ELEVEN

65 Horace, *Ars Poetica*, ll. 170–72. The name of Aristarchus, a Homeric scholar of Alexandria in the second century BC had become proverbial for the good critic. Sir John is excusing himself for troubling about small things. He claims that it is

the duty of a friend to bother about such things, lest inattention to detail brings the friend's work into disrepute: '[such a critic] will prove to be an Aristarchus. He will not say, "Why should I give offence to a friend about trifles?" Those trifles will bring that friend into serious trouble.' The passage continues: '*in mala derisum semel exceptamque sinistre* / if once he has been laughed down and given an unlucky reception' (translation by H. Rushton Fairclough, Loeb Classical Library). *Humana parum cavit natura:* 'Human nature does not sufficiently guard against'.

66 'I have published successively the various books up to the fifth volume which will conclude my treatise, *The Mechanism of the Heavens*, and in that I give a historical analysis of the researches of geometricians on the subject, this has made me reread with particular attention Newton's incomparable work on the mathematical principles of natural philosophy, which contains the germ of all his research. The more I have studied this work, the more admirable it seems to me, especially in taking me back to the period when he published it. But at the same time that I feel the elegance of the synthetic method according to which Newton presented his discoveries, I recognise the indispensable need for a deeper analysis of the very difficult questions that Newton could do no more than skim over by synthesis. I see with great pleasure your mathematicians committing themselves now to the analytical method and I do not doubt that in following this method with the wisdom appropriate to your nation they will be led to important discoveries.'

67 Quaternion system: quaternions are complex numbers of the form $w+xi+yj+zk$ where w, x, y, z are real numbers and i, j, k are imaginary units that satisfy certain conditions.

TWELVE

68 *Orage*: whenever, that is, the politics were likely to be stormy.

69 Washington's stepbrother and guardian was married to Anne Fairfax. At the outbreak of the American War of Independence, Mary Somerville's father was serving on a British ship on the North American station. George Washington invited him as family to visit. But the war prevented the meeting and Lieutenant Fairfax, as he then was, was reprimanded for being in correspondence with the enemy (http://www.groups.dcs.st-and.ac.uk/~history/Mathematicians/Somerville.html).

70 Between 1765–67 the Champ de Mars, now the park in which the Eiffel Tower stands, was a parade ground. On 14 July 1790 at the Fête de la Fédération the King, the Assembly, delegates from the provinces and the army took an oath at the Autel de la Patrice to uphold the new Constitution.

71 The Brocken spectre or Brocken bow is supposed to have been first observed on the Brocken, the highest of the Harz Mountains in West Germany. It is as Mary Somerville describes, a magnified shadow of the observer cast against mist or cloud below the level of the summit. The shadow is surrounded by coloured fringes caused by the diffraction of the light. The phenomenon is sometimes given as the naturalistic explanation of the strange apparition seen by George Colwan in Hogg's *Confessions of a Justified Sinner* (1824).

72 *Juste milieu*: 'moderate', 'not extreme'.

THIRTEEN

73 Jean Etienne Montucla, *Histoire des mathématiques* (1758).

74 *Sic itur ad astra*: the phrase from Virgil, *Aeneid*, IX, 641 is usually translated 'Such is the way to the stars'. Mary Berry misuses it slightly here, apparently to mean 'thus to go to the stars'.

75 Sidereal astronomy: that which pertains to the stars.

76 This letter is certainly misdated, since Sir John did not go to the Cape until 1833 and he made his first observation from Feldhausen on 22 February 1834. Mary Somerville was made an honorary member of the Astronomical Society on 13 February 1835.

77 In 1831 Exeter Hall in the Strand opened for Evangelical meetings. It had a large hall which seated 3500, a smaller one that seated 600, and 21 committee rooms. In 1843, 300 people had to be turned away when Prince Albert addressed a meeting for the promotion of Christian Unity.

FOURTEEN

78 The Roman Campagna, the country surrounding Rome, was a favourite subject in the landscapes of Claude and Poussin (see n. 102). The area which had declined into malarial marshes began to be reclaimed for agriculture in the late 1870s.

79 The Pincio was laid out as a Romantic park on the Pincian Hill by Giuseppe Valdier in 1809–14. It adjoins the Villa Borghese and is the largest public garden in the centre of the city.

80   The *vetturino* is actually the coachman but, by extension, is used for the vehicle.

81   *Agoni* are freshwater shad found in the Lombardy lakes, called after their shape, since an *agone* is a pack-needle.

82   The Maremma is the Tuscan marshes.

83   The Liberal Party effectively grew out of the Whigs. After the 1832 Reform Act, the aristocrats, mostly Whigs, began to attract support from the middle class and even from some radicals. Sometimes the first Liberal administration is said to be that of Lord John Russell in 1846. By 1855 the administration of Palmerston attracted the label, although the first fully-fledged Liberal administration was that of Gladstone in 1868.

84   Floods in Rome were fairly common until the end of the 19th century, when embankments were constructed along the Tiber. The 'Lungotevere' ('along the Tiber') roads were built at the same time.

FIFTEEN

85   Gum-cistus: a shrub of the genus *Cistus*, which yields laudanum.

86   In his *Histoire naturelle des oiseaux* ('Natural History of Birds') 1771, 10 vols., Georges Louis, Comte de Buffon (1707–88) so characterises the large-eared night owl. The large 'ears', or 'horns', are actually tufts of feathers above the eyes.

87   A *villegiatura* is a country or holiday place.

88   *Stornelli* are Tuscan folk songs with three-line stanzas; they are often improvised. *Rispetti* have eight-line stanzas; the form has also attracted composers.

89   *Grosso gatto*: 'large cat', when what is intended is a 'large cake'. The confusion is with the French *gâteau*; the Italian for 'cake' is *torta*. *Costolette alla sorella*: 'cutlets in the manner of the sister'. Perhaps she was trying to find the Italian for sorrell, which is actually *acetosa*. *Pulini i lampi* would mean to 'clean the flashes of lightning'; Italian for 'lamps' is *lampade*. *Peau* means skin in this usage. The lady wanted to say that she had come in person, not that she was 'Venus in person', but she uses the wrong part of *venir*: she should have said *venue en personne*. Presumably, Mary Somerville wants to protect Elizabeth Barrett Browning from having told a slightly bitchy story. It is worth remarking, however, that Mary Somerville must have been upset by Barrett Browning's belief in spirit-rapping: see p. 277. Yet she clearly admires her otherwise.

90 Via del Corso, usually simply called 'Il Corso', has been one
    of the important thoroughfares in the city since Roman times.
    It runs from the Piazza del Popolo to the Piazza Venezia; it is
    straight, almost a mile long, but surprisingly narrow, so that
    both pavements and road are always crowded, even now
    when the movement of private traffic is restricted.

91 The Great Comet of 1843 has no other name and we need not
    hope to see it again, since it has an orbit of 512.57 years.

92 The original edition has the following note: 'The vessel on
    board which this bust was shipped for England ran on a shoal
    and sank, but as the accident happened in shallow water, the
    bust was recovered, none the worse for its immersion in salt
    water.'

93 *Rococo* style probably derived from the French *rocaille*, shell-
    or pebblework; the term refers to a style of interior decoration
    first introduced in France in the early 18th century. The style
    developed from Baroque but was lighter and more frivolous,
    characterised by gilded carving, light backgrounds and mir-
    rors.

94 Modena ceased to be ruled by the Grand Dukes after its
    representatives declared it part of Italy in 1859. This was
    confirmed by the plebiscite of 1860.

95 Castello Estense is the former palace of the Dukes. It is a
    massive quadrilateral surrounded by a moat and approached
    by drawbridges.

96 The Mausoleum of Theodoric was begun by Theodoric the
    Ostrogoth. It is hewn out of stone without mortar and
    crowned by a monolithic roof.

97 The Roman city of Iguvium, which became Eugubium, was
    sacked by the Goths but became a free commune in the 11th
    century. The Eugubian tables, preserved in the Palazzo dei
    Consoli at Gubbio are fundamental documents for the study
    of the Umbrian language.

98 The Elgin Marbles, ancient Greek marble statues from the
    Parthenon, were sold to the British Museum in 1816 by Lord
    Elgin for £35,000. He had saved them from the Turks who
    were using them for target practice during their occupation of
    Athens. James Rich (1787–1820) travelled extensively in the
    East. When he was the East India Company's representative
    at Baghdad, he amassed oriental collections which were
    purchased by the British Museum after his death from
    cholera at Shiraz. Fragments of the sculptures which adorned
    the Mausoleum of Halicarnassus are in the British Museum:

this ancient Greek tomb was built (363–361 BC) as a monument to Mausolus of Caria by his widow. The archaeologist, Sir Austen Henry Layard (1817–94) excavated the Assyrian capital of Nineveh and its co-capital, Nimrud, finding masterpieces of cuneiform literature. Gigantic statues of winged bulls were transported from Nimrud.

99   Turner's studio was not usually found to be a welcoming place, yet the rich and the famous regularly turned up there. *The Times* of 10 November 1856 describes it thus:

> In that desolate house – 47 Queen Anne Street, West – from 1812 to 1851, lived Joseph Mallord William Turner, the greatest landscape painter of the English school. Hanging along a bare and chilly gallery on the first floor of that gloomy house, stacked against the walls, rolled up in dark cupboards, flung aside into damp cellars, the rain streaming down the canvasses from the warped sashes and paper-patched frames of the ill-fitting skylights, were collected some of the noblest landscapes that were ever painted, while piles of drawings even more masterly, and reams of sketches, the rudiments and first thoughts of finished works, were piled away in portfolios, and cupboards, and boxes, in every nook and corner of the dark and dusty dwelling.

100   In heraldry the wyvern is a winged dragon with two feet like an eagle's and a serpent-like barbed tail.

101   The Torlonia and Borghese families became connected in the later 19th century. Among the 19th-century representatives of the families, Prince Giuseppe Torlonia was a Roman banker; Camillo Fillipo Borghese married Napoleon's sister Pauline.

102   Claude Lorrain (Claude Gellée: 1600–82), the French landscape painter, settled in Rome from 1626. He is famous for his paintings of an idealised Roman countryside, often including small biblical or classical figures. Nicholas Poussin (1594–1665) also painted classical scenes in the Roman countryside but the narrative is always much more prominent than in Claude and his classicism more severe. These painters, along with the Italian, Salvator Rosa (1615–73), who painted sublime and rugged landscapes, provided ways of seeing and interpreting the natural world for more than a century.

103 The Piazza della Bocca della Verità is named from a large disc representing a human face on the wall outside the church of Santa Maria in Cosmedin. The open mouth is supposed to close on the hand of any perjurer who dares to place it within. It is actually a slab that once closed a drain.

SIXTEEN

104 'Regelation': 'refreezing'. An example would be ice melted by pressure which refreezes on the release of that pressure.

105 The charming village of Anif has a church with a late Romanesque tower. The Gothic château Mary Somerville refers to may be the neo-Gothic *Schloss* of the prince-bishops of Chiemsee, now private property. Aigen is situated at the mouth of the Schöffau valley, on the boundary between Salzburg province and Upper Austria. The *Schloss* at Aigen is in a beautiful natural park.

106 'That's a queer story, that one about Adam and Eve, who were punished as fitted their crime; but the serpent had to be condemned to crawl on its belly all its life, can you tell me, Monsieur, if before that it had paws?'

107 Vallombrosa is a valley about 20 miles east of Florence. It has a number of literary associations (e.g. Milton, *Paradise Lost*, i, 303) and is a famous beauty spot.

108 *Pancratium maratimum*: a Mediterranean lily or sea daffodil, from the Greek for bulbous plant.

109 The Battle of Solferino (1859) was a very bloody one and organising relief for its wounded made (Jean-)Henri Dunant take the first steps towards founding the Red Cross as an international relief agency. Dunant was awarded the Nobel Peace Prize in 1901.

110 The Zouaves are a body of light infantry in the French Army. They were originally recruited from the Algerian Kabyle tribe of Zouaoua, but afterwards were French soldiers distinguished by their physique and their dashing appearance, assisted by their retaining the original oriental uniform.

111 James Macpherson (1736–96) claimed to have discovered remains of the poetry of the legendary poet, Ossian or Oisin, in the Highlands and published his 'translations' between 1760 and 1763. Controversy over whether the poems are better described as 'forgeries' than translations has raged more or less ever since. see *The Poems of Ossian and Related Works*, ed. Howard Gaskill, with an Introduction by Fiona Stafford (Edinburgh; Edinburgh U.P., 1996).

SEVENTEEN

112 'God, great in great things, greatest in the least.'

113 Notes from the original edition: 'The *Resistance*, ironclad, commanded by Captain Chamberlayne, then absent on sick leave.' 'Captain Henry Fairfax, my mother's nephew, then Commander on board the *Resistance*, senior officer in the absence of the captain.'

114 There can be little question that Garibaldi was betrayed at Aspromonte. He had been agitating in Sicily for an attempt on Rome. He proceeded with a private army, with the Prime Minister almost certainly colluding, until the collusion became public and Garibaldi was speedily denounced. The clash with Italian troops at Aspromonte in Calabria was a flagrant breach of trust. Garibaldi, although imprisoned, was quickly pardoned. He himself did not pursue the matter lest Italy suffer.

115 Claude François Millet de Chales, *The Elements of Euclid Explained*, trans. William Hallifax (1696).

116 Vassar College in America was established in 1865 but Girton was the only female college established in Britain in Mary Somerville's lifetime.

EIGHTEEN

117 Encke's comet is a faint comet having the shortest orbital period, 3.3 years. It was the second comet to have its orbital period established and was named after the discoverer of its period, Johann Franz Encke (1791–1865), rather than, as is more usual, the person who first saw it (Pierre Méchan). Encke made his discovery by working out that the comets of 1786, 1795, 1805 and 1818 were all the same comet.

118 A *portantina* is a kind of sedan chair.

119 There were three episodes of severe eruptions of Vesuvius during Mary Somerville's Italian period: 1861, 1868 and 1872. All of these concluded in an eruptive stage during which the mouth of the volcano was almost continually open. Although Mary Somerville calls 1868 the 'great eruption', 1861 was more severe, but the Somervilles were not in the Naples area at the time. In 1861 there were several days of violent shuddering after the eruptions, accompanied by dull roaring sounds. The town of Torre del Greco was severely damaged. The 1872 eruptions went through similar stages to 1861 but without, as Mary Somerville says, the same damage to Torre del Greco, which had been rebuilt in the interim.

Accounts of the 1872 eruption remark the destruction of Massa di Somma and the adjacent San Sebastiano and the fate of the unfortunate sightseers.

120 *Trachelium cæruleum* is a member of the *Campanula* genus. Popularly known as throatwort, it is supposed to be good for afflictions of the neck.

121 Mary Somerville was denounced by the Rev. William Cockburn (1773–1858) in the course of his long-running attack on the new geologists, whose discoveries threatened fundamental readings of the Bible (EP, p. 53).

Bibliography

Mary Somerville, *The Mechanism of the Heavens* (London; John Murray, 1831); *Preliminary Dissertation to the 'Mechanism of the Heavens'* (London; John Murray, 1831); *On the Connexion of the Physical Sciences* (London; John Murray, 1834); *Physical Geography*, 2 vols. (London; 1848); *On Molecular and Microscopic Science* (London; 1869); *Personal Recollections from Early Life to Old Age, with selections of her correspondence by her daughter, Martha Somerville* (London; John Murray, 1873; reprinted New York; AMS Press, 1975); *An Unpublished Letter of Mary Somerville, with a Comment by F. E. Hutchison, reprinted from the Oxford Magazine* (Oxonian Press, 1929)

Further reading

W. H. Davenport Adams, *Celebrated Englishwomen of the Victorian Era* (London; F. V. White, 1884)

Margaret Alic, *Hypatia's Heritage: A History of Women in Science from Antiquity to the Late Nineteenth Century* (London; The Women's Press, 1986)

Selma Brody, 'Mary Somerville's Influence on George Eliot', *George Eliot–George Henry Lewes Studies*, 34–5 (Sept. 1998), 1–12

William Chambers, *Stories of Remarkable Persons* (Edinburgh; Chambers, 1878)

Julian Lowell Coolidge, *Six Female Mathematicians* (New York; Scripta Mathematica, 1951)

Millicent Garrett Fawcett, *Some Eminent Women of Our Times: Short Biographical Sketches* (London; Macmillan, 1889)

Eva Hope, *Famous Women Authors* (London; W. Scott, 1890[?])

Alice Jenkins, 'Mary Somerville as Autobiographer', Juliet John and Alice Jenkins, eds., *Rethinking Victorian Culture* (London; Macmillan, 2000)

Jane McKinlay, *Mary Somerville, 1780–1872* (Edinburgh; University of Edinburgh, 1987)

Charlene Morrow and Teri Perl, eds, *Notable Women in Mathematics: A Biographical Dictionary* (Westport, Conn.; Greenwood Press, 1998)

Kathryn Neeley, ed., *Mary Somerville: Science, Illumination and the Female Mind* (Cambridge; Cambridge University Press, 2001)

Lynn M. Osen, *Women in Mathematics* (Cambridge, Mass.; MIT Press, 1974)

Elizabeth Chambers Patterson, *Mary Somerville, 1780–1872* (Oxford; Somerville College, 1979)

Elizabeth Chambers Patterson, *Mary Somerville and the Cultivation of Science, 1815–1840* (The Hague; Martinus Nijhoff, 1983)

Arthur Gay Payne, *Mrs Somerville and Mary Carpenter* (London; Cassell, 1892)

Allie Wilson Richeson, *Mary Somerville* (1941). Reprinted from *Scripta Mathematica*, vol. VIII, no. 1 (March 1941)

George Barnett Smith, *Women of Renown: Nineteenth Century Studies* (London; Allen, 1893)

Julia Swindells, 'Other People's Truths? Scientific Subjects in the *Personal Recollections* of Mary Somerville', Pauline Polkey, ed., *Women's Lives into Print* (Basingstoke; Macmillan, 1999)

Margaret E. Tabor, *Pioneer Women: Caroline Herschel, Sarah Siddons, Maria Edgeworth, Mary Somerville* (London; The Sheldon Press, 1933)

Lucy Bethia Walford, *Twelve English Authoresses* (London; Longmans, Green, and co., 1892)

Mona Wilson, *Jane Austen and Some Contemporaries* (London; Cresset Press, 1938)

Mary Somerville is also included in the 'Dictionary of National Biography' and a number of other collections of biographies of famous women, mostly dating from the late 19th or early 20th century, and a number of them are intended for children or adolescents.

There is also a most useful entry on Mary Somerville, with links to biographies of scientists that she knew, and a brief bibliography, at the St Andrews University history of mathematics site: http://www.groups.dcs.st-and.ac.uk/~history/index.html

Index

Abbotsford: 79, 397
Abercromby, James, Baron
    Dunfermline: 130, 405
Abercromby, Sir Ralph: 130, 405
Aberdeen: 91
Aberdour: 21
Abrantès, Laure Junot, née
    Permon, Duchesse
    d'Abrantès: 153, 303
Academy, The: xxxv
Académie des Sciences (Paris): 141,
    278
Academy of Natural Science
    (Florence): 189
Accademia Pontoniana: 273
Accademia Tiberiana: 193
Acton, Guglielmo (William): 268,
    273, 303
Adam, Sir Frederick: 203, 217,
    303
Adam, Lady: 203
Adams, John Couch: xxvi, 235,
    303, 312, 347
Adelaide of Saxe-Meiningen,
    Queen: 153, 304
Africa: 73, 94
Agnesi, Madame: xxviii,
Aigen: 239, 411
Airy, Sir George Biddell: xxviii,
    90, 146, 174, 219, 235, 304,
    366
Alban hills: 197
Albano: 194–199, 206
Albany, Countess of: 96, 304
Albrizzi, Countess: 91, 304
Alexander I of Russia: 74, 401
Alembert, Jean le Rond, Duc d':
    137, 305
Alfieri, Vittorio, Conte: 96, 304,
    305

Allerly: 31, 398
Alps: 85, 189, 243, 245
Amalfi: 272
Amélie, Queen of France: 153,
    305
American Philosophical Society at
    Philadelphia: 181
Amici, Giovanni Battista: 189,
    305
Ampère, André Marie: 151, 305,
    310
Ancona: 206, 225
Andes: 91
Anif: 239, 411
Antinori, Vincenzio, Marchese:
    189, 306
Antonelli, Giacomo, Cardinal:
    100, 306
Apennines: 194, 211
Apreece, Mrs (see Davy)
Arabian Nights: 17
Arago, (Dominique) François
    (Jean): 87–89, 150, 156, 167,
    306, 311, 395
Archerfield: 104
Arco, Countess Irene: 239
Arcoeuil: 89–90, 151, 289
Argyll, George Douglas
    Campbell, 8th Duke of
    Argyll: 288, 306; *Reign of
    Law*, 288
Arquà: 211
Aspromonte: 271, 412
Assisi: xliii, 98, 205, 403
Atlantic Ocean: 110
Atrio del Cavallo: 274–275, 295–
    296
Augustine of Hippo, Saint: xlii,
    267
Aurora Borealis: 24, 284, 398

Austen, Jane: 118, 359; *Pride and Prejudice*, 118
Australia: 282
Austria: 230, 251

Babbage, Charles: xxiv, 65, 115, 141, 225, 293, 307, 350, 362, 365
Babylonian antiquities: 217
Baden Baden: 189
Baffin Bay: 111
Baia: 291
Baillie, Agnes: 213–214
Baillie, Joanna: xxviii, xxviii-ix, xxxvi, xli, xliv, 97, 117, 165, 207, 212–214, 307, 310, 323, 326, 329, 338, 342, 373, 375, 401, 404; *De Monfort*, 117, 343, 344, 404; *The Family Legend*, 118, 307, 405
Baillie, Dr Matthew: 117, 307
Baily, Francis: 83, 162, 185, 308
Bannister, John: 40, 308
Barbauld, Anna Laetitia: 308–309
Barbieri-Nini, Marianna: 250, 309
Barclay family: 95, 113, 309, 404
Barthe, Félix: 157, 309
Bartolommei, Ferdinando, Marchese: 260, 309
Barton, Suffolk: 126
Basle: 189
Bass Rock; 104
Basso del, fort: 251
Beaufort, Sir Francis: 143, 309
Becher, Sir William: 117
Becker, Karl Ferdinand: 128, 310
Becquerel, Antoine César: 151, 310
Bedford: 170
Beechwood Park, Hertfordshire: 120–122
Bell, Lady: 155
Bell, Sir Charles: 155, 310
Bellegarde, Countess: 239
Bellagio: 187
Beluchistan: 192
Belvedere, fort of: 251
Bengal: 75
Berchtesgaden: 239

Berry, Marie-Caroline de Bourbon-Sicile, Duchesse de: 154, 310
Berry, Mary: 166–167, 178, 310, 348, 407; *Comparative View of Social Life in France and England*, 178; *Memoirs*, 179, 348
Bible: 26, 76, 246, 413
Biel: 104
Billington, Elizabeth Weichsel, Madame: 49, 311
Biot, Jean-Baptiste: 66, 87, 89, 91, 141–143,150, 311
Birmingham: 85, 402, 405
Blackheath: 183
Blackwood's Magazine: 52, 384
Blair, Hugh: 45–6, 311
Blair, Mrs: 45
Blake, Miss, of Danesbury: 218
Blücher, Field Marshal, Prince von: 74, 401
Bologna: 102, 230
Bonaparte, Lucien: 100, 177, 311
Bonar family: 64, 96
Bon-Brenzoni, Caterina, Countess: 240–242; *I Cieli*, 242
Bonn: 129
Bonnycastle's *Introduction to Algebra*: 41
Bordeaux, Henri, Duc de: 208, 311
Borghese, Pauline: 99
Borghese, Prince Camillo Fillipo: 223, 410
Borneo: 246
Boswell, Sir Alexander, of Affleck: 56, 399
Boswell Claude Irvine, Lord Balmuto: 42, 312
Boswell, Miss: 43
Boulton, Matthew, junior: 85, 402
Boulton, Matthew, senior: 402
Bourbon family: 230
Bouvard, Alexis: 89, 109, 150, 312
Bouvard, Jean-Louis-Eloi: 157, 312

Bowditch, Henry Ingersoll: 180, 363
Bowditch, Nathaniel: 180, 312, 363
Bradley, James: 90, 312
Brand or Brande, William Thomas: 105, 313
Brenner pass: 240
Brewster, Sir David: xxviii, 30, 54, 84, 313, 342, 398
Bristol Philosophical Institution: 143
British Museum: 107, 217, 409
Broglie, 3rd Duc de: 152, 309, 313
Broglie, Duchesse de: 152–153, 224
Broglie, Prince de: 224, 228
Brongniart, Alexandre: 156, 313
Brougham, Henry Peter, Baron Brougham and Vaux: xiii, 68, 131–132, 135, 145, 163, 167–168, 176, 190–192, 200, 221, 313–314, 342, 374, 400; *Dissertation* on the 'Principia', 191
Brown, Montagu Yeats-: 272, 314
Brown, Rawdon Lubbock: 208, 314
Brown, Robert: 94
Browning, Elizabeth Barrett: 181, 203, 314, 408
Brussels: 128
Buchan (see Erskine)
Buchan, Captain: 111
Buckland, William: 106, 224, 315; 'Bridgewater Treatise', 106
Buffon, Georges Louis, Comte de: 197, 408; *Histoire naturelle des oiseaux*, 408
Buller, Charles: 145, 315
Bunbury, Sir Charles: 126, 315
Bunbury, Sir Henry: 126, 315
Bunbury, Lady: 126, 315
Bunsen, Robert Wilhelm: 109, 233, 267, 316, 344
Buoncompagni or Boncompagni di Mombello, Carlo: 260, 316

Burns, Robert: 39, 42, 360
Burntisland: xi, xxii, xxix, xxxiv, 3, 7, 9–11, 17, 20–27, 28, 36–37, 41–42, 55, 61, 64, 67–68, 78, 269, 281
Buyukdéré, Constantinople: 206
Byron, Ada, (see Lovelace)
Byron, George Gordon, 6th Baron: xliv, 96, 316, 329, 349, 355, 358, 359
Byron, Lady Noel (Annabella (Anne Isabella) Milbanke: 125, 316, 349, 358

Caesar's *Commentaries*: 29
Calabria: 284, 291
Callet's *Logarithms*: 66
Camaldoli: 248
Cambridge: 62, 132, 138–139, 141, 146, 191, 293
Campbell, Lady Charlotte: 50
Campbell, Colonel John of Shawfield· 50
Campbell, Lord: 26
Campbell, Rev. Dr: 26
Campbell, Thomas: 116, 179, 316
Camperdown: 57–58, 61, 77, 217, 400
Campo Morto: 100
Canada: 73
Canning, Lady Stratford: 206
Canning, Stratford, 1st Viscount Stratford de Redcliffe: 206, 317
Canova, Antonio: 99, 187, 317, 322, 334, 379
Cape of Good Hope: 73, 129, 170–171, 173, 407
Capellini, Giovanni: 270, 317
Capo Miseno: 291
Capri: 291
Capua: 100
Carignan, Prince: 260, 317
Caroline, Queen: 119,178, 313, 340, 348, 405
Castellamare: 298
Catalani, Madame Valabrèque: 117, 317
Catherine II, the Great, of Russia: xii, 336

Cavour, Camillo Benso di, Count: 230, 244–245, 260–262, 316, 317, 333, 357, 362

Cervara: 229

Ceylon: 105

Chales, Claude François Millet de: 273, 412; *The Elements of Euclid Explained*, 412

Chambers, Robert, *Vestiges of the Natural History of Creation*: 226

Champollion, Jean-François: 107, 318

Chantilly: 87–88

Chantrey, Sir Francis Leggatt: 121–122, 143, 159, 318, 334

Chapone, Hester: 23, 318; *Letters on the Improvement of the Mind, addressed to a young lady*, 23

Charles, Archduke: 208, 318, 319

Charles X (1757–1836) King of France: 120, 154, 310, 319, 345

Charles Albert, King of Sardinia-Piedmont: 238, 240, 319

Charters, Samuel: 2, 7

Charters, Thomas: 9

Charters, William Henry: 28, 33–35, 37

Chenu, Emma: 278

Cheviots: 59

Chigi family: 198, 319

China: 112, 281

Chiusi: 205, 212

Choiseul, Étienne François, Duc de: 8, 319

Christchurch College: 106

Città della Pieve: 212

Civita Vecchia: 100, 225

Clapham Common Society: 113, 309

Clairault's *Figure of the Earth*: 66

Clarke, William: 147, 319

Claude Lorrain: 229, 410

Clerk, Lady Mary: 56

Clerk, William of Eldin: 76, 79, 319

Cobbe, Frances Power: xvii–xix, xxv, xxxiii, xxxv–xxxvi, 247, 263, 289, 304, 320

Cockburn, Rev. William: 413

Coke, Thomas William, Earl Leicester of Holkham: 158, 320

Colà: 240–243, 320

Colbert, Auguste-Napoléon-Joseph, Marquis de Chabanais: 151

College of the Risurgenti: 217

Coltman, Justice: 400

Como: 187–188

Condé, Prince de: 88, 320

Congo: 94

Cooper, James Fenimore: 153, 320–321

Corcelles, Madame de: 150

Corri, Natale: 39, 321

Corunna: 151

Cowe, Miss: 35

Craig, Sir James Henry: xxxiv, 73, 321

Craw, Mr: 41

Cromek, Robert Hartley: 197, 321

Cuvier, Georges, Baron: 90–91, 320

Dana, James Dwight: xxxviii, 180, 322

Daniell, Samuel: 73, 322

Dante: 5, 122

Darwin, Charles Robert: xxxix, 287, 289, 322; *Descent of Man*, 288; *Origin of Species*, 287, 350

David d'Angers, Pierre-Jean: 156, 322

Davis, Paulina Kellogg Wright: 279, 323

Davy, Lady (née Kerr, formerly Mrs Jane Apreece): 68, 179, 202–203, 323

Davy, Sir Humphry: 87, 167, 313, 323, 329, 354

Dawes, William Rutter: 218, 323

De Candolle, Augustin Pyrane: 92–95, 324

De Filippi, Filippo: 268, 324

De la Rive, Auguste Arthur: 168, 324

De la Rive, Gaspard: 92, 168, 324
De Morgan, Augustus: 65, 141, 324, 350
Deserto, the: 291
De Vico, Padre Francesco: 193, 216, 325
De Winter, Admiral: 58
Dick, Thomas: 83, 402; *The Sidereal Heavens*, 402
Dickens, Charles: 213–214
Don family: 47
Don Quixote (Cervantes): 77, 401
Donati, Giovanni Battista: 251, 325
Dora: 244
Doria, Giacomo: 246, 325
Doria, Teresa, Marchesa: 246, 268, 273, 325
Douglas of Cavers: 49
Drum: 79
Duchênois, Catherine Josephine Rufuin, Mademoiselle: 90, 325
Dudley, John William Ward, 1st Earl of Dudley: 179, 325
Duncan, Adam, Viscount: 57–58, 325–326, 400
Dunfermline: 23, 55
Dupin, (François Pierre) Charles: 152, 326
Dupin, André Marie Jean-Jacques: 152, 156, 326
Dysart: 43

Eclipse, 1870: 285
Edgeworth, Maria: xxxvi, xli, 126–127, 163, 213, 326
Edinburgh: xii, 7, 12–13, 20, 28, 30, 33–34, 36, 39, 42–44, 52–53, 59, 72, 75–76, 78, 119–120, 221, 239; Assembly Rooms, George Street, 33, 49; Castle, 33; Princes Street, 53; Queen Street, 221; Tolbooth, 12, 397
Edinburgh Review: 68, 84, 157, 221, 314, 342, 348, 374, 384, 400–401
Edwards, Henri Milne: 151, 326, 372

Elcho Castle: 45–46
Elegant Extracts (Vicesimus Knox): 44, 399
Elgin marbles: 217, 409
Elgin, Thomas Bruce, 7th Earl of Elgin: 44, 330, 361, 377
Eliot, George: xvi
Elliot, Gilbert, 2nd Earl of Minto: 2, 8, 52, 327
Elliott, General Henry: 221
Elliott, Janet Somerville: 9, 32, 74, 221, 264–265
Elphinstone, Mountstuart: 192, 327
Elwin, Rev. Whitewell: 291
Ely, Marchioness of: 292
Encke's comet: 286, 412
English Channel: 113
Epping Forest: 120
Erskine, David Stuart, 11th Earl of Buchan: 52, 327
Erskine, Thomas, first Baron Erskine: 36, 327, 378
Esher: 125
Este family: 211
Euclid: 38–39, 41
Eugénie, Empress: 64, 359
Eugubian tables: 211, 409
Euler: 66; *Algebra*, 66; *Isoperimentrical Problems*, 66

Fairfax, Admiral Sir Henry: xii, xiv, xxx, 96, 155, 182–183, 263, 268, 327
Fairfax, Baron: 150, 182
Fairfax, Margaret Charters, Lady Fairfax: xii, xli, 1, 11, 15–16, 28, 46, 155, 328
Fairfax, Mary (see Somerville)
Fairfax, Mrs Mary, of Gilling Castle: 100, 220
Fairfax, Samuel: xii, 9, 12, 27–28, 58
Fairfax, Sir Thomas: xii
Fairfax, Sir William George: 62
Fairfax, Vice-Admiral Sir William: xii, xxxii, xxxiv, 6–7, 11, 15, 57, 62, 77, 182–183, 328, 400, 406

Falkner or Falconer, Hugh: 257, 328
Fanshawe, Catherine Maria: 179, 329
Faraday, Michael: xxiii, xxviii, 92, 236–238, 257, 323, 324, 329, 381, 382
Feldhausen: 174, 407
Ferdinand, Archduke: 252
Ferguson, Sir Adam: 79, 329–330
Ferguson, James, _Astronomy Explained on Sir Isaac Newton's Principles_: 65, 400
Fergusons of Raith: 58, 78, 104, 178, 190, 330, 365, 377
Ferrara: 211; Castello Estense, 211, 409
Fiesole: 249
Fifeshire: 104
Finlayson, Donald: 75
Finlayson, George: 75, 105, 330
Fiorelli, Giuseppe: 102, 330
Firth of Forth: 104
Flamsteed, John: 169–170, 330
Flinders, Matthew: 94, 314, 331
Florence: 96, 98, 122, 181, 187, 189–190, 196, 230, 246–265 (_passim_), 266; Campanile, 251; Cascine, 252, 254, 256; Casa Corsini, 254; Casa Guidi, 181; Duomo, 251, 261; Lung'Arno, 251; Maglio, 262; Palazzo delle Crocelle, 253; Palazzo Pitti, 98, 189, 252, 261; Palazzo Vecchio, 253, 259; Pergola, 231; Piazza dei Signori, 251; Piazza del Prato, 254, 260; Piazza dell' Indipendenza, 251; Piazza San Marco, 262; Ponte Carraja, 261; Porta San Gallo, 252; Santa Croce, 122; Uffizi, 98; Via del Mandorlo: 246
Foligno: 98
Fontainebleau: 92
Forth: 221
Foscolo, Niccolò Ugo: 122, 331
Fotheringham, Miss: 95

Foucault, Jean Bernard Léon: 244, 331
Fox, Charles James: 126, 315
Francoeur: _Elements of Mechanics_, 66; _Mathematics_, 66
Franklin, Sir John: 111–112, 331
Franklin, Lady: 111
Frascati: 100, 197–198
Fraunhofer, Joseph von: 109, 332
Frederick William II of Prussia: 74, 401
Freiburg: 78
Frere, Sir (Henry) Bartle Edward, 1st Baronet: 299, 332
Frolic: 272
Fry, Elizabeth, (née Gurney): 113, 118, 332

Gaetani, Don Michelangelo, Duke of Sermoneta: 201, 273, 332
Gaimard, Joseph-Paul: 112, 332
Galignani: 201
The Gamester (Edward Moore): 40, 399
Garda, Lago di: 240, 243
Garibaldi, Guiseppe: xxxviii, 245, 271, 333, 360, 381, 412
Gasparis, Annibale de: 273, 333
Gasperone: 100
Gassiot, Jean-Pierre: 267, 333
Gay-Lussac, Joseph Louis: 91, 151, 311, 333
General Committee for Woman Suffrage: 279
Geneva: xxiii, 92, 169
Genoa: 225, 240, 245–246, 260, 266, 272
Genzano: 197–198, 217–218
Geographical and Statistical Society of New York: 181
Geographical Society at Florence: 282
George III: 17, 63, 116, 327, 334
George IV: 77, 118–119, 330, 405
Gibson, John: 187, 201–202, 247, 334, 340–341
Ginori, Marchesa: 262, 334
Girton College: 280, 400, 412
Glaisher, James: 85, 334

Glover, John: 86, 334
Graham, James: xlii
Grand Duke, (see Tuscany).
Grant, Anne (Mrs Grant of
    Laggan): 74, 335
Granville, Lady: 153
Granville, Lord James: 130, 153,
    335
Greenland: 110
Gregory, James: 77, 335
Gregory XVI, Pope: 99, 193, 229,
    231, 335
Greig, Agnes Graham: xiii, xxxi,
    xxxiv, xliii, 199, 207, 217,
    269, 336
Greig, Sir Alexis Samuilovich: 62,
    336
Greig, Mary Fairfax (see
    Somerville)
Greig, Samuel: xii, xxxv, 4, 61,
    63
Greig, Admiral Sir Samuel
    Carlowitz: xii, 336
Greig, William George: xiii
Greig, Woronzow: xiii, xxxi-
    xxxiv, xliv, 64, 75, 80, 146,
    199-200, 207-210, 214, 217,
    223-225, 226-227, 243, 258-
    261, 272, 336, 350
Grimsel: 157
Grisi, Giulia: 116, 177, 230, 337
Gubbio: 207, 211
Gulf of Salerno: 291
Gurney family: 113
Gurney, Hudson: 108, 121-122,
    337, 361
Guy's Cliff (Warwickshire): 220

Hague, The: 130
Haiti: 113
Halicarnassus marbles: 217, 409
Hall, Sir James, 4th Baronet: 78,
    337
Hall, Lady Helen: 78
Halley's comet: 82-83, 169
Hales, Stephen, *Vegetable Staticks*:
    94, 395
Halifax (Nova Scotia): 217
Hallam, Henry: 160, 176, 337,
    364

Hamilton, Elizabeth: 74, 337
Hamilton, Sir William Rowan,
    Lectures on Quaternions: 291,
    338
Handel: 95, 266
Hankey, Mrs: 122
Hardy, Thomas: 36, 338, 380
Haüy, René-Just, Abbé: 78, 338
Hay, Robert: 292
Herbert, Auberon Edward
    William Molyneux: 299, 338
Herodotus: 38, 398
Herschell, Caroline Lucretia:
    xxvii, 86, 141, 171, 339
Herschel, Sir John: xiv-xv, xix,
    xxiv, xxvii, xxxvi, xxxvii, xl,
    xli, 65, 86, 109-110, 135-138,
    141, 145, 162, 170, 173-175,
    213, 215-220 (*passim*), 226-
    228, 232-236, 290, 293, 339,
    360, 362, 376, 407
Herschel, Lady (John): 170, 218-
    220, 235-236
Herschel, Matilda Rose: 218, 220
Herschel, Sir William: 86, 109,
    171-172, 339
Highlands: 76, 262, 411
Hill, Dr: 45
Himalayas: 192, 257
Hobhouse, Sir John Cam, Baron
    Broughton de Gyfford: 96,
    339 340, 358
Holland: 23, 35, 129, 400
Holland, Sir Henry, 1st Baronet:
    176, 232, 251, 340
Holyrood: 119-120
Home, John: 39, 311, 340;
    Douglas, 39, 340
Homer: 75
Hope, Sir Archibald: 19
Hope, James, (later Hope Scott):
    81, 340
Hope, Lady: 19
Horace: 70, 138, 405
Hosmer Harriet Goodhue: 247,
    340-341
House of Commons: 145, 174, 259
Huggins, Sir William: 175, 340
Humboldt, Alexander von: xxvii,
    89, 94, 129, 227, 232-235,

314, 341, 395; *Ansichten*, 234, 395; *Kosmos*, xxvii, 112, 227, 232–235, 363, 371
Hume, David: 17, 341; *History of England*, 17, 341
Hypatia: xxviii

Imperial and Royal Academy of Science, Literature and Art (Arezzo): 217
India House: 192
Inglis, Sir Robert: 113, 404
Innsbrück: 240
Ireland: 218
Irving, Washington: 180, 341–324
Ischia: 291
Italian Geographical Society: 283
Ivory, Sir James: 65, 162, 185, 342
Jameson, Robert: 78, 342
Janssen, Pierre-Jules César: 290
Japan: 112, 281
Jedburgh: xii, xxix, 3, 8–9, 29, 30–32, 54, 59, 72, 79, 81, 221
Jedburgh Abbey: 221
Jeffrey, Francis, Lord: 221, 314, 342, 374, 400
Johnson's *Dictionary*: 18
Johnston, (Alexander) Keith: 238, 343; *Atlas of Physical Geography*, 238
Jones, Tibby: 32

Kane, Dr: 112
Kater, Captain Henry: 106, 176, 343
Kater, Mary Frances Reeves: xxvii, 95, 106, 176, 343
Kean, Edmund: 117, 343, 352, 404
Kelso: 221
Kelso Chronicle: xxxi
Kelso Mail: xxxi
Kemble, Charles: 40, 343
Kemble, Frances Ann, 'Fanny': xvi, 223, 343–344, 340, 351
Kemble, John: 39, 90, 117–118, 344, 404
Kenilworth: 220

Kent, Victoria of Saxe-Coburg Gotha, Duchess of Kent: 162, 344
Ker, Anne (of Nisbet): 45
Kinghorn: 10, 67
Kirchhoff, Gustave Robert: 109, 267, 316, 344
Kirkcaldy: 78
Königsee: 239
Kosloffsky, (Koslofski) Petr Borisovich, Prince: 153–154, 344–345

Lablache, Luigi: 117, 337, 345
Lacroix, Sylvestre François: 65–66, 142, 150; *Traité du calcul différential et du calcul integral*, 65–66
Lafayette, General Marie Joseph Gilbert Motier, Marquis de: 149–150, 154, 157–158, 345
Lagrange, Joseph Louis, Comte de: 66, 89, 148, 244, 345–346, 365
Lajatico, Cino: 260
Lajatico, Marchesa: 254, 260–261
Lamarck, Jean-Baptiste de Monet, Chevalier de, *Flore francaise*: 93, 395
Lansdowne, Sir Henry Petty-Fitzmaurice, 3rd Marquis of Lansdowne: 179, 346
Laplace, Marquise, de: 88, 90, 151, 155
Laplace, Pierre Simon, Marquis de: xi, xiii, 87–89, 109, 133, 136–138, 147–148, 289, 320, 346, 350, 368; *Analytical Theory of Probabilities*, 66; *Mécanique céleste*, xi, xiii, 66, 68–69, 89, 131, 138, 148, 191, 234, 289, 312; *Système du monde*, 89, 147, 366
Lariccia: 198
Larrey, Dominique-Jean, Baron: 92, 346
La Vernia: 248
Lavoisier, Antoine Laurent: 152, 347
Layard, Sir Henry Austen: 218

Legendre, Adrien Marie: 142
Leghorn (Livorno): 260
Leith: 24, 55, 59
Leopold's Krone (near Salzburg): 239
Leslie, Sir John: 75, 347
Leverrier, Urbain Jean Joseph: 235, 304, 347
Lindley, *Observations on the Structure of Fruits and Seeds*: 93, 395
Lindsay, Lady Charlotte: 178–179, 347–348
Linton: 221
Lister, Lady Theresa (afterwards Lewis): 179, 348
Liston, John: 117, 347
Livingstone, David: 299, 348
Loch Ness: 45
Lockhart, John Gibson: 80, 348–349, 351, 384
Lombardy: 253, 255, 257
London: xiii, xxiii, 48, 60–63, 73–74, 85, 95, 122, 127, 184–185, 277; Albemarle Street, 176; Camden Hill, Kensington, 109, 175; Chelsea, xiii, 118, 125, 127, 132–133, 149, 159, 166; Chelsea Hospital, xiii, 125,185; Curzon Street, 178; Exeter Hall, 177, 407; Greenwich, 90; Greenwich Royal Hospital, 58, 400; Hampstead, 122; Hampton Court, 257; Hanover Square, 87, 104, 108, 116, 118, 122; Lansdown House, 145; Temple Barr, 74; Trafalgar Square, 224; Twickenham, 179; Westminster Abbey, 118–119; Westminster Hall, 118
Longfellow, Henry Wadsworth: 182, 349
Loreto: 206
Louis, Joseph-Dominique, Baron: 156–157, 349
Louis I, King of Bavaria: 239, 349

Lovelace, Ada Augusta Byron King, Lady Lovelace: xxiv, xxvii, 125–126, 349
Lowood: 74
Lowry, Joseph Wilson: 86, 350
Lowry, Mrs Joseph: xxvii, 86
Lubbock, Sir John William: xxiv, 275, 350
Lucchesi, Luigi: 271
Lugo: 211
Lyell, Sir Charles: 35, 118, 350
Lyell, Mary Horner, Mrs Charles: xxvii, 35, 351

Macaulay, Thomas Babbington: 116, 179, 187, 351
Macaulay, Zachary: 113, 404
Macdonald, Jacques-Etienne-Joseph-Alexandre, Duc de Tarante: 157, 351
Macdonald, Lawrence: 48, 202, 206, 224, 351
Mackintosh, Sir James: 116, 128–130, 153, 179, 352
Maclane, Miss Clephane: 96, 352
McClintock, Sir Leopold: 111
MacPherson, Samuel Charters: 277, 352
Macready, William Charles: 117, 352
Majendie or Magendie, François: 155, 352–353
Malibran, Mme Maria Felicita Garcia: 116, 177, 230, 353
Malta: 30
Malthus, Thomas Robert: 176, 353
Marcello, Benedetto: 99, 353
Marcet, Alexander John Gaspard: 92, 353–354, 367
Marcet, Jane Haldimand: xxvii, 92, 127, 168–169, 329, 353–354; *Conversations on Chemistry*, 92, 353–354
Maremma: 100, 189, 408
Margaret, Crown Princess of Italy: 292
Marlow: 65
Marmont, (Auguste-Frédéric-Louis) Viesse de, Duc de Raguse: 208, 354

Mars, Mademoiselle (Anne-Françoise-Hippolyte): 90, 354

Martineau, Harriet: xvi, 321, 354–355

Mary Somerville: 143

Maskelyne, Nevil: 90, 355

Massa di Somma: 291, 296–297, 413

Massa, Nicolas-François-Sylvestre Régnier, Duc de Massa: 157, 355

Maury, Matthew Fontaine: 180, 355; *The Physical Geography of the Sea*, 180

Mazzini, Guiseppe: 229, 355, 368

Melbourne, William Lamb: 116, 355–356, 370

Melville family: 34, 37

Melville Island: 111

Menabrea, Luigi Federico: 255, 282–283, 356

Menaggio: 188

Mezzofanti, Guiseppe Caspar: 102, 240, 356

Milan: 58, 95, 225, 240, 253; Palazzo di Brera, 98, 403

Mill, John Stuart: 277–278, 356; *The Subjection of Women*, 277, 356

Miller, Hugh: 78, 356–357

Miller, Lady: 45

Milman, Henry Hart: 176, 357, 359

Milton, John: 32, 40

Mincio: 251

Minghetti, Marco: 255, 357

Miniscalchi, Count Erizzo: 240, 243–244, 357

Miniscalchi, Countess: 240

Minto, Earl of, see Elliot

Mirbel, Brisseau de, *Éléments de physiologie végétale et de botanique*: 94, 395

Mitford, Mary Russell: 118, 357; *Our Village*, 118, 357

Mocenigo, Countess: 208, 357–358

Modena: 258–259, 409

Modena, Grand Duke of: 210

Moncreiff, Miss: 40

Monferrat (near Asti): 245

Monge's *Application of Analysis to Geometry*: 66

Mont Cenis: 85, 402

Montalembert, Charles- (Forbes-René), Comte de: 177, 358

Montalembert, Madame de: 177

Monte Cavo: 200

Monte Porzio: 198

Monte Santangelo: 291

Montucla, Jean Etienne: 161, 407

Monza: 95, 403

Moore, Thomas: 116, 176, 358

More, Hannah: 74, 358–359, 404

Moretti, Countess (see Bonar)

Morning Post: xi

Morton, Earl of: 21

Munich: 109, 239; Odeon, 239

Murchison, Lady: 100, 106

Murchison, Sir Roderick Impey, 1st Baronet: 99, 106, 282, 292, 359; *Silurian System*, 282

Murray, Christian of Kynynmont: 2, 8

Murray, John: 82, 176, 200, 237, 289, 359

Musselburgh: xii, 18–20

Naldi, Giuseppe: 87, 359

Napier, General Sir William: 126, 315

Napier, Lady Sarah: 126, 315

Napier, Richard: 126, 315

Naples: xiii, 5, 100, 101, 160, 162, 187, 258, 273–302 (*passim*); Campo Santo, 302

Napoleon, Emperor: 89, 92, 99, 154, 303, 311, 330, 331, 346, 364, 367

Napoleon, Prince Jêrome: 254, 256

Napoleon III, Emperor: 64, 253, 313, 359, 378

Nasmyth, Alexander: 38, 53–54, 359–360, 398

Negri, Commendatore: 283

Nélaton, Auguste: 271, 360

Nemi, Lake of: 200, 217

Nettuno: 197
Neusatz, Hungary: 206
Newhaven: 13
New Holland: 94
New Zealand: 282
Newton, Sir Isaac: 65, 108, 148,
170, 238, 257, 305, 329, 330,
360, 406; *Principia*, 65, 132
Newton Don (Kelso): 47
Nice: 253
Nicolai, Baron: 63
Nightingale, Florence: 101, 360
Normanby, Lady: 250
Normanby, Sir Constantine
Henry Phipps, 1st Marquis
of Normanby: 250, 360–361
North British Review: 84
North Polar region: 276
North Sea: 21
Northesk, William Carnegie, 7th
Earl of Northesk: 24, 361
Novara: 230
Novello, Clara Anastasia,
Countess Gigliucci: 266, 361

Oberland: 262
Oddi-Baglioni, Conte: 204
Ogilvie, Miss: 37
Old English Baron (Clara Reeve):
54, 399
Olmütz: 150
O'Neill, Miss, Lady Becher: 117,
361
Opie, Amelia: 118, 361
Orvieto: 207
Ossian: 55, 262, 311, 411
Ostia: 206, 273
Oswalds of Dunnikier: 8, 44
Oswald, Elizabeth: 44, 327, 361–
362
Oxford: 106

Pacific Ocean: 110
Padua: 211
Paestum: 101, 403
Palitzch, George: 82
Palli, Lucchesi, Marquese: 154
Panceri, Paolo: 273, 362
Pantaleone, Diomede: 228, 362
Papal States: 100

Paris: xxiii, 75, 90–2, 99, 149–
159, 167, 289; Champs de
Mars,157, 407; Jardin des
Plantes, 90–91, 403; Louvre,
98
Parma: 98, 259
Parry, Sir William Edward: 111–
112, 362, 369, 371
Pasta, Giudetta (Maria
Constanza), née Negri: 116,
177, 230, 309, 362
Patterson, Elizabeth Chambers:
xviii, xx–xxi, xxiii, xl, xliii,
367, 382; *Mary Somerville,
1780–1872*, xviii, xl; *Mary
Somerville and the Cultivation
of Science, 1815–1840*, xviii, xl
Peacock, George, Professor, Dean
of Ely: 65, 140–141, 362
Peel, Sir Robert: xxviii, 143–144,
174, 363
Peirce, Benjamin: 286, 363
Pentland, Joseph Barclay: 91,
238, 363
Percy, Charles, Lord: 220, 363
Percy, Lady (Charles): 220
Percy, Lady Susan: 229, 363
Persia: 246
Perugia: 204–205, 207, 212; Casa
Oddi-Baglioni: 204
Peruzzi family: 255, 363
Peschiera: 240
Petit-Brie: 156
Petrarch: 211
Philibert, J. C., *Elémens de
botanique et de physique*: 94,
395
Phillips, John: 275, 364
Pianciani, Padre: 193, 364
Piano di Sorrento: 291
Piedmont: 230, 251, 255–256, 259
Pillans, James: 75, 364
Pinkie: 19
Pisa: 189
Pistoia: 199
Pius VII, Gregorio Barnaba
Chiaramenti: 99, 364
Pius IX, Giovanni Maria Mastai-
Ferretti: 229, 250, 306, 364–
365

Pizzifalcone: 275
Plana, Giovanni Antonio Amedeo,
    Baron: 244, 306, 365
Platoff, Count Hetman: 74, 401
Playfair, John: 68, 75, 77, 365
Plücker Julius: 267, 366
Po: 244
Poinsot, Louis: 89, 150, 366
Poisson, Siméon Denis: 66, 89,
    150, 161, 185, 366
Pompeii: 102, 403
Pond, John: 90, 366
Ponte Molle: 193
Pontécoulant, Philipe Gustave le
    Doulcet: 150, 366–367
Portici: 102, 296
Posilipo: 291
Potter, Mr: 143
Pottinger, Sir Henry, 1st Baronet:
    192, 367
Poussin, Nicholas: 229, 410
Pozzo di Borgo, Count: 154, 367
Pozzuoli: 291
Prévost, Pierre: 92, 143, 367
Primrose, Miss: xxi, 18
Procida: 291
Prony, (Gaspard-François-Clair-
    Marie) Riche, Baron de: 150,
    367
Provence: 190–191

Quarterly Review: xxvi, xli, 80, 82,
    157, 232, 308, 325, 348, 359,
    384, 400–402
Quebec: 77, 401
Quetelet, Lambert Adolphe
    Jacques: 128, 367–368

Radcliffe, Ann: 118; *The Mysteries
    of Udolpho*, 54, 399; *A
    Romance of the Forest*, 54, 399
Radetzky, Josef, Count of Radetz:
    240, 368
Ramsay family: xxxi, 46
Ravenna: 198, 207; Basilica of St
    Apollinaire in Classis
    (Sant'Apollinare Nuovo),
    211; Mausoleum of
    Theodoric, 211, 409; San
    Vitale, 211

Recoaro: 231
Reed, Mr: 24
Rémusat, Madame de: 150
Repulse: 24, *398*
Resistance: 268–269, 412
Rhine: 129, 207
Ricasoli, Bettino, Baron: 252,
    257, 260–262, 368
Rich, James: 217, 409
Richard, Louis-Claude, *Analyse de
    Fruit*: 93, 395
Rigny, Mademoiselle de: 156
Rigny, Henri Gauthier, Comte
    de: 157, 368
Riviera di Chiaja: 275
Robertson, John: 37, 39, 368–369;
    The Elements of Navigation,
    37, 39, 368
Robinson Crusoe (Defoe): 17
Rocca del Papa: 198
Rogers, Samuel: 116, 179, 321,
    325, 369, 374
Rohan, Mademoiselle, de: 87
Roman Campagna: 5, 186, 193–
    194, 197, 206, 225, 229, 292,
    407
Rome: 48, 98–100, 134, 185–187,
    192–195, 201–204, 205, 210,
    222–230 (*passim*), 254, 265,
    297; Cancelleria, 228; Corso,
    203–204, 409; Ghetto, 193;
    Palazzo Lepri, 192;
    Pantheon, 193; Piazza de la
    Bocca de la Verità, 229, 411;
    Pincio, 99, 187, 193, 407; St
    Peter's, 98–99; Tiber, 193,
    205; Via dei Condotti: 192
Rosetta, Egypt: 107
Ross, Sir James Clark: 111–112,
    201, 369, 371
Rosse, William Parsons, 3rd Earl
    of Rosse: 172–173, 217, 369
Rossi, Count Pelligrino: 228, 306,
    369
Rossini, Gioacchino Antonio:
    230, 369–370, 362
Rosslyn, Earl of: 43
Royal Academy (Dublin): 143
Royal Astronomical Society:
    xxvii, 141, 175, 323, 376, 407

Royal Geographical Society: 282
Royal Institution: 87, 105, 107, 236, 313, 323, 354, 403
Royal Italian Geographical Society: 244
Royal Society (London): 109, 112, 143, 173, 227, 307, 313, 355, 376, 382
Rubini, Giovanni Battista: 177, 230, 370
Rumford, Thompson, Benjamin, Count Rumford: 87, 152, 370, 403
Russell, John 1st Earl:145, 370, 408
Russia: 61, 154
Rutherfurds of Edgerton: 31, 371

Sabine, General Sir Edward:12, 371
Sabine, Elizabeth Juliana, Lady Sabine: xxvii, 112, 371
Sacro Speco (Subiaco): 228
Salmon, *Higher Algebra*: 286
Salzburg: 239
St Gothard Pass: 231
San Germano: 187
San Sebastiano: 297
Santa Fiora: 190
Santa Lucia: 295–296
Santa Maria degli Angeli: 98, 403
Saturday Review: xxv–xxvi, xli
Saussure, (Nicolas) Théodore de, *Recherches chimiques sur la végétation*: 94
Savoy: 253
Say, Jean-Baptiste: 169, 371
Scarlett, Sir James: 252, 257, 371
Schlegel, August Wilhelm von: 129, 371
Schwartzenberg, Friedrich (Johann Josef Cölestin) Cardinal: 239, 371
Scoresby, William: 110–111, 372
Scott, Charles: 80
Scott, (Charlotte) Sophia: 80
Scott, Sir Walter: xxviii, xviv, 79–81, 153, 287, 330, 340, 348–349, 351, 352, 364, 371, 374, 375, 402; *Guy Mannering*, 80,

402; *Waverley Novels*, 79; *The Memorie of the Somervilles*, 80
Sebright, Sir John Saunders, 7th Baronet: 120–121, 151, 372
Sedgwick, Adam: 146–147, 224, 292–294, 372
Sermoneta, see Gaetani
Serret, *Cours d'Algèbre Supérieure*: 286
Sèvres: 156,
Shakespeare, William: 5, 22, 30, 32, 39–40, 90, 129, 352; *Coriolanus*, 40; *Cymbeline*, 39; *Hamlet*, 40; *Macbeth*, 40; *Othello*, 40
Shee, Sir Martin Archer: 61, 372
Sheepshanks, Rev. Richard: 147
Sheridan, Caroline (Mrs Norton): 179, 202, 356, 372–373, 356, 378
Sheridan, Helen Selina (Lady Dufferin, Countess of Gifford): 179, 202, 372, 378
Sheridan, Jane Georgina (Duchess of Somerset): 179, 372–373, 378
Shiriff, Emily: 126
Sicily: 73, 126, 257, 286
Siddons, Sarah (née Kemble): 39–40, 90, 117–118, 343, 344, 373, 404–405
Siena: 97, 190–191, 199, 400
Silliman, Benjamin: 95, 180, 322, 373
Simplon Pass: 95
Sind: 192
Sismondi, J(ean)-C(harles)-L(éonard) Simonde de: 92, 373
Sismondi, Madame (Miss Allen): 92
Slitterik (Slitrig): 32, 398
Slough: 86
Smart, Admiral Sir Robert: 268, 373
Smith, Patty: 101, 114
Smith, Sir (William) Sidney: 153, 373

Smith, Rev. Sydney: 68, 97, 116, 176, 314, 342, 361, 364, 374, 376, 400
Smith, William: 100, 114, 373
Smyth, Admiral W H: 169–170, 330, 373
Società Geografica Italiana, see Italian Geographical Society
Società Protettrice degli Animali: 248
Société de Physique et d'Histoire Naturelle (Geneva): 143
Society for Diffusing Useful Knowledge: 131
Society of Friends: 107
Society of Natural History (Italy): 270
Solferino: 252, 259, 411
Somerville, James Craig: xxxiv
Somerville, John, Lord: 79
Somerville, Margaret Farquar: xiii, 104, 124
Somerville, Martha Charters (aunt): 2, 9, 375
Somerville, Martha Charters (daughter): xiii-xlii (*passim*) 1–302 (*passim* as editor), 104, 127–128, 188–189, 200, 206, 208, 219, 224, 253, 255, 257, 259, 267, 269–270, 272, 295–296, 298
Somerville, Mary Charlotte: xiii, xvii, xxxiii, 1, 104, 127–128, 188–189, 206, 208, 224, 253, 255, 267, 269–270, 272, 295–296, 298
Somerville, Mary Fairfax Greig
On the Connexion of the Physical Sciences, xi, xxiii, xl, xli, 84, 110, 156, 159–163, 171, 201, 217, 233, 235, 238, 267; *On Molecular and Microscopic Science*, xi, xl, 267, 272; *The Mechanism of the Heavens*, xi, xxviii, xli, 140–143, 145–146, 150, 161, 176, 185, 206, 233, 350, 362, 406; *Personal Recollections*, xi-xlv (*passim*); *Physical Geography*, xi, 84, 91, 189,

192, 201, 232–234, 238, 243, 281, 282; 'Preliminary Dissertation', 163, 165
Somerville, Rev. Dr Thomas: xii, xxx, 2–3, 8, 29, 70–71, 72, 74, 79, 124, 263–264, 375
Life and Times, 70–71, 263–264, 375
Somerville, Samuel: 74, 79, 375
Somerville, William: xiii-iv, xxiv, xxvi-xxvii, xxx, xxxiv, xxxv-xxxvi, 69, 70–264 (*passim*), 375
Sonnino: 100
South Africa: 70, 281
Sopwith, Sir Thomas: 159, 375
Sorrento: 5, 272, 290–291, 297–298
Sotheby, William: 120, 375
South, Sir James: 109, 175–176, 376
South America: 274
Sparks, Jared: 182, 376
Sparre, Comte de: 87
Sparrow, Lady Olivia: 177, 376
Spectator: 17
Spencer, Earl: 57
Spencer, William Robert: 116, 179, 376
Spezia: 112, 186, 266–273 (*passim*)
Spitzbergen: 110
Spottiswoode, William: 286, 376
Stabilini, Girolamo (Hieronymo): 39, 376–377
Staël, Anne Louise Germaine Necker, Madame de: 91, 130, 152, 323, 361, 377–378; *Corinne*, 91, 377, 403
Stanley, Arthur Penrhyn, Dean of Westminster: 44, 377
Stanley, Lady Augusta: 44, 377
Stanley, Sir Henry Morton: 299, 348
Strange (dancing master): 33
Stewartfield: 31
Stuart, Prince Charles Edward: 96, 304
Stuart, James of Dunearne: 56, 399

Subiaco: 228
Swinton, James Rannie: 48, 295, 378

Tait, Peter Guthrie, *On Quaternions*: 286
Talleyrand-Périgord, Charles Maurice de: 157, 378
Talma, François-Joseph: 90, 378
Tavolata: 194
Terracina: 196
Texel: 57, 400
Thelwall, John: 36, 338, 378, 380
Thiers, Louis Adolphe: 228, 378
Thomson, George: 39, 379
Thorwaldsen Bertel: 99, 187, 334, 379
Thornton, Henry: 113, 404
Thurn, Countess of: 210
Thurn and Taxis, Prince of: 208, 379
Thury, (Louis-Étienne François) Héricault, Vicomte de: 154, 380
Tibet: 192, 257
Times, The: 224, 410
Tivoli: 206
Tooke, (John) Horne: 36, 338, 378, 380
Torlonia, Princess (Colonna): 222, 410
Torre del Greco: 296, 412
Transactions of the Geographical Society: 192
Trendelenburg, Friedrich Adolf : 128, 380
Trieste: 206
Tuckerman, Rev. Joseph: 182–183, 380
Tuileries: 118, 149, 153
Turin: 107, 244–245, 260, 266–267; Casa Cavour, 244
Turner, Joseph Mallord William: 196, 218, 410
Tuscany: 255–256, 258
Tuscany, Leopold II, Grand Duke of: 189–190, 250, 254, 255, 380–381
Tusculum: 198
Tweed: 79, 188, 232

Tylor, Sir Edward Burnett, *Researches on the Early History of Mankind and the Development of Civilization*, 289
Tyndall, John: 236, 267, 275, 381

Umbria: 98
United States: 113, 162, 180–181, 276, 277, 282
Usedom, Guido, Conte von: 273, 381

Val di Susa: 245
Vallombrosa: 248, 411
Varignano: 271
Vatican: 98, 187, 240
Veii: 206
Veitch, James, Laird of Inchbonny: xl, 81–84, 381, 402
Venerable: 57, 217, 398, 400
Venice: 96, 98, 207–210, 212–213, 217, 253; Accademia, 208; Bridge of Sighs, 209; Grand Canal, 208, 210; Piazza San Marco, 208–209
Vesuvius: 101, 273–275, 284, 291, 294–297, 403, 412
Viareggio: 249
Victor Emmanuel II, King of Italy: 230, 254, 284, 317, 333, 381
Victoria: 268–269
Victoria, Queen: 119–120, 162, 294, 340, 344, 377
Victoria Medal: 282
Villa Borghese: 194, 407
Villa Capponi (near Florence): 273
Villafranca: 253
Virgil: 29, 407
Vogt, Professor: 270, 382
Volscian Mountains: 100

Wallace, John: 69
Wallace, William: xxiii, 65–66, 69, 382
Wardlaw, Miss: 49
Warten, Joseph: 206

Warwick Castle: 220
Washington, George: 150, 182, 327, 342, 376, 406
Waterford, Marchioness of: 202
Waterloo: 75
Watt and Boulton's manufactory: 85, 402
Wedderburn, Captain: 35
Wellwood, Sir Henry Moncreiff: 40, 74, 76, 382
Wemyss family: 27, 55
Werner, Abraham Gottlob: 78, 382–383
West Indian Colonies: 113
Whewell, William: xxvi, xli, 62, 138–140, 147, 228, 293, 362, 383
White, Lydia: 179, 383
Wilberforce, William: 113, 374, 404
Wilkes, Admiral Charles: 180, 383
Wilson, Andrew: 192, 384
Wilson, John: 51–52, 399; *Isle of Palms*, 52, 384
Wilson, Mrs: 50

Wilton (Hawick): 32
Windermere: 51
Windsor: 63
Wiseman, Nicholas Patrick Stephen: 198, 384
Wolfe, General: 77, 401
Wollaston, William Hyde: 105–6, 108, 120–122, 127, 176, 343, 375, 384–385
Wollstonecraft, Mary: xxiv, 361
Woronzow, Catherine, Countess of Pembroke: 63, 385

Xenophon: 38, 398

Yarmouth Roads: 7
Yetholm: 221
Young, Alexander: 180
Young, Charles Mayne: 40, 385
Young, Thomas: 106–108, 167, 176, 221, 337, 343, 385
York Cathedral: 6, 300

Zanetti, Ferdinando: xxxvii, 249, 385
Zouaves: 258, 411